ROUTLEDGE LIBRARY EDITIONS:
SLAVERY

Volume 6

FORCED MIGRATION

FORCED MIGRATION

The Impact of the Export Slave Trade on African Societies

Edited by
J. E. INIKORI

LONDON AND NEW YORK

First published in 1982 by Hutchinson University Library

This edition first published in 2023
by Routledge
4 Park Square, Milton Park, Abingdon, Oxon OX14 4RN

and by Routledge
605 Third Avenue, New York, NY 10158

Routledge is an imprint of the Taylor & Francis Group, an informa business

Introduction, editorial matter, selection and arrangement © 1982 J.E. Inikori
Individual chapters © their authors and original publishers

All rights reserved. No part of this book may be reprinted or reproduced or utilised in any form or by any electronic, mechanical, or other means, now known or hereafter invented, including photocopying and recording, or in any information storage or retrieval system, without permission in writing from the publishers.

Trademark notice: Product or corporate names may be trademarks or registered trademarks, and are used only for identification and explanation without intent to infringe.

British Library Cataloguing in Publication Data
A catalogue record for this book is available from the British Library

ISBN: 978-1-032-30942-2 (Set)
ISBN: 978-1-032-33028-0 (Volume 6) (hbk)
ISBN: 978-1-032-33041-9 (Volume 6) (pbk)
ISBN: 978-1-003-31786-9 (Volume 6) (ebk)

DOI: 10.4324/9781003317869

Publisher's Note
The publisher has gone to great lengths to ensure the quality of this reprint but points out that some imperfections in the original copies may be apparent.

Disclaimer
The publisher has made every effort to trace copyright holders and would welcome correspondence from those they have been unable to trace.

Forced Migration
The Impact of the Export Slave Trade on African Societies

Edited by J. E. Inikori

Hutchinson University Library
Hutchinson University Library for Africa
London Melbourne Sydney Auckland Johannesburg

HUTCHINSON UNIVERSITY LIBRARY FOR AFRICA

Hutchinson & Co. (Publishers) Ltd
An imprint of the Hutchinson Publishing Group
17–21 Conway Street, London W1P 5HL

Hutchinson Group (Australia) Pty Ltd
30–32 Cremorne Street, Richmond South, Victoria 3121
PO Box 151, Broadway, New South Wales 2007

Hutchinson Group (NZ) Ltd
32–34 View Road, PO Box 40–086, Glenfield, Auckland 10

Hutchinson Group (SA) (Pty) Ltd
PO Box 337, Bergvlei 2012, South Africa

First published in 1982

Introduction, editorial matter, selection and arrangement © J. E. Inikori 1982
Individual chapters © their authors and original publishers

The paperback edition of this book is sold subject to the condition that
it shall not, by way of trade or otherwise, be lent, resold, hired out or
otherwise circulated in any form of binding or cover other than that in
which it is published and without a similar condition including this
condition being imposed on the subsequent purchaser

Set in Times

Printed in Great Britain by The Anchor Press Ltd
and bound by Wm Brendon & Son Ltd
both of Tiptree, Essex

British Library Cataloguing in Publication Data
Forced migration.
   1. Slave-trade – Africa – Addresses, essays, lectures
   2. Africa – Social conditions – Addresses, essays, lectures
   I. Inikori, J. E.
   306'.3   HT891

ISBN 0 09 145900 1 cased
      0 09 145901 X paper

Contents

List of maps		7
List of tables		7
Preface		9
Acknowledgements		11
	Introduction	13
1	African slavery and other forms of social oppression on the Upper Guinea Coast in the context of the Atlantic slave trade *Walter Rodney*	61
2	The role of slavery in the economic and social history of Sahelo-Sudanic Africa *Claude Meillassoux*	74
3	Kayor and Baol: Senegalese kingdoms and the slave trade in the eighteenth century *Charles Becker and Victor Martin*	100
4	The import of firearms into West Africa, 1750 to 1807: a quantitative analysis *J. E. Inikori*	126
5	Slavery and the slave trade in the context of West African history *J. D. Fage*	154
6	The Oyo Yoruba and the Atlantic trade, 1670 to 1830 *Peter Morton-Williams*	167
7	Effects of the Atlantic slave trade on some West African societies *Albert van Dantzig*	187
8	The trade of Loango in the seventeenth and eighteenth centuries *Phyllis Martin*	202
9	The Portuguese slave trade from Angola in the eighteenth century *Herbert S. Klein*	221

10	The impact of the slave trade on East Central Africa in the nineteenth century *Edward A. Alpers*	242
	Notes and references	275
	Select bibliography	341
	Index	345

Maps and tables

Maps

1	The main towns between Old Oyo and the Atlantic ports before 1830	185
2	West Central Africa	204

Tables

1	Curtin's estimates compared with those made since 1976	21
2	Sex composition by African region of origin of 43,096 slaves imported into Jamaica, 1764–88	23
3	Enslaved people as a percentage of the total non-slave population	95
4	Kayor and Baol in the eighteenth century: table of events	104
5	Figures on the trade in captives in Kayor and Baol	108
6	Quantity of gunpowder annually exported from England to West Africa, 1750–1807	132
7	Prices of guns exported to West Africa, 1796–1807	133
8	Guns imported into West Africa from England, 1796–1805	133
9	Slaves purchased by European nations annually	134
10	Regional distribution of imported firearms	138
11	An analysis of 64,828 guns imported into West Africa from 1757 to 1806	142
12	Clapperton's and the Landerses' route through Egbado to Oyo	178
13	Estimates of the African slave exports from Angola in the eighteenth century	224
14	Slave trade from Luanda, Angola, 1723–71	225
15	Slave exports from Luanda, Angola, by month, 1723–71	226

8 *Tables*

16	Slave exports from Luanda, Angola, by season, 1723–71	227
17	Slave exports from Luanda, Angola, by port of destination, 1723–71	228
18	Legal carrying capacity of ships and number of slaves actually carried, 1762–5	229
19	Children, by category, shipped from Luanda, 1726–69	230
20	Income and expenditures of seven slaves shipped to Rio de Janeiro in 1762	231
21	Slave exports from Luanda of the Pombaline slave trade companies and Brazilian ports of destination, 1756–88	236
22	Slaves exported from Mozambique, 1818–30	246
23	Slaves exported from Kilwa Kivinje, 1862–9	268

Preface

Scholarly study of African history, centred on Africa rather than as an extension of European history, has gone on now for about three decades. Over this relatively short period of time a lot has been achieved in making the African past more intelligible to the knowledgeable man. But, our understanding of the African past and, therefore, the African present, remains very much blurred by the failure of many of the pioneers in African historiography to locate the external slave trade of over four centuries in its proper position among the major factors in the African historical process. The activities surrounding this unusual international trade of immense magnitude have been so important in determining the nature of the relationship between Black Africa and the rest of the world, and in shaping the internal structures of the region's societies, that without a proper understanding of the slave trade factor, *ipso facto*, there can be no proper understanding of the African historical process.

For the past decade or so several scholars have been carrying out detailed researches to establish the facts and the analytical framework for the interpretation of these facts in order that the slave trade factor may be better understood. This collection of papers represents an attempt to present to the students of African societies what is now known about the subject. Some of the papers provide detailed information about certain sub-regions or sub-themes, while others deal with analytical frameworks explicitly linking the external slave trade to processes within Africa. The information and the analytical concepts which they collectively make available can be more profitably utilized if directed toward an explanation of Black Africa's backwardness in the late nineteenth century, which can be linked up with colonial rule to explain contemporary economic underdevelopment in Black Africa.

For a proper understanding of the impact of the export slave trade on African societies, the subject must be conceived in the context of Black Africa as a region in which developments taking place in some parts provide the conditions for the transformation of all the individual parts and the whole region as an entity. This point is important because the economic development process requires stimulating links which spread over a wide contiguous geographical area, in addition to links with economies outside the base region. Consequently, an external relationship which produces a serious adverse impact on some parts of the base region retards the development of all the parts, individually, and the whole region as an entity. This is the more so if the parts directly affected are the ones with resource endowments to play the role of growth poles. Thus, while detailed empirical research has to be carried out at the level of narrow geographical areas, the information dug out must be analysed in the context of the broad region within which the parts could have realized their potentials for development.

It should also be stressed from the onset that the impact of the external slave trade on African societies must not be looked for only in direct terms. The slave trade was a major economic activity which went on for several centuries. Like all economic activities, the character of the commodity involved determined the kind of conditions created both for the rest of the economic sector and for the non-economic spheres of society. The conditions so created influenced in a complex manner the totality of the social process – the economic, the political, the cultural, etc.

The subject of the external slave trade and African societies remains an open one. We have not tried to say the last word on the subject. It is our hope that the present collection will stimulate further interest in the examination of the relationship between the external slave trade and the African historical process.

I would like at this point, to express my gratitude to all those who contributed in different ways toward the production of this book. I am grateful to Professor A. E. Afigbo of the University of Nigeria, Nsukka, Michael Crowder and Dr Paul Richards, general editors of Hutchinson University Library for Africa, who read and made helpful comments on the introduction. A part of the introduction was presented at a seminar of the Centre of West African Studies, University of Birmingham, while I was there as a John Cadbury Visiting Fellow. I wish to thank all those whose comments helped me in writing the final draft, in particular, Professors A. G. Hopkins, J. D. Fage, Jan S. Hogendorn, Dr Peter Mitchell and Mrs Marion Johnson. It must be said, however, that I am entirely responsible for any shortcomings in the introduction, the selection of papers, the arrangement and the editorial matters.

J. E. Inikori
Zaria, July 1981

Acknowledgements

Hutchinson Education and the editor are grateful to the following authors and their publishers for permission to reproduce the articles included in this book:

Walter Rodney and Cambridge University Press for 'African slavery and other forms of social oppression on the Upper Guinea Coast in the context of the Atlantic slave trade'

Claude Meillassoux for 'The role of slavery in the economic and social history of Sahelo-Sudanic Africa' (and R. J. Gavin for the English translation)

Charles Becker, Victor Martin and the Société Française d'Histoire d'Outre Mer for 'Kayor and Baol: Senegalese kingdoms and the slave trade in the eighteenth century'

Cambridge University Press for 'The import of firearms into West Africa 1750 to 1807: a quantitative analysis'

J. D. Fage and Cambridge University Press for 'Slavery and the slave trade in the context of West African history'

Peter Morton-Williams and the Historical Society of Nigeria for 'The Oyo Yoruba and the Atlantic trade, 1670 to 1830'

Albert van Dantzig and the Société Française d'Histoire d'Outre Mer for 'Effects of the Atlantic slave trade on some West African societies'

Phyllis Martin and Oxford University Press for 'The trade of Loango in the seventeenth and eighteenth centuries'

Herbert S. Klein and the Economic History Association for 'The Portuguese slave trade from Angola in the eighteenth century'

Edward A. Alpers and Heinemann Educational Books for 'The impact of the slave trade on East Central Africa in the nineteenth century'

*To the memory of
Professor Kolawole Ogungbesan
and Dr Walter Rodney*

Introduction

The export slave trade from Africa began early in the Christian era with exports to the Muslim world through the Sahara, the Red Sea and the Indian Ocean. By the ninth century AD the annual volume of exports to the Muslim World had become quite significant, and continued so up to the nineteenth century. For the period up to the fifteenth century the Muslim territories around the Mediterranean and beyond were the main slave importing regions of the world, fed by supplies both from Europe and from sub-Saharan Africa. In the fifteenth and sixteenth centuries Western European countries led by Portugal and Spain embarked upon voyages of exploration which gave rise to the establishment of European colonies in parts of the Atlantic territories and Indian Ocean Islands. The great need for labour to exploit the resources of these colonies added a new sector to the export slave trade from Africa – the trans-Atlantic slave trade. This new branch quickly came to supersede the older one in annual export volume. For over four centuries both sectors of the trade went on simultaneously, removing millions of persons – men, women and children – from sub-Saharan Africa.

For a long time studies of the export slave trade from Africa placed emphasis on topics other than those directly related to historical processes in Africa. In 1956 Professor K. O. Dike drew the attention of professional historians to the neglect of the African aspects of the export slave trade. 'As yet,' he said, 'no comprehensive assessment of the African middle men's position in the Atlantic slave trade exists; few if any studies have displayed the real magnitude of the revolution brought about by the prohibition of the traffic from 1807 or the full effects of abolition on the existing native governments.'[1] By focusing on the impact of abolition on the societies of the Niger Delta area of present-day Nigeria, Dike's book remains an important contribution along these lines. In general, this book has had great impact on the study of African history from the African standpoint. But, surprisingly, more than two decades since the publication of Dike's work no detailed and comprehensive analysis of the impact of the export slave trade on

14 *Introduction*

African societies exists.² It is only recently that scholars have begun to move from the traditional areas of slave trade studies – the organization of the trade, its profits, its sufferings, the numbers game, abolition and its politics – to the analysis of the trade's impact on African societies. The results of these recent research efforts are still to be found mostly among conference and seminar papers,³ some published, others not, and in scholarly journals. Yet, with the growing interest in the study of African underdevelopment, Africanists are more than ever before eager to know how the export slave trade may be fitted into the processes leading to underdevelopment in Africa. It is in response to this growing demand that the present effort has been made to bring together in one volume some of the papers relating to the subject.

The papers included in this collection deal with such issues as, the impact of the export slave trade on demographic processes in Africa; the relationship between the export slave trade and the institution of slavery in Africa; the consequences of the export slave trade for political processes in Africa; and, finally, the relationship between the export slave trade and economic underdevelopment in Africa. Each chapter is preceded by editorial comments which focus upon the central issues of each paper as they relate to the main theme of the collection. The introductory chapter is therefore composed as a self-contained contribution to the collection.

Focus and analytical framework

The central theme of the discussion in this chapter is the relationship between the export slave trade and the degree of economic backwardness which prevailed generally in Black Africa by the middle decades of the nineteenth century. It is now generally accepted that earlier writers greatly underestimated the volume of trade, the extent of manufacturing, and the level of technological development in sub-Saharan Africa by the late nineteenth century. But the fact still remains that in terms of market institutions and the organization and technology of agriculture and manufacturing, Black African economies by the middle decades of the nineteenth century were backward not only in relation to the economies of Europe and North America, but also in relation to the major Asian economies, China and India. While there were important commercial and manufacturing sectors, the economies of sub-Saharan Africa by the mid nineteenth century were, in general, characterized by a very low level of market development. There was scarcely any land market to talk about. There was little or no developed wage-labour market. Agriculture was generally uncommercialized, subsistence production and extensive cultivation overwhelmingly predominating. Handicraft manufacturing was still at a low level of organization and technology, the great skills of artisans in places like Kano notwithstanding. In fact, the commercialization of peasant crafts, with merchant capitalists imposing their control (through their distribution of the raw materials and the marketing of the finished products) over semi-independent peasant manufacturers was generally absent in the organization of handicraft manufacturing. Internal transport facilities, in terms of roads and instruments of transportation, remained poorly developed. This state of affairs, when compared with the prevailing situation in Europe, Asia and much of the New World at this time, shows Black Africa as the most economically backward major region of the world. This huge gap in economic development between Black Africa and the other major regions of the world is easily discernible in the observations of European visitors to Africa in the late nineteenth century. Yet, no such great gap is discernible in the observations of Arab and European visitors to the region in the first half of the present millennium.

These efforts to show the demographic, social and political impact of the export slave trade on African societies are directly connected with our central concern to prove, with detailed analysis and evidence, the strong relationship between that trade and African economic backwardness by the middle decades of the nineteenth century. Our view of the economic development process has much in common with the 'organic totality' version of the base-superstructure model, with a dialectical interaction, over time, between economic, political and cultural factors, with the economic factors playing the leading role in this process.

The organic totality version of this model sees society as an organic structure. The material base of this structure is made up of the fundamental conditions of production, including the natural environment and man himself, with his hereditary traits. The superstructure is made up of the sphere of the political state, with its laws, and the cultural sphere, with its science, philosophy, art, religion, morality and customs. Over time, there is constant interaction between the material base and the superstructure. The character of the material base conditions that of the superstructure. But once so conditioned, the character of the superstructure facilitates the functioning of the material base. A major change in the base brings about a major contradiction between the base and the superstructure. This contradiction creates obstacles for the proper functioning of both the base and the superstructure until over time a new equilibrium is established between the material base and the superstructure. This version which allows for a two-way relationship between the material base and the superstructure frees the model from the economic determinism of the version which sees only a one-way relationship between the base and the superstructure.[4]

The analytical framework presented here shares some common elements with this version. In our view, the rise of many important kingdoms and empires in Black Africa between the fifteenth and mid nineteenth century took place in circumstances closely related to the export slave trade. Consequently, the political and cultural spheres of these kingdoms and empires were all structured in accordance with the economic conditions provided by the export slave trade. The harmony arising from this structural adaptation facilitated the operation of the slave trade for several centuries. But in so doing, it consolidated the dominance of dependency forces by preventing the growth of other forces capable of bringing about self-sustained economic development. These latter forces are related to population growth and commodity international trade.

In general, the present analysis is organized around the basic assumption that before the twentieth-century rise of powerful modernizing governments, employing coercion and the forceful instruments of central planning, self-sustained modern economic development (as manifested in the form of technology and organization of production) took place only after a general commercialization of economic activities. In order to appreciate the arguments that follow, it is pertinent, therefore, to raise the theoretical question of what factors operate over time to move a predominantly subsistence economy to a predominantly commercial one. It is an important part of my assumption that there are only two central factors to which others in the process are secondarily related. These two factors are population growth (an internal factor, which could also be related to the external one) and overseas commodity trade (an external factor).

The logic of these assumptions is simple enough to be taken for granted. In fact, the theoretical framework has been built up in some detail around the evolution of market and other institutions in Western Europe from the Middle Ages by certain economists who have taken an unusual interest in institutional development.[5] Recent publications by specialists in medieval social and economic history have tended to provide general support for this theoretical model.[6] The development of market and other institutions in sub-Saharan Africa since the late nineteenth-century expansion of population and seaborne commodity trade provides similar general support.

The issue of factors affecting demographic change is somewhat more

Introduction 17

problematic and has stimulated quite a lively debate since the time of Malthus.[7] We therefore consider it necessary at the outset to draw attention to an aspect of the subject which does not seem to have been given sufficient attention. Because the demographic debate has been centred on societies where land had become a scarce resource it has not been thought necessary to distinguish between demographic behaviour in land-surplus traditional societies and demographic behaviour in land-scarce societies. A proper understanding of the demographic process requires that we first distinguish between these two types of society.[8]

Logic and historical evidence show that in land-surplus traditional societies the natural tendency of uncontrolled high birth-rates to exceed high death-rates by a margin large enough to allow a slow and steady population growth is only interrupted by three agents – protracted and destructive wars; plague (whose outbreak may have nothing to do with the state of the economy and whose spread may be related to the ecology); and climatic change. In the absence of these phenomena, the population goes on expanding, albeit slowly. The pressure of population on cultivable land within areas of earlier settlement is taken off by the movement of cultivators to previously unsettled or lightly settled areas, in waves of internal colonization. One of the indirect demographic consequences of protracted wars is that the widespread sense of insecurity which they engender prevents the movement of extra populations to uncultivated but good lands, thus creating an artificial scarcity. If the favourable period is long enough, the tendency is for all the available good land to become fully occupied. At this point intensive agriculture with important changes in technology are forced on the society and this gradually raises the optimum ratio of population to cultivable land. As can be shown for medieval Europe, 'Population growth drove nobles, farmers and peasants to look for new land and improved techniques: more land and improved techniques in turn supported further population growth.'[9]

It is only when Boserup's thesis is placed in the context of a land-surplus traditional society, with limited opportunity for overseas trade in agricultural commodities, that its contribution can be appreciated. In this kind of society changes in the organization and technology of agriculture are dependent on population growth, and not the other way round, as Malthus would want us to believe. And this is the major contribution of Boserup's thesis.[10] A land-surplus society involved in large-scale overseas trade in agricultural commodities over a long period of time, such as the United States from the eighteenth century, will depend more on export demand for change, with population growth through natural increase and net gains from migration playing a secondary role.

In both cases, however, the long-term result of population expansion and continuing export demand, is the commercialization of agriculture, with land becoming a private property and a very scarce resource. At this point we are in the second type of society. Here population growth depends more strongly on developments outside agriculture: the growth of employment opportunities outside agriculture, or major developments in medicine and the expansion of medical facilities which keep more people alive, irrespective of resource constraint.

The thesis of proletarianization advanced by David Levine is quite interesting. But it does not really add anything to our knowledge of the demographic process. Levine's argument is that before the large-scale proletarianization (that is, dependence upon wage-labour for subsistence) of peasants and artisans in England, 'late age at marriage and, to a lesser extent, restriction of fertility within marriage' operated as 'effective methods of demographic regulation', but after 1750, 'the proletarianization of peasants and craftsmen undermined the efficacy of these controls'.[11]

But Levine's own evidence shows that the demographic behaviour of the peasants and artisans before 1750 was a response to land scarcity and inadequate opportunity for non-agricultural employment. As he says himself:

Members of each new generation were expected to wait until their fathers retired or died before assuming control over their family farms or workshops. For this reason, peasants and artisans adopted a prudent, calculating approach to marriage.[12]

Being dependent on the availability of opportunities for independent employment, the growth of such opportunities provides a sufficient explanation for the elimination of this mode of behaviour. This is why European migrants who went to land-surplus North America in the seventeenth and eighteenth centuries were not restrained by culture from having large families. In fact, this point is borne out by Levine's qualification to his argument. As he puts it:

When employment became available to all who were willing to sell their labour in the market place, it became more difficult to maintain the equilibrium mechanism of postponed marriage because men (and women) reached their earning capacity at an early age and no longer had any reason to defer marriage.[13]

This is why deceleration in industrial growth in industrialized societies, some decades after the industrial revolution, also leads to deceleration in population growth.[14]

It is hoped that the foregoing discussion will make clear the import of the analysis which now follows. We begin with the demographic consequences of the trade. The emphasis on the demographic impact should be understood in terms of the economic consequences of underpopulation.

The demographic impact

The impact of the export slave trade on demographic processes in Africa has attracted a great deal of attention since the eighteenth century when the first efforts were made to abolish the trans-Atlantic trade. It was early realized that no meaningful discussion of the subject can be made without some estimate of the total numbers actually exported. Thus participants in the discussion tried to provide some figures. But, for a long time very little effort was made to provide a systematic estimate of the total numbers involved in the two sectors of the trade – the trade to the Muslim world and the trans-Atlantic trade. In 1969 Professor P. D. Curtin reviewed the literature on the trans-Atlantic trade and found the published estimates wanting in many respects.[15] Curtin became convinced that these earlier global estimates of the Atlantic slave trade were exaggerated. Based on this conviction, Curtin set out to produce, using published data, what has become one of the few systematic estimates of the volume of the Atlantic slave trade.[16]

It is important to point out that Curtin was not the first modern writer to conclude that earlier estimates of the Atlantic slave trade were exaggerated. Without any elaborate calculations Professor K. O. Dike stated more than two decades ago that the figure of 10 million put forward by some writers as the number of persons exported from West Africa by way of the Atlantic trade between 1450 and 1850 was an exaggeration. Dike suggested that 'five to six million seem nearer the mark.'[17] Curtin's more elaborate calculations produced about the same result for West Africa, that is, about 6 million persons exported during the whole period of the Atlantic trade.

My own assessment of Curtin's estimates has shown that the global figures are much too low.[18] Subsequent publications arising from new research also support this conclusion. Of these subsequent publications, that by Leslie B. Rout, Jr., has been particularly critical of the said figures. As Rout puts it:

Philip Curtin's importation census is a laudable effort, but one with definite weaknesses. This scholar divides the slave trade into two major periods, 1521 to 1773 and 1773 to 1807. Unlike Brito Figueroa, he makes no particularly serious effort to study the *licencia* [legally recognized] trade. As to the contraband slave traffic up to 1773, Curtin recognizes its existence, but his conclusion that this trade was 'extremely difficult to estimate' does nothing to further our knowledge concerning the issue. Ambiguous also are the bases upon which Professor Curtin chose to accept some statistics while rejecting others. In tabulating his totals for 1773 to 1807, he accepts the figures given by Elena Fanny Scheuss de Studer and Brito Figueroa for the illegal traffic to Venezuela and the Rio de la Plata region. For some unexplained reason, however, Curtin completely ignores Humboldt's measurement of the contraband Cuban traffic. Omissions of this sort do little to strengthen the credibility of Curtin's computations.[19]

Table 1 summarizes the independent estimates made since my own assessment of Curtin's and Anstey's estimates.[20] In general, it can be said that there is now some consensus among specialists that Curtin underestimated the volume of the Atlantic exports. The problem is to determine the magnitude of the underestimate. The independent estimates made since my own assessment of Curtin's and Anstey's figures, and my own repeated re-examination of the subject, assure me that a 40 per cent upward adjustment of Curtin's global figure is quite reasonable. This brings the Atlantic exports to a total of 15,400,000. This is a total addition of about 4,400,000 to Curtin's figures. My own estimate of the British trade in the eighteenth century alone, Stein's estimate of the French trade in the eighteenth century, and the estimate by Eltis of total African exports for the roughly twenty-year period, 1821 to 1843, already account for about 1,800,000 of this number. This leaves about 2,600,000 to be accounted for by underestimates of the Portuguese trade and the whole trade of the sixteenth and seventeenth centuries for which the evidence indicates a much greater level of underestimate, as can be seen in part from Leslie Rout's comments on the Spanish trade. As we move from mere guessing to systematic estimates based on recorded evidence, the well known problem of incomplete data will mean that all estimates may contain some degree of underestimate.

No satisfactory analysis of the consequences of the export slave trade for African demographic history can be made without including the export of slaves to the Muslim world. The most detailed global estimates of the volume of this branch of the trade are those by Raymond Mauny[21] and Ralph Austen.[22] While the grand totals presented by both writers are in close agreement, their distribution of the volume over time is radically different. For the period 1400 to 1900, during which the Atlantic and Muslim exports ran concurrently for most of the time,

Introduction 21

Table 1 *Curtin's estimates compared with those made since 1976*

Author	Component estimated	Estimated number of slaves	Curtin's estimate for the same component	Percentage difference
J. E. Inikori	British slave exports from Africa 1701–1807	3,699,572	2,480,000[1]	49.2
L. B. Rout, Jr.	Slaves delivered to the Spanish Indies 1500–1810	1,500,000	925,100[2]	62.1
D. Eltis (*a*)	Trans-Atlantic slave exports from Africa 1821–43	1,485,000	1,104,950[3]	34.4
D. Eltis (*b*)	Slave imports into Brazil 1821–43	829,100	637,000[4]	30
Robert Stein	French slave exports 1713–92/3	1,140,257	939,100[5]	21.4

Sources and notes:
J. E. Inikori, 'Measuring the Atlantic slave trade: a rejoinder', *Journal of African History*, vol. XVII, no. 4 (London 1976), p. 614; L. B. Rout, Jr., *The African Experience in Spanish America 1502 to the Present Day* (Cambridge: Cambridge University Press 1976), pp. 61–6; D. Eltis (*a*), 'The export of slaves from Africa, 1821–1843', *Journal of Economic History*, vol. XXXVII, no. 2 (London 1977), p. 429; D. Eltis (*b*), 'The direction and fluctuation of the Transatlantic slave trade, 1821–43: a revision of the 1845 Parliamentary Paper', in Henry A. Gemery and Jan S. Hogendorn (eds.), *The Uncommon Market: Essays in the Economic History of the Atlantic Slave Trade* (New York: Academic Press 1979), p. 289; Robert Stein, 'Measuring the French slave trade, 1713–92/3', *Journal of African History*, vol. XIX, no. 4 (London 1978), pp. 515–21. Stein states that his estimate is 'some 17 per cent higher than Curtin's' (p. 518). This is a minor error of arithmetic. Stein's figure is higher than Curtin's by $\frac{201,157}{939,100} \times \frac{100}{1}$, which is 21.4 per cent. For Curtin's figures in the table, see Curtin, *Census*, table 41, p. 142, for (1), p. 268, table 77, for (2), pp. 234 and 280, tables 67 and 80, for (3), p. 234, table 67, for (4), p. 170, table 49, for (5).

Mauny's estimate of 10 million[23] is much greater than that of Austen. For this reason, it will help our argument to use Mauny's figures. But we think that Austen's examination of the evidence is more thorough, although a large margin of error, either way, is still to be expected, because of the weak data-base of the trans-Saharan trade. Austen's figures are therefore employed in our analysis.

For the trans-Saharan exports, Austen's figure for the whole period,

AD 650 to 1900, is 9,387,000 slaves.[24] And for the Red Sea–Indian Ocean trade to the Muslim world, total export from AD 800 to 1890 is estimated at 5,000,000.[25] The over-time breakdown of the estimates shows that for the trans-Saharan trade, total export from AD 900 to 1500 was 4,813,000, and from 1500 to 1880, 3,956,000. By making use of Austen's annual averages, the East African portion of the estimate can be broken down to periods comparable with the trans-Saharan portion. This gives a total export of 2,100,000 slaves for the period, AD 800 to 1500, and 2,900,000 for the period from 1500 to 1890.

Thus the total export of people from sub-Saharan Africa to the Muslim world and to the European colonies can be put at 29,787,000, that is, about 30 million. Taking only the period during which exports to the Muslim world and to the European colonies ran concurrently, that is, from 1500 to 1890, the total comes to 22,256,000, that is, about 22 million.

To make a proper judgement as to how the numbers exported affected demographic processes in sub-Saharan Africa we need to know something about the sex and age composition of the people exported. The preference of the employers of slave labour in the Americas, as reflected in the instructions given to the captains of slave ships, was one female to two male slaves. In addition, they were to be persons in their prime of life, that is, between the ages of 16 and 30. In the case of the female slaves the captains were often told to buy only those with 'round breasts', thus emphasizing the age limits. These general instructions have for long remained the only basis for historians' judgements about the sex and age composition of the persons exported by way of the Atlantic trade. However, new researches have begun to turn out hard data on the basis of which firmer conclusions can be made. In Table 2, we present the sex composition by African regions of origin of 43,096 slaves imported into Jamaica in 125 separate cargoes over the period 1764 to 1788.

The regions to the north of West Africa, that is, Gambia, the Windward Coast and the Gold Coast, show in the table a sex structure which agrees generally with the one indicated in the instructions to the captains of slave ships – one female to two male slaves. The same thing is generally true for Gabon and Angola. But for Whydah, Benin, Bonny and Calabar, the proportion of female slaves is significantly higher than the one-third proportion usually mentioned. In fact, for Benin the proportion of female slaves is slightly higher than that for male slaves. This shows that even after the ban on the sale of male slaves had been removed in the 1690s, Benin did not 'produce' proportionately as many male slaves as were available elsewhere in Africa. It would be an

Table 2 *Sex composition by African region of origin of 43,096 slaves imported into Jamaica, 1764-88*

African region	Number of cargoes	Total number sold	Number of males	Number of females	Male %	Female %
Gambia	4	659	475	184	72.1	27.9
Windward Coast	11	2,679	1,761	918	65.7	34.3
Gold Coast	47	16,741	11,176	5,565	66.8	33.2
Whydah	12	4,813	2,783	2,030	57.8	42.2
Benin	5	1,319	659	660	49.96	50.04
Bonny	19	8,203	4,632	3,571	56.5	43.5
Calabar	21	6,634	3,904	2,730	58.8	41.2
Gabon	1	154	106	48	68.8	31.2
Angola	5	1,894	1,291	603	68.2	31.8
Totals	125	43,096	26,787	16,309	62.2	37.8

Source: PRO, CO. 137/88, Appendix nos. 1, 2, 3 and 5, pp. 20-23 and 25.

interesting topic of research to try and discover the factors that made for these regional variations in the sex structure of the people exported.

At the bottom of the table, we have tried to work out the overall sex structure for the 43,096 persons imported. This shows that male slaves formed 62.2 per cent while female slaves formed 37.8 per cent of the total. Here the disproportionate representation of Gold Coast figures in the table must be pointed out. The Gold Coast figures represent approximately 38 per cent of the total number of cargoes and 39 per cent of the total number of slaves. But Bonny, which actually exported much larger numbers of slaves than the Gold Coast at this time, has approximately only 16 per cent of the cargoes and 19 per cent of the number of slaves. The relative over-representation of Gold Coast figures and under-representation of figures from the Bight of Biafra (Bonny and Calabar) means that the actual weight of the higher ratio of female slaves from the latter region, as indicated in the table, has been much reduced. Interpreted in this way the information in the table indicates that the sex ratio of the people exported from the west coast of Africa in the eighteenth century was in the neighbourhood of 60 per cent for men and 40 per cent for female slaves.

Information relating to 25,051 slaves exported by the Dutch free traders between 1730 and 1795 also supports this conclusion. The proportions here are 59.1 per cent for male slaves and 40.9 per cent for female slaves.[26] For the seventeenth century the information we have relates only to the Dutch trade. One set of information relating to 5150 slaves exported between 1636 and 1645 gives sex ratios which agree with those for the eighteenth century. These are 59.7 per cent for male slaves and 40.3 per cent for female slaves.[27] But another set of information relating to 36,121 slaves exported between 1675 and 1740 shows somewhat different ratios. These are 70.0 per cent for male slaves and 30.0 per cent for female slaves.[28] If the latter set of information alone is related to the Dutch slave trade of the eighteenth century there would appear to be a change over time in the sex ratios.[29] But this seems unlikely considering the first set of information relating to the period 1636 to 1645. It is probable that the African regions which predominated during different periods of the Dutch trade account for the variations in the ratios.

We also have some information on 6039 slaves imported into Jamaica between 1781 and 1786, and on 14,113 imported into all the British West Indies in 1795. But these are not broken down into African regions of origin.[30] When these are taken together with our earlier data for the seventeenth and eighteenth centuries, we thus have sex ratios for 129,570 slaves spread over these two crucial centuries of the Atlantic trade. Of this figure the male slaves numbered 82,669, being 63.8 per cent, and the female slaves numbered 46,901, being 36.2 per cent. Following the earlier argument, we take the operative ratios for the Atlantic trade as 60 per cent male and 40 per cent female slaves.[31]

Not all of the data from which the sex ratios are taken contain information on age composition. Information relating to age is shown only for cargoes totalling 88,545 slaves. Of this number, 12,828 are stated as youths, the others being entered as adults or 'grown slaves'. The cargoes in question are also spread over the seventeenth and eighteenth centuries. From these figures the proportion of youths comes to 14.5 per cent. For the British trade, height seems to have been the only criterion for distributing the slaves between youths and adults. Youths were defined as those below 4 feet 4 inches, while those above this height were described as adults.[32] As yet we do not have any hard data on the age distribution of the adult slaves. The point should be made, however, that the sex structure revealed by the available hard data comes very close to the ratios specified in the captains' instructions. This shows that the composition of the products sold reflected the character of what the buyers demanded. If this was true of the sex composition of the slaves there is no plausible reason why it should not be true for the age composition.

While the European buyers preferred male to female slaves, the opposite was the case for the buyers in the Muslim world. The demand for slaves in the Muslim world was largely for domestic service, including concubinage. For this reason female slaves were the preferred commodity in the Muslim trade. It is generally believed that the sex ratio in the Muslim trade was one male to two female slaves. Very little hard data exist for this generalization but census evidence relating to the population of black slaves in Egypt in the nineteenth century shows that the ratio of male to female slaves was about 1:3.[33] To be conservative, we may take the sex proportions in the Muslim trade to be 67 per cent female and 33 per cent male.

We can now apply the sex proportions established for the European and Muslim slave trades to the total numbers exported in each trade in order to determine the number of males and females exported. For the whole period of the Muslim trade this comes to approximately 9,640,000 female, and 4,750,000 male slaves. For the whole period of the Atlantic trade the comparative figures are 6,160,000 females and 9,240,000 males. Thus, during the whole period of the export slave trade from sub-Saharan Africa, 15,800,000 female slaves were exported, being about 53 per cent of the total, while 13,990,000 male slaves were exported, being 47 per cent of the total. If we restrict ourselves to the period during which the two sectors went on concurrently, that is, from about 1500 to 1890, the proportions are slightly changed owing to the greater weight of the Atlantic trade. The number of female slaves in the Muslim trade during this period is 4,590,000, and 2,260,000 for male slaves. Thus, for the period 1500 to 1890, 10,750,000 female slaves were exported from sub-Saharan Africa, being 48 per cent of the total, and 11,500,000 male slaves, being 52 per cent of the total.

From these figures, it can be seen that when the European and Muslim trades are taken together the number of males and the number of females exported are about equal. Therefore, the secondary impact of the export slave trade on demographic processes in sub-Saharan Africa should be expected not from changes in the sex composition, but in the age composition of the populations, since those exported were people in the prime of life.

Having examined the evidence relating to the total number of slaves exported to the Muslim world and the European colonies, and to the age and sex composition of those exported, it must now be emphasized that the numbers exported formed only a part (and most likely a much smaller part) of the total population losses suffered by sub-Saharan Africa as a result of the export slave trade. This point is usually appreciated by historians. For example, Professor Fage states that:

substantial numbers of other lives must have been lost to Africa as a result of the operations involved in securing slaves, i.e. in the wars and raids by which a large proportion of them were enslaved, or in the famines and epidemics which could follow from such activities. Further lives must have been lost in bringing the slaves down to the coast and in keeping them in captivity until purchasers could be found to buy them and ships to take them away.[34]

But Fage's conclusion that 'there is no means whatsoever of even guessing at what this additional loss of life may have been overall'[35] is not helpful, particularly when it is used as an excuse for ignoring these quantitatively important components in the overall assessment of the impact of the export slave trade on African demographic processes. For some of the components, some systematic assessment is possible, although the research required is still only being thought about.[36] For others a review of the qualitative evidence can help to form some impression.

In January 1721, the officials of the English Royal African Company resident on the Gold Coast wrote to their employers in England concerning mortality among the slaves held awaiting the arrival of ships. They reminded their employers that:

We have at several times acquainted your honours of the great detriment the slaves' hole is to their healths for want of its being lined and a platform raised and which we are not capable of getting completed for want of deals etc., as indented for, so that notwithstanding all our care to accept of none but good slaves from any of your factories yet we have lately had a great mortality besides a number of them very much reduced and in a bad state of health. . . .[37]

In general, the weakened condition of the slaves at the time of reaching the export centres, the poor physical conditions to which they were subjected while waiting for purchasers and the final journey to the importing territories, together with the poor feeding they received during this period, occasioned frequent outbreaks of epidemics among them. Of all the export centres, evidence relating to Mozambique is by far the most comprehensive. Edward Alpers has shown that in 1819, of the 10,442 slaves held at Mozambique for sale to exporters 1200 died before they could be purchased, and of the 9242 purchased by the Brazilians in that year 1804 died at Mozambique before the slave ships left for Brazil. On the basis of such quantitative evidence and other qualitative ones, Alpers suggests that about 25 per cent of the export slaves brought to Mozambique in the 1820s and 1830s died every year before the numbers actually exported left the coast for Brazil.[38] In fact, the 1819 figures show that the slaves who died at Mozambique, both before purchase by the Brazilians and before the ships left the coast, were approximately 40 per cent of the 7438 slaves actually exported.

The final export centres were not the only centres for the bulking of export slaves. Bulking was done at various centres in the interior. The slaves often moved from depot to depot before their arrival at the final export centres. And at these various depots in the interior the same mortality experienced at the export centres occurred. Describing the interior slave market at Ujiji, situated east of Lake Tanganyika, Professor R. W. Beachy writes:

Near the slave market lay an uncultivated piece of ground, the cemetery, where not only the dead, but the dying, too, were cast. Hyenas, very numerous, gorged on human flesh, and were so sated that bodies were left half-devoured.[39]

Great numbers also died in the march from one depot to another before finally arriving at the export centres. Here again, we have some evidence relating to the East African slave trade. Many of the slaves sold at the Ujiji market were brought from territories west of Lake Tanganyika. These were collected from depots to the west and transported in canoes across the lake to Ujiji. Beachy states that during the crossing of Lake Tanganyika the 'slaves were made to sit doubled up in the bottom of the canoes, so closely packed that by the time Ujiji was reached a quarter had succumbed, although the distance across the lake, depot to depot, was scarcely 200 miles.'[40] It is shown that of 300 slaves collected from Manyema (to the west of Lake Tanganyika) by one Said bin Habib, only 50 got to Unyanyembe alive.[41] Many deaths during the long march to the coast were often caused by deficient supply of food to the slaves.[42]

From the available evidence, therefore, it can be guessed that mortality between the time of first acquisition and the time of final exportation could not have been less than 50 per cent of those actually exported.

When we come to population losses due to slave raids and slaving wars, and the famine and epidemics arising from these activities, it becomes quite difficult to find any hard data. There is a lot of evidence showing the unusual frequency of wars during the slave trade era. But these wars have not been individually studied in detail, in terms of deaths during military operations. It may be argued that direct losses arising from casualties in battle were small because the wars were usually on a small scale. Even allowing for possible exaggeration, the comments of European slave traders during the period show that the scale of these wars was much greater than is often thought. Mr Lamb's eye-witness accounts of the wars of Dahomey in the early eighteenth century are particularly instructive.[43] The Yoruba wars of the nineteenth century may not have been typical. But, at least, a modern writer commenting on the scale of these wars has said:

It seems beyond doubt, therefore, that on occasion – both before and after the introduction of firearms – casualties were numerous and serious, and Burton's attempt, on slender evidence, to minimize the determination with which these wars were fought must be rejected. Even so, the toll of life among non-combatants in the wars seems likely to have been at least as high as that among the warriors, whether from famine, as at Ijaye and Owu, or by the unprovoked slaughter of those unlucky enough to be caught in the track of the armies, like the Egba farmers along the River Ogun.[44]

Apart from those who died during military operations, slave raiding and wars had other consequences for the demographic process. The political and social upheavals which they engendered had serious negative effects on economic activities. They seriously restricted the inter-regional flow of goods. Opportunities and incentives for innovation in agricultural technology were severely restricted. To procure protection against the activities of slave gatherers, security became a far more important determinant of the choice of settlement than economic considerations, thus restricting the opportunities and incentives for economic growth and development in sub-Saharan Africa. This produced a serious negative impact on the demographic process in the area during the slave trade era.

While there is hardly any writer who now seriously disputes this, there seems to be some confusion in the discussion. This arises from the apparent lumping together of two questions which ought to be separated. One of the questions is whether the wars of the slave trade era had serious negative effects on the populations of sub-Saharan Africa during that period. The other is whether these wars were caused by the demand for export slaves.

This confusion seems to be present in Professor Fage's analysis of West African population movement from 1500 to 1850. In all the publications by Fage on the slave trade since 1969 there is none in which he disputes the fact that the wars of the slave trade era had negative effects on West African population. Fage's analysis, therefore, ought to produce a declining population for West Africa from 1650 to 1850, even on the basis of Curtin's low estimate. But, on the contrary, Fage postulates a growing population for West Africa during the era of the export slave trade, putting the total West African population at 20 million by 1500, 25 million by 1700, and 28 million by 1850.[45] In all these calculations no account is taken of exports to the Muslim world; no account is taken of losses due to wars; and no account is taken of losses between points of capture and points of final exportation.

Fage's analysis seems to suggest that he is not actually concerned with the broader issue of how West African population developed over the centuries. His main argument is that the Atlantic slave trade had no noticeable impact on African populations. For this purpose he argues that slave raids and slaving wars were not due to the Atlantic slave trade, because they would have occurred even without that trade.[46] Apparently this is why Fage does not include losses from wars and raids in his calculations, although there seems no justifiable reason for ignoring losses between points of capture and points of final exportation. The point to be made here is that while one may argue that the wars and raids were not due to export demand and therefore population losses arising therefrom should not be attributed to the Atlantic trade, in order to show how the whole of West African population developed over the centuries those losses must be taken into account.

When proper account is taken of all the new factors affecting demographic processes in West Africa from 1500 to 1880, the evidence points strongly to a significantly declining population from 1650 to 1850. This comes out when all the additional losses discussed earlier, together with exports to the Muslim world, are added to Fage's calculations. When this is done, whether with Curtin's low estimates or with a 40 per cent upward revision of those estimates, the result shows a significant net deficit in West African population at the end of each year's slave exporting activity during the period considered by Fage.[47] The conclusion that West African population was declining absolutely from the middle of the seventeenth century to the middle of the nineteenth, is further strengthened by the implication of the age and sex composition of the slaves exported for birth rates. The evidence we displayed earlier about the age and sex structure of the slaves points strongly to the conclusion that birth rates in Africa were significantly depressed during the period 1650 to 1850.

The foregoing argument is one which is supported by the implications of recent discussions on African populations. In a recent paper Professor J. C. Caldwell argues that the implications of the growing data on African demography indicate that substantial natural population increase in Africa has not been confined to the second half of the twentieth century, but was already an important feature of some areas during the previous fifty to seventy-five years.[48] In the face of this evidence Caldwell could not reconcile the Willcox/Carr-Saunders/Durand figure for African population in the sixteenth century with the twentieth-century figures. He was therefore forced to conclude that the actual population of Africa during this early period was 'probably less than half that number'.[49]

But at the same conference in which Caldwell presented his paper, Professor Thurstan Shaw presented a paper in which he demonstrates, with the benefit of archaeology, that the figure of 20 million for West African population in AD 1500, derived partly from the Willcox/Carr-Saunders/Durand estimate, is in general agreement with the facts and expectation when extrapolated backwards to 500 BC.[50] Taking Shaw and Caldwell together what comes out is that the Willcox/Carr-Saunders/Durand estimate of African population in AD 1500 is not an exaggeration. What is wrong with earlier discussions of African demographic history is the presentation of a stationary population from the seventeenth to the nineteenth century. When it is recognized that the African population was in fact declining from about 1650 to 1850, Caldwell's problem of reconciling the sixteenth-century figures with those of the twentieth century is at once eliminated.

The import of Caldwell's argument is that the population of sub-Saharan Africa in the nineteenth century has to be much smaller than was previously thought for it to grow at the discovered high rates and produce the relatively small size of African population in the 1950s and 1960s. This argument appears convincing. Our point of disagreement is whether this smaller-than-thought African population in the nineteenth century was due to a decline over time from a much higher level in the sixteenth century, or to a sixteenth-century population size smaller than the one estimated by earlier writers. Caldwell holds that the latter explanation is the correct one. On this we differ. But this view still means that the effects of the export slave trade produced a declining population in Africa up to the middle decades of the nineteenth century. If the size of the African population in the sixteenth century was much smaller than that indicated by previous estimates, then the effects of exporting the known numbers of slaves annually from this small population would have been still more devastating. If the population figures employed in Fage's calculations are reduced by a half, as Caldwell suggests, our argument for a declining population would be even more strongly supported.

It seems clear, therefore, that the existing evidence strongly supports the conclusion that the population of sub-Saharan Africa was declining from the seventeenth to the nineteenth century. We often forget that while the slave trade and its disturbances were taking their toll, the African population had also to contend with natural demographic calamities arising from climatic change and plagues which afflicted all continents periodically during these centuries. The African demographic predicament was that the slave trade and its disturbances made it impossible for time to heal the wounds inflicted by nature, as was the case in other territories.

It is appropriate at this juncture to bring in the issue of what the population of sub-Saharan Africa would have been without the export slave trade. Caldwell's judgement on this subject is that all the persons exported through the Atlantic trade would have produced 'no more than about four million' descendants.[51] This rather curious calculation arises from some factual historical errors. First, it is based on the assertion that 'only about one-sixth of the slaves were females. . . .'[52] In relation to the evidence we displayed earlier, this is a staggering error of over 100 per cent. Second, the calculation implies that subsistence conditions in Africa would have made it impossible to maintain all the descendants that would have been produced by those exported. This is contrary to the facts of African history. Land, the main source of subsistence, remained abundant in relation to population. The growth of population which began in the late nineteenth century after the abolition of export slave trade was not checked by inadequate supply of the means of subsistence. In fact, the substantial expansion of agricultural export production, and the increase in food production to feed the growing numbers, were all achieved between the mid nineteenth and mid twentieth centuries through the movement of cultivators into previously uncultivated lands. It was the discovery of this fact that inspired the vent-for-surplus theory by development economists. It has been shown that even in Senegal, where export cash-crop production developed very early in the nineteenth century, the maximum population densities that the available land could sustain under traditional methods of cultivation were not reached until around the middle decades of the twentieth century.[53] What is more, the whole argument about low population density in pre-colonial Africa being due to the low population holding capacity of the agricultural land, arising from poor soils, has been subjected over the years to continuous deflation. Evidence from the Kano close-settled zone of northern Nigeria, the densely populated portions of Ibo land and Ibibio land of southeastern Nigeria, the hill-top settlements of the Mandara mountains, the Jos and Adamawa Plateaux, and from other places in Africa, shows that land conditions constitute no insurmountable obstacle to high population density in most of sub-Saharan Africa.[54]

There is, therefore, a great deal of evidence to show that African soils can stand intensive cultivation under proper care, and that historically African cultivators successfully adopted intensive cultivation techniques wherever the ratio of population to accessible cultivatable land demanded it.

This being the case, a more useful question to ask is how many descendants the 30 million Africans exported would have produced over time by about 1880, had they been left in Africa. To answer this question we have to bear in mind that the people exported were in the prime of life and, therefore, at their reproductive peak. We also have to bear in mind that the survival rate which obtained in Africa during the slave trade era was reduced by the adverse conditions created by the export slave trade.

Bearing these in mind we can search for evidence relating to the rates of reproduction among the exported Africans in the territories where they were employed as slave labourers. Unfortunately, for most of the slave importing regions, because of the extremely harsh conditions under which the slaves worked, negative rates of natural increase operated among them until late in the nineteenth century. Since it is obvious that negative rates would not have operated among the exported Africans had they been left in Africa, this evidence is not usable. The only usable evidence we have for comparison, relates to about 430,000 Africans imported into the United States of America largely after the middle of the eighteenth century. It has been shown that between this time and 1863, these Africans produced a black population of about 4,500,000.[55]

Before speculating on the rate of reproduction implied by these figures some comments are necessary. In the first place we must raise the United States import figure by 40 per cent in the light of what we discussed earlier about the magnitude of error in Curtin's estimates. This means that the black population of 4,500,000 in the United States by 1863 was produced by 602,000 slaves imported from Africa. Second, it is important to note that because slave imports into the United States were concentrated in the late eighteenth century, it actually took the imported Africans only about one century to produce the black population of 1863. By the time a large number of Africans began to arrive in the United States in the second half of the eighteenth century, the first one million Africans to leave Africa as a result of the export slave trade had done so for more than 100 years. It should also be noted that the harsh conditions of slavery, the psychological effects of slavery on the fecundity of female slaves, and the strange disease environment, all operated to depress the rate of reproduction among the imported Africans in the United States.

On the other side of the coin, some people have argued that the mortality rate in tropical Africa was higher than that in the United States, even among the imported Africans. In fact, Caldwell argues that pre-colonial West Africa was probably

the most unhealthy major region in the world. Death rates were almost certainly the world's highest (presumably close to 50 per thousand with a life expectancy at birth under 20 years) and population numbers were sustained only by equally high birth rates, achieved only by placing great cultural and social stress on high fertility values.[56]

However, as we shall show later, the population of tropical Africa by 1500 relative to world population of that time, together with demographic processes in Africa between 1850 and 1945, shows that Caldwell is exaggerating. It would seem that he has taken the mortality rates which operated under conditions created by the export slave trade as the normal rates for pre-colonial Africa.

The point may also be made that the slaves in the United States received some modern medical attention, however minimal the effect may have been for their health. All told, there were certainly some factors which operated to raise the rate of reproduction among the Africans imported into the United States between 1750 and 1863. But when these are set against those which operated as depressants, it is not easy to decide the direction of the net result. For the sake of argument, let us assume that all the points made above notwithstanding the reproduction rates which operated among the Africans in the United States between 1750 and 1863 were twice the rates that would have operated among all the Africans exported had they been left in Africa. Under this assumption the 30 million Africans exported would have produced an additional population of a little over 112 million by around 1880, had they been left in Africa.[57]

If we had no other evidence not much weight would be placed on this kind of calculation. But the evidence relating to the population of Africa by 1500, and to the growth of African population between 1850 and World War II, shows that in the absence of modern medicine natural conditions in tropical Africa are not particularly hostile to population growth. During the period 1850 to 1939 the available modern medical facilities were restricted to a tiny minority of Africans in the limited urban centres. The vast majority of Africans continued to depend on traditional medicine as their forefathers had done for centuries. Surely the explanation for the population growth of the period cannot be attributed to the availability of modern medicine. The ending of the export slave trade which allowed internal and external trade in the products of the African soil to expand, thereby producing improved social and economic conditions, must to a great extent provide the explanation for the population expansion of the period.[58]

These improved economic and social conditions are often related strictly to colonial rule.[59] The implied argument seems to be that incessant warfare, slave raiding, political fragmentation and instability, underdeveloped infrastructures for large-scale inter-regional and local trade, were all due to independent processes operating within sub-Saharan Africa. Then came colonial rule to suppress these internal processes and to build the needed infrastructures for the expansion of internal and external trade.

However, we shall show later that the unusually violent conditions which prevailed in sub-Saharan Africa up to the eve of colonial intervention were largely due to the export slave trade and its aftermath. But another important point should be made at this juncture. Before the late nineteenth century when some governments began to embark on large-scale infrastructural developments as part of a planned programme to achieve national economic development, the building of economic infrastructures was usually the outcome of private entrepreneurs' response to economic pressures. The economic infrastructures which supported the first industrial revolution in the world – that of Britain in the late eighteenth and early nineteenth centuries – were all built by private entrepreneurs. The profitable conditions which made this kind of investment attractive to these private entrepreneurs were created by the interaction of expanding external and internal trade.

This process of historical development is not limited to western societies. There is some evidence to show that had the conditions been right African societies were capable of responding in the same way. The 1872 constitution of the Fante Confederation gives some idea of possible independent African response to opportunities for economic modernization. Some of the aims of the leaders of the Confederation as contained in article eight of the constitution are instructive:

That it be the object of the Confederation:
 i To promote friendly intercourse between all the kings and chiefs of Fanti, and unite them for offensive and defensive purposes against their common enemy.
 ii To direct the labours of the Confederation towards the improvement of the country at large.
 iii To make good and substantial roads throughout all the interior districts included in the Confederation.
 iv To erect school-houses and establish schools for the education of all children within the Confederation, and to obtain the service of efficient schoolmasters.
 v To promote agricultural and industrial pursuits, and to endeavour to introduce such new plants as may hereafter become sources of profitable commerce to the country.
 vi To develop and facilitate the working of the mineral and other resources of the country.[60]

The efforts of the Asante government to modernize the country's economy and administration in the last quarter of the nineteenth century, are even more reflective of the response of the African bourgeoisie to economic conditions. Thanks to the monumental work by Ivor Wilks, these modernization efforts have been generously

Introduction 35

documented.⁶¹ They included attempts by the government to have a railway constructed in the country. The first attempt was made in 1892, and a second in 1895.

The Ghanaian bourgeoisie were not alone in their response to the changing economic conditions under the impact of commodity trade in the nineteenth century. The Egba rulers of south-western Nigeria showed a similar response. In 1908, one of their spokesmen declared:

I think the worst enemy of the Egbas will admit that no other nation has been more active in road making than the Egbas. For the last six or seven years the Alake has busied himself with nothing more than Roads! Roads! Roads! Roads! and Markets! Even before the Lagos Government rose to this, we have broken down numberless houses in order to have good roads in the town and there are a number of roads from the farm districts into the town of very good lengths and use.... It is the road constructed that the Egba Farmers' Association are now taking advantage of to establish a waggon service.... But we cannot make roads which are not useful.⁶²

The last sentence of the quote is worthy of note. It underlines the point we made earlier about the conditions necessary for either the independent bourgeoisie or their representatives in government to invest in the improvement of transport facilities. The Egba chief demonstrated that the African bourgeoisie and their governments were aware of the fact that transport facilities could not be provided before the volume of trade made such investment economic. This is why it looks like putting the cart before the horse, when analysts talk of lack of transport facilities hindering trade in Africa. Of course, historically the provision of transport facilities stimulated the growth of trade. But, in the first instance, it was the volume of trade that attracted investment in the development of transport, except in cases where such developments were related to military purposes as was the case in the Roman empire. The same point is well demonstrated in medieval Europe where, it is said,

roads would not be improved so long as economic growth did not put sufficient pressure on people who were to use them and since economic growth depended partly on good roads and large ships, transportation was enmeshed in a closed circle. To pry the circle open, the Commercial Revolution needed the collaboration of producers and consumers everywhere, the merchants providing the spark, the whole society offering the fuel. It was a long process....⁶³

It does not make any economic sense for one to argue that the European traders and the African merchant princes would not have seen their own self-interest in the development of internal transport facilities if and when the expansion of commodity trade and production made it necessary. The important point about the export slave trade is that it did not create any pressures in Africa for the improvement of internal transport facilities, since the commodity involved carried itself on its own feet. The transport problems created by the trade were in shipping and were taken care of in Europe. It is thus easy to understand why all the major developments in internal transport facilities in Europe, especially in England in the second half of the eighteenth century, failed to filter down to Africa through the agency of the European traders, as American food crops did before the slave trade came to dominate African overseas trade. The argument here is that in the absence of the export slave trade, the growth of external and internal trade in the products of the African soil would have stimulated infrastructural developments in sub-Saharan Africa before the twentieth century.

One of the few attempts to deal with the issue of what the population of Africa would have been in the absence of the export slave trade includes an assumption which contains some of the elements of our foregoing analysis. This is the effort by Dr Mitchell to construct a hypothetical growth curve of West African population from AD 1500 to 2000, had the export slave trade not occurred.[64] The assumption in question is that the opening up of sea trade with other parts of the world caused the rate of population growth in Africa to increase from the 1.2 per 1000 per annum of the period before 1500 to the high growth rates of about 30 per 1000 per annum of the recent decades.[65] Unfortunately, however, Mitchell does not deal with the issue of how the operation of the export slave trade delayed the point in time when the high growth rates began to operate. My own view, briefly stated, is that the growth of sea trade in African commodities such as pepper, gold, cloth, wood, ivory, etc., in the fifteenth and sixteenth centuries encouraged a gradual increase in population growth rates in the sixteenth century. Had this sea trade in African commodities continued to grow over the seventeenth, eighteenth and nineteenth centuries, this increase in population growth rates would have continued and the twentieth-century high rates would have been achieved in the late eighteenth or early nineteenth century. But, as we shall show later, because the export slave trade prevented the growth of sea trade in African commodities with other parts of the world, the increase in population growth rates was stopped while the export slave trade lasted. It was not until the middle decades of the nineteenth century when the export slave trade had declined sufficiently to allow the growth of sea trade in African commodities did the increase begin again. Hence, the high rates could not be achieved until the middle decades of the twentieth century.

We can now relate the foregoing argument and direct evidence to our

Introduction 37

estimate of 112 million additional population in sub-Saharan Africa by about 1880 had there been no export slave trade. The important thing about the figure is not whether it would have been the exact additional population, but that it indicates an order of magnitude. And this order of magnitude is strongly supported by the analysis based on the application of economic and demographic theory to direct and indirect evidence. The generalization that flows from this analysis is that the low population density of sub-Saharan Africa during the pre-colonial period was the direct product of the export slave trade and its attendant disturbances. It is to be expected that in the absence of the export slave trade different parts of sub-Saharan Africa would have experienced different rates of natural population increase over time. But ultimately, population pressure on resources in areas experiencing higher rates of growth would have forced some people in such areas to move to those regions with lower rates and, therefore, lower densities. This has been the historical course of population movement the world over. And this is what the Ibo of South-eastern Nigeria have been doing during the present century.

The fact that some parts of sub-Saharan Africa managed to record some increase in their population during this period when the overall population of the region was declining would suggest that there were areas which experienced serious depopulation. The evidence of ethnolinguistic continuity on the Guinea coast established by Dr Hair does not invalidate this point.[66] In order to prove or disprove the negative demographic impact of the export slave trade at the micro level, one has to distinguish between the victim regions on the one hand, and the slave-'producing' and slave-selling regions on the other. The states on the Guinea coast were largely slave sellers and partly slave 'producers'. Therefore the Guinea coast is the wrong place to look for evidence of negative demographic impact of the export slave trade. More important, one does not need evidence of total extermination or displacement of whole ethnic groups to establish substantial negative demographic repercussions of the export slave trade and its disturbances, as we have shown. The serious demographic impact of the Thirty Years War on German States has been well established, yet there is no evidence of ethnolinguistic discontinuity in those states.[67]

In the same way, the assertion by Fage that 'West African communities sold slaves for export with some regard to their capacity to do so without causing serious damage to their populations and economies and their chances of growth',[68] misses the point. The Muslims in the Sudanese states who raided their non-Muslim neighbours for slaves, the Nupe armies that raided some Yoruba territories in the fifteenth and sixteenth centuries, the Oyo armies that raided the Mahi and other northern territories in the seventeenth and eighteenth centuries, the Asante and Dahomean armies that fought wars and raided their neighbours for slaves, and the Ijebu who instigated kidnapping, raiding and warfare in Yorubaland in the late eighteenth century, were not interested in taking care to avoid 'causing serious damage' to the population and economies of the 'foreign' societies they raided and against whom they waged wars. Even in places like Akwamu and the Senegambian states that tended to raid and sell the peasants within their own kingdoms or empires, it does not seem that the authorities took any care to avoid 'causing serious damage to their populations and economies'. If they did, how does one explain those social and political upheavals connected with slaving operations in these areas, which are now well documented?[69]

The export slave trade and internal slavery

The relationship between the export slave trade and internal slavery in Africa has become one of the central themes in the analysis of external slave trade impact on African societies. In the face of growing attack on the immorality of their lucrative trade, the British slave traders in the late eighteenth century argued that the export slave trade was merely incidental to slavery and slave raiding in Africa and not the cause of those evils as the abolitionists claimed. In other words, the slave traders were arguing that slavery, slave raiding and slave trade had always been part of African historical processes, even before export slave trade began. By the nineteenth century the view of the British slave traders had become fashionable among most European travellers to Africa. Lord Lugard asserted that 'slavery has been an African institution for a 1000 years' and that 'you could not send three men on a mission, or two would combine to enslave the third'.[70]

In the light of these assertions Walter Rodney examined the history of the Upper Guinea coast where slavery had become common in the nineteenth century, in order to discover the circumstances in which the institution developed. In a paper published in 1966, Rodney demonstrated convincingly that the nineteenth-century institution of slavery which existed in the Upper Guinea coast was not indigenous to the region, but rather developed directly from the export slave trade. What existed in the Upper Guinea coast before the growth of the export slave trade was 'a small number of political clients in the households of the kings and chiefs of the area'.[71] Rodney holds that there are indications that the Atlantic slave trade stimulated the growth and development of the

Introduction 39

institution of slavery in other parts of Africa as it did in the Upper Guinea coast area.

The Rodney thesis provoked a number of reactions. Notable among these is the one by Fage.[72] Fage accepts Rodney's thesis as it applies to the Upper Guinea coast but rejects its application to other parts of Africa. For African territories outside the Upper Guinea coast, Fage argues that the growth and development of the institution of slavery was associated with the growth of export trade in African commodities, first in the Sudanese states and later in the states nearer to the coast. As Fage puts it:

In a situation in which there was an abundance of land but a scarcity of people, traditional village societies based on ties of kinship and engaged in subsistence agriculture were unable to take advantage of all the opportunities arising when they were touched by growing external demands for scarce and valuable commodities such as gold, salt, copper or ivory. There was a shortage of people available to act as traders and carriers, to work in the mines, to provide the political organization and military security to enable trade to flow freely, or to provide food and other support [for] those withdrawn from the subsistence sector to engage in these new activities. The solution lay in the emergence of kings powerful enough to impress labour and to secure tribute; and the growth of monarchies with their courts and craftsmen, officials, priests and soldiers serving the needs of their courts and governments, meant that the process of converting ordinary men into slaves, clients or tributaries was further accelerated.[73]

Thus, according to the Fage thesis, powerful states together with their military organizations emerged in response to the need to impress labour to produce commodities for export. To find empirical evidence to support this hypothesis one has to examine the volume and the mode of production of export commodities in sub-Saharan Africa before the expansion of slave exports from the tenth century onward. The point in time when the powerful states of pre-colonial Africa emerged and the circumstances under which they developed their military character will all be important supporting evidence.

From the point of view of value, the most important commodity exported by way of the trade across the Sahara and the Atlantic trade before the growth of export slave trade was gold. Evidence from the Akan gold mines shows that gold production at this time was labour intensive.[74] But on the basis of evidence relating to the Sahelo-Sudanic areas, Professor Claude Meillassoux states that, 'The production of gold was mostly the work, not of slaves belonging to a ruler, but of independent populations'.[75] This statement is in general agreement with the evidence of John Barnes who was resident in West Africa in the eighteenth century for thirteen years, and was the British governor of Senegambia from 1763 to 1766. In 1789 Barnes told a committee of the British House of Commons that in areas of West Africa where gold was obtained from mines, the gold so collected was distributed to the different people working for it: 'the Prince has a share; the clergy have a share; and the labouring workman has the remainder. Whoever sells his share, it is his own property what he receives in exchange'.[76] The indication, therefore, is that servile labour of any form was not very important in gold production.

In the Atlantic trade, pepper was the next important export commodity. But there is no evidence that the pepper sold in places around the Sierra Leone coast and in the Benin trading area was produced by slave labour. In the case of Benin, the pepper, cotton cloth and other export commodities sold to the Europeans in the fifteenth and sixteenth centuries were obtained by the rulers largely through trade with the neighbouring peoples.[77] Again, Dike's account of the peopling of the Nigerian Delta area does not show that early commodity trade with the Europeans stimulated the growth of slavery in this area. Dike shows that free migration of people into this region had been going on before the fifteenth century, mainly from Benin. But between 1450 and 1600 there was a large movement of free peoples into the region in connection with the development of commodity trade with the Europeans. It was during this period that the delta city-states were founded. According to Dike, 'once the states were founded and the settlers' position as middle men consolidated, fresh voluntary migrations from the hinterland to the coast were practically impossible'.[78] Henceforth the inflow of new populations during the era of the export slave trade became dependent on the accumulation of slaves by the great traders of the delta city-states. This account does not show that the Niger Delta societies were employing slave labour in export activities before the growth of the export slave trade in this area, from the seventeenth century onward. On the contrary, it shows that free labour was forthcoming from the hinterland during the era of commodity export trade.

That there was no automatic connection between the growth of commodity trade and slavery in the period before the growth of export slave trade in Africa is further demonstrated by the early trade of the Yao, east of Lake Nyasa. For centuries they traded to the coast with tobacco, hoes and skins in exchange for calico, salt and beads. During this period of commodity trade the Yao are said to have known nothing about the value of slaves. As the Fishers put it:

Then the coast people offered them guns and powder, asking in return for ivory

Introduction 41

and slaves; and before long, the Yao were refusing to accept any other commodities from their contacts in the interior. The slave trade became so much a part of the Yao national heritage that the children played a game, much like snakes-and-ladders, in which beans represented traders and slaves on their way to the coast; the loser was said 'to have died on the way'.[79]

Moving to the timing of the formation of powerful states with their elaborate military organizations and the circumstances of their formation it becomes even more difficult to sustain Fage's hypothesis. Apart from Benin which was already a powerful state before the arrival of the Europeans, all the other militarily powerful Guinea states – Akwamu, Denkyira, Asante, Whydah, Dahomey – developed their military character and power after the middle decades of the seventeenth century, that is, during the era of the export slave trade.[80] If the elaborate military machines of those states were developed in order to impress labour for the production of export commodities, then it is odd indeed that they were established when commodity export production was already declining seriously as the export slave trade was expanding. In the case of Oyo which developed its military character and power before it became involved in the Atlantic slave trade, the evidence indicates that this may have been in reaction to slave raids from the north.[81]

Everything considered, therefore, it can be demonstrated that the historical facts are largely against Fage's hypothesis. The evidence does not show that the development of commodity export trade across the Sahara led to the growth of powerful states using elaborate military machines to impress labour for export production before the expansion of the export slave trade across the Sahara. In the same way, the use of military machines to capture free individuals in the Atlantic hinterland occurred largely after the middle decades of the seventeenth century when Atlantic commodity trade was in decline and so was not connected with the production of commodities for that trade.

In contrast to Fage's thesis, Professor Meillassoux's analysis of the processes leading to widespread slavery in sub-Saharan Africa provides many details which very much strengthen Rodney's thesis. Meillassoux puts the growth and spread of military aristocracies, associated with powerful military states, at the centre of the institution of slavery in the Sudan and the coastal areas. As he puts it:

The evidence gives the picture of slavery linked with some aristocratic forms of society: court slavery, military slavery, and plantation slavery, devoted to the reproduction of the dominant class and its means of domination, that is war and the administration of war.[82]

Meillassoux argues that the origin of these military states, both in medieval Sudan and later in the areas to the coast, was directly connected with the growth of export slave trade, first across the Sahara, and later across the Atlantic.

Slaving activity and the permanent military deployment that it engendered, explain better than the production and trade in gold, the constitution of aristocratic and warlike states. Certainly one cannot overlook the importance of gold bearing resources for states that controlled their circulation and which, by making possible the purchase of horses and other goods, consolidated the force and the prestige of the princes. But the gold trade does not explain the features of the medieval states. The failure of the Mali rulers' *military* attempts to seize the gold mines is well known; as soon as force was used, the miners abandoned their places and production stopped for lack of producers. Great war machines were not designed for establishing permanent organised productive activity, nor for its control.[83]

Both the timing and the circumstances of the development of the military states in the Sudan and later in the area nearer to the coast make Meillassoux's conclusion far more relevant to the historical facts. Whether for purposes of aggression or defence these states developed their military machines in circumstances closely associated with the export slave trade. What is more, the captives procured by the armies of these states were not employed by the kings to produce goods for trade. As Meillassoux rightly points out, 'in commerce, the king used the slave more as an object in the transaction than as a producer'. It was only after the abolition of the export slave trade that some of them like the king of Dahomey tried to employ their captives in the production of export commodities as a form of adjustment to the new situation.

The Rodney–Meillassoux line of analysis has been adopted by a number of scholars, in particular, Martin Klein and Paul Lovejoy. While extending the Rodney–Meillassoux argument in the light of evidence from archival records and extensive field work, the latter have added some new points. They argue in the Meillassoux way that the export slave trade directly and indirectly led to the rise of militaristic states and to the dominance of a military class. But an important point is added, that:

the participation of states in the production of slaves helped keep slave prices low and account for the tendency toward extensive slave use. Domestic employment of slaves became pegged to the existence of the foreign market and its supply. This relationship between internal consumption and export demand was a pattern that later extended to the non-Muslim areas near the coast.[84]

This argument implies the operation of the economies of scale in slave

Introduction 43

'production' as a result of the existence of large external demands to which large-scale producers, the states, responded. As the authors argue, the resulting deflated levels of slave prices, together with the negative consequences of slave 'production' for economic development, seriously hampered the development of alternative forms of labour.

Some writers have tried to discount the important role of external demand in stimulating the growth and development of internal slavery in Africa by citing the increase of internal slavery after export demand had been cut off.[85] In reply, Martin Klein provides three answers:

First, centuries of slave trading have left Africa with social and economic structures adapted to the capture, trade and exploitation of slaves. Second, the demand for tropical products made the exploitation of slave labour within Africa increasingly remunerative. Third, new and more efficient weapons made it easier for smaller groups of men to impose their will on larger populations and thus facilitated slave raiding.[86]

The first answer is certainly the most important explanation and this is made clear in Klein's analysis.[87] But Klein's answers still leave much that should be brought into the explanation. One important point to note is that private slave holding (as opposed to state holding) in Africa was for both economic and status reasons.

For those who held slaves in order to employ them to produce commodities either for the export market or the domestic market or both, the question arising is why they preferred this form of labour. The answer certainly revolves around the relative prices of different forms of labour. Klein and Lovejoy have looked at the conditions which affected the 'production' and prices of slaves in relation to other forms of labour. But they have not seriously examined the conditions which affected the supply and prices of these other forms of labour.

Empirically and conceptually it is possible to indicate a number of conditions for the supply of non-servile labour. The most important condition is population growth which raises the ratio of population to cultivatable land. This leads to the development of private property rights in land. As population growth continues, a point will be reached when all available cultivatable land has been taken up and a landless class begins to build up. At this point people who are unable to secure enough land to provide adequate subsistence will move into some form of non-agricultural self-employment, like trading or handicraft production, or into share-cropping or free wage-labour, depending on the prevailing economic and political conditions. This process can be encountered in the history of many parts of the world that experienced long periods of population expansion. This was true of Western Europe from the Middle Ages.[88] It has also been shown that the decline of slavery and the growth of a free labour market in Egypt from the late 1880s onward was very much associated with population growth in that country.[89] But in sub-Saharan Africa the export slave trade effectively prevented population growth during the 300 years or so preceding the growth of European demand for African commodities in the nineteenth century. This seriously affected the supply of non-servile labour. It was the interaction between the situation arising from this, and the social, political and economic structures inherited from the era of the export slave trade, that led to increased slavery and slave raiding in some places in the late nineteenth century, when the production of commodities for export and for internal exchange called for more labour than was available.

However, low population alone does not provide a full explanation. Land for subsistence agriculture continued to be in abundant supply in many parts of Africa in the first half of this century, yet there was a massive movement of free labour to places where wage employment was available. The reason for this is that wage employment in these places offered higher standards of living than could be procured from subsistence agriculture. In some cases share-cropping, which made it possible for peasants to engage in both subsistence and cash-crop agriculture, was devised. This was an important way of procuring labour for the rubber industry in the Urhobo area of present-day Bendel State in Nigeria. But in the nineteenth century, it would seem, the political, economic and social structures inherited from the export slave trade era still made it cheaper to procure slaves than to pay wages sufficiently higher than incomes in subsistence agriculture or to adopt share-cropping. Thus, the conclusion by Martin Klein, that it is not

> an exaggeration of the slave trade's role to suggest that the most important effect of centuries of slave trading was not in the loss of peoples but in the adaptation of social and political structures to the trade and the resulting failure to develop[90]

is important in stressing the consequences of those structures for subsequent developments. But it has to be qualified in order to stress the equally important role of population losses.

As for those who held slaves for purposes of social status, the question to ask is why they preferred this form of showing off their material achievement. And the historical evidence indicates that there were many – particularly among the wealthy middle men in the export slave trade of the Niger Delta – who manifested their material success in this way.

Introduction 45

Professor Igbafe states that:

The possession of a large number of slaves was, in pre-colonial Benin, an index of a man's social status and the degree of respectability which he could command in the estimation of the people.[91]

For the Cross River area of South-eastern Nigeria, Dr Latham says:

The profits of commerce were not invested in capitalistic production. Instead, any surplus above the demands of commercial liquidity was converted into slaves, the most desired and status-conferring possession in Cross River society.[92]

The explanation for this behaviour is to be found in the fact that opportunities for capital investment outside the slave trade were limited. In addition, commercialization and, therefore, monetization of the African economies at this time had been very much restricted, although trade and commercial intercourse were widespread. All this restricted opportunities for the accumulation of real wealth and for various forms of ostentatious consumption.

The fact is that the export slave trade contributed in no small way to the limited commercialization and monetization of African economies at this time, as can be seen from different sections of our analysis above. To this extent, therefore, the export slave trade helped in creating conditions which favoured the accumulation of slaves as a status symbol, and so, increasing internal demand for slaves. As Igbafe has shown in the case of Benin, after the slave trade was cut off, 'the growth of trade and the use of currency ultimately created a new standard of wealth which gradually readjusted the situation'.[93]

It is clear, therefore, that the export slave trade to the Muslim world and across the Atlantic was a major factor in the growth and spread of slavery in sub-Saharan Africa. This conclusion does not depend on whether or not there were some forms of limited servitude in some parts of sub-Saharan Africa before the growth of export slave trade. The crucial issue is what the export slave trade did to the extent and character of slavery in the region. It is particularly important to note that the historical evidence shows that there were no large-scale slave-producing and slave-selling states in sub-Saharan Africa before the expansion of the export slave trade from the tenth century onward. The emergence of such states was directly associated with the export slave trade.

Political consequences

We have seen that there are conflicting views about the demographic impact and about the relationship between the external slave trade and internal slavery. But it would seem that there have been more heated disagreements on the political consequences than on any other aspect of the trade's impact on African societies. The main area of contention is the extent to which African states fought wars deliberately to acquire captives for export. In a broader sense, the issue is the extent to which one can explain political conflicts, whether between states or within states, in terms of the export slave trade.

These issues have tended to evoke a great deal of emotion, obscuring the historical reality. There are some who consider it degrading to the level of civilization achieved by pre-colonial African states to accept that pre-colonial African rulers fought wars in order to acquire captives for export. This attitude seems to have arisen from a reaction to the 'savage Africa' hypothesis propagated by colonial rulers to justify colonial rule. W. D. Cooley writing in 1845, lamented the tendency among European reporters of presenting nothing remarkable about Africa except an 'extravagant bad taste with which they relate incredible barbarities perpetrated by natives'.[94] As Kjekshus puts it:

Cooley here pointed to a general assumption that a state of barbarism reigned in Africa, that the writer had not so much to prove this as to confirm it, and that the more solidly this impression could be embedded in the readership the greater would be the glory of bringing Christian light and civilization, trade and administration to peoples suffering as much from self as from slavery.[95]

In reaction to the savage Africa hypothesis scholars of African origin demonstrated convincingly that pre-colonial African states were not barbaric, but on the contrary, they reached a high level of cultural civilization. In the context of this general thrust it was thought, for reasons which are not altogether clear, that to explain political and social conflicts in economic terms – especially the slave trade – diminishes the level of civilization in pre-colonial Africa. Conversely, it was thought that attributing conflicts within or between states to 'political' factors within Africa raises the level of civilization in pre-colonial Africa. Thus, after criticizing European characterization of the Ashanti wars, Kwame Arhin concludes:

Our examination here shows that whatever may have been the origins, in the sense of reasons, of the Ashanti wars, there was developed the notion of uniting principally the Akans in political subjection to the Ashanti king. Whether one believes that this notion sprang from economic motives or from the fairly universal human desire to create larger political aggregates, especially in locally contiguous areas with cultural homogeneity, depends on one's view of human nature or of history in general; or in some cases, on whether or not one believes that the African was different from others from the point of view of the considerations that shaped his history.[96]

This reaction to the savage Africa hypothesis seems to have had some influence on writers of non-African origin as well. For example, Curtin states that:

Africa was supposed to be a savage continent made that way largely by the slave traders. As 'savages,' the Africans had been seen only as victims, never as men in command of their own destiny, having a serious role to play in their own history.... If they said that African states had had real and legitimate interests, which they pursued through diplomacy and wars – that they were not mere puppets in the hands of the slave traders – the new Africanists could be accused of trying to shift the burden of guilt for the horrors of the trade from European to African heads.[97]

This type of approach to the impact of the export slave trade on African societies beclouds the issues. One does not have to accept the savage Africa hypothesis in order to show that the slave trade to the Muslim world and across the Atlantic was a major cause of social tension and political conflict, both within and between states, in pre-colonial Africa. Nor does one have to propound a 'savage Europe' theory in order to show that the industrial revolution, which began in eighteenth-century Britain and then spread to the continent, led to social tension and political conflicts in Europe. It is quite easy and logical to accept the view that pre-colonial African states reached a high level of cultural development and at the same time demonstrate that the export slave trade increased social tension and political conflicts within and between these states.

A number of writers have actually tried to show that the increased social tensions and conflicts within and between African states during the slave trade era were due to internal processes in Africa to which the export slave trade was *merely* incidental. While this seems to be the position of Professor Fage, there is some contradiction in the development of his argument. At some point, Fage states that pre-colonial African rulers fought wars deliberately to acquire captives, not for export but to use them to produce goods for sale. As he puts it:

The prime motive for warfare and raiding in Africa, then, was not to secure slaves for sale and export, but to secure adequate quantities of this resource and to diminish the amounts available to rivals.[98]

We argued earlier that the historical facts make it abundantly clear that there were no large-scale slave-producing states in pre-colonial Africa before the expansion of the export slave trade to the Muslim world and across the Atlantic. But, if for the sake of argument we accept Fage's hypothesis, the question which arises is whether the Muslim and

48 *Introduction*

Atlantic demands for slaves did not greatly expand the need to gather slaves far more than were previously needed. If the answer is in the affirmative, as should be expected, is it not logical to expect this to equally increase the incidence of slave raiding and warfare fought deliberately to acquire captives?

The main point here, however, is that elsewhere Fage tries to show that pre-colonial African rulers did not engage in slave raiding or wage wars deliberately to acquire captives.[99] This argument is supported with reference to the oft-cited statements of King Kpengla of Dahomey (1774–89) and King Osei Bonsu of Ashanti (*c.* 1801–24). It is here that the contradiction arises.

The position of Dov Ronen is clear and without contradictions. Writing about Dahomey, the author states that the rulers of Dahomey fought wars deliberately to acquire captives. But the aim was not to sell them, rather, it was to use them for ceremonial sacrifices during the annual customs. According to Ronen:

Human beings were needed for the Customs; and since no Dahomean could be sacrificed (except those guilty of major crimes), other humans had to be captured, which was done in the Annual Wars which preceded the Annual Customs. It cannot be proved unequivocally that all wars were waged for the purpose of acquiring captives for the annual ceremonies, but it also appears incorrect to assume that Dahomey was a slave trading state in the sense that it waged wars solely, or mainly, for the purpose of capturing slaves for sale. It appears that the socio-religious aspects of war were far more important than its economic aspects.[100]

Again, this conclusion is derived from the reported statement of King Kpengla of Dahomey. It would seem that historians who derive their conclusions from the reported statements of the kings of Dahomey and Ashanti do not critically examine the circumstances in which those statements were made. The king of Dahomey made his statement in the 1790s when the great debate to abolish the slave trade was on in Britain. The king of Ashanti made his statement in 1820 when the painful process of adjusting to the situation created by the abolition of the slave trade was still in progress. That these kings were aware of the moral condemnation of the slave trade in Europe at the time of their interview is very clear in their statements. If one realizes the extent to which the rulers of these two states were involved in the export slave trade one would see that there is enough reason for these rulers to make that trade look less evil, less immoral and less harmful to African societies, as the European slave traders also tried to do at the time. Some portions of Osei Bonsu's statement are rather revealing:

the white men who go to council with your master, and pray to the great God for him, do not understand my country, or they would not say the slave trade was bad. But if they think it bad now, why did they think it good before. . . . If the great king would like to restore this trade, it would be good for the white men and for me too, because Ashantee is a country for war, and the people are strong; so if you talk that palaver for me properly, in the white country if you go there, I will give you plenty of gold, and I will make you richer than all the white men.[101]

It would seem somewhat naïve to expect these rulers to admit that they waged wars simply to acquire captives, in the face of the moral condemnation of this type of activity at the time, even if that was what they were doing. The statement by Osei Bonsu that 'I cannot make war to catch slaves in the bush, like a thief',[102] shows his awareness of the moral implications. This is not to say that there may not be some element of truth in what these kings are reported to have said. The issue here is that it is important to take into account the circumstances in which these statements were made.

The serious factor in Ronen's argument is his belief that the number of people annually needed in Dahomey for ceremonial sacrifices was so large that the rulers established elaborate military machines to go to war annually to acquire such people. This conclusion seems to have arisen from Ronen's failure to take into account the origin of the Dahomean state system, particularly its military character, and from his exaggerated view of human sacrifice in Dahomey. The militaristic nature of the Dahomean state was developed either for defence or for aggression, or for both in circumstances closely related to the export slave trade.[103] The huge Dahomean army was not called into being, in the first instance, for purposes of gathering captives for sacrifice. As for the numbers involved in the Dahomean sacrifices, these would seem to have been grossly exaggerated in the same way as those for Benin have now been shown to have been exaggerated.[104]

Ronen concludes his paper by asking historians to free 'traditional Dahomey' from 'the moral accusations of existing on trade in humans as well as from the white man's generosity of attributing to it, almost as a compensation, a complex centralized political system'. This, taken together with the rest of Ronen's paper, implies that it is more honourable to be accused of waging wars to acquire human beings for sacrifice than for export!

With the deepening controversy over the relationship between export demand for slaves and warfare, some scholars have tried to apply the techniques of econometric history to produce an answer. The assumption behind the application of this method is that if African states waged wars deliberately to produce slaves in response to export

50 *Introduction*

demand, then there should be a strong correlation between the quantities of slaves supplied and the prices offered over time. If no strong correlation is discovered then slave supplies were a result of internal political processes unrelated to the economic influences of profits and prices. The end result of this approach is a dichotomy between two models of warfare – a 'political warfare' model and an 'economic warfare' model.

Phillip LeVeen applied this method to the supply of slaves from the whole of sub-Saharan Africa to the Atlantic trade from 1690 to 1850. On the basis of his result LeVeen concludes that: 'there is evidence to support the contention that profit-oriented slave-raiding did occur and was an important method of enslavement'.[105] But the application of the same method to Senegambia by Curtin produced a contrary result.[106]

The main weakness of this approach to the problem is the false dichotomy which it establishes between political causes and economic causes of wars. This is revealed clearly in Curtin's conclusion that 'political enslavement obviously responded to African conditions while economic enslavement had its roots in the American plantations'.[107] The unanswered question here is the extent to which the export slave trade itself contributed to those 'African conditions' leading to war.

The argument that African rulers in their political decision-making processes were not affected in some important way by the economic gains to be made from the export slave trade would seem to make a Diogenes[108] of these rulers. But all the efforts made by some of them to monopolize the slave trade within their states do not show that they were above economic desires as the Greek philosopher seems to have been. If these rulers valued the gains to be made from the slave trade to the extent of making all the efforts to monopolize it as they did, there is no tenable ground for arguing that economic considerations relating to the slave trade could not have influenced their political decision-making processes. It is true that some analysts have employed the economic factor in a simplistic fashion, and so undermined the complexity of the relationship. This has tended to make their analyses look to some historians like variants of the outmoded colonial scholarship. But the answer is not the application of a simplistic political model that excludes economic influences. In order to provide a realistic explanation we have to look for an analytical framework that combines both the economic and non-economic processes.

Meillassoux, Hopkins, Klein and some others, have tried to provide this kind of framework in their various contributions.[109] The emphasis here is on the influence of the export slave trade on the character of the African states, particularly their militaristic character which gave the

Introduction 51

warrior class a great deal of influence in state matters. This also relates to the extent to which the vested economic interests of some groups within the states determined the direction of national interest. By examining issues of this nature it is possible to show that wars which may validly be said to be political in origin also had deep economic connections.

Apart from these considerations, it must be said too that the export slave trade in many other ways created conditions for political warfare not specifically directed towards the acquisition of slaves for export. The kidnapping and sale for export of a few traders or other individuals from neighbouring territories, often led to complicated political problems ending up in some major wars. Good examples are the political complications which arose from the activities of the Ijebu slave traders in the western towns of the Ife kingdom, which eventually led to the Owu War in Yorubaland in the early nineteenth century.[110] Similar political situations have been documented for Senegal and states in East Africa.[111] Similarly, the proliferation of firearms in connection with the slave trade, as shown in Chapter 4 in this book, contributed in some important ways to the incidence of warfare in sub-Saharan Africa during the slave trade era.

Thus, it can be said that the export slave trade was a major cause of social conflict and warfare in pre-colonial Africa. This was so not because most of the wars of the period were specifically directed towards the acquisition of captives for export. Certainly some wars were so directed, and there were slave raids specifically to acquire captives for export. But the more important element is that the export slave trade helped to create values, political and social structures, economic interests, social tensions and inter-group or inter-territorial misunderstandings, all of which encouraged frequent warfare.

Economic consequences

The ultimate result of the consequences of the export slave trade for African demographic processes, the expansion of internal slavery, the increase of social tensions, political conflicts and warfare, was economic underdevelopment in sub-Saharan Africa. A proper understanding of this subject requires that we differentiate between private costs and benefits, and social costs and benefits. For a macro-study of the subject, private costs and benefits should include the costs and benefits of individuals or groups of individuals, as well as the costs and benefits of individual towns or small sub-regions involved in the trade. Social costs and benefits should then relate to larger sub-regions, such as West

52 *Introduction*

Africa, south-west Africa (including the Loango coast area and Angola, broadly defined), East Africa, or the whole of sub-Saharan Africa. At the level of private costs and benefits, we have to distinguish between the slave-producing and/or slave-selling areas and the victim areas.[112] Some of the existing studies relate only to slave-producing and slave-selling areas.[113] Of course, implicit or explicit generalizations made for all of sub-Saharan Africa from such studies will be erroneous. My analysis is centred on social costs and benefits for the whole of sub-Saharan Africa.

One subject that is only just beginning to receive the attention of scholars is the opportunity cost of the export slave trade for African economic development. The central issue here is the extent to which the export slave trade prevented the growth and development of commodity trade between sub-Saharan Africa and the rest of the world. Because this question had never been examined in detail until recently,[114] some writers have suggested that in the absence of the slave trade there would have been no trade at all between sub-Saharan Africa and the rest of the world. This is implied in Klein's statement that:

> Economic relations first with the Mediterranean and later with the Americas were influenced by the relative absence of products the outside world wanted. Gold, ivory, spices and hides were exported north in the Middle Ages, but often this was inadequate to pay for luxury products, weapons, and skills that Africa's trading partners had to offer. With the growth of the Atlantic slave trade, the importance of slaving increased. Many societies exported nothing else, and few had anything to offer that would have attracted European traders without the lure of slaves (certain exceptions were the gum of Senegal, the gold of the Volta River area and the ivory of Benin, but none of these came close to the slave trade in total value).[115]

Curtin rightly criticized this assumption, 'that Africa had virtually nothing but slaves to sell, leaving a choice of slave trade or no trade at all'. But he agrees that 'this may have been nearly true for other regions', except for Senegambia, 'where the average slave exports from the 1680s through to the 1830s came to only about 52 per cent of the total value of export trade'.[116]

What these and other writers expressing similar views have done is to show the extent to which the export slave trade dominated the external trade of sub-Saharan Africa for many centuries. In fact, we have shown elsewhere that the export of slaves constituted over 90 per cent of West African Atlantic trade during the period 1750 to 1807, when the average annual value of West African Atlantic trade was £4.5 million.[117] What has not been given proper attention, however, is to show that it was the export slave trade which in various ways made it impossible for other forms of trade to develop. The disturbances which attended the production of captives for export were not conducive to the development of commodity production for export. Furthermore, on the African side, there was a massive withdrawal of labour and skills from the peaceful production and distribution of commodities to the military production and distribution of slaves, as the slave trade was seen to be more profitable. As Hopkins observes, 'even when palm produce prices were at their highest in the middle of the nineteenth century, it still did not pay producers to turn from exporting slaves to shipping palm oil'.[118] On the European side, so long as African slaves were available to exploit the rich natural resources of the Americas, the slave trade and the exploitation and distribution of those resources remained far more attractive and profitable than the development of commodity trade in Africa. This is why attempts by European merchants to develop commodity production and trade in Africa during the slave trade era remained half-hearted and unsuccessful.[119] The irony of the situation is that the export slave trade lowered Africa's comparative advantage, while increasing that of the Americas, in the development of commodity production and trade with Europe. The Americas were richer in natural resources, while Africa was richer in human resources, both in quality and quantity. In the absence of the export slave trade the comparative advantages of both regions would have operated differently to provide European merchants with much greater incentives to encourage the development of commodity production and trade in Africa.

The argument that Africa lacked commodities the outside world wanted evades the point. It may be valid to say that because of transportation costs it would have been difficult to develop export trade in bulky goods across the Sahara. But this is not true of the Atlantic trade. What was lacking was demand, not commodities. We know better now than Say[120] did in his day, that it is demand (or anticipated demand) that gives rise to production in a market economy. Historically, we know that the growth of European trade with the New World from the sixteenth century was not based on commodities the New World was producing in commercial quantities before the arrival of the Europeans. In other words, what attracted the Europeans to the New World was not a pre-existing commodity trade into which they fitted themselves. Rather, the production of the commodities that came to form the centre of the trade, such as sugar, were developed in the different parts of the New World, through trial and error, by Europeans looking for commodities that could be produced in the New World for which markets already existed or could be anticipated in Europe. We also know that apart from palm produce and one or two other commodities whose production had existed in Africa for several centuries, the great expansion of commodity export production that occurred in Africa in the late nineteenth and twentieth centuries was based on the development of new commodities in response to demand.

The question, therefore, is not whether commodities already existed that could have been attractive to, and retained the interest of, European merchants in Africa. The relevant question is what prevented the kind of trial and error efforts that were made in the New World in the sixteenth, seventeenth and eighteenth centuries, and in Africa in the nineteenth and twentieth centuries, from being made and producing the expansion of commodity international trade in Africa in the sixteenth, seventeenth and eighteenth centuries. The answer to this latter question, as has been demonstrated, lay with the export slave trade.

It has been argued that climatic and physical conditions would have made it impossible for West Africa to develop export production of sugar in the absence of the export slave trade.[121] Whether this is correct or not, the important point is that the development of commodity export production in Africa in the absence of the slave trade did not have to depend on sugar. The European merchants knew a host of other commodities they could have tried. And they frequently mentioned these in their correspondence.[122]

It is thus beyond reasonable doubt that the extremely low level of commodity export trade in sub-Saharan Africa up to the middle of the nineteenth century was the direct outcome of the export slave trade. The loss of the economic developmental effects that would have been associated with the expansion of commodity export trade during a period of over 300 years constitutes the greatest opportunity cost of the export slave trade for African economies. The long-term consequences of this cost are the greater still, because this was the very period when commodity export trade was acting as a powerful engine of growth and transformation for the economies of some other regions in the Atlantic basin. Hence, the export slave trade helped strongly in relegating the African economies to the periphery of the Atlantic area which came to form the centre of the world economic order in the nineteenth and twentieth centuries. Once so relegated, that situation tended to be self-perpetuating, especially under colonial rule. What worsened the situation is that the export slave trade by its nature could not stimulate any positive development, infrastructural or institutional, in the African economies. While preventing the stimulus that commodity export trade would have produced, all the slave trade did was to create social and political structures hostile to peaceful economic development.

Commodity production for consumption within Africa was also

stultified by the export slave trade. The uncontrolled importation of cheap textiles and other manufactured goods from Europe and the oriental world retarded the development of manufacturing in Africa.[123] Some historians do not properly appreciate this point. Hence Fage says:

> It has sometimes been argued that the increasing imports of European goods like cloth, metals and metalware, and spirits undermined indigenous African economic activities and was socially deleterious. But there is considerable evidence that Africans were often discriminating in their purchases. It is probably more to the point to argue that they bought only those goods which they regarded as better value than their own products, and that the net result was an increase, not a decrease, in African production and economic activity generally. There was probably also an increase in general living standards, even though new distinctions were being made between rich and poor, haves and have-nots. Thus, the increase in imports of Indian, European or American cloth meant that more people could afford to clothe themselves rather than that local manufacture ceased (or, so far as there is evidence, declined).[124]

This argument seems to have arisen from a wrong application of neo-classical economics to issues of structural and general economic transformation. There is no historical example of an economy in which the technology and organization of industrial production were transformed during a period of uncontrolled importation of cheap foreign manufactures. Certainly, the British people bought oriental textiles in the seventeenth and early eighteenth centuries because they regarded them as better value than their own products. But when the cheap and good quality oriental textiles were found to be retarding the development of British textile industries their consumption in England was prohibited early in the eighteenth century. It was this wise action of the British government which enabled the cotton textile industry in Lancashire to expand to the point where further demand pressure forced it to transform its organization and technology, thereby creating the environment for the late eighteenth- and early nineteenth-century industrial revolution in England. It has been shown that continental European countries which failed to adopt the British protectionist type of measures against the oriental textiles could not develop any important modern cotton-textile industry in the eighteenth century.[125] In the United States where the cotton-textile industry played a major role in the industrial transformation, import control has also been shown to have been crucial in the development of that key industry.[126] This is why it is reasonable to expect the uncontrolled importation of cheap foreign manufactures to have retarded the development of domestic industries in Africa during the slave trade era, a situation which was carried over to colonial rule. In fact, it has been shown that the large-scale import of oriental and European textiles took the Gold Coast market away from Benin textiles in the seventeenth century.[127]

Apart from this long-term cost in the retardation of industrial development, it has been shown that the Atlantic slave trade also produced a short-term welfare cost. The application of a static theory of gains from international trade shows that the loss of output resulting from the sale of produce was greater than the amount of goods received in exchange.[128]

Having effectively prevented the operation of stimuli from commodity export trade, the external slave trade still did not allow the operation of internal forces to bring about the transformation of African economies over time. Underpopulation arising from the slave trade prevented the operation of population pressures that would have created favourable conditions for the transformation of manufacture and agriculture.

Directly and indirectly, the inability of the manufacturing sector of African economies to develop beyond the handicraft stage can be partly attributed to the low population of the regions and its dispersion. Low population directly affected the level of demand for manufactured goods in pre-colonial Africa. And through its retardative effects on the growth of trade and specialization, underpopulation acted as a double force effectively holding down the growth of demand for manufactured goods. The consequence of this was that, in the absence of stimulating demand pressure, there was no incentive for rapid and widespread change in the organization and technology of manufacture in precolonial Africa.

The consequence of underpopulation for the agricultural sector was more immediate. The extremely low ratio of population to cultivatable land encouraged wide dispersion of population in many areas of sub-Saharan Africa. In the end, low population, in absolute terms and its wide dispersion, led to extensive, rather than intensive, forms of cultivation, which made subsistence production and local self-sufficiency predominant. Because land was never a scarce resource, no market for land developed and agriculture generally remained uncommercialized. The underdevelopment of African agriculture between 1600 and 1900 was thus due to underpopulation and lack of external demand for agricultural commodities, both of which were the direct product of the export slave trade.

From the point of view of the superstructure of pre-colonial African states, conditions associated with the export slave trade were not conducive to the development of institutions and infrastructures essential for economic development. Historical evidence shows that the

Introduction 57

differing economic interests of the dominant classes of society determine whether private resources and state powers are used for development or underdevelopment purposes. The conditions determining those interests in the first instance are created by economic, social and political processes over time. In seventeenth- and eighteenth-century Britain, owing to a combination of factors, the dominant classes had vested interests in the production and distribution of commodities. Consequently, they directed private and public efforts to provide the institutions, the infrastructures and other requirements for economic development which helped to transform the British economy under stimulating internal and external demand pressures. The same thing is true of the United States of the late eighteenth and nineteenth centuries, Germany of the nineteenth century and Japan of the nineteenth and twentieth centuries, for example. But in Africa of the slave trade era, owing to the economic and political conditions created by external demand for slaves, the dominant classes had their vested economic interests in the production and distribution of captives. In this way, there was neither economic nor political incentive to use state powers and the private resources at the disposal of the dominant classes to develop institutions, infrastructures and other requirements for the production and distribution of commodities. On the other hand, the prevalence of social structures based on slave-holders and slaves in many of the states encouraged a lop-sided pattern of income distribution which adversely affected the extent of the domestic market for mass consumer goods.

Again, the increased social tensions, political conflicts and warfare associated with the export slave trade were extremely harmful to economic development. They helped to limit the growth of trade by raising the cost of moving commodities from one area to another under conditions of widespread insecurity. Warfare and raids also limited the expansion of trade in another way. Areas easily accessible to trade and other external contacts were also the ones exposed to raids and invasions. Under the prevailing conditions of actual and anticipated insecurity, low value was placed on easily accessible areas while a premium was placed on defensive sites that were of necessity difficult to link commercially with other areas.[129] Since limited trade also means limited specialization, we can understand why deficient demand was a major barrier to the transformation of the various sectors of pre-colonial African economies.

Thus it is clear that the export slave trade operated in various ways to retard the development of the economies of sub-Saharan Africa during the period the trade lasted. Fage is obviously wrong in arguing that because large-scale emigration in the nineteenth century did not have destructive effects on the economies and societies of Western Europe, therefore the export slave trade could not have had adverse effects on African development.[130] The simple fact is that the loss of population occurred in Africa at the very moment when population pressure was required to stimulate institutional and other developments required for economic transformation. In Western Europe large-scale emigration occurred in the nineteenth century after many centuries of international commodity trade and population growth had already produced a fairly high level of modern economic development. In fact, by this time, what Rostow calls the take-off into self-sustained economic growth had already taken place, or was in the process of taking place, in some of the countries, and population was growing fast in response to the economic change. With the institutional arrangements that had already been developed, the migration of a part of the rapidly growing population made it possible for the pace of technological innovation to be maintained, leading to further economic development rather than underdevelopment, as was the case in sub-Saharan Africa. It is important to add that while emigration from Western Europe was voluntary and therefore peaceful, the slaves exported from Africa were produced through violence which was, therefore, socially disruptive.

Conclusion

To conclude the chapter, it should be stressed that the literature on the slave trade contains a variety of arguments. Some of these originate from a basic conviction on the side of some writers, that the impact of the export slave trade on African societies had earlier been exaggerated. This is probably true in some cases.

Recent researches, however, now show that when properly understood it is easy to demonstrate the great adverse effects of the trade on African societies without exaggeration. Growing information relating specifically to the trade, and to African history generally, has helped greatly in this respect. But what has probably contributed more is the growing number of new analytical concepts being brought into the discussion by scholars sufficiently acquainted with modern tools of economic, social and political analysis. This is why a growing number of experts in the field now easily accept the ramifications of the adverse impact of the trade on African societies.

This is exemplified by the report of experts who met in Haiti in 1978 under the auspices of UNESCO to discuss various aspects of the trade.[131] As stated in the report, the experts agreed that:

the traditionally organized authorities, for example in Jolof, Cayor, Balol, Songhay, Congo and Zimbabwe, were in various ways and at various times, confronted with the pressure of European and Muslim demands for slaves. They were all upset by this pressure. . . . Such upsets were accompanied by an increase of social tensions, a worsening of servitude, especially quantitatively and by a transformation of the former processes of social integration that the various forms of personal dependence provided in African society prior to the fifteenth century.

And on the economic impact of the trade, it is stated in the report that 'none of the experts present disputed the idea that the slave trade was responsible for the economic backwardness of Black Africa'.[132]

Viewed against the information assembled in this chapter, and the arguments built upon it, there is no doubt that the experts are right in their conclusion. The available evidence makes it clear that the total number of persons exported from sub-Saharan Africa to the Muslim world and the European colonies could not have been less than 30 million, during the whole period of the trade. The violent process of producing the persons exported led to a considerable loss of lives, directly and indirectly. Also, the age and sex composition of those exported make it abundantly clear that birth rates must have been seriously depressed during the period. All this evidence, when related to African demographic data in the period before 1500 and those between the late nineteenth and the first half of the twentieth century, shows beyond reasonable doubt that underpopulation in pre-colonial Africa was the direct result of the export slave trade.

Politically, the export slave trade placed an economic value on the individual persons rather than on their labour. Consequently, powerful states had no commanding economic interest in dominating weaker states politically in order to exploit the labour of the people and the natural resources of such states. Rather, the powerful states saw the weaker ones as a source of people to be captured and exported. In this way, conditions associated with the slave trade did not encourage the growth of large and stable political units, contrary to the argument of some historians. Added to this, by encouraging the dominance of the warrior class the national interests of the stronger states were directed towards the prosecution of wars, while the weaker states were forced for reasons of defence, also to become militaristic. As a result of all this, a new social formation emerged based on the dichotomy between slaves and slave-holders – the oppressed and the oppressors.

In the end, underpopulation and the political and social distortions arising from the slave trade created conditions entirely hostile to the process of economic transformation. To make matters worse, the stimulating influence of commodity export trade could not operate as the slave trade prevented the development and growth of all other forms of trade. Sub-Saharan Africa thus developed over the slave trade era as a periphery of other economies in the Atlantic area. And once that position was firmly entrenched, it tended to be self-perpetuating, particularly under colonial rule when there were no independent national governments to reverse the trend.

1 African slavery and other forms of social oppression on the Upper Guinea Coast in the context of the Atlantic slave trade
Walter Rodney

Editor's comments

In the literature on the Atlantic slave trade from Africa one often encounters the view that by the time European slave traders arrived on the west coast of Africa, African rulers already had in their possession large stocks of slaves. Thus, it is argued, when the European traders demanded slaves in exchange for their goods the African rulers, like cattle owners, were faced with an economic choice: whether it was more economically profitable for them to sell some part of their stock for the European goods (which included firearms) or retain it all. Invariably, it is said, they opted 'rationally' to sell some part of their stock of slaves. And so, the growth of the Atlantic slave trade, from this point of view, depended on the previously accumulated stocks of slaves by African rulers. In the present chapter Walter Rodney tests this hypothesis against empirical evidence relating to the Upper Guinea Coast of West Africa. On the basis of the evidence Rodney holds that the growth of the Atlantic slave trade from this region of West Africa was not based on any pre-existing stock of slaves in the possession of some privileged groups. On the contrary, he explains, the growth of slavery in the region was directly linked to the growth of the export slave trade. From this finding, Rodney suggests that the circumstances under which slavery expanded in other parts of Black Africa may have been similar to those of the Upper Guinea Coast. This broader question is taken up in Chapter 2, below, by Professor Meillassoux.

It has come to be widely accepted that slavery prevailed on the African continent before the arrival of the Europeans, and this indigenous slavery is said to have facilitated the rise and progress of the Atlantic slave trade. According to P. D. Rinchon, 'from the earliest days of the

This paper was first published in the *Journal of African History*, vol. VII no. 3 (1966), pp. 431–43. It has been reprinted here by permission of the author and the publishers. [Ed.]

trade, the majority of the Negroes were living in a state of servitude, and the native chiefs did not have far to seek for the human merchandise'.[1] Daniel Mannix, in one of the most recent accounts of the Atlantic slave trade, contends that 'many of the Negroes transported to America had been slaves in Africa, born to captivity. Slavery in Africa was an ancient and widespread institution, but it was especially prevalent in the Sudan'.[2] In the opinion of J. D. Fage, 'the presence of a slave class among the coastal peoples meant that there was already a class of human beings who could be sold to Europeans if there was an incentive to do so.... So the coastal merchants began by selling the domestic slaves in their own tribes'.[3] The main purpose of this brief study is to test these generalizations with evidence taken from the Upper Guinea Coast – the region between the Gambia and Cape Mount.

Not only did the Upper Guinea Coast have a lengthy association with the Atlantic slave trade, beginning in the 1460s and extending over four centuries, but it is also a very useful example as far as the present problem is concerned, because the so-called African 'slavery' was known to be widespread in this region during the colonial period, and emancipation was eventually brought about by the intervention of the metropolitan powers involved. Sometimes, what obtained was a quasi-feudal exploitation of labour by a ruling *élite*, who received the greater portion of the harvest.[4] More often than not, however, the 'domestic slaves', as they have been categorized, were members of their masters' households. They could not be sold, except for serious offences; they had their own plots of land and/or rights to a proportion of the fruits of their labour; they could marry; their children had rights of inheritance, and if born of one free parent often acquired a new status. Such individuals could rise to positions of great trust, including that of chief.[5]

Quite obviously, R. S. Rattray's well-known description of the Ashante 'slave',[6] which is cited in most discussions on this subject,[7] is fully applicable to the Upper Guinea Coast. Rattray was primarily concerned with the 'slave child' (*Odonko ba*), whose privileges were quite different from those of his parents and foreparents. On the Upper Guinea coast, too, the servants born in the household were distinguished from the individuals who were recruited from captives of war or from those pledged and not redeemed. These latter were vulnerable to sale, being exchanged for goods as well as serving as currency in a number of transactions such as marriage payments. During the latter part of the nineteenth century, after the Atlantic slave trade had ceased to be conducted from the Upper Guinea Coast, one of the major problems facing the administration of the colony of Sierra Leone was the persistence of the internal slave trade, mainly supplying

Slavery and other forms of social oppression 63

victims to the Mande and the Fulas.⁸ Thus, an examination of the society of the Upper Guinea Coast at a relatively recent date does reveal the presence of a category of slaves, as well as agricultural serfdom and personal service, which are represented here as 'forms of social oppression', though in many cases the oppression was extremely attenuated.

In seeking the roots of the indigenous slavery and serfdom of the Upper Guinea Coast, and in attempting to juxtapose these phenomena with the Atlantic slave trade, one is struck by the absence of references to local African slavery in the sixteenth or even the seventeenth century, when such evidence could reasonably be construed to mean that the institution preceded the advent of the Atlantic slave trade. Sometimes, the word 'slave' was indeed used, but so loosely as to apply to all the common people. For instance, the Jesuit Alonso de Sandoval reported that, when he was in Cartagena in the early seventeenth century, a priest who came over on a slave ship told him that all the talk about the injustice of slavery was nonsense, because all the Negroes were slaves of absolute kings. Sandoval then went on to pinpoint the king of Cassanga on the river Casamance as one such absolute monarch whose subjects were his slaves.⁹ In this arbitrary and figurative sense, the word 'slave' is equally applicable not only to the common people of Europe at that time but also to the proletariat of the capitalist world.

There is only one clear instance where labour services on the Upper Guinea Coast were associated with the limitation of the privileges of free men. In Sierra Leone at the beginning of the seventeenth century, when a subject was in danger in one kingdom he could flee to the court of another king and place himself at the mercy of the latter. He became the 'slave' of that king, either remaining in his service or liable for sale (to the Europeans).¹⁰ At that time, local customs were already influenced by the presence of slave-buying Europeans, as well as by the arrival of an alien Mande ruling element some decades previously; but the essentials of the practice almost certainly preceded these two external factors. In 1507 the Portuguese chronicler Valentim Fernandes made a statement which could refer to nothing else: 'The king has no servants other than his slaves. Sometimes a young stranger arrives and seeks the protection of the king, who looks upon the young man as his own.'¹¹

When the occasional references to 'slaves' on the Upper Guinea Coast in the sixteenth and seventeenth centuries are carefully scrutinized, they therefore point, at the very most, to the presence of a small number of political clients in the households of the kings and chiefs of the area. If they were to have constituted the pad for launching the Atlantic slave trade, it would never have left the ground.

It is difficult to believe that any observers could possibly have overlooked features such as chattel slaves, agricultural serfs, or even household servants if these had been numerous and markedly disprivileged. Several of the sixteenth- and seventeenth-century Portuguese descriptions of the Upper Guinea Coast are replete with details of the structure of African society on that section of the West African littoral; and the only distinction that they consistently emphasized was the one between rulers and subjects – the *fidalgos* and *plebeus*.[12] For the neighbouring Senegambia, Valentim Fernandes left testimony that the Wolof nobles had several households, each comprising a wife, children and 'slaves', the latter working six days for the mistress and one day every week for themselves.[13] Alvares de Almada in 1594 also referred to Fula 'slaves' ruling the Wolofs.[14] Both these writers dealt with the area between the Gambia and Cape Mount at great length, without mentioning any similar phenomena.

On matters of trade, even more than on matters of ethnographic interest, the early Portuguese chroniclers were scrupulous in recording details. In the sixteenth and seventeenth century they knew of the trade routes between the Futa Djalon and the coast, linking the littoral peoples with the Mande and Fula of the interior. Yet, in enumerating the products exchanged, they never once mentioned or hinted that slaves were involved in this commerce.[15] Cloths, pieces of dried indigo and iron bars were noted as being the circulating media in the barter economy of the Upper Guinea Coast, but never slaves in the early period. Non-mention in such circumstances is presumptive of non-existence.

Though one can identify no African slavery, serfdom or the like on the Upper Guinea Coast during the first phase of European contact, that region was one of the first sections of the West African coast from which slaves were exported; and in the sixteenth century the transfer of Africans from the Upper Guinea Coast to the Spanish Indies was already a significant undertaking. No slave class was necessary to make this possible, because there was in existence a fundamental class contradiction between the ruling nobility and the commoners; and the ruling class joined hands with the Europeans in exploiting the African masses – a not unfamiliar situation on the African continent today.

While the view that African slavery and 'domestic slavery' preceded and stimulated the Atlantic slave trade has been given wide currency, no thought has been spared for any other possible connection between the two. Was it merely coincidence that it was only after two and a half centuries of slave trading that the vast majority of the peoples of the Upper Guinea Coast were said to have been living in a state of subjection? Curiously enough, Mungo Park, though he added his authority to

Slavery and other forms of social oppression   65

the pro-slavery arguments, had posed this question, while absolving himself from answering it. After describing what amounted to both chattel slavery and household service in the Senegambia and the western Sudan, he wrote: 'How far it is maintained and supported by the Slave Traffic which, for two hundred years, the nations of Europe have carried on with the natives of the coast, it is neither within my province, nor in my power to explain.'[16]

It is a striking fact that the greatest agents of the Atlantic slave trade on the Upper Guinea Coast, the Mande and the Fulas, were the very tribes who subsequently continued to handle the internal slave trade, and whose society came to include significant numbers of disprivileged individuals labouring under coercion. The sequence of events points in the very direction in which Mungo Park had not cared to look too closely. In the first place, the political and religious dominance of the Mande and Fulas over the littoral peoples of the Upper Guinea Coast in the eighteenth century was based on a mixture of motives, among which the desire to sell more slaves to the Europeans featured prominently. Thus the Atlantic slave trade can immediately be identified as being partly responsible for the vassalage to which the coastal tribes were reduced. In the second place, the raiding of individuals for sale to the Europeans encouraged the marauding tribes to retain numbers of their captives to serve their own needs. When, for example, the Mandinga *Farim Cabo* raided his neighbours to obtain captives for the slave ships, he retained a small proportion for his own needs.[17]

One of the most direct connections between the Atlantic slave trade and the nineteenth-century pattern of social stratification and oppression on the Upper Guinea Coast lay in the fact that numbers of Africans were captured with a view to being sold to the European slavers, but they remained for greater or lesser periods (or sometimes for ever) in the service of their African captors. To begin with, there was usually a time-lag between capture and the moment when a buyer presented himself. Then, there were always individuals whom the Europeans rejected for one reason or another; while the African merchants also decided against carrying through the sale under certain circumstances.

De Almada related that on one occasion on which the Portuguese refused to buy some 'pieces' who had been kidnapped by Fulas, the latter killed the victims.[18] Such action might have been taken in isolated instances, but, in general, persons who were offered for sale and who were not purchased by the Europeans were utilized for the economic benefit of their African captors. C. B. Wadstrom, an activist in the movement for the colonization of Sierra Leone, addressed himself to interviewing those engaged in the Atlantic slave trade in the area on this specific point. First, there was the testimony of the chief of Port Loko, who affirmed that those captives whom the Europeans did not buy were always put to work on the coast. Secondly, 'two other intelligent native traders mentioned the great number of slaves now confined on the coast for purchasers: one trader had no fewer than 200. . . . They said that the slaves would certainly not be put to death; for nobody was ever put to death, except in war or for crimes.' Further questioning by Wadstrom revealed that, when the average price of slaves fell from 160 'bars' to 120 'bars', the king of the Fulas, to bring the European slave traders to terms, forbade his subjects to carry any slaves down to the coast. As a consequence of this manoeuvre, the Fula, Mandinga and Susu territories had become full of slaves who were set to cultivate rice.[19]

For the sake of safety the captives were put to work in small groups.[20] Ever since the seventeenth century (and perhaps earlier) it had been the habit of the Mandinga *Farim Cabo* to disperse his captives among his own subjects, expecting to have them returned when a buyer was available.[21] Those captives thus became for a while literally 'household slaves' of the Mandingas. At any given moment, therefore, two of the components of the domestic slave population of the Upper Guinea Coast as viewed by observers at the end of the eighteenth century would have been, first, captives drafted into alien tribes in servile disprivileged positions, as by-products of the Atlantic slaving industry, and, secondly, the real products, who were stock-piled in bond for export.

The majority of the tribes of the Upper Guinea Coast were active participants in the Atlantic slave trade, and most of them must have retained supplies of slaves for domestic consumption. But the Mandingas, Susus and Fulas stood well to the fore – partly because of their own key role in the slaving operations on the Upper Guinea Coast, and partly because they succeeded in reducing many of the littoral peoples and the inhabitants of the Futa Djalon to a state of vassalage, under the banner of Islam. Military conquest and political ascendancy involved in most cases nothing more than the payment of tribute, but in some instances the Mande or Fula ruling class were directly superimposed on the subjugated peoples. The latter were not dispersed within individual households, but were grouped together in villages, which were economic units producing for the benefit of the master class.

During the latter part of the eighteenth century, some of the Mandinga chiefs on the Upper Guinea Coast had 'slave towns' with as many as 1000 inhabitants.[22] Travelling in Sierra Leone in 1823, Major Laing found that Falaba, the capital of the Sulima Susus, had its own 'slave town', Konkodoogorée. Intense agricultural activities were carried on there, and the fields in that area were the best tilled and best laid out that Laing had seen in his travels.[23] The 'slave town' was known to the Fulas as the *rounde*. The inhabitants (*rimaibe*) worked under the supervision of a *satigi* who was not himself a free man, although he had the full confidence of the Muslim *Alimamy* or chief of the *diwal*, and was in complete control of the *rounde*. At the end of each harvest, the *satigi* immediately dispatched a bundle of reeds to the *Alimamy*, with the number of stalks indicating the number of loads of grain harvested.[24] This situation has been justifiably equated with serfdom, and it was most prevalent in the Futa Djalon after the success of the Muslim *Jihad*.[25]

It was also at the tail-end of the Atlantic slave trade that evidence was forthcoming about the existence of an internal trade in slaves, and there is every reason to believe that this was an accurate reflection on the date that it came into being. Captain Canot, who was familiar with the Upper Guinea Coast in the 1820s and 1830s, wrote vividly on both the Atlantic slave trade and the internal slave trade, implicitly linking the two. With the Atlantic slave trade as the main preoccupation of the Susus and Fulas, 'a man, therefore, becomes the standard of prices. A slave is a note of hand that may be discounted or pawned; he is a bill of exchange that carries himself to his destination and pays a debt bodily; he is a tax that walks corporately into the chieftain's treasury.' As far as the home market was concerned, the victims not only became agricultural labourers, but men were required as personal attendants and women as wives or concubines.[26]

While one major contribution to the rise of 'domestic slavery' on the Upper Guinea Coast was made by the coastwards thrust of the interior peoples and their involvement in the slave trade, an equally great contribution was being made by the European forces acting on the littoral from the seaward side.

In the forts and factories of the Royal African Company, a distinction was made between 'sale slaves' and 'castle slaves' or 'factory slaves'. Both were acquired in the same way, but, while the former were destined to face the Middle Passage, the latter were retained around the forts and factories to help in the conduct of trade.[27] The directors took some interest in these 'castle slaves'. In 1702 they issued instructions that a Negro overseer should be appointed over them. They were to be converted to Christianity, given names, taught to speak English, and be allowed to have one wife (another 'castle slave'). Perhaps the most important provision from the company's point of view was that the 'castle slaves' should be taught skills to enhance their value and utility. Such workers were not to be sold or transported overseas except for great crimes.[28]

Apparently, no record remains of the number of 'castle slaves' in the forts of York and Bence Island and their subsidiary factories, but in 1702 it was felt that there were too many in Sierra Leone, and that some should be transferred to Cape Coast Castle.[29] However, some years later there was talk of shortage. At least, the directors had been made to understand that it was cheaper to use their own slaves than to hire African servants, and they gave their factors authority to purchase slaves for the factories.[30] Walter Charles, the last of the chief factors of the Royal African Company in Sierra Leone, was certainly convinced that, if the company used their own slaves, it would be cheaper and more convenient; and he urged that some 'castle slaves' should be sent to Sierra Leone from the Gambia establishments.[31] The same situation was to be found in the Portuguese trading centre of Cacheu, where the captain-major argued in 1694 that it cost too much to get the help of the Africans.[32]

Apart from the trading companies, private European traders also owned slaves on the coast, so that altogether the numbers of Africans bought by Europeans and remaining in servitude on the Upper Guinea Coast were considerable. The practice probably began with the arrival of Portuguese ships in the fifteenth century, giving rise to the term *grumete* ('sailor's slave'). In practice, the *grumete* (or *grometto*, as the English came to use the word) was seldom a chattel. More often than not he was a wage-earner, and in many cases African rulers on the Upper Guinea Coast voluntarily sent their children to live with the Europeans and to serve as auxiliaries in the coastal trade.[33] There was a somewhat similar practice in the nineteenth century, involving the sending of children from the hinterland to the colony of Sierra Leone to learn 'white man fashion'. However, these children were usually only unpaid servants, and, when they grew old enough to realize that they were free, they were sold to the Mande and Fula traders.[34]

Some of the Africans purchased by and remaining in the service of the resident Europeans were little better off than slaves in the New World. The 'castle slaves', like their American counterparts, were branded with their owners' marks.[35] When a 'castle slave' committed a crime his punishment was often brutal. In February 1682 the Bence Island factor reported that some of the 'castle slaves' had stolen, and he had executed one as an example.[36] Escape and rebellion led to the same fate. If the 'castle slave' was not sold, or did not die an early natural death, then he could look forward to being freed when he was 'old and useless'.[37] With the private traders, it was equally obvious that unmitigated chattel slavery prevailed at times. Occasionally, the owners displayed those fits of sadism which afflict those who hold absolute power over human life.

When in 1694 Francisco Vaz, member of a prominent Afro-Portuguese trading family, cruelly disposed of twelve of his slaves in his Nunez emporium, the matter reached the ears of the Conselho Ultramarino.[38] In the latter years of the eighteenth century John Ormond, thirty-five years a slave trader in Baga territory, was notorious for amusing himself at the expense of the lives and limbs of his servants, in much the same way as his contemporaries in Sainte Domingue.[39]

The servitude directly introduced on to the Upper Guinea Coast by the Europeans slowly assumed an African character. The slave owners were originally white and foreigners, but the late eighteenth century saw the emergence of powerful mulatto slave-trading chiefs, who were said to own large numbers of 'domestic slaves'. Wadstrom explains that 'if an African slave is impertinent he is sold. The children of such are occasionally sold also. But with the rich traders this is not common.'[40] The rich traders he refers to were mulattoes like the Caulkers and the Clevelands, the progeny of English slave dealers and African women. They kept 'slaves' not only to serve as crews on the coastal and riverain vessels and to act as porters, but also to provide labour for the production of food and manufactures, which indirectly facilitated the Atlantic slave trade. In the latter part of the eighteenth century Chief William Cleveland (grandson of the original white Cleveland, who died in 1758) had a large 'slave town' on the mainland opposite the Banana Islands. The inhabitants were employed in cultivating extensive rice fields, described as being some of the largest in Africa at the time, and equalled only by the Susu plantations which were also employing forced labour. In another smaller village, whose people were said to have been owned by Cleveland, there was a thriving mat and cotton industry.[41]

Whether as agricultural labourers or sailing *grumetes*, whether as temporary members of households or as permanent residents of *roundes*, a large number of Africans on the Upper Guinea Coast at the end of the eighteenth century had been reduced to servile status through the agency of the Atlantic slave trade. A few quickly emerged as trusted servants and lieutenants, but the majority signalled their oppression by rebelling or escaping when the opportunity presented itself. They had every reason for so doing; because, having been spawned by the Atlantic slave trade, they in turn constituted the section of the society most liable to be exported. Again it is from Captain Canot's account that the interrelationship between the two phenomena most clearly emerges. When, on one occasion, Canot visited Timbo, the capital of the Futa Djalon, the inhabitants of Findo and Furto, two slave settlements on the outskirts of the city, fled in consternation on hearing that he wanted slaves. They knew that they were earmarked as the first to be exported; and, as it turned out, flight did them no good, because they were hunted by Fulas on horseback, and Canot was provided with his coffle to return to the waterside.[42]

The village of local slaves thus became a warren supplying the Europeans. This was the ultimate degradation to which the Atlantic slave trade had brought the African society of the Upper Guinea Coast. Without a doubt, as far as this region is concerned, to speak of African slavery as being ancient, and to suggest that this provided the initial stimulus and early recruiting ground for slaves exported to Europe and the Americas is to stand history on its head.[43] When the European powers involved in the area (namely Britain, France and Portugal) intervened to end slavery and serfdom in their respective colonies, they were simply undoing their own handiwork.

While it is the main concern of this paper to demonstrate that the generalization that the Atlantic slave trade was at its inception stimulated by African slavery and 'domestic slavery' cannot be sustained when applied to the Upper Guinea Coast, the validity of the thesis as a whole is open to question. The weaknesses of the generalization can be seen by reverting to the three statements quoted at the outset.

No attempt was made by Rinchon to substantiate his sweeping assertion that the majority of the Africans lived in a state of servitude. Nor does he define 'servitude', and it does seem that he is using the word in a very arbitrary and imaginative sense. Propositions stated in this manner cannot be entertained.

J. D. Fage is very careful in defining 'domestic slavery' and circumscribing the numbers involved; but he feels that it 'nevertheless' gave a fillip to the Atlantic slave trade. This highlights a certain contradiction. The 'domestic slave' was the member of a royal or noble household. What reason is there to suppose that the ruling class would first dispose of the affinal members of their own family? Perhaps the continued employment of the term 'slave', however qualified, has some bearing on the conclusion. Rattray himself ended by referring to the 'so-called "slaves" '; and, though perhaps the label 'domestic slave' is meant to express this idea, it carries with it the same associations with the Americas which the pro-slavery interests were at pains to provoke, especially since the literature on American slavery has already made familiar the distinction between the domestic or household slave and the field slave on the basis simply of their place of work; while it is well known what constituted the principal 'domestic institution' of the Old South.[44]

To recognize that 'domestic slavery' is a misnomer is to avoid much confusion, and it does not mean losing sight of the possible existence within fifteenth- and sixteenth-century West African coastal society of authentic chattel slavery and other forms of social oppression such as serfdom and household service with limited rights and onerous obligations. If these can be shown to have prevailed, then the Upper Guinea Coast would be atypical in its social structure and the link with the Atlantic slave trade would appear extremely credible. But it is quite remarkable that so far no contemporary fifteenth- or sixteenth-century evidence for any West African coastal region has been marshalled behind this imposing generalization.[45]

On the question of identifying African slavery, Mannix gives a much more acceptable picture, legitimately citing Mungo Park to establish a distinction between household servants on the one hand and captives and newly purchased slaves on the other. However, when Park added that these social institutions were ancient and widespread in Africa, he was speculating rather than making a factual observation, so that it is pointless to echo him.[46] It is similarly inconclusive to give a modern ethnographic description (as Fage seems to have done) and leave the impression that this was part of the ancient and traditional order of things in Africa. Here it will be useful to take as an example the contention that people could be enslaved in punishment for a civil or criminal offence, and to test it with evidence from the Upper Guinea Coast.

In describing the societies of the littoral peoples of the Upper Guinea Coast the Portuguese did not omit mention of the regime of law and punishment. It was reported at the beginning of the sixteenth century that the Temnes had no capital punishment, while only murder was punishable by death among the Bulloms. The main punishments were in the form of fines. Adultery, for instance, was easily resolved, the offending male paying the damages.[47] Deprivation of liberty was not listed as a legal penalty at this early date. It makes its appearance in the seventeenth century, when the process of law had become warped under the pressure of the Atlantic slave trade, and there was hardly an offence which did not carry the penalty of sale into the hands of the Europeans.[48] When, therefore, a modern ethnographic survey of the region indicates that 'punishments formerly included' enslavement for a wide variety of crimes, this itself needs to be placed in historical perspective rather than accepted as historical evidence.[49]

The examples of African slavery documented at an early date which immediately spring to mind come from the western Sudan, with its large centralized expansionist states and its developed system of production and distribution. Not only were slaves exported across the Sahara, but peoples in the region were also being reduced to vassalage and made captives in the large-scale wars that were fought in the open savanna. Their labour was then exploited within an economy which was characterized by some amount of specialization. These would seem to be the prerequisites for a society to incorporate slaves, serfs and the like.

In many respects the Senegambia was an extension of the western Sudan, and so was the Gold Coast area around Mina. The Africans around Mina actually purchased slaves from the Portuguese in the fifteenth and early sixteenth century, those slaves being brought from other sections of the coast and exchanged for gold.[50] In the Senegambia the pattern was even more instructive. As indicated earlier, the Portuguese chroniclers did report 'household slaves' among the Wolof. They also recorded that the district was exporting slaves in directions other than westwards to the Atlantic. In fact, by a curious cycle of barter, the Portuguese took slaves from the Upper Guinea Coast in the sixteenth century and exchanged them for iron from the Wolofs. The latter apparently handed on most of the slaves to the Moors, while the Portuguese took the iron and bartered it for further captives on the Upper Guinea Coast, making a surplus which was destined for the Spanish Americas.[51] Richard Jobson also bore witness in 1620-1 that slaves were traded inland from the lower and middle Gambia, though 'among themselves . . . they make little use thereof'.[52]

Two issues would be worth pursuing on the basis of the Mina and Senegambia examples, especially the latter. The first is the extent to which these societies were representative of the West African littoral; and at a glance it would appear that there were far greater areas where the social structure was parallel to the Upper Guinea Coast. The second matter to be noted is the tremendous increase in local slavery in the Senegambia between the voyages of Jobson and Mungo Park – separated by nearly two centuries in which the ruling class had committed itself to a slaving partnership with the Europeans. Quite obviously, Mungo Park's question must have been quite pertinent to the Senegambia,[53] even though slavery and serfdom were encountered in some measure before the arrival of the Portuguese caravels. There must have been some connection between the status quo at the end of the eighteenth century and the Atlantic slave trade.

A random selection of examples drawn from farther afield indicates the likelihood of a widespread impact of the Atlantic slave trade along the lines followed on the Upper Guinea Coast. The Nyamwezi were the great traders in ivory and slaves who supplied the coastal slaving towns in the vicinity of Zanzibar. While they were travelling between the coast and their sources of supply deep in the interior, their lands were worked by slaves acquired for that purpose.[54] In the case of the Nike of eastern

Nigeria, the correlation between their participation in the Atlantic slave trade and their accumulation of slaves was even more definite. Nike acted as the northern agents of the Aro, and were among the principal recruiters of slaves in eastern Nigeria. In the process, they acquired great tracts of land and large numbers of captives remained in their hands, giving rise subsequently to mitigated forms of household service.[55] In this respect, the Ashanti may well repay investigation.

The Nyamwezi and the Nike would correspond to the Mande and Fula of the Upper Guinea Coast; while the resident European and mulatto slave traders of the Upper Guinea Coast also had counterparts elsewhere, notably in Angola. There too, 'sale slaves' were employed in agricultural activities for a period of time, while some were kept permanently on the coast. When the Portuguese sought to abolish slavery in Angola in the nineteenth century, what was involved was the ownership of Africans by whites and mulattoes.[56] This can be maintained without contradiction, even if it can be proved that there were tribal slaves within the hierarchical society of the Congo–Angola area in the fifteenth and sixteenth centuries, and that these constituted the first victims of the Atlantic slave trade. However, while this latter hypothesis has been shown to be unsatisfactory in many respects, there seems to be at least a *prima facie* case for the counter-assertion that many of the forms of slavery and subjection present in Africa in the nineteenth and twentieth centuries and considered indigenous to that continent were in reality engendered by the Atlantic slave trade.

2 The role of slavery in the economic and social history of Sahelo–Sudanic Africa

Claude Meillassoux (translated by R. J. Gavin)

Editor's comments

It is generally recognized that by the late nineteenth century slavery was widespread in Black Africa. But only a handful of writers have gone beyond a static description of the institution as it existed in the nineteenth century, to a detailed analysis of the circumstances under which it developed its varied characteristics and expanded. This is what Professor Meillassoux has done in this paper. Some of the issues raised by Walter Rodney in Chapter 1, are here taken up and worked out in detail. The detailed analysis in the paper shows that the development and expansion of slavery in pre-colonial Africa were both linked originally to export demand for slaves. This export demand, first from the trans-Saharan trade, and later from the Atlantic trade, led to the emergence of powerful military states, with their military aristocracies, giving rise to the growth of aristocratic and state slavery. In places where the growth of internal exchange followed the expansion of the military states, Meillassoux explains, aristocratic and state slavery paved the way for mercantile slavery producing goods for internal exchange. The paper is based on the researches of several scholars whose results were published in a collective work edited by Meillassoux himself. It provides an important link between the export slave trade and economic, social and political processes in pre-colonial Africa, which is central to the debate on the impact of the export slave trade on African societies. In many ways it complements and strengthens the arguments advanced by Walter Rodney in the previous chapter.

This paper was first presented at an international conference held in Kano, Nigeria, 5–10 January 1976. It has been included in this collection by permission of the author and the organizers of the conference.

Slavery, a historical fact

The historical development of Africa up to the colonial period produced several distinct economic and social zones. The different circumstances under whose pressure these zones emerged provided slavery with many different frameworks for its genesis and evolution. This is illustrated by the contributions to a collective work: *L'Esclavage en Afrique Précoloniale*[1] which represents the most advanced state of research on this issue and whose contents provide the background and the inspiration for the discussion that is set out here.

The contributions to that study were concerned with populations resident in the area stretching from the Sahara to the Equator. A thorough study of these groups must distinguish between a number of historical zones: the Saharan desert region of the nomads, through which contact between the Maghreb and the Sudan was established; the Sahelo-Sudanic region (from Senegal to Songhai) situated between the desert and the forest, and comprising populations that have for more than ten centuries been in contact with Maghrebo-Sahalian civilizations; the Voltaic zone, the hinterland of the last named, which evolved in relationship with, but in opposition to the latter; the Senegambian region, affected by the ancient continental, economic and social currents, and by the more recent impact of European trade; the 'Benin' zone, more heavily affected by European trade, whose political evolution came later, its hinterland experiencing the conquest or influence of neighbouring peoples; lastly, and similarly, the Congolese coast and the populations situated in the sphere of influence of the trans-Atlantic slave trade.

One cannot here retrace the history of each of these historical zones, even though such an undertaking, directed towards the significant features of economic and social evolution, would be indispensable to a more profound study. Being unable to undertake this, I will limit myself to two points. Geographically I will concentrate on the Sahelo-Sudanic zone, where the development of slavery was at once very ancient and instructive. In tracing its history I shall set out only what seems to me relevant in relation to the problem before us (the aims and the extent of warfare, the development of exchange, the function of states). By reference to this region I hope to be able to characterize, briefly, the objective conditions of developments in the others. This summary and rather arbitrary procedure has as its sole object to suggest some socio-historical structures that will enable us to set out in a preliminary way, a differential examination of the evolution of slavery in the various parts of Africa.

1 Sahelo-Sudanic slavery

(a) From empires to traders

The Sahelo–Sudanic zone appears on the historical scene in Africa as the oldest supplier of the external slave trade in the direction of the desert and the Mediterranean. The most ancient references to the slave trade concern Fezzan.[2] But from the eleventh century onward, the effects of this traffic were being felt in West Africa. Edrissi[3] mentions several times that the population of the desert and of the Sudanic states (Barisa, Silla, Tekrur, Ghana, Ghiyaro) were reducing to captivity the people of Lam-lam (a name given to the countries of the central part of West Africa, including Mallol), 'transporting them to their own country and selling them to merchants who come there and take them elsewhere'.[4] The Lam-lam, he explains, 'are continually the victims of incursions by the peoples of the neighbouring countries who reduce them to captivity by means of various stratagems, and who carry them off to their country to sell them to merchants by dozens; at present a considerable number come from there destined for the Western Maghreb'[5]. Elsewhere, Edrissi explains the tactics of the slave raiders of Ghiyaro[6]. The historical data for this region in relation to slavery and the slave trade are already summed up in this short extract:

the presence of political formations organised through contact with the peoples of the Maghreb; the presence of merchants and the organisation of commercial networks stretching from the Sudan to the Maghreb; the existence of populations that are apparently particularist and pagan, victims of the raids of military states. How large were the latter? What, in this perspective, was the function of warfare which we know was a constant activity of medieval states? The link between war and the capture of slaves is not clearly established by the texts of the Arab authors. We know, however, from the more recent examples drawn from African history in the eighteenth and nineteenth centuries, that military organisation, warlike enterprise, was essentially directed to this end, whether we consider the army of the kings of Segu, that of El Hajj Umar or of Samory, or the annual conquests of the rulers of Benin. Likewise in the Middle Ages, it seems probable that armies were, above all, instruments for the supply of slaves.

From the eleventh century onward Ghana already disposed of a numerous army and cavalry. Al-Bakri says that the king could mobilize 200,000 warriors, of which 40,000 were armed with bows and arrows, plus cavalry.[7] War was continuous and regarded as being holy: 'The king of Silla [a kingdom probably situated on the Senegal river] *always* wages war with the blacks who are plunged in *infidelity*' (my italics).[8] 'The Bani Lemtouna wage jihad in fighting with the blacks'.[9]

The role of the Almoravids in supplying markets with slaves is not clear. But many indications suggest that these holy men were involved in this business to a not inconsiderable extent. It is known that there were slaves by the thousand in Awdaghost[10] and that in 1054–5, at the sacking of the town, the Almoravids seized all that they found there,[11] no mention being made of any emancipation of those captured. We know also that Ibn Yacin took a third of the possessions of those that joined his camp, among which one can expect that there would have been a number of slaves.

In the fourteenth century, the data that Al-Omari provides about Mali is similar to that of Al-Bakri on Ghana, the Mali army numbered 100,000 men, 10,000 of them horsemen[12] and the rulers '*constantly* waged jihad and were on *continual* expeditions against the pagan negroes'.[13] According to the *Tarikh el Sudan*,[14] the king of Mali conquered Songhai, Timbuktu, Zagha, Mina, Bahena and the bordering countries as far as the ocean. Only the merchant town of Jenne succeeded in resisting his repeated blows. The trade in slaves from this period onward was one of the major activities and one of the principal resources of the political and military formations that were situated on the Sahelo-Sudanic zone: Tekrur, Ghana, Mali, Ghiroy, Silla. During the following centuries, warfare continued to be a permanent feature of the history of Songhai. The Chi Suleyman Dama 'spent *his whole reign* on warlike expeditions'.[15] Soni Ali '*was employed* in warlike expeditions and conquests of countries'.[16] He conquered the Baram the Nunu Sanbadja, Timbuktu, Jenne, the country of the Kunta, Borgu and Gurma without counting his battles with the Mossi, which we will come back to later.[17] Askia Muhammad conquered Bagana, Air,[18] Kingi,[19] Kusata.[20] Sultan Muhammad Benkan had such an appetite for warlike expeditions that he exhausted the patience of the people of Songhai with them, so it is said. The chronicles chant on thus, the interminable list of wars and expeditions up to the end of the Askias.[21]

The chroniclers do not often explain what the causes or the consequences of these wars were. Edrissi's reports relate that they contributed to the supply of slaves. The chronicles relate that there was booty but do not always tell us what the booty was.[22] When we are given details slaves are mentioned in practically every case. According to Rouch[23] certain wars by Soni Ali against the Dendi or the Tuareg 'had no other object but to furnish Songhay with soldiers'. Some of the information is more precise: in 1501, Askia Daud made 'a victorious incursion into Mali, in the course of which he took numerous slaves. . . .' including the daughter of the king. We hear that the inhabitants of three urban areas were 'by origin, the remainder of the booty gathered in Mossi country by Al

Jadj.[24] Others came from Askia Muhammad's expeditions in the distant Kusata country. After an expedition by Askia Ismail into Gurma (a region which constantly attracted Songhai attacks), 'the booty was such that a slave sold at Kagho for 300 cowries at that time'.[25]

After the Moroccan invasion, which contributed to the disruption of the political structures, internal security broke down, the people 'devoured each other'[26] and, above all, *free men* were now being reduced to slavery[27] and this considerably upset the chronicler. The Bambara seized Songhai women, Qadi Mansur vanquished Askia Nuh and reduced to captivity all the Songhai accompanying him 'men and women, young and old, praise singers of both sexes'.[28]

At Chenekou, the Moroccans 'took a large number of persons, men and women, holy men and men trained in the law'. But while one of the conquerors released his prisoners, others sold theirs.[29]

The lands of origin of the peoples brought together or conquered by Songhai provide evidence of enormous population movements (Wangara, Kaniaga, Bitu, Mali, Jafunu,[30] etc.). Since the eleventh century in fact, these wars were distinguished by their increasing seriousness. Distances seemed no obstacle to armies that currently operated more than a thousand kilometres from their base. They employed cavalry although the majority of the men were foot soldiers. We have little information on the organization and tactics of these armies. Here one must put forward a few hypotheses. First of all, all of the wars were not of the same magnitude. In the eighteenth and nineteenth centuries, Mungo Park and the Bambara[31] distinguished between two types of armed enterprise: one consisted of raids executed by a restricted number of individuals, the other involved mounted expeditions in which a greater number of soldiers participated. In both cases the object was the capture of slaves. One must also distinguish, I believe, between wars which represented the bloody expression of the settlement of accounts between kingdoms, armies versus armies, princes versus princes, and which were carried out with a certain degree of formality; and the great expeditions, bringing along thousands of men to the pillage of some distant country, in the course of which no quarter was given. When the capture of men involved long distance movement, it was then that the capacity of kingdoms to mobilize a numerous force and to organize, transport and supply these troops that gave these kingdoms their real superiority over pagan populations, as much as the use of war horses.[32]

These wars in effect were self perpetuating, they created the conditions of their own development by contributing to the evolution of tactics and armament. Simple ambushes or the 'razzia', at first sufficient to capture slaves among ill-defended populations, stimulated among the latter more efficient methods of defence,[33] the constitution of fortifications and the establishment of military organizations capable of fighting back. The escalation in defensive provisions encouraged the emergence of other military aristocracies devoted to the defence of vulnerable village communities but which also turned to aggression and slave raiding. Consequently military expeditions were directed ever further afield against populations which were still ill protected, or were launched ever more powerfully against the better protected communities closer at hand. These large armies, mostly composed of ill-armed foot soldiers, were no doubt quite undisciplined.[34] Their movements perhaps resembled more the surge of a migrant horde, ravaging villages in its path, than the manoeuvres of an ordered military formation. Battles were probably no more than an aggregation of single combats. The main aim of these troops was above all the pillage of poorly defended villages. Despite their numbers, they were only really formidable when launched against ill-armed peasants, who were frightened by the horses, the noise of the guns, the sheer size of the attacking force. When confronted by organized and trained soldiers, however, such armies seem to have possessed a quite limited capacity for resistance, as the encounter between the Songhai armies and the Moroccan troops would seem to demonstrate.[35] The latter's military organization and their use of firearms,[36] enabled them, as from the sixteenth century, to avoid deploying so many men. The number of the Moroccan soldiers who conquered Songhai, probably did not exceed 3000.[37]

The Mossi kingdoms were established as a result of a different conjuncture of historical circumstance. Mossi armies made several attempts to break through to the north toward the Saharan market for slaves. There was the invasion of Timbuktu in 1337, of Walata in 1480 or earlier in 1447,[38] of Masina in 1465. In each of these attempts, they clashed with Sahelian states and especially Songhai.[39] The failure of these sallies in turn provoked reprisals by the rulers of Songhai. Askia Muhammad organized a holy war in 1498 against Mossi, 'carrying off their children into captivity'.[40] Cut off from their markets in the direction of the Sahara, victims of predatory wars, the Mossi turned in upon themselves and formed themselves into powerful states, but states which were devoted above all to defence.

Functioning as a protector to the people against capture by the men of the Sahel, the Mossi military aristocracy brought about an exceptional degree of social and political integration among the population. This aristocracy was not affected by the concurrent pressure of the merchants and Islam. The *Naba* were never muslims, and had no pretext for holy war. Their foreign wars, after the attempts to break through to the north, were not on the same scale as those carried out by their northern neighbours. Slavery, instead of gravitating around export requirements, tended to centre upon the crown. Palace demand accentuated its aristocratic character and polarized its development. The royal slaves that Izard deals with (1973) were the descendants of men captured during a distant expedition into Bamana.

It was only later, in the nineteenth century, that Naba Baongo (Baongo, 1855-94), the twenty-sixth successor of the founder of the dynasty, had 'the idea of selling captives taken in war'. (Before him, however, Mossi warriors had previously associated themselves with Songhai bandits to furnish the demand.) So, it was only in the nineteenth century that the Mossi kingdom appeared as a supplier of slaves to the European slave trade.

The opportune conversion of the princes to Islam – a conversion which did not at first affect the generality of the population – gave them a moral justification for fighting and enslaving the 'pagans'.[41] Muslim *marabouts*, who are known to have been closely associated with commerce, were interested in inciting the rulers thus to furnish the slave market.

This slaving activity and the permanent military deployment that it engendered, explains better than the production and trade in gold, the constitution of aristocrats and warlike states.[42] Certainly one cannot overlook the importance of gold-bearing resources for states that controlled their circulation and which, by making possible the purchase of horses and other goods, consolidated the force and the prestige of the princes.[43] But the gold trade does not explain the *character* of the medieval states. The failure of the Mali rulers' *military* attempts to seize the gold mines are well known; as soon as force was used, the miners abandoned their places and production stopped for lack of producers.[44]

Great war machines were not designed for establishing permanent organized productive activity, nor for its control. The production of gold was mostly the work not of slaves belonging to a ruler, but of independent populations. The peaceful merchants who maintained contact with these gold panners were more suited to preserving the social conditions of production than destructive warriors.

Warriors and brigands, on the other hand, were useful when the seizure of property and men was effected by the destruction of the groups that produced them, that is to say, by pillage and theft.

The glory and the ruin of the Sudanese 'empires' and the shift from west to east of the great political formations – a shift which is often attributed to the exhaustion of the gold deposits which made the fortune

Slavery in economic and social history 81

of each in turn[45] – is explained as well, if not better by a double phenomenon: first of all by depopulation due to the flight of populations subjected to razzias,[46] secondly by the conquest and progressive civilization of the pagan populations that remained. In the first case, there was the exhaustion of the human resources, in the second case, exhaustion of the *social* resources that could supply slaves in large numbers. Military expansion in fact ended up with a progressive expansion of the subjected territory, by a transformation of the area of razzias into administered zones, that is to say by the political subjection of populations which, from being strangers open to capture, became subjects. Besides, wars in this region were always accompanied by the extension of organized and *professional* commerce, by the infiltration and implementation of Islamized traders – a circumstance which was not to be found in more southerly regions. The simultaneous propagation of military conquest, state administration, commerce and Islam, favoured the civilization of the subjected populations, and thus their formal incorporation as subjects of the political formations. When this happened, the source of slaves dried up. Territorial conquest thus opened up two possible paths; the state could modify its mode of exploitation and partially or completely give up the seizure of its inhabitants to concentrate rather on the exploitation of their labour or the acquisition of their surplus – the producer would then generally acquire the status of a 'civilized man' which would protect him from capture by his own ruler, as well as other rulers: or the ruler could persist in drawing upon the human resources of his subjects but in doing so would be unable to justify his civil authority and would see his power decline.

It is generally characteristic of strong states that they protect their citizens from subjection. Thus it was with the Mossi. The *Tarikh el Sudan* tells of the elaboration of a statute protecting the free man from being subjected to servitude and providing for the redemption of those wrongly so subjected. In the case of the lower classes, Askia Muhammad had established a compromise: certain 'tribes' only had their children taken for exchange against horses.[47]

This Sahelo-Sudanic zone, in which were to be found the great states that supplied slaves to the Mediterranean countries and the Sahara, with long experience of wars, conquests and commerce, were also the especial area of development of indigenous slavery.

Al-Bakri briefly mentions its existence in the eleventh century. In the fourteenth century, Ibn Batuta notes it in the Sudanese states and especially in Mali. He saw there, slaves of both sexes, children and adults, above all palace servants,[48] royal soldiers,[49] concubines[50]. Some were employed as porters,[51] others in the copper mines. They were the object of corporal punishment[52] and could be donated as gifts.[53] Some references provide evidence of a trade in slaves involving women and young men,[54] and the trans-Saharan trade in slaves (600 girls brought by caravan across the desert).[55] It is also known that in return, the Malian court received a few Turkish slaves of good quality.[56]

The *Tarikhs el Fattash* and *el Sudan* provide more precise information on the forms of slavery that predominated in the kingdom of Gao.[57] In the sixteenth century, the slavery described by the *Tarikhs* mainly concerned the court, its supply with foodstuffs and its administration. The documents speak of enslaved farm labourers, organized and supervised on plantations for subsistence production to provide for the needs of the king, his followers, his army, as well as those of the poor. The court slaves seem to have constituted a corps of supernumeraries.[58] Some women slaves were retained to ensure the reproduction of the clan: all the Askias, except one, were sons of concubines.

The king was supplied from distant regions, but no description is given of the trade. We know indirectly that some merchants at Gao were involved in it.[59] For the king, when he engaged in trade, the slave was more the object of a transaction than a producer. According to manuscript C of the *Tarikh el Fattash*,[60] the Askia disposed of the children of three 'tribes' to exchange them against horses. There is also a lot of talk of gifts of slaves, sometimes accompanied by donations of land, the generous bounty of a highly religious monarch, who thus earned the praise of the authors of the chronicles.

Thus the phase of domination by the medieval states of the Sahel corresponded to that of the constitution and domination of a military class, which grew out of plundering warfare. The evidence gives the picture of a slavery linked with these aristocratic forms of society: court slavery, military slavery, plantation slavery, devoted to the reproduction of the dominant class and its means of domination: war and the administration of war.[61]

Although the product of slave raiding was eventually sold, it would be wrong to consider this military class as being based on commerce. Its principal activity was war; war shaped its social organization and modes of domination as well as the character of the slavery that grew up around it. By contrast with the merchants, in fact, the plundering aristocrats did not sell in order to buy other products for later sale. Their involvement in commerce was most often limited to immediate exchange.[62] They were in no way intermediaries in market circuits. They went no further than transforming free individuals into commodities by their capture. It was the traders who took these products in charge, lived and profited from commerce, and organized themselves socially as a function of this activity.

(b) From merchant cities to Muslim aristocracies

Meanwhile a mercantile economy was developing parallel with this building of empires (although the sources make less mention of the former than the latter). The presence of merchants, markets, towns or quarters peopled by traders, organized networks, commercial circuits, money (cowries, pieces of copper, or money of account commodities) is mentioned throughout the Sahel.[63] The gold trade cannot alone explain this organization. This *mercantile* commerce was established and penetrated everywhere, it followed the progress of armies and sometimes preceded them.

The emergence of Sahelian and Saharan towns, almost all of them dependent upon external provisioning, the development of Islam and of the use of clothing, the enrichment of nomad transporters, created a growing demand for the *product* of Sudanic agricultural and craft labour. The *dura* (millet) consumed in Awdaghost was imported from the Sudan. Timbuktu, according to the *Tarikh el Sudan*[64] was, since its foundation, an entrepôt for grain. Jenne was above all a great market for foodstuffs (fish, millet, onions, rice, baobab leaves, condiments) and craft products (cotton, cotton textiles, woollen textiles – Kassa) that were bound for northern markets. The foodstuffs stored in the town enabled it to hold out for seven years, seven months and seven days, says the *Tarikh el Sudan*[65] (in other words a long time) against the siege of Soni Ali.

At first confined within the Saharan towns, then in the Sahelian towns, or in the merchant quarters of the capitals, the traders, ideologically protected by Islam, dispersed, established themselves further and further to the south, took up residence in villages under the protection of local lords. The Islamo-Sahelian civilization thus reached the savanna and drew its populations into a more and more complex network of social and political relationships. The rhythm of this movement of merchants, towns and markets toward the savanna is not well known. Mauny estimates that it began as far back as the fourteenth century and that by 1500, the broad lines of inter-regional commerce in the interior of West Africa were well established.[66] (Wadan, Singetti go back to the fifteenth century.) In the sixteenth century the frontier towns, Walata, then Timbuktu, Jenne, Gao, among others, were established and their activity continued despite the Moroccan invasion in 1590.[67] The appearance as residents of Islamized merchant families however should not be confused with the Islamization of populations, which often took place later.[68] This slow, progressive penetration of merchants, accompanied the setting up of organized commercial networks, the substratum of an eventual political organization.

The states, depending upon their military organization which enabled them to bring slave-commodities on to the market, benefited from the existence of commerce. But the latter was not in their hands. The outlet for their booty, the importation of horses (which, for a long time, came from North Africa),[69] and prestige goods, depended upon the organization of merchants. The latter thus emerged as a class associated with the military class, but also competitive with it and tending to weaken its power. The development of commerce, which was associated with the prosperity of states, was also the starting point of their ruin if they did not succeed in exercising absolute control over it.[70] While slave-based production developed, as we believe it did, slavery ceased to be the privilege of sovereigns and court personnel. It extended to the rest of the population, each community being capable of becoming an employer of slaves, whose product they released on to the markets. What one sees emerging then, in step with the weakening of the empires, is a mosaic of chiefdoms and mercantile towns of variable size, a diffusion of productive slavery among the peasant communities, a substitution of the trade in products for the trade in men.

This development of a merchant class was perceived by the older generation of historians and by M. Delafosse in particular, as the sole consequence of the dispersal of the Soninke populations of Wagadu (Ghana), a dispersal which seems hardly to have ceased since the destruction of that state by the Almoravids in the eleventh century. This represents a rather simple view of history and in addition it involves a confusion – also started by Delafosse – between Soninke and Marka.[71] In fact, the Marka do not have, any more than the Jula (when this refers to families professionally engaged in trade), any particular ethnic origin.[72] However, ethnic identity was in no way a determining factor. If the merchants were almost always described as 'strangers', this was for socio-economic reasons that are perfectly explicable.[73] The multiplication of Jula and Marka, their dissemination and their growing influence, resulted from the development of an economic conjuncture and not from any accident of history or an innate predisposition of certain 'races' towards commerce.

Behind the political organization of states, therefore, the power of cities and merchant strongholds was built up, and these tried, throughout their history, to escape from imperial tutelage, with in some cases durable success, as with Jenne. Mercantile power, backed by

Islam, was everywhere interwoven with the power of warrior aristocracies, a thread of a different colour, which might at any moment change the tint of the whole fabric. Ghana collapsed, Mali dissolved, while the mercantile towns that established themselves in their orbits, Awdaghost, Walata, Jara, Tishit, Wadan, survived them and perpetuated their commercial activity along the same routes, prospering less perhaps thenceforward from the slave-trading line of business and more from the commerce in mercantile goods, the products of slave labour.

In the sixteenth century, the mercantile economy had already taken shape. In addition to the northward slave trade, whose importance is still difficult to estimate, and to the gold trade, there was now a real business in commodities, which penetrated through almost the whole Sahel, dealing in the products of agricultural and craft labour, and creating a local demand for slave producers. The last empire, that of Gao, fell to pieces under the effects of the Moroccan conquest: the Sultan's proconsuls little by little lost control over the caids and pashas placed under their authority. Power was being decentralized, and this seems also to have been the index of the declining importance of slave catching as compared with the trade in commodities. The capture of slaves no doubt diminished and their domestic reproduction probably played a more and more important role. The forms of political organization were transformed. In place of centralized powers, we have either federations or fortified villages, placed under the authority of families charged with the organization of defence (sometimes holding power in rotation), or we have fiefdoms dominated by a local dynasty ruling over a small number of agglomerations, or mercantile towns, which, to protect themselves, organized a militia or engaged mercenaries.

The chronicles, which are preoccupied especially with the glorious exploits of the warrior aristocracies, say little of those social formations, which did not engage like the others, in spectacular exploits. The absence of chronicles similar to the *Tarikhs*, the discreet silence of the historians during the first half of the seventeenth century, are an indication of the wakening of the great military aristocracies and the probable emergence in place of them, of prosaic bourgeois societies, more concerned with routine production than with warlike adventures.[74]

The existence of these towns in the seventeenth century and the employment of slave producers by their Jula or Marka inhabitants, are attested to by the traditions collected by C. Monteil[75] in the Segu and Kaarta regions: these villages called 'Soninke' in the midst of Bamana people were noted for the easy circumstances, and on occasion the wealth, that gave them a sort of pre-eminence over the Bambara *dugu* [villages]: this prosperity rested upon the labour of a servile population which the Soninke had acquired by commercial practices.

These villages, according to the same author, seem to have enjoyed quite extensive political independence. The importance of Kong, that mercantile town *par excellence*, which played a role in the savanna comparable to that of Jenne in the Niger bend, had its foundation, if we are to believe Binger, in the fourteenth century,[76] but had attained its political independence in 1790.[77] The appearance of Jula merchants, according to the same author, took place during Soni Ali's reign in Songhai, that is to say at the same period.[78]

The European slave trade was to challenge, without however stopping, this rise of the merchants, and was to offer the warriors an opportunity to recover their position on the political scene.

The emergence of Segu as a political formation, in the depths of the savanna, as from the second half of the seventeenth century, resulted from this conjuncture of events. The demand for slaves produced a new insecurity. Villages seized each other's women and children; robber bands were formed; federations of *togere* (bandits) were organized. Bamana traditions relate how the Kulibali, a warrior clan from Kaarta, acting as mercenaries for a merchant town, seized power on the occasion of a conflict with the civil authorities.[79] The birth of the state of Segu, under the authority of Biton Kulibali, was marked by armed conflicts with the merchant towns established in the neighbourhood[80] and above all with the town of Kong which on two occasions launched unsuccessful attacks on Segu.[81] One can guess in fact that mercantile power was disturbed at the emergence of a rival force primarily based on war. Later a *modus vivendi* was established between Segu and certain mercantile communities, in particular those of the Marka acting in an indispensably complementary capacity to the military economy (Bazin, 1972). The organization of the *ton-jon* (*ton:* the law, regulated society; *jon:* the subject, the dependant) of Segu illustrates the formation of a military democracy originally composed of chiefs of associated bands, all equal to one another, designating one among them as *primus inter pares*, but only allowing him limited power. Among these Bamana warriors, as among the Malinke or among hunters, two types of selection were practised: election and the lottery. In the time of Biton Kulibali, the leaders of Bamana raids were chosen by drawing of lots, each warrior or bandit considering himself to be of equal value. This egalitarian formula however did not suppress rivalries among the *ton-*

jon, which rather quickly led to the predominance of one among them, Ngolo Jara who, arrogating to himself hereditary power, substituted a dynastic order for election by a *coup d'état*.[82] These barons were not all nobles, any more than the king. In the case of a number of them, their recruitment resulted from their capture. Ngolo Jara himself, was by origin no more than a hostage given by his village as a guarantee for the payment of tribute. Booty was 'the price of their life',[83] all were dead men resuscitated. They had no children, they had only captives. This state of being warriors, soldiers bound almost for life to their profession, weighed upon all the citizens of Segu, for this was in effect the condition for being a citizen and the rulers themselves did not escape from it.[84] Segu's profession was war and the capture of men. Its social organization reflected its military organization. Villages were peopled by the importation of prisoners, who together reconstituted pseudo-clans. The bonds of kin were rivalled by comradeship in arms. Segu was at that time a great supplier of the 'slave-commodity'. Some of the slaves were sent to the Guinea coast or Gambia in exchange for muskets and European goods; others were sold to the Marka, traders and employers of slaves, situated within the ambit of the kingdom but retaining their autonomy.[85] The latter produced mercantile goods and foodstuffs for exportation or for the court. The rest of the captives were retained by the soldiers, either for exchange, or to work the land. Thus the human booty could be divided into two categories each with its own market: the men for the European slave trade, women and young people for the internal trade, for agricultural or domestic service, or to be sold to the Marka.

The trade with the Marka, both to provide an outlet for the slaves and to secure a part of their subsistence, limited the employment of field slaves by the Bamana of Segu. (The captives they retained were more often enrolled in the army and used for raiding.) This subordinated Segu's economy to that of the merchants. The Segu warriors could only retain their dominance by the periodical exercise of violence. Da Monson, one of the rulers of Segu, said that the Marka were like fields of millet grain, that had to be cut down from time to time to allow them to grow more strongly.

Unlike the rulers of the medieval states and Songhai, the Bamana kings never made use of religious pretexts for reducing men to captivity.

The state of Masina on the other hand, which was established around 1818, as a mechanism of defence against Bamana raids and aggression, took a muslim stance. Masina, mainly peopled by herdsmen of Fulani origin, was organized under the tutelage of warrior and rival chiefs, the Ardo-en, each having no more than a limited area which they weakly administered. In consequence their populations were a prey to the repeated incursions of Segu troops, sometimes with the complicity of the Ardo-en themselves. To resist the military organization of the Bamana, Masina also adopted, on the initiative of Sheku Ahmadu, a constitution – but a theocratic one: the government, carried on by a college of *marabouts* recruited by co-option, brought the military chiefs under civil control, organized the economy and public security in an effective manner, and soon acquired the capacity to conquer and raid for slaves in its turn. This political construction became the refuge of a merchant class who enjoyed there a degree of security unprecedented in any Sudanic state: protection of persons (a war was waged against Kaarta to save a rich trader Jawambe from the exactions of the Masai);[86] protection of property, (mercantile goods were legally protected, even against requisition by the army in time of war).[87] Masina served as a springboard for this class to invest mercantile towns, like Jenne for example, that was thus rid of its pagan Songhai elements;[88] in other words one might say that Masina endowed this class with a real military power. Sheku Ahmadu and his *marabouts* however professed to be ascetics. They themselves were not involved in trade. They represented a clerical class which politically declared itself to be possessor of a powerful and coherent ideology and capable of offering an alternative to the antecedent aristocracies in this economically transformed world. To a greater extent than the aristocracies in fact, they respected wealth and listened to its demands. In this clerical state, social inequalities however had not disappeared. Castes and slavery remained, by the declared will of Sheku Ahmadu, who considered free men, members of the castes, and slaves as being of different species, incapable of being amalgamated.[89] On slavery, the principal document that we have[90] provides little information. By contrast with the centralized, military states, there was state slavery and private slavery. Prisoners of war, who belonged to the state and who did not practise Islam, were assigned to agricultural work on public land up to the time that their conversion and completion of their religious education emancipated them and permitted their eventual integration into the society. Such at least was the doctrine, in conformity with the precepts of Islam.[91] We do not however know how many of them reached this status and to what extent the equilibrium between new captures and state needs, allowed for such emancipation. There were also private slaves who, in theory, should have participated in the wars as auxiliaries[92] except when their owners paid the tax levied on all those not mobilized. Some were assigned to artisanal castes to work at the production of armaments. We have no other information about their activity.

While Masina represented a political construction arising out of an alliance between commerce and Islam, it is clear that the Omarian tempest that broke upon the whole Sudan in the middle of the nineteenth century, in the name of Tijjani-ism, was less a religious than a warlike enterprise, devoted to the capture of men. Despite his piety, Al Hajj Umar was first of all a warrior, making use, no doubt, of the means provided by Islam to gather together his *talibe*,[93] but then subjecting them to an efficient military discipline; he invoked orthodoxy, but did so in order to transform other muslims into miscreants who became the justifiable prey for his attacks, which reduced them to the state of dead men or legitimate captives; he made use of written Arabic, but more as a means of administration than of learning.

Al Hajj Umar attacked without distinction the pagan Bambara of Segu and the pious rulers of Masina, the muslim towns and the chiefs who indulged in *dolo*.[94] The most obvious result of his military action was the placing on the market of a considerable quantity of slaves; women and children in particular. The men, now more difficult to sell because of the slowing down of the trans-Atlantic slave trade, were massacred, if they were not already slaves.

The ideological interpretation that has been given (the 'fanaticism' of the 'holy war'), to these wars, rests upon some very shallow religious pretexts: a bead more or less in the rosary; one position of the arm, during the prayer, preferred to another . . . were these wars really so disinterested? The issue clearly shows that this was not so. They were concerned more than any before them with goods and property in considerable quantities, among which slaves stood first in rank. They had the effect of supplying with slave producers almost all the Sahelian populations at the expense of those people that had remained the most particularistic and the least protected in the savanna.

The reason why these slave-supplying wars broke out with such force at a time when the trans-Atlantic slave outlet was closed off, was no doubt that the economic development of the Sudanic zone was already capable of offering a market for such abundant merchandise. Productive slavery, commercial slavery, had reached such a stage of development that it generated this type of enterprise. The growth of production alone however does not provide a sufficient explanation for the extent of these slave-raiding wars conducted by Al Hajj Umar, Samori and their emulators. One must here take into account a circumstance which contributed, by reducing the yield of these wars, to their intensification. During the trans-Atlantic slave trade, there was an outlet for the totality of the captives, for there were two separate markets for slaves. The first, the European market, absorbed *adult men*, whatever their social condition might be, free men or recaptured slaves, but offered a low demand for women and children. The other, the continental African market, provided a demand above all for women and children, but had little use for adult men except recaptured slaves.[95] In this fashion an outlet was found for the totality of the captures.

When the American markets were closed off and the trans-Atlantic trade disappeared, there was no outlet for the male captives of free origin: from then onward, they were usually massacred on the battlefield. Only the recaptured slaves, the women and the children picked up in the conquered villages, were kept. But to this extent the profit of war was reduced, for the effort involved in waging war was of the same order, whether only a part of the loot was saleable or the totality. For war to remain profitable, it had to be intensified, attacks had to be made upon more numerous populations, military operations had to be multiplied. Despite the growth of production, the African market was now however prepared to absorb such a quantity of slaves. We know that during the second half of the nineteenth century the price of slaves fell and with it, the profits of war that created the propensity to supply yet more captives and seek yet more conquests.[96] Looked at from the point of view of the employers of slaves, this fall in price encouraged the use of slaves in production, especially as the armies provided an outlet for the sale of agricultural products. While the productivity of war declined, the yield of the slave increased. Merchants and peasant exploiters of slaves gained therefore from an unprecedented flood of available labour onto the market, at prices that made possible an amortization of investment in it as fast as the conditions of their reproduction were transformed.

On the other hand they lost political power to a new dominant class, that of the muslim warrior aristocracy which, from the time of Al Hajj Umar onward, was opposed both to the class of pagan military aristocracies and to that of the technocratic *marabouts* (such as we have seen in Masina). Thus, as soon as Islam became the dominant ideology, the social group to which it reached, diversified, at the same time as the functions formerly performed by other classes fell into its hands. Thenceforward there was a tendency toward a confusion between the control of armed force and of ideology, the one dominating the other or vice versa. Masina and Qadiriya muslims had succeeded in subordinating the warriors to the clerical *marabouts*; the Tijjaniya subordinated the *marabouts* and the Islamized merchants to a muslim warrior aristocracy.

The wars of Al Hajj Umar, like those of Samori were to complete, at the end of the nineteenth century, the profound transfers of populations that had begun two centuries before in this zone. The prophet pulled along behind him Futanke, Bunduke in great numbers who occupied the villages of Kaarta that had been emptied of their inhabitants and they spread out as far as Masina. Samori in the same way pulled along with him troops recruited along his route, deported entire populations, while his captures extended from the Sahel and the savanna into the forest. The social transfers that followed from the shifting of captives, the deportation of populations, the removals of the soldiery, the flight of raided populations, the movements of merchants: the constant threat hanging over everyone of being captured as well as the desire of each to enjoy the servitude of others, contributed to the establishment of an interleaved social entity, extending over thousands of kilometres and whose constituent parts, clans, castes and classes, knew each other, opposed each other, united with each other in familiar fashion across wide areas. Between such units, numerous, diverse and often compulsive alliances were formed, which by their interlacing constituted a 'symplectique'[97] social fabric, resulting in a specific social order whose ethnic particularisms tended to disappear in favour of the extension of a sphere of diffused socialization which penetrated to the heart of each state, each clan. A society was forming that was open to elaborate forms of power but reticent to absolutism: a society shimmering with intrigue, in which each element, anxious to retain its liberty and its prestige, sought the alliance that would assure it the security to develop, move forward and progress in this complex and dangerous world, and which feared on the same grounds, betrayal that could bring about secular subordination and shame.

(c) Slavery in the colonial period

The French occupation occurred when the wars, commerce and slavery were in full flood.[98] The ruin brought about by the wars and which travellers and military men insisted upon, could not conceal the intense mercantile and productive activity of the region.[99]

The official reports on slavery, drawn up in 1894 and 1905, Archives Senegal Series K, provide evidence, biased of course, but nevertheless unrivalled, on this situation.

Let us note that the phenomena examined in this study are replicated in other regions. M. Klein[100] notes the role of the Yoruba civil wars in the same period, the commercial wars in Sierra Leone, the slave raiding of the Fulani Emirates of Zaria, Adamawa, Kontagora and Senegambia as sources of supply for a growing demand for slave producers.

The introduction to the general report of 1894[101] stated that the slave-supplying zones shifted in the periods before and after the conquest. Formerly situated in Bundu, Bambuk, the basin of the Bafing, Kingi, the region of Nioro and Bamana country, they shifted to the right bank of the Niger, toward the states of Samori and Tieba, Kenedugu and, further to the west, Futa Jallon. Certain regions such as Kayor, Baol, which exported slaves at the time when the warrior aristocracies dominated[102] became, after 1904, importers of slave producers brought from the country of the Moors.[103]

The internal traffic in slaves was intense. It confirmed the geographical displacement mentioned above. The administrator of Jenne[104] stated that the slaves bought from Kenedugu especially, and from Mossi, went toward Julaso, Warkoi, then San, Baramandugu, Banamba, Timbuktu; at Sokolo[105] the captives from the same source were bought by Moors, people from Nioro and Medina. From that town, the slaves went toward the lower Senegal, to be resold in Kayor or in zones along the banks of the Senegal.[106] The Moors resold their slaves at Basikunu, Nere, Khaleifa, and to the inhabitants of Sokolo.[107] Jula traders[108] imported slaves from Tukoro and Toma country. The Marka prospected Mossi and the Bobo country, sending their merchandise toward the markets already mentioned.[109] Wasulu, Buguni, Kuranko, Konian, Tolu and Kisidugu were countries which only exported slaves and imported none. They supplied Bamako,[110] Banamba,[111] and Kankan.[112]

The markets of Segu, Barweli, Markaduguba, Boge Kulala (Genekalari), Suba, Samfulala, were supplied by Jula from Kenedugu or Samori's country.[113] Kenedugu remained one of the last supply centres even when the French were allied with the local ruler against Samori.[114] Later official reports[115] mention the existence of former slave markets at Tsienso (Cercle de Kutiala), Safara and Kaho (Cercle de Bandiagara), Baramandugu, Tuge (Cercle de Jenne) and Barweli (Cercle de Segu). According to this document the supplying regions were above all Mossi, Gurunsi and Lobi (that is to say, the country south of the Niger), while the consuming regions were the Sahel and the south Saharan zone.

Toward the afforested south, a trade found its outlet in the direction of Baku, on the Gold Coast, and Grand Bassam, through Nigene, Bawle, Kong, Tiasale[116] or by the markets of Kwajuko (Cercle de Salekama), Makosu (Cercle de Warebo) and Kifibo.

A survey of these movements reveals the operation of two principal markets: the old continental market which continued to absorb slave producers to supply the demand for grain and cotton by the towns and the Sahara; the new coastal market which now, instead of exporting slaves, employed them near the European factories and canteens for the production of the articles demanded by the legitimate trade (that is, the trade in commodities). For as Klein justly remarks, (1971) and Fage also, (1969) the switch-over from the slave trade[117] encouraged slavery in regions where, for the reasons examined above (absence of a market for commodities), it had up to then been confined to the Palace. This was the maraboutic revolution: the production of groundnuts for the benefit of the Islamized merchants.

The archives provide innumerable references to the 'price' of slaves in terms of barrels of salt, gunpowder, bundles of various articles, cowries, imported coin, etc.[118]

According to the writer of the report on Bafulabe:[119]

> the value of captives depends on their sex, women being always preferred to men. It depends also upon their geographical origin: captives from Segu and Bamako are preferred, for they will eat any couscous on offer. By contrast, the captives from the southern and south western countries and Futa, who are used to eating rice, do not take well to food made from maize, millet or fonio, with a resultant complete loss when they are sick.[120]

The price of a slave was settled by negotiation between the parties and therefore varied considerably according to the individual's physical characteristics, his age, his or her sex, the use he was to be put to, his feeding habits and the distance from his place of origin.[121] And all varied with the fortunes of war. When Samori, in his last extremity was seeking arms and especially food supplies for his army in movement, prisoners were exchanged at the rate of 8 to 12 for a single horse, a man for a bale of cassava.[122] Finally, the value of the slave depended also upon the capacity of the different populations to make profitable use of them.

What should be noted here is the existence of an organized commerce in slaves with its personnel, its markets, its pricing system, that covered a considerable extent of West Africa and involved therefore a large number of marketable articles.

As a result of the wars and the consequent deportations of individuals from supplying to consuming zones, slave holding in the nineteenth century was very unevenly spread. It was unknown among some populations or only existed in its patriarchal form: Serer, Jola in the Casamance, Kisi, the populations in the coastal forest area and Wasulu, the Samo of Upper Volta, the Tenda and Basari of eastern Senegal, etc. Where slave holding did exist, the proportions between enslaved and free were variable. The enquiries made by the colonial authorities mentioned above, provide figures that can serve as no more than indicators because of the way in which they were collected (estimates, partial censuses that differed in form from region to region, variable definitions of social categories, etc). Between one report and another concerning the same district the figures sometimes varied up to double the value. Deherme[123] who tried to make a synthesis of these documents, estimated that a quarter of the population of West Africa was enslaved: 200,000 in Senegal, 600,000 in Haut Senegal–Niger, 250,000 in Dahomey, a like number in the Ivory Coast, 450,000 in Guinea.[124] By making use of these documents one can only arrive at a partial and approximate table of the distribution of slave holding as in Table 3.

Numerous corrections have to be added to the figures in this table. Their grouping by regions in particular conceals differences between populations living in the same region. Boutillier[125] demonstrates in his triple study of the populations of Buna, the important differences observed between the merchant Jula, the peasant Kulango and the old aristocracies. Certain figures, on the other hand, such as those for Gumbu, have been confirmed by recent investigations.

The great variations in the proportions of the enslaved reveal the different capacities of the several populations for the employment of a distinct class of producers and hence of the variation in the relations of production.[126]

From this rapid historical overview which has concentrated on the elements that relate to slavery, it emerges that this institution, whether it fed the external slave trade or internal production, whether it contributed to the creation of military empires or merchant cities, has played a major role in the economic and political development of the Sahelo–Sudanic zone.

Slavery has left behind deep traces which are still perceptible today, deep-rooted prejudices, the sequels of exploitation that have scarcely been overcome. These bear witness to the entrenchment and the functionality of this institution in pre-colonial society. Up to today, marriages between children of the free and descendants of slaves, even in the most progressive milieux, come up against bitter resistance, and even among emigrant workers from these regions, slave descendants often have to protest against the impositions of their former masters, even though the latter are subjected to the same general conditions as themselves.

Slavery was in no way a superficial feature of the organization of these societies; history cannot be understood if one ignores it.

2 Slave trade without commerce

Other regions of West and Equatorial Africa appear in a different light by comparison with this historical presentation of the circumstances

Slavery in economic and social history 95

Table 3 *Enslaved people as a percentage of the total non-slave population*

−10 per cent	10 to 20 per cent	about 25 per cent	about 1/3
Serer du Baol (K 27)	Gurma (K 22 f. 11)	Kinji (K 21)	Tumbuktu (K 19)
Bobo (K 19)	Podor (K 18)	Bamana sud (K 19)	Bobo Julaso (Mande) (K 19)
	San (K 19)	Jenne (id)	Kankan (Fulbe) (K 14)
	Kutiala (K 19)	Sigiri (K 14)	Bafulabe (K 14) (1)
	Bemba (sedentary) (K 19)		Nioro (40%) (K 19)

about 50 per cent	about 2/3	about 75 per cent	more than 100 per cent
Gumbu (K 19)	Sikasso (K 19)	Say (K 25)	Jula de Kong (400%) (K 21)
Dagana (K 18 and 25)	Bakel (K 18 and 25)	Kong (K 25)	
Gao (K 19)	Rio Pungo (K 25)		
Bassam (K 25)	Dingiray (id)		
Assinie (id)	Gijume (K 19)		
Jugu (id)	Jawara (id)		
Kwande (id)	Kingi (id)		
Beyle (id)			
Labe* (id)			
Kayes (id)			
Sikasso			
Tumbuktu			
Diori			

Note: *2/5 in K 19
Source: Dakar Archives, Series K.

that accompanied the development of slavery in the Sahelo–Sudanic zone. The forest and coastal zones of West Africa were distant from the economic heart of the continent as well as from its warlike turbulences. The penetration of savanna warriors and traders generally stopped at the edge of the forest which was hostile to the horses of the former and the pack animals of the latter. When the European slave trade opened up and was established on the coast, it did not deeply penetrate these regions, it did not send merchants to the interior, above all it did not provide a significant market for the product of agricultural and craft labour. It demanded, above all, men. There was a major difference between the regions involved in the continental commerce in the *products* of labour and those where the export of the *agents* of labour predominated. In the former, the producing community represented an outlet for slaves, who, by their production, contributed toward the supply of internal markets. Their labour-power remained at the disposal of the continental economy and participated in its prosperity. In the coastal zones, the traders bought first of all men, and that demand obliterated that for commodities and compromised the production of the latter.

Because of the nature of the goods received in exchange for slaves (arms, horses for war, alcohol for the aristocracies and their war boys who raided for slaves, textiles, gewgaws for the courtesans), the slave trade represented an almost total loss of productive wealth to the societies involved in the traffic.[127]

The situation on the coast under the impact of the slave traders reproduced, it would seem, that created by the trans-Saharan slave trade in its early stages: the formation of aristocratic and military states in contact with the slave traders, the military exploitation of the hinterland where wars, slave raids and kidnappings were propagated. In the military states, the slave trade favoured a specific form of palace slavery, little different no doubt from that which prevailed during the middle ages on the fringe of the Sahel. In Dahomey, as among the Abron,[128] the king employed slaves on his fields and his plantations to provide for the court. Cada Mosto[129] tells us that the slaves of Burba Jolof[130] cultivated his lands, while the other captives were sold to the Moors against horses and other goods.

By contrast it seems that private slavery was not widely known. The rulers, evidently, wanted to reserve the privilege to themselves and only on occasion accorded it to their close followers. The people in general did not have access to this means of production by which it would have found itself in a position to penetrate the international market and acquire the means to economic emancipation[131] especially as the employment of slaves would not have augmented the revenue from tribute (cf. below).

Again by contrast with what happened in the Sahel, internal commerce did not develop either. Exchanges were dominated by the foreign slave trade which was carried on directly by the king (or his agents) with the slave traders. This type of relationship did not encourage the establishment of an intermediary class of professional merchants. Of course there were the muslim merchants in Senegambia who came in from the interior, but they belonged to the continental commercial zone. They did not arise from the exchange with the slave traders which they were frequently kept out of by the aristocrats. In Dahomey it was officers of the king, not traders, who negotiated transactions with the Europeans.[132]

Slavery in economic and social history 97

In the Abron country,[133] the Jula merchants stopped at Bonduku in the north of the country where the mercantile and artisanal fringe was situated. Abron country supplied, in particular, two products of the robber economy, ivory and gold. While the production of neither was a royal monopoly by right, the ownership of the agents of labour, the slaves that panned for gold and those involved in transport were largely reserved to the ruler. This, according to Terray, provided him with the bulk of his revenue, more than the tribute from his hypothetical control of trade.

With regard to what is correctly referred to as trade, the transactions carried on by the ruler or his representatives with the European slave traders, were not as far as he was concerned *commerce* – or trade – properly speaking, they were immediate exchange. The merchandise coming into his hands lost its mercantile quality and became social goods destined for distributive channels in the form of gifts and favours. They were not resold for profit.[134]

In the context of a slave-holding system that was restricted to the royal sector and a very circumscribed production – that of gold – slave labour did not participate in the supply of an internal market; it supplied only the court and royal trade. The advantage that the ruler derived from this situation resulted from his reserving to himself the production and the outward movement of export products, while as a corollary, he opposed commercial production by his subjects. Thus he protected himself against a double danger: that of seeing his subjects emancipate themselves by getting access to production and commerce; and that of seeing an omnipresent merchant class rise up within his state.

Power, when it is held and exercised by a military class, thus preserves the existence of enclaves in which tribute paying and royal gift-making circuits predominate and in which the internal market does not develop.

In Equatorial Africa likewise, the coastal states, like the Kongo kingdom, exercised a control over the transactions engaged in with the slave traders, transactions which also had an administrative character as can be seen from the documents of the period.[135] This form of 'staple' trade was not calculated to propagate *commerce* in the hinterland: money – in the strict sense of the word[136] – was not disseminated there. The slave markets were only to be found on the coast in contact with the European merchants. Among the populations of the interior, according to Bonnafe and Rey (1974), the transactions were carried on between elders and chiefs, man to man, as between 'comrades in the trade', right from the coast to very far in the interior, without the intervention of professional merchants. By their form as well as by their content, these transactions remained limited to a whole series of obligations and promises, even though the latter were propagated from one to the next, over long distances. They were the basis for alliances, the occasion for the exchange of symbolic gauges of trust, but they did not give place to a social organization of commerce, mercantile networks, or the establishment of a merchant class.[137] Although exchanges of artisanal products, iron in particular, are mentioned, it does not seem that the labour of enslaved men was devoted to the production of mercantile goods for exchange. For lack of a sufficient outlet for the product of slave labour, productive slave-holding could not develop. So while the slave trade encouraged enslavement on a dramatic scale, the captives were above all the objects of exportation. Rey notes that their insertion into domestic production made them otherwise and almost necessarily 'kinsmen'. The strength of enslaved individuals maintained within the ranks of the population of the interior remained very small, of the order of three per thousand, according to Bonnafe, among the Kukuya.[138]

While war, capture, violent withdrawal from the place of origin, was the dominant mode of enslavement in the savanna region, loss of rights was frequent among the populations of the tropical forests as a means of desocializing the individual and making him grist for the slave trade. Neither were the captives the objects of an avowed commerce. The transactions were disguised as customary transfers of subordinates resulting in deprivation of rights by the subject in a more or less arbitrary fashion.[139]

Anti-social persons or those reputed as such, convicted of repeated contraventions of social norms, were driven out of the group and deprived of all relationship with it. The condemned Anyi received a symbolic brand to light the route of his exile;[140] the Kukuya mother pressed out a few drops of milk from her breast, rejecting and renouncing her unworthy progeniture.[141] The individual thus cut off from his people was either sold or ostracized. The Kuni used a stratagem which reveals the degradation of this institution under the effect of gain. When the fines levied upon anti-social persons were too heavy, they were paid by a few associated titled men instead of by the parent and the former were then given full charge of the offender.[142] Traditional practices were thus converted into disguised sales. This perversion of the mechanisms of social control is mentioned also by Terray[143] and Bonnafe.[144] Among the Kukuya peoples studied by the latter, the procedure for removal of rights paralleled the form of capture practised in particular conditions: the titled men would invite each other – and in mutual fashion – to come and seize their recalcitrant subjects, the raider then disposing of them at will. This police service thus at the same time served as an appreciable source of profit.

One can see then that it is not sufficient to consider natural local factors (today they are called 'ecological'), to discover the conditions for the development of slavery. Nieboer believes that slavery develops in agricultural societies where land is abundant in relation to the available work force and where men rather than material are employed in production. These no doubt constitute conditions favourable to the utilization of a cheap agricultural workforce, but for it to be servile other historical circumstances must operate. What history tells us is that the development of this particular productive relationship is linked with the contacts that permit the transfer of individuals from one society to another. This in effect is what characterizes the essence of slavery and there lies its logic.

History enables us to realize that slavery, that is to say the employment of slaves and not just their capture, develops along with population transfer; that it was more considerable in the zones that were subjected to wars of conquest and centralized power than in zones where ethnic particularisms persisted; that the external slave trade encouraged aristocratic and royal slave-holding, but prepared the way also for mercantile slavery; that when the latter developed, it established itself at the expense of the former, as the support for an eventual political power with a 'bourgeois' tendency, thanks to the establishment of an organized, diversified, specialized internal commerce, concerned more and more with the products of labour. In consequence, slavery appeared in different guises according to the combined respective developments of the factors involved: the form of warfare, population transfer, external slave trade, internal commerce, the nature of production, the evolution of the political, social and ideological forces that underpinned them.

History thus separates out the regions that experienced different conjunctures and moments of evolution. The general economic conditions that we have examined, the form and content of the social relationships and political forces that were established within this framework, no doubt do not explain the totality of the observed variants. However, they situate research within a primary objective context which will contribute toward clarifying its various aspects.

3 Kayor and Baol: Senegalese kingdoms and the slave trade in the eighteenth century

Charles Becker and Victor Martin
(translated by Linda Zuck)

Editor's comments

In recent years the appeal is frequently made in academic conferences for studies of the impact of the export slave trade on African societies to include detailed field work, made up of physical observations in slave catchment areas and oral evidence. The present chapter is the outcome of detailed researches in that direction, combining the use of archival evidence, physical observations and oral tradition. On the basis of their evidence, the authors hold that the Atlantic slave trade was a major cause of political conflict, warfare, social tensions and frequent famines, in the Senegalese kingdoms studied. The social structures and the economic life of the kingdoms were seriously affected by these upheavals. On the issue of slavery, the authors show that the institution was already established in these Senegalese kingdoms before the arrival of the Europeans, as we would expect from Meillassoux's analysis in Chapter 2. But even so, it is argued, the growth of the Atlantic slave trade greatly expanded the number of slaves in these kingdoms. As stated by the authors, the details of their researches, of which the present chapter is just a summary, will soon be published in book form.

This paper aims to examine certain consequences of the slave trade in the Senegalese kingdoms of Kayor and Baol.

The present study is a summary of research carried out on the history of Senegambia and the Wolof states.[1] The methodological framework may be summarized as follows:

1 The history of the Senegalese kingdoms may first be explored using 'internal' sources, amongst which oral tradition (village, family,

The original French version of this paper was published in a special edition of *Revue française d'histoire d'outre-mer*, Tome LXII nos. 226–227, 1er et 2e trimestres, 1975, pp. 270–300. The translated version is being published here for the first time by permission of the authors and the publishers.

provincial, dynastic tradition) occupies a privileged status. Also included among these sources are sociological, linguistic and ethnological studies, which throw light upon the history of settlement and socio-political structures.

2 Second, what we may call 'external' sources, which are the European documents on the subject. In fact on several points relating to social history, archive documents are very brief and appear to be manifestly erroneous interpretations. The incomplete and often prejudiced nature of these sources forces a critical attitude upon the historian. Foreign texts may be used for a 'history of European establishments in Senegal' which is quite different from a 'history of Senegal'.

The available documents show clearly – despite more or less deliberate gaps and errors – that the archives deal chiefly with trade and European settlement and are only marginally concerned with the Senegalese kingdoms and people. The very fact that most European authors do not even feel the need to name the king they are dealing with is symptomatic of their underlying attitude; and this illustrates immediately the limited nature of 'external' source material.

Nevertheless, when reconstructing the history of Kayor and Baol, the collation of external and internal sources proves interesting and brings to light certain important facts.

Internal sources present this period as one of socio-political disturbance, marked by a number of civil wars, continuous conflict between Kayor and Baol, and frequent battles with other neighbouring kingdoms. They also record the alliances established between noble families and the leaders of neighbouring kingdoms; the leading role played by the maternal line of the Gedj family; the movement of population as linked to political events, in particular when certain princes and fallen kings were exiled; and the consolidation of muslim groups who acquired sufficient strength to organize armed resistance against their sovereign at the end of the eighteenth century. Yet these sources hardly even mention the link between the political situation in Kayor and Baol and the European slave trade. Occasionally the trade in firearms is mentioned, but the slave trade is generally passed over in silence.

In contrast, the external sources emphasize the commercial relations between the Europeans and the Damel (the King of Kayor) and the Tegn (the King of Baol). More often than not these records minimize the importance of the slave trade in Kayor and Baol. Since it was known that most slaves were brought from the African interior by Dyula merchants and were sold in Galam or Gambia, it has generally been concluded that the slave trade along the Senegalese coast was very insignificant, both numerically and in terms of its impact on society. This thesis, which is upheld by most European historians, does not stand up in the light of the documentary evidence in the archives. In fact, after a careful perusal of the written sources, which we undertook in order to question traditional ideas and in particular to establish an accurate chronology, we are quite convinced that the slave trade, and Atlantic trade in general, had considerable influence in breaking up traditional society and transforming the social, political and religious structures.[2] There was a close connection between the black slave trade and the internal disturbances which European sources describe in detail. Although in the eighteenth century, and even in the seventeenth, there had been some European proposals for agricultural development of the lands along the Senegalese coast, in order to solve the problems of provisioning the traders and possibly with a view to exporting produce to Europe, European relations with the Senegalese kingdoms were principally centred on the slave trade. Even the precursors of a new type of exploitation had as their first consideration that the eighteenth century was in Kayor and Baol, as elsewhere, the century of the slave trade.

Thus an analysis of the history of Kayor and Baol in the eighteenth century breaks fresh ground in the study of the conditions of trading in the Senegambian coastlands, and also illuminates the internal effects of the trade.

Brief history of the Damel and the Tegn

Despite certain divergences, historical tradition and written sources allow us to trace the chronological framework of the political events and changes which took place in eighteenth-century Kayor and Baol. Tradition provides us with reliable and precise information[3] which European documents frequently corroborate. Also, obvious mistakes in oral tradition can be rectified from written sources, and questions passed over in silence by 'traditionalists' can be explored in the archive material.

Table 4 sets out a chronology of the Damel and the Tegn and is followed by a commentary on the events which took place during the reign of each sovereign.

A number of general remarks may be made on the history of Kayor and Baol from this outline chronological table.

1   The two kingdoms, both ruled by the Fall dynasty, underwent similar development during the eighteenth century. This was characterized by internal and external conflicts, and by countless attempts to unify the two thrones. We can see that six sovereigns succeeded in holding the title of Damel-Tegn. Written sources often evoke French fears of a possible union of the two countries. The frequent efforts to unify Kayor and Baol may be seen as a form of resistance to the European commercial hegemony and foreign encroachments on local political power: in fact, the intermittent union that existed during a period of seventy-eight years under six of the kings who reigned between 1695 and 1809 inconvenienced the Europeans, and afforded these sovereigns a powerful position in relation to commercial transactions.

2   The predominance of the maternal line of the Gedj family from Latsukabe at the end of the seventeenth century should be observed. By an extremely able domestic policy, Latsukabe successfully prepared for the continuing matrilineage at the head of Kayor and Baol throughout the major part of the eighteenth century. The Dorobé, supported by other maternal families that had been ousted from power, managed to expel the Gedj on only two brief occasions.[4] The rise of the Gedj family under the remarkable reign of Latsukabe can be shown to be connected with the development of the European slave trade. In fact, according to a report on Kayor and Baol published recently,[5] Latsukabe bought arms from the French on several occasions in order to consolidate his own position and that of his family. With the help of the power that he acquired within his country, he was able to resist French attempts – Brue's in particular – to impose a commercial monopoly on the Senegalese kingdoms. The internal divisions of the Gedj, after Latsukabe, did not jeopardize the family's power; they made use of their numerous *dyami* (captives), who were hardened to war and well armed, in order to maintain control.

Although it had some influence, the opposition among the three branches of the paternal Fall family[6] was only of secondary importance during the eighteenth century in the face of the rise of the Gedj.

3   Numerous conflicts took place during the eighteenth century, often over successions. Oral tradition mentions about forty battles during this period. Written sources suggest that tradition omits a number of disturbances and makes no reference to the countless 'raids' on the Serer lands which were part of Kayor and Baol. Also, these sources sometimes give details about pretenders whom we are not able to identify with certainty from tradition.

However, it seems that the political history of Kayor and Baol was

Table 4 Kayor and Baol in the eighteenth century: table of events

Period	Damel*	Damel–Tegn*	Tegn*	Main events
1695–1720		Latsukabé T.Y, G		Mbassin's victory over the Dyolof (c. 1700). Imprisonment of Brue (1701). Battles of Ngania (against the Sine), Ndab and Barar. Battle against the Moors at Ngangaram (c. 1719). The Gedj family became established in Kayor.
1720–6	Maysa Teindé Wedj T.Y., G.		Tyé Kumba T.Y., G.	Numerous wars between Kayor and Baol (written sources).
1726–36	—		Mali Kumba T.Y., G.	Continuation of conflicts between Kayor and Baol.
1736	—		Makodu Kumba Diaring T.N., G.	*Tegn*, defeated at Sangay Mbol, flees to Saloum.
1736–49		Maysa Teindé Wedj		Battles of Ndiang, Ndoukouk, Barar against pretenders. Siege of Maka, the capital, by Makodu.
1749	Maysa Bigé Ngoné T.Y., G.		Tyé Yasin Issa T.Y., G.	Beginning of the civil war between the Gedj and the Dorobé. Tyé Yasin, driven out by Mawa, dies at the siege of Maka. Maysa Bigé Ngoné is driven out by Mawa after the four battles at Khokh, Ndob, Ndiourki and Diamsil.
1749–54		Mawa T.Y., D.		Preparation for the wars of 1754. Alliances with neighbouring kingdoms.
1754	Biram Kodu Ndumbé M, D.		Mawa	Biram takes Kayor for a month, but is driven out by Mawa. Mawa is assassinated at Lambaye.
1754		Mawa		
1756	Biram Kodu Ndumbé (2nd reign)		Makodu Kumba Diaring (2nd reign)	Maysa kills Biram at Sanguère (1756).

1756–7	Maysa Bigé Ngoné (2nd reign)	—	Leading a coalition, the king of Dyolof Birayamb fights Maysa at Bittiwe and becomes king.
1757–8	*Buurba* Birayamb	—	Maysa kills Birayamb at the battle of Mbal and becomes king again.
1758–63	Maysa Bigé Ngoné (3rd reign)	—	
1763–6	Madior M., G.		Madior, a weak king, is defeated by the king of Walo (*brak*) at Khatta, Diamsil and Ngol.
1766–78	Makodu Kumba Diaring		Imposed by the *brak* at Kayor. Besieged at Khandan, his capital, by Madior. Makodu beats Madior at Gouye-Tody and kills him at Saté-Lâ.
1778–86	Biram Fatim Penda T.N., G.	Amari Ngoné Ndéla T.Y., G.	Amari is driven out of Baol by Biram in 1786 after a period of tension between Kayor and Baol.
1786–90		Biram Fatim Penda	
1790–1809		Amari Ngoné Ndéla	Kayor and Baol taken by Amari. Revolt of the Muslims of Ndiambour who are beaten at Palo and Pire. Secession of Cape Verde after the defeat of Amari (c. 1795). Invasion of Kayor by Abdul-Qadir who is beaten at Bounkoy in 1796. Exile of Birima Fatma Tyub, Amari's nephew, who defeats his uncle's troops at Ndio (Sine).

*The abbreviations which follow the names of the damel, tegn, and damel-tegn correspond respectively to the paternal line:
(T.Y. = branch descended from Tyé Yasin
T.N. = branch descended from Tyé Ndela
M = branch descended from Madior)
and to the matrilineage:
(G = Gedj
D = Dorobé)
All kings in the eighteenth century had the patronymic Fall

marked by considerable agitation and this can be linked directly with the slave trade.

4 The development of Kayor and Baol in the eighteenth century was connected with that of neighbouring kingdoms who were also in contact with European traders. This link was the result of kinship ties which united ruling families, and also of alliances which were being entered into. Several deposed kings or pretenders took advantage of their exile to form coalitions and wage war against Kayor and Baol. All the neighbouring countries welcomed these defeated leaders and frequently allied with them in battle. Relations between the various sovereigns were characterized by a concern to preserve a certain balance of power between the kingdoms, and this preoccupation was largely a result of European pressure.

5 The eighteenth century saw the rise of a social class linked to the kings and pretenders. A distinction can be made between the provincial leaders, nominated by the king, and the warrior slaves, who were in the service of aristocratic families. The two groups were frequently engaged in a struggle for power, which modified appreciably their attitude towards the peasantry. Along with the kings, they were led into taking part in Atlantic trade, buying rifles, gunpowder and alcohol, and selling slaves and provisions to the traders.

6 The eighteenth century drew to a close with muslim upheavals at Ndiambour and Cape Verde, and with the invasion of Kayor by the *almamy* Abdul-Qadir. These episodes, which took place at the end of the great slave-trading century, illustrate the more or less latent tension between those in political power and the Islamic communities. This religious opposition accompanied Nasir Al-Din's movement, which was widespread in Kayor between 1673 and 1677, and forced the Fall dynasty to cede power temporarily to a muslim chief, the Qadi Ndiay Sall. The 'war of the *marabouts*' which was led by Nasir Al-Din, was fought against all the kings who were then heavily engaged in the slave trade. The objective was both the establishment of pure Islam and an end to the raids and tyranny of the kings.[7] It is reasonable to conclude with B. Barry, however, that these wars, although fought in the name of Islam and involving all the kingdoms in contact with Saint Louis, in fact represented

> the first signs of the consequences of the negro slave trade, which resulted in wars and pillaging in order to obtain the European merchandise which was arriving henceforward in great quantities.[8]

Senegalese kingdoms and the slave trade, 18th century 107

The slave trade in Kayor and Baol from written sources

Archive sources give us a rather unsatisfactory account of the extent and effects of the slave trade in Kayor and Baol. They provide us with sets of figures relating to European intervention in the country's politics. They also give some idea of the socio-political effects of the European trade.

The main product which Europeans sought after in Kayor and Baol was 'ebony wood', that is, slaves. Nonetheless, the dependence of the trading posts on neighbouring kingdoms for basic supplies, such as wood and water, was very real and influenced trading conditions. The sovereigns often took advantage of this trump card by refusing to provide essential supplies; kings exercised some authority over the traders in this way and assured themselves a position of power, but breakdowns in trading were always only temporary.

Numerical data

Written sources are extremely inadequate for Kayor and Baol. It is possible to provide fairly accurate figures of numbers of slaves who embarked at Saint Louis and at Gorée,[9] but it is very difficult to determine where they came from and to give the exact number from each kingdom. Table 5 summarizes the information concerning Kayor and Baol. Note that:

— figures are incomplete for certain periods.
— they often correspond to one day's trading or to a single trade transaction.
— the figures often relate to one or two neighbouring kingdoms, or to estimated areas.
— on the whole, they are official French figures; trading with un-authorized and English traders hardly appears, although it is referred to on several occasions.

This table suggests a number of things:

1 An average which can be established from the figures quoted gives us an estimated number of 2–300 slaves sold per year to French traders by the kings of Kayor and Baol. However, the largest transactions involved more than 500 captives sold to the French in a single year. We may also note that the sale of blacks was interrupted from time to time, according to the written source, by wars waged between the kingdoms.

2 Official French figures suggest that English trade diverted the slaves either via illegal traders to Portudal (principal trading post in

Table 5 Figures on the trade in captives in Kayor and Baol

Year Period	With Damel	Damel debt (a)	With Damel-Tègn	Damel-Tègn debt (a)	With Tègn (a)	Tègn debt (a)	Saint-Louis area (b)	Gorée area (c)	References (d)
end of 17th cent.			500 a year						Labat, t. IV, p. 232
beginning of 18th century			2–300 per year						Ibid., id.
1701			321 in 12 days						Arch. dép. L-A C 739, 29.6.1702
1704							50?	300?	Arch. dép. L-A C 740, 1704
1705							50?	100–150?	Arch. nat., C⁶ 3 14.9.1705
1706			56+						Arch. nat., C⁶ 3 and Bibl. nat. n.a.f.
1716				110+					Arch. nat., C⁶ 6, 6.6.1720
1718									Arch. nat., C⁶ 14 (s.d.)
Oct 1719			366	80					Arch. nat., C⁵ 5, 3.10.1719
Dec 1719				62					Arch. nat., C⁵ 5 and 6
1720		31				31			Arch. nat., C⁶ 6, 26.8.1720
Aug 1720					8+				Arch. nat., C⁶ 6, id.
Sept 1720		44+			41+	10+			Arch. nat., C⁶ 6, 28.3.1721
Dec 1720	70+								Arch. nat., C⁶ 6, id.
end of 1720		41+			49+	70+			Arch. nat., C⁶ 6, id.
May 1721	81+			53+	22+	18+			Arch. nat., C⁶ 6, 24.5.1721
beginning of 1722									Arch. nat., C⁶ 7, 3.5.1722 (trading with the English)
Mar 1722	70+	24							Arch. nat., C⁶ 7, 26.3.1722
May 1722	Damel sends slaves to the Gambia								Arch. nat., C⁶ 7, 16.7.1722
Mar 1722	62+								Arch. nat., C⁶ 7, 3.5.1722
Aug 1722	49+	43			95+	28+			Arch. nat., C⁶ 7, 27.8.1722
Sept 1722	300?				55+				Arch. nat., C⁶ 7, 28.12.1722
1722	5–600 captives possible per year with Damel and Tègn								Arch. nat., C⁶ 7, 1.6.1722
1723					300?				Arch. nat., C⁶ 7, 27.4.1723
July 1723	40+								Arch. nat., C⁶ 7, 18.8.1723

Date	Description	Number	Source
1723	trading with Damel and Tègn in 1723 very much lower than anticipated		Arch. nat., C⁶ 7, 18.12.1723
Mar 1724	no trading of slaves with Damel and Tègn during the preceding 6 months		Arch. nat., C⁶ 8, 28.3.1724
May 1724		40+	Arch. nat., C⁶ 8, 25.5.1724
June 1724	19+		Arch. nat., C⁶ 8, 18.6.1724
1725	the difficulty of combating illicit slave trading	50?	Arch. nat., C⁶ 9, 21.7.1725
1725		170	Arch. nat., C⁶ 9, 18.6.1725
Jan 1726		107	Arch. nat., C⁶ 29, 26.1.1726
July 1726		40+ 41	Arch. nat., C⁶ 10, 7.7.1726
Jan 1731	16+		Arch. nat., C⁶ 10, 6.9.1731
Aug 1732	4+ (c. 100 captives promised by Damel)	40+	Arch. nat., C⁶ 10, 23.8.1732
July 1733			Arch. nat., C⁶ 10, 12.7.1733
1736–7	Damel-Tègn has done no trading during this year and convokes the English	135 (1 year)	Arch. nat., C⁶ 11, 31.5.1737
1737	30+		Arch. nat., C⁶ 11, 20.5.1737
June 1737	38+		Arch. nat., C⁶ 11, 4.7.1737
July 1737	Damel-Tègn has sold only 95–100 slaves to the French in 1 year		Arch. nat., C⁶ 11, 2.8.1737
1737–8		130 per year	Arch. nat., C⁶ 11, 4.7.1738
1738–41		220–50 per year	Arch. nat., C⁶ 27 bis p. 91 (Pruneau de Pommegorge)
1738–41	Gorée has supplied more than 300 slaves over 2 years		Arch. nat., C⁶ 12, 30.7.1741
1741	Gorée has supplied the usual number during the year		
1741	6+ (sold to the English at Portugal)		
June 1741	50+		Arch. nat., C⁶ 13, 29.7.1751
beginning of 1752	42+		Arch. nat., C⁶ 13, 30.6.1751
beginning of 1753	50+ (sold to the English)		Arch. nat., C⁶ 13, 24.2.1752
Jan–June 1753	400 slaves sold to the French during the year; this seems to be the highest figure achieved by a Damel-Tègn with the French		Arch. nat., C⁶ 14, 10.2.1753
			Arch. nat., C⁶ 14, 20.6.1753
Oct 1753	100 slaves taken from Gorée after a war between Kayor and Sine		Arch. nat., C⁶ 14, 25.10.1753
1753		500	Arch. nat., C⁶ 14, 25.10.1753
July 1753 } July 1754		540	Arch. nat., C⁶ 14, 11.7.1754
1754	over 500 slaves sold by Damel-Tègn after a civil war		Arch. nat. C⁶ 27 bis (Pruneau de Pommegorge)
Jan–July 1754		400 350	Arch. nat., C⁶ 14, 11.7.1754

(Continued overleaf)

Table 5 *(continued)*

Year Period	With Damel	Damel debt (a)	With Damel-Tègn	Damel-Tègn debt (a)	With Tègn (a)	Tègn debt (a)	Saint-Louis area (b)	Gorée area (c)	References (d)
1754	numerous refugees from Kayor sold by Brak at Saint-Louis								Arch. nat. C⁶ 14, 3.6.1754
1754-5							600	500	Arch. nat. C⁶ 14, 31.7.1755
1756	much trading following the wars between Kayor and Baol								Arch. nat. C⁶ 14, 16.10.1756
1757-8	Buurba Birayamb becomes the king of Kayor and refuses, in the name of Islam, to sell slaves and does not buy alcohol								PRO, CO 267/12, 31.3.1758
1763 onwards	60 per year							250 per year	Arch. nat., SOM, DFC, Gorée
—									
1765	300 possible with Damel	130-50?			3-400?				Arch. nat., C⁶ 23 mémoire s.d.
c. 1765		100-150 per year							PRO, CO 388/52, 17.2.1765
1766					100?				Arch. nat., C⁶ 15, mémoire s.d.
1774					80+ (carried off by the English)				Arch. nat., C⁶ 17, 24.7.1774
1775 onwards								2-300 per year	Arch. nat., C⁶ 29 (Le Brasseur)
1775	numerous slaves sold to Saint-Louis. The Moors took 8000 captives from Brak in less than 6 months, many of whom are refugees from Kayor								Arch. nat., C⁶ 18 (État...1783)
1776			170-200 possible with Damel-Tègn					300?	Arch. nat. SOM, DFC, Gorée (Le Brasseur)
1776		100 per year							Arch. nat. SOM, DFC, Gorée (Le Brasseur)
1778	50-80?				50-80?				Arch. dép. L-A. C 739
c. 1778									Arch. nat., C⁶ 17, 5.3.1778
c. 1784							5-600 per year		Arch. nat., SOM, DFC, Senegal 2.8.1784
1786							120?		Arch. nat., SOM, DFC, Senegal 18.11.1783
1787	250?			250?			600	300	Goldberry, t. II, pp. 27 and 205; Arch. nat., C⁶ 19, 24.1.1787

NOTES FOR TABLE 5

Note: the figures in the different columns of the table relate to slave trading with the Damel, Damel–Tègn and Tègn, and the respective debts of these kings.

The three columns headed 'debt (a)' give the figures showing how much each of the kings owed. In effect, the system of commerce sometimes permitted loans of merchandise of a value equivalent to a certain number of captives, loans which the kings undertook to repay in the form of captives. Thus the figures in these columns show the number of captives to be handed over by the different kings in exchange for goods that had been given on loan. A number on its own shows the total debt of a king, while a number followed by a + shows a debt contracted during one trade.

The figures in the two last columns, (b) the Saint-Louis area and (c) the Gorée area and (c) relate to the slave trading carried out in the Saint-Louis area with the Walo, the Kayor and the Fouta (b) and in the Gorée area with the Kayor, the Baol and the Sine (c).

The sign + following the number of slaves bought from a king indicates that the captives were supplied in a single transaction. When followed by the sign ? the figure is an estimate or a possible number of slaves that could have been bought from one or several kings.

The system of references (d) has been simplified, but makes it possible to find the texts quoted. (The documents mentioned here will be used in more detail in an article that is to follow on the Kayor and the Baol in the eighteenth century for which references will be more complete.) The abbreviations are as follows:

Arch. nat., C⁶ = Archives nationales, documents from the files in the series Colonies C⁶
Bibl. nat., n.a.f. = Bibliotheque nationale, Département des Manuscrits, nouvelles acquisitions françaises
Arch. nat., SOM = Archives nationales, section Outre-mer; DFC. = Dépôt des Fortifications des Colonies
Arch. dep. L-A = Archives départementales de la Loire-Atlantique
PRO, CO = Public Record Office, Colonial Office (Documents passed on by M. B. Barry)
Labat = *Nouvelle relation de l'Afrique occidentale* (Paris: Cavelier, 1728)
Goldberry = *Fragments d'un voyage en Afrique, fait pendant les années 1785, 1786 and 1787* ... (Paris: an X, 1802)

Baol), or to English trading posts in Gambia, or to Saint Louis during the English occupation, between 1758 and 1779.

3   An illicit slave trade existed, referred to in a document dated 1725. It is virtually impossible to estimate the extent of this traffic which was probably not actively suppressed because of arrangements agreed between the captains and the agents of the French companies.

4   It is almost impossible to estimate the extent of the buying and selling of slaves in Kayor and Baol by mulattoes. Local traders bought slaves inland or at the trading posts themselves, and then resold a large number of them to the companies. The English encouraged this system of trading more than the French; they tried to surround themselves with 'brokers' to aid trading with the Senegambian kingdoms.[10] Some of the blacks bought and sold by the Moors undoubtedly came from Kayor and Baol.

5   During the first half of the eighteenth century, French traders accepted debts, often unwillingly, from the kings of Kayor and Baol, who borrowed goods and repaid with slaves. These loans were very common until the middle of the century. Several trade documents distinguish between 'reimbursed' slaves, 'traded' slaves, and slaves 'on loan'. The extent of this latter group exceeded the number of slaves actually delivered in certain sales, and partial repayment was often a condition of further advances. Incidentally, a sovereign's debt was considered hereditary by French traders. On the death of Latsukabe in 1720, his debt was divided up between his two successors. Several kings challenged this carrying over of their predecessors' debts, and temporarily ceased trading.

6   Although the exact origin of slaves is not always evident, they seem to have been taken captive in the following ways:
— during civil wars
— during wars against neighbouring kingdoms
— during raids on outlying provinces, and often on Serer lands
— during periods of famine

It seems that many men taken captive during wars and raids were not sold, but were integrated into the conquering society; others were sold to Europeans immediately or shortly after being captured. The relations of the traders with Kayor and Baol, which were necessary if the trading posts were to be provided with fresh supplies, often broke down and trade ceased temporarily, and this would bring about an increase in the number of captives in Wolof society.[11]

French trade policy and its consequences

Much documentary material about French trade policy is available, and it clearly illustrates the more or less direct intervention of administrators in the political life of the Senegalese kingdoms. It would seem that this policy was intended to keep Kayor and Baol under the rule of two separate kings, in order to facilitate the growth of trade. On a number of occasions suitable pretenders were provided with arms and ammunition and encouraged to wage war with a view to dividing the two kingdoms. On the other hand, the sovereigns were often raiding each other's land, following deliveries of rifles and gunpowder. Sometimes, when wars between the Damel and the Tegn caused prolonged breakdowns both in slave trading and in the supply of basic provisions, the French tried to bring about a reconciliation between the adversaries: the agreements they recommended had the purpose of re-establishing normal trading activity and allowing each king to concentrate on profitable pillaging of his own land.

Protection of trade by the military was limited to the two principal trading posts at Saint Louis and Gorée, which were defended by a garrison whose size varied according to the needs of the time. There was scarcely any armed intervention within the kingdoms of Kayor and Baol, except in areas in close proximity to the trading posts. The French administrators advocated intervention on a number of occasions to end the trade blockade imposed by the Damel and to punish the 'insolent' king, but they were unable to put their plans into action because of lack of means.

The sale of arms was reserved almost exclusively to kings and leaders. Thus the 'Observations on the Island of Gorée by M. de Rochelave, Governor, to M. Ronoface, his successor' in 1772, emphasized the importance of not arming the 'commoners' as this might 'dissuade the kings from looting' and of only arming the leaders.[12] This attitude, which prevailed in the eighteenth century, shows clearly that Atlantic trade was a strong contributory factor in the deterioration of social relations, arming the princes and weakening the peasants. It is clear that the complacent descriptions of the 'tyranny of kings towards their subjects' almost always omit to mention the responsibility of the traders who created this situation in order to obtain their slaves and provisions.[13]

As in neighbouring kingdoms, the traders had to pay trading dues, customs duties, to the sovereigns and kings of Kayor and Baol. The payment of these dues took place every year; on Muslim holidays or on opening a trade transaction, special customs duties to the king were paid. These mostly took the form of military supplies. Moreover, the Damel and the Tegn always insisted upon the regular payment of these taxes: several breakdowns in trade were caused by irregular payment of customs dues. Finally, it seems that collection of customs taxes was a powerful motive in all the succession conflicts and attempts at unifying Kayor and Baol.

French policy was hampered by English rivalry throughout the eighteenth century.[14] The kings of Kayor and Baol were able to take advantage of this opposition at certain times, to collect higher taxes and sell slaves and supplies at a higher price. However, this competition led the French traders to intervene, depending on their interests, on behalf of, or against the sovereigns of the two countries. Large numbers of gifts, deliveries of arms, encouragement of supposedly favourable alliances, and incitement to war were amongst the main tactics used to secure the development of French trade.

Various texts illustrate clearly the nature of the relations between the kings of Kayor and Baol and French traders,[15] and show the role played by the latter in the political life of the coastal kingdoms.

In 1687, a few years before the reign of Latsukabe, the division of Kayor and Baol was encouraged:

the said Sr Hugollein and Mathelot will not fail immediately upon their arrival at Portudal to send a white man quickly with the King Thin (Tegn)'s present, letting him know of our arrival. Let it be made known to him that we have learnt that he is at war with the Damel king, and that we will be happy to supply him with arms, gunpowder lead and other things should he be in need of them, and that we are glad to be of service and hope to remain on the best of friendly terms; that henceforth no company other than our own will trade at Portudal, and will always be stocked with excellent goods, and that should the English or any other nation arrive, we will seize their cargoes; he may also be told that after his hoped for defeat of the Damel king, he will take several men captive and send them to Gorée where we will trade them for good quality merchandise, and finally get the king to undertake to supply us promptly with a substantial number of slaves, since we are in grave need of them at Gorée.[16]

On the death of Latsukabe in 1720, the director of Saint Robert tried to gain the good will of the two successors, and announced to the Damel that:

I am aware that he and his brother the Thin have rivals who are ready to wage war against them, that there are even those who have made it known they will support them, and that they will soon send me captives if I will supply them with arms and gunpowder; but he may depend upon it that as long as he shows good faith in his dealings with the Company, I will only listen to his enemies if it be in his interests to do so. I thought it necessary to speak in these terms to the new Damel in order that he should acquit himself promptly.[17]

Senegalese kingdoms and the slave trade, 18th century   115

Since the wars between the successors of Latsukabe were harmful to commerce, the director Dubellay tried to bring about a reconciliation between the Damel and the Tegn in 1724, so that the latter might begin selling him slaves again who would be taken captive during raids:

Despite M. Dufour and myself remonstrating with the kings Thin and Damel to bring them to peace, this has been of no use since the Damel has been advised to the contrary by the Marabouts, since according to public opinion the Thin would not keep away, this being why they have only traded in a small way at Gorée, and why they do not dare to raid their neighbours nor their subjects, as they are used to doing, being content merely to take precautions against each other in their own domains for fear of being caught unawares; it seems that this war is not likely to end soon, for otherwise the company could take advantage of their greed for goods by the number of slaves they would be able to provide, if they were at peace, and I shall endeavour to bring this about, and to make its trade flourish in all the establishments within its concession.[18]

The same year, Dubellay wrote to the director of Gorée, Lafore, in identical terms:

The Company orders me sir to direct you to urge the kings Thin and Damel with gifts and solicitations to come to a peaceful settlement, pointing out to them that it is in both their interests, because they would then be in a position to raid their enemies, that is, the Serer, and to pillage their subjects when they were displeased with them, as Damel Latir fal [Latsukabe Fall] did.[19]

In 1731, when Walo and Kayor were threatened with invasion by the Moors, the French decided to support the Wolof kingdoms:

[21 January 1731] We learn that the Akalifa Moors have made an alliance with Syratik king of the country of the Fulani Moors to put Giuogomaye, a relation of Damel, on the throne of Kayor in revenge for the fact that the Damel had handed over to Hamar, the Moorish leader, a party of Akalifas who had taken refuge with him; they have even, so it is claimed, asked Brak to let their troops pass through his country, but it is highly probable that Brak will oppose this with all his might, since it is not in his interests to allow the Moors into his country: it is true that the country would be ruined if the Moors were in Kayor, and the Company's trade completely destroyed on the Senegal river and in Gorée, and so M. Levens [the director of St Louis] who is well aware of the consequences has no doubt what action to take; on the 22nd, he will find Jambar and recommend him to send a man to Brak to assure him that despite the war he is waging with us, if he needs help with arms, gunpowder, or even a few boats to stop the Moors from entering his land, I will supply him with them, reserving the right to recommence the war between us, or make peace, if Brak is willing to pay us what he owes.[20]

The position in relation to Damel-Tegn Maysa Teindé Wedj who took over Baol in 1736, is defined in a number of documents of the Gorée

Council and the Saint Louis Council, written in 1736 and 1737. Thus the Gorée Council notes:

> It would be essential for the good of the Company's trade that the Tegn's kingdom which Damel has just conquered, should be taken over by someone else, so that Tegn's kingdom would no longer be in a position to communicate with the English, since the latter cannot get through Portudal ... whereas Damel as master of both kingdoms is in a position to do without us: we might manage to drive him out of Tegn's country by supplying his rival with arms and ammunition, as his rival is very keen to recommence war, if only he had the means. On that supposition, we could reach some compromise by which we might assure repayment of the advances which would have been made for this enterprise.[21]

In 1753, the High Council of Senegal, directed by Estoupan de La Brue, drew attention to the large numbers of slaves purchased from the Damel-Tegn Mawa, who had been exchanged exclusively for arms, as well as to the refusal to allow this sovereign to contract debts:

> We have paid no heed to the Damel's persistent attempts to squeeze loans from us. In the end, he ceased asking and we are now on good terms with him. During the year he has sold us more than 400 slaves and to our knowledge none of his predecessors have ever done such abundant trade with us. As this king takes almost exclusively arms and ammunition in exchange for his captives, we have very few rifles left for trading.[22]

Shortly afterwards a *Statement on Senegal* in 1754 recommended setting up a station on Cape Verde peninsula to remedy the problem of provisioning Gorée. It also outlined the way to deal with Mawa:

> The Damel, who is the most powerful king on the coast, owes his greatness entirely to King Brak, who aided him in his conquests ... so, since there is no one to balance his power, all our trade depends on him. And it is from his country that we take almost all of our slaves. Thus, the only policy called for is to keep his friendship, without seeming to fear him, that is to say, to put into practice that prudent firmness which makes such an impression on the minds of the blacks, who, more than other men, have a high regard for their own interests. As this king frequently pillages his subjects, it is hardly surprising that he is able to supply us with plenty of blacks and little in the way of food supplies in times of scarcity. And yet the Island of Gorée needs them for itself and for the Company's vessels which put into port there.
>
> I cannot see any reason why the Company should not establish a port at Gorée; on the contrary, the more the king sees this island regularly frequented with heavy vessels, the more he will be inclined to have some consideration and respect for us; also, the more he will rid himself of his wrong-headed idea of not allowing poultry to be raised in his country, for he will be made to see that it will be to his advantage.

Senegalese kingdoms and the slave trade, 18th century 117

In order to fulfil this aim, a piece of land must be obtained from him in the large area where we are looking for fresh water for Gorée and the vessels. Once this land, which contains about 39 acres, has been granted to us, we shall be able to keep it safe from attack at little cost, create pasture-land and raise cattle and poultry. By these same means, facilities for obtaining supplies of fresh water would be secured – water not available at present on the Island of Gorée and which the king can, at any time, for a mere whim, prevent us from obtaining. As his only aim is to plunder his subjects, we would soon see villages forming around this small establishment whose inhabitants would seek our protection.[23]

In 1764, Poncet, the Governor of Gorée made a proposition to the Damel Madior to encourage him to attack the *buurba Dyolof*, in order to weaken both kings and so prepare for conquering Bambouk:

Poncet intends to have war declared against the King Buurbayoloff, his enemy, by the King Damel, whom he is sure of, in order to weaken both of them so that neither of them can oppose his passage if the court agrees to the conquest of Bambouc.[24]

Poncet himself writes in his letter:

[Kayor] belongs to the Damel whom I am sure of, our interests are entirely linked to each other . . . as for the interests of Yoloff, whose king is called Buurbayoloff, I am not sure whether he will give me any difficulty, but if he refuses to come to terms with me, I will have Damel wage war against him. The Kings of Kayor and Yoloff fall out as soon as they become kings – for it is in Buurbayoloff's interest to weaken the King of Kayor. I will point out to them where their interests lie, and give to Damel gifts of gunpowder and bullets so as to get him to attack Buurbayoloff; I could even supply him with a detachment, and field artillery.[25]

In 1773, English policy towards the Damel–Tegn Makodu, who traded with the English at Saint Louis and with the French at Rufisque and Gorée, encouraged war between this sovereign and his rival:

[O'Hara] has been supplying [the Damel] with gunpowder against a king he has deposed, and at the same time he is supplying the unfortunate king, so that he may regain his throne. In this way, by getting them to fight each other, the English were assured of the exclusive supply of slaves.[26]

From 1777–8, Le Brasseur proposed a reversal in French policy, which, until then, had always prevented the Moors from seizing Kayor and Baol. Despite his initial hesitation,[27] Le Brasseur sent a *Plan for Revolution in the Kingdoms of Kayor and Baol* to the minister in 1778, which would be furthered by:

secret treaties, which we could negotiate shrewdly with the Moors, a subtle, ambitious and war-like nation, and besides that a constant plague to the Negroes, who fear them in all those characteristics whose most terrifying effects they have always experienced in the past, witness the total loss and destruction of Brak's Kingdom, neighbouring the Damel's, where they left only enough inhabitants to make an annual raid worthwhile . . . ; this revolution brought about in our two kingdoms, like the one the English brought about in Brak, would be equally advantageous to cultivation in America and the peace and safety of the Island of Gorée. You will see, My Lord, that the Guyana Company will not be adversely affected if this plan is carried out in Kayor and Baol, who annually produce scarcely 100 negroes, although they are just as heavily populated as other parts of Africa where trade is far more abundant.[28]

The general outlines of French commercial policy towards Kayor and Baol are well enough illustrated by the texts quoted in this essay. The history of these two kingdoms shows that this policy was not always successful, but nonetheless it helped to build up an atmosphere of insecurity, and led to the increase in wars and raids which characterized the eighteenth century.

The internal consequences of the slave trade

With the information obtained from internal sources and archive documents it is possible to discuss the impact of the slave trade on the societies of Kayor and Baol. In the eighteenth century there was a tremendous upheaval in the socio-political structures of these two coastal kingdoms. The changes which arose are closely connected with the development of European trade, and French trade in particular, which was concerned with exporting as large a number of slaves as possible. The economic context of this trade largely determined the outbreaks of internal disturbances and civil wars, and the increasing frequency – if, indeed, it was not the cause, of raids on the peasant Wolof and Serer populations, as well as the frequent campaigns against neighbouring countries. This continuing unrest brought about a socio-political crisis whose consequences were felt until the nineteenth century. The colonizers were then able to take advantage of the situation provoked by the trade of the previous century, and claimed to justify their action by the specious argument that they were 'liberating the enslaved peoples from oppression by their tyrannical rulers'. Now this trade system, desired and imposed by the Europeans was very different from the trans-Saharan slave trade in method, and also involved greater numbers.[29] It took the form of exporting blacks who were supplied by the local leaders, to whom was given the responsibility for capturing them, either through wars or raids, and who were supplied with arms for this purpose. A study of the history of Kayor and Baol largely confirms

Senegalese kingdoms and the slave trade, 18th century

the conclusions of Suret-Canale about the social consequences of the trade:

Europe could, as a general rule, avoid having to hunt for slaves itself... and in this way the Africans became the architects of their own ruin, for the sole benefit of the slave trader. Instead of productive activity, the most lucrative occupation became war with its long trail of human and material destruction – war to acquire slaves for the trade.

It was then, and only then, that permanent insecurity, wars, and incessant raids, and the misery and famine that come in their train, became permanent features of black Africa.

The African slave trade was not the culmination of a process of internal development, but was the result of persuasion, of external intervention.[30]

In Kayor and Baol, the slave trade was set up by the Europeans. It brought about untold misery, led rulers to collaborate with the Europeans and compromise themselves on numerous occasions, and also aroused peasant resistance, which was mainly Muslim in origin.[31] There can be little doubt that the changes which took place during the eighteenth century were almost entirely the direct consequences of the slave trade. They affected the entirety of Kayor and Baol society and may be analysed at different levels.[32]

1 Demography and the settlement of villages

Figures from written sources show us that the number of slaves exported was substantial. Oral sources inform us that wars caused deaths. However, Kayor and Baol were not depopulated as much as other African areas. The real demographic effects of the slave trade are difficult to evaluate, but it is possible to establish population movement inland, and a change in social structures. The history of settlement patterns and village traditions clearly shows a marked depopulation of border areas in the eighteenth century. These were where the frequent raids took place and were thus very unstable areas. Also, a number of villages were established which were ruled by the princes or *tyedo*, and their fate was thus very much tied to that of the King.[33] Also, the raids and wars were responsible for famine, even more so than adverse climatic conditions, and for the deaths that resulted.

2 Economic life

The frequent famines during the eighteenth century may be linked with the development of the slave trade. The wars frequently took place during the seasons when agricultural work was crucial, and disrupted the sowing or harvesting. The irregular production of millet was largely due to the wars and raids, which took the attackers, as well as the attacked, away from the fields. Millet, a basic crop, and oxen, were often stolen from the peasants at a time of scarcity by the leaders and their soldiers. Thus the rural groups suffered the effects of shortages most savagely.[34]

Levying 'taxes' was often the pretext for these extortive practices. The revenue from these collections was partly destined for the king, and partly for the king's representatives who were responsible for the collection. The use of these sinecures for commercial and military purposes became general: the products collected (millet, cattle and slaves) were mostly sold for arms, alcohol, shoddy goods, and materials.

The demand for European goods came from the middle layers of society who were in the leader's service, and from the aristocracy. The purchase of certain types of product from the European traders no doubt contributed to the decline of the local Wolof industries (weaving, dyeing, metal work) and of stock breeding, and to the gradual cessation of the manufacture of traditional agricultural production (cotton, palm oil, tobacco).

3 Socio-political organization

The most significant changes took place in the social and political structure, and the relations between the different levels of society. The effects of the slave trade have already been outlined above, but deserve to be analysed in greater detail. Although the kings were appointed by an assembly representative of the whole of society, and were subject to their dismissal, they abused their powers, and it was scarcely possible to control them. Despite the frequent errors and the consequent erroneous judgements contained in European accounts of the authority and 'tyranny' of the Kings, they do illustrate clearly the changes which occurred in the relations between the sovereign and his subjects. The characteristic features of government were recourse to force, an inordinate use of the right of the state to nominate to government office and the growth of the military potential. The peasant and Islamic revolts can only be understood in this context.

The chiefs, nominated by the kings, surrounded themselves, as did the kings, with a category of people at their service, the *tyedo*,[35] but also with caste people such as *griots* (dependants who would sing their praises), and *laubee* craftsmen (blacksmiths in particular). The *tyedo* were mostly captives of the crown, belonging, in fact, to the sovereign's or prince's family. Thus the *dyami-Gedj* (captives of the matrilineal Gedj), in the eighteenth century acquired a privileged position in the socio-political structure of the two kingdoms, a position which would remain theirs in the following century. The preponderance of the *tyedo* and *dyami* in the council which elected and controlled the kings weakened the strength of peasant representation: several traditional conflicts between kings and *lamans* (peasant leaders, withholders of land dues), resulted in victory for the sovereign, with the support of his family and the *tyedo*. The leaders (chiefs) and *tyedo* were characterized by their inclination for military activity. They took part in domestic and foreign wars; consequently they were armed.

The decline in the role of the *laman*, who were still able to make the Damel destitute in the seventeenth century,[36] is linked to the weakening of the *dyambuur* peasants (free non-caste men), who may be referred to by the term *badolo*. The worsening of the material lot of the peasants provoked a number of reactions: moving away to the Islamized areas where there was some assurance of security; the tightening up of Serer groups, which resulted in autarchy and a well-organized defence against the pillaging; the passing of *dyambuur* into the *dyami* (captives) caste in order to gain protection from their leaders in exchange for their work and change in conditions. Whichever course of action the peasants took, it certainly seems that they were the group that suffered most from the consequences of the slave trade, and lost their position in the socio-political edifice. The change in the balance of power was detrimental to them.

Current sociological analysis shows that the proportion of *dyami* in the villages of Kayor and Baol was very high. This phenomenon can be understood in the light of the explanations given above and manifests the social change that took place in the eighteenth century.[37]

Before the rise of the slave trade, Kayor and Baol society, with the exception of most Serer groups, was made up of a caste of slaves. The development of the slave trade was accompanied by the swelling in number of this caste, and also by the growth of the power of the *farba* (captive leaders) and the *tyedo* captives.

With the support which they either gave or refused to kings and pretenders, these captives were able to gain considerable influence in political life. The growth in the size of the slave caste during the eighteenth century is closely connected with the existence of the slave trade. The wars, internal conflicts, and raids, led the peasants to accept their condition as *dyami*, and to yield a multitude of captives to the warriors. The relatively low number of slaves of Kayor–Baol origin, exported by the Europeans, may be explained by the fact that a large number of men taken captive were not sold but were integrated into

Wolof society as *dyami*. Some kings – and the French did not appreciate such behaviour – objected to the massive sale of slaves, and preferred to retain new slaves within their own kingdoms, keeping some in their own service, and sending others to dignitaries (leaders of provinces, and heads of the Muslim Wolof and Moorish families).[38]

4 Relations with neighbouring communities

As we have already pointed out, more or less direct European intervention caused the countless conflicts which characterized relations between Kayor and Baol, and between those two countries and their neighbours. The political aims of the traders, which were to sow dissension amongst their clients, were frequently fulfilled.

Relations with the borderlands were marked by pillaging of border villages, and wars, whose motive was often to remove the support which these borderland areas had agreed to give to fallen kings or to exiled enemy princes. The frontier areas were the most affected, and became depopulated; provinces which were particularly menaced by these conflicts were reinforced by stationing warriors among the peasant groups.

Despite the kinship links which united the Damels and Tegns with the sovereigns of the Walo, Dyolof, Sine, Saloum and the Fouta, the tensions between them were frequent and serious: this indicates that all the kingdoms concerned entered into the game organized by the European traders.[39]

The profound changes that took place during the eighteenth century were the precursors of the nineteenth century Muslim revival and the Islamic resistance to French military colonization. In Kayor and Baol they were the origin of *Mouridisme*, which was a dual protest movement aimed against French colonization and against the regime of the *tyedo* inherited from the previous century's slave trade.

With regard to Kayor, several historians have put forward the idea of a 'superficial Islamization' before the 'massive nineteenth century conversion'. This theory cannot be accepted neither for Kayor nor for Baol, since information tallying both with tradition and with written sources indicates that Islam was already deeply rooted in the Wolof.[40] It is certainly the case that the Serer groups which were attached to both kingdoms conserved their traditional religion and rejected Islam until very recent times, with the exception of a certain number of villages in the centre of Baol and to the east which were 'Wolofized' and converted *ipso facto*: the Serer who became Wolof in this way were called *Mbalongiafén*, a word which means mixture, or cross-breed. Amongst

Senegalese kingdoms and the slave trade, 18th century   123

the Wolof themselves, Islam infiltrated social and political life profoundly from the Fall dynasty onwards, and no doubt began earlier. In the eighteenth century, several Muslim centres existed throughout Kayor and Baol. The religious leaders were either Wolof, 'Wolofized' Toucouleur, or Moors who had settled in the country in earlier periods.

The best known Wolof Islamic centres were those at Pire, Longor, Coki, and Ndiambour, where a strict religious teaching was given by teachers who kept close links with Arab and Moorish Islam.[41]

During the eighteenth century the political policy consisted in dealing tactfully with the religious leaders and the Muslim groups under their rule, but also in taking advantage of the internal division within the Islamic 'party'. This policy took the following form:

— nominating men whose loyalty could be relied on to the post of Qadir Kayor (who was responsible for justice according to Muslim law), but also recognizing the specific jurisdiction and thus the real power, of these dignitaries;

— accepting the hereditary characters of the functions and prerogatives devolving upon Muslim families;

— maintaining the (previously recognized) rights and privileges of Moorish and Wolof religious leaders;

— carefully avoiding raids on Muslim communities, except when there was open rebellion against the authority of the king or the princes;

— sending certain leaders' sons to Koranic schools;

— offering of gifts by the King and princes in exchange for the services rendered by the *marabouts*.

These gifts were traditional and often took the form of captives. They were a reward for prayers in favour of the leaders, and for the supply of Talismans, called *téré* or *galadj*, whose use became general both for ensuring conquest and for affirming power in war with neighbouring countries.

This policy had the effect of consolidating the Muslim party and regrouping Islamic forces, which were able to ally beyond the state frontiers. The 'war of the *marabouts*' at the beginning of the great age of slave trading – with the taking of power by the Qadi Ndiay Sall in Kayor and the assassination of the Damel Ma Faly who drank alcohol – was a warning to the princes of Kayor and Baol. They were on their guard throughout the eighteenth century against Muslim groups and their leaders. At the end of the eighteenth century, direct attacks against the political power then held by the Damel-Tegn Amari Ngoné Ndela, showed that the Muslim party had not disarmed during the slave-trading century. The Muslim protestation against the system of selling slaves in exchange for guns and alcohol, and against the attitude of the rulers, took a violent form at this time, and to a great extent assured its credit in the nineteenth century at the time of resistance to French military colonization. Despite the collaboration of certain Islamic factions linked to the princes during the eighteenth century, the Muslim community kept its distance from power, and even gained sympathy from the ruling classes. It protested against the slave trade and the raids, and in the end it fought the king with arms. Because of its attitude in the eighteenth century, Islam substantially consolidated its position in Kayor and Baol society and laid the foundations of its future predominant role.[42]

At the end of this study three general points come to light:

First, from the last quarter of the seventeenth century and throughout the eighteenth century, the intervention of European trade, which bought slaves and sold arms and alcohol, caused a profound upheaval within Kayor and Baol society. It would seem that the trade was more or less directly responsible for the conflicts, wars, raids and famines which characterized this period, and was also a determining factor in the social, political, economic and religious changes that took place during this time.

Second, during the seventeenth century, before 1675, Atlantic trade was not primarily concerned with slave trading, and the exchanges with Kayor and Baol, as with the other coastal kingdoms, were far more diversified. From the end of the seventeenth century there developed a Franco-English rivalry to the exclusion of the other European nations which negotiated with Kayor and Baol. Whilst the transactions in the seventeenth century to a great extent involved products other than slaves,[43] and took place on a more or less equal footing between traders and suppliers, from the eighteenth century onwards French and English commerce imposed new objectives and methods, and changed the nature of relations with the sovereigns of these countries. The acquisition of slaves became the major concern of the French and English, who sought to impose their commercial hegemony on the leaders of Kayor and Baol, essentially by giving or selling them arms.

Despite the opposition of several Damel-Tegn to this policy, and the interruptions in trading which sometimes prevented the commercial establishments from being supplied with basic provisions and slaves, and despite the mistakes, and the poor organization of trade, which are revealed by several texts, European negotiators on the whole were extremely successful, and created a situation in Kayor–Baol which allowed them to reap the maximum profit.

Third, the reorganization of colonial trade, with the gradual abolition of slave traffic,[44] was accompanied by the beginnings of the policy of annexation of Senegalese territory. In the middle of the nineteenth century, French military activities often worked at the request of and in the interests of the trader. The unwarranted intrusion in the internal affairs of Kayor and Baol, which went as far as installing or removing kings by force, together with taking possession of lands and provinces dependent on these kingdoms, aroused a resistance, the main antagonist being Lat Dior Diop, which lasted about thirty years. The analysis of these movements, in particular the participation of different groups of society, illustrates just how serious the consequences of the slave trade in the eighteenth century were.

Summary

A study of different historical sources shows the importance of the slave trade, and of European trade in general, in the development of the Senegalese kingdoms of Kayor and Baol in the eighteenth century. The profound socio-political changes which took place during this period were influenced by the rise of European commerce and by the specific conditions of the slave trade along the Senegambian coast. Written sources give fragmentary information about the number of slaves exported by the two kingdoms, and describe clearly the nature of foreign intervention in the political life of these countries. The commercial relations between European traders and local leaders initiated the important changes in social, economic, political and religious life.

Despite the relatively small number of slaves sold to the Europeans by the Damel and the Tegn, it is not possible to dismiss the internal consequences of the slave trade. The eighteenth century in Kayor and Baol was characterized by these effects, which were the result of European trade: political instability and the struggle for power, wars with neighbouring kingdoms and the looting of the peasants by princes or *tyedo*, a marked modification of social groups and the relations between them, the integration of captives who were not sold to Europeans into Wolof society, and the movements inspired by Islam as a reaction against the chiefs who were dealing in the slave trade.

4 The import of firearms into West Africa, 1750 to 1807: a quantitative analysis
J. E. Inikori

Editor's comments

The relationship between the export slave trade and the widespread distribution of firearms in pre-colonial Africa on the one hand, and the consequences of that distribution on the other, form an important part of the debate on the impact of the export slave trade on African societies. The present chapter, based on a large body of private and official records, shows that large quantities of guns and powder were annually imported into West Africa in the late eighteenth century, directly connected with the export slave trade. The evidence indicates a strong relationship between the imported firearms and the process through which the export slaves were acquired: forceful capture. In particular, the evidence about Bonny indicates the inaccuracy of the view that a majority of slaves exported through this port in the eighteenth century were acquired through judicial processes. The paper, 'The import of firearms into West Africa in the eighteenth century,' published recently in the *Journal of African History*, vol. XXI no. 1 (1980), by W. A. Richards, shows that firearms were also important in the acquisition of slaves in West Africa in the first half of the eighteenth century.

In 1971 a number of articles dealing with various aspects of firearms in Africa appeared in the *Journal of African History*.[1] These articles raised a number of questions. To some of these no conclusive answers were given: in particular, to those relating to the quantities of firearms and ammunition annually imported into Africa over particular periods; their types and quality; the uses to which they were put; and the impact of those uses. These issues have received very little further attention

This paper was first published in the *Journal of African History*, vol. XVIII, no. 3 (1977), pp. 339–68. It has been reprinted here by permission of the publishers.

since the appearance of those articles. It is therefore proposed to shed some light on these questions in the present paper.

The scope of the paper is limited in various ways. Geographically it is limited to the west coast of Africa from Senegambia to north of the River Congo. The time period covered is only the second half of the eighteenth and the first decade of the nineteenth centuries. The paper deals essentially with quantities. But the quantitative analysis throws some light on many of the questions relating to firearms in West Africa during the period covered by the paper.

I

Government legislation relating to the exportation of firearms and ammunition from England to other countries and the extant private records of gunmakers and merchants make it very clear that guns and gunpowder were very important commodities in eighteenth-century West African trade. In the eighteenth century, it was a regular practice for the government in England to prohibit the exportation of firearms and ammunition in war-time. But, because these dangerous commodities formed the backbone of English trade to West Africa at this time, the merchants in the trade regularly petitioned the government in times of war to grant them special licences which made West Africa an exception to the general law.

In the *Acts of the Privy Council Colonial Series IV 1745–66*, reference is made to 'a very large number [of these licences] for ships engaged in the African trade'[2] granted between 1756 and 1763. Hardware, one of the merchants involved, states in his petition to Pitt:

Your petitioner being concerned in the trade to Africa has (as the Custom House Cocketts will appear) loaded on board the ship *King George* at Liverpool gunpowder and arms as part of the cargo of said ship agreeable to His Majesty's Licence of the 5th October 1756 a copy whereof is annexed.

He further adds that 'the above gunpowder and arms are of an inferior kind and have always been a necessary part of the cargoes of ships trading to Africa'.[3] The point made in Hardware's petition, that gunpowder and arms were always 'a *necessary* part of the cargoes of ships trading to Africa', was repeated indirectly and in a stronger form by another merchant, in Liverpool, in 1775. Writing to his business friends, this merchant reported that

Since your first there has been nothing done in the African business here, owing to a prohibition on arms and powder wch is a material part of an African ship's cargo, but within three days past find that licence is granted to those ships upon certain restrictions wch encourages the merchants to begin to fit out again.[4]

The very high demand for guns which prevailed in West Africa in the eighteenth century is reflected in the fact that £1 sterling of guns had a much greater purchasing power in West Africa than £1 sterling of other goods. The trade of the *Fly* on the Windward coast in 1787,[5] may be used as an illustration. The vessel carried textiles, guns, brass kettles, brass pans, and other goods. The average prices of the selected goods in England were, textiles, 22s. 5d. per piece; guns, 7s. 8d. per gun; brass kettles, 4s. 1d. per kettle; and brass pans, 2s. 5d. per pan. The account of the vessel's trade on the coast was drawn up in bars. This account shows that the average prices of these commodities on the coast were: textiles, 4.5 bars per piece; guns, 5.38 bars per gun; brass kettles, 1.74 bars per kettle; and brass pans, 1 bar per pan. Thus, £1 sterling of textiles was worth 4 bars on the coast, £1 sterling of guns 13 bars, £1 sterling of brass kettles 8.5 bars, and £1 sterling of brass 8.3 bars. These relative values varied somewhat from region to region and over time. But the superior purchasing power of guns relative to other goods remained generally true.

The general pressure on gun manufacturers whenever the volume of English trade to West Africa was on the increase is a further proof of the great demand for guns in the trade. This can be shown for the periods 1751–4, 1771–5 and 1790–2, which were periods of expansion in English trade to West Africa. For the first and second periods, the private records of one of the largest firms producing guns for the West African trade, the firm of Farmer and Galton[6] of Birmingham, show clearly the extent of the pressure. In March 1754, Samuel Galton reported to his partner that every gun manufacturer was pressing the workmen for locks.

> Willets sent to Darleston to let the workmen know he'd give 14d. each for musqts. & Perkins, Guest, etc. who supply Adams, Hadly & Jordan seem to beat in his tract that the workmen expect soon to have them at 10d. each filing & 6d. forging.[7]

By the middle of the year, orders were still pouring in, as Galton stated in June:

> We have now on hand orders for a great number of guns to be supply'd in the course of this month & more orders are expected from Liverpool, Lancaster & Bristol . . . this being holiday week 't will hinder us a great deal. We shall be very hard set in getting locks & barrels. . . .[8]

Up to the very last month of the year the firm of Farmer and Galton was still battling with the orders which continued to be heaped upon it. The two partners seem to have disagreed as to the best method of handling them. Mr Farmer insisted on all the orders being supplied, but Samuel Galton thought this was impossible. In a letter of 9 December 1754, Galton declared:

I can readily assure you that the guns for Captn Picket & many more can be got up in less time than they are required in, but as there's already more than 6000 required in the immediate time if we aim at supplying great [parts] of these perhaps may be more likely to disappoint Picket. . . . I think there is very little affinity in the gun trade & Manchester, as the manufacturers in those goods keep severally a stock on hand & can readily supply another whereas at this time each manufacturer in guns hath orders for more than [he] can supply and at this time Hadley [is] endeavouring to get our workmen. . . .[9]

The evidence from the records of Farmer and Galton thus shows that at the beginning of our period the gun manufacturers in Birmingham were under great pressure of demand from merchants in Liverpool and the other ports trading to West Africa.

Again, the private papers of Farmer and Galton show clearly that the expansion of English trade to West Africa in the 1770s created great pressures on the gun manufacturers. Under these pressures the manufacturers in Birmingham were forced into a cut-throat competition for workmen to execute their orders for guns. In the course of this, some of the manufacturers incited the workmen into a violent demonstration against the firm of Farmer and Galton on 27 and 28 November 1772. The legal suit which followed showed that the firm of Farmer and Galton received a large number of orders for 'Sham Danish' guns in 1772. In the course of January alone the orders on the firm's books were 15,900 guns 'and upwards'. One order from Liverpool was for 6410 guns.[10]

For the 1790-2 boom period in English trade to West Africa, the private papers of the Bristol slave-trading firm of James Rogers & Co contain much information on the volume of demand for guns by merchants trading to West Africa. In his search for guns, one of the firm's ship captains wrote in July 1792:

[I] have just treated upon the gentlemen in the gun business and have got Mr Galton and Grice to take up part of the order for the *Jupiter* to be supply'd, in all, Septr. and it was with the greatest difficulty I could prevail upon them to do that as they declared they must disoblige several of their Liverpool friends on so doing.[11]

Galton & Son had earlier written to James Rogers & Co. in June informing them that

On Saturday we shall advise of all that we can possibly send for the ship *Pearl*, the *Friendship*, the *Sarah & Rodney*. We sent to Mr. Whately agreeable to our promise to Capn. Simmons to give him half the order of the *Pearl* but he like us could not effect it. We entreat you not to wait, for our difficulties accumulate upon us & we are every day declining orders. . . . We have offended some of our oldest friends at Liverpool by sparing the last guns to you.[12]

Writing on the same day, another Birmingham gun manufacturer, Joseph Grice, informed James Rogers & Co:

In answer to your favour of the 25th inst. containing an order for sundry guns it would have given me pleasure to have supplied them if it had been in my power. I could by no means undertake an order of that magnitude in double the time specified.[13]

Again, another Birmingham gun manufacturing firm wrote on the same day to Rogers & Co, echoing the same complaints about the pressure of demand for guns:

We are favoured with your Mr Bower's letter of the 25th instant & are sorry to have no alternative but to refer you to ours of the 22nd in which we speak very sincerely of our concern at being unable to execute the *Hornet*'s order. To undertake any part of it would be equally unjustifiable in us, as we are already under more engagements for guns than we expect to be able to supply. Therefore to bind ourselves by another promise to you wou'd be more injurious to you than serviceable otherwise we shou'd immediately have done it with great pleasure.[14]

These letters, among many others, make it very clear that the gun manufacturers were under very great pressures of demand from merchants trading to West Africa during the period of expansion, 1790-2. On the whole, the evidence so far adduced should make it sufficiently clear that demand for guns in the West African trade was very great during our period. It was not for nothing, therefore, that while the bill to abolish the slave trade was being debated in the British parliament, the gun manufacturers in and around Birmingham petitioned the House of Commons that the abolition of the slave trade would be extremely detrimental to them, because 'by such abolition the greatest, and perhaps only, efficient nursery for artificers in the art of manufacturing arms, would be destroyed'.[15]

But, important as firearms and ammunition were in West African trade at this time, we have no estimates of the quantities annually imported over particular periods. The only statement we have which gives some idea of the annual volume of imports was made in 1765 by Lord Shelburne, to the effect that for the preceding twenty or twenty-five years Birmingham had practised 'gunmaking to a prodigious amount for exportation . . . [and] send annually above a hundred and fifty thousand to the coast of Africa, some of which are sold for five and six-pence a-piece. . . .'[16] No one has tried to prove or disprove this statement. Hence, references to the volume of firearms and ammunition annually imported into West Africa in the eighteenth century remain largely conjectural.

It is possible to remedy the situation by piecing together the evidence available in official and merchants' private records. The British customs ledgers of imports and exports,[17] which have been surprisingly neglected by Africanists, contain year by year quantity and value of gunpowder, lead and shot, and gunflints exported from England to the West African coast in the eighteenth century and later. The figures for gunpowder are shown in Table 6. The table shows a complete time series of the quantity of gunpowder imported annually into West Africa from England during the second half of the eighteenth century. For the fifty-eight years from 1750 to 1807, a total of 49,130,368 lbs of gunpowder were imported, giving an annual average of 847,075 lbs. During the same period an annual average of just over 200,000 lbs of lead and shot were imported from England.

However, for reasons which are not at all known, guns exported to West Africa from England are neither regularly nor properly entered in the customs ledgers of the eighteenth century. Some 'iron ordnance' weighing 530 cwt are entered for the 'outports' (Liverpool, Bristol, Lancaster, etc.) in 1750. Similar entries are irregularly made for London between 1753 and 1768. Then from 1775 to 1780, 'iron, being arms by licence' and 'iron ordnance by licence' are separately entered for London only, every year. The entries are in weight and value. In 1775 the quantity of 'iron being arm by licence' was 1184 cwt 2 qr, and 'iron ordnance by licence', 600 cwt. Aggregate figures of firearms exported from England to West Africa are entered only for the seven years, 1797 and 1802 to 1807 (inclusive). For these years, the entries show only the official value and no quantity.

Thus the British customs ledgers of imports and exports are not very helpful in providing information on the quantity of guns exported to West Africa in the eighteenth century. Very fortunately, the account prepared for the British House of Commons in 1806 by William Irving, the Inspector General of Imports and Exports of Great Britain, shows the official and real values of ordnance and small arms exported from England to the coast of Africa for ten years, 1796 to 1805. Private records of English merchants trading to the coast of Africa show the prices of various types of guns (6530 in all) exported to the African coast

Table 6 *Quantity of gunpowder annually exported from England to West Africa, 1750–1807*

Year	Quantity lbs	Year	Quantity lbs
1750	272,402	1779	198,442
1751	361,812	1780	182,750
1752	449,691	1781	323,664
1753	510,176	1782	352,055
1754	200,141	1783	1,035,471
1755	354,199	1784	1,146,150
1756	327,211	1785	1,563,400
1757	269,052	1786	1,412,300
1758	389,344	1787	1,258,400
1759	436,355	1788	1,482,475
1760	470,864	1789	1,288,200
1761	501,525	1790	2,056,350
1762	470,493	1791	1,581,175
1763	700,310	1792	1,760,825
1764	754,478	1793	491,850
1765	186,110	1794	919,300
1766	866,126	1795	435,710
1767	691,743	1796	769,190
1768	867,512	1797	1,114,750
1769	778,995	1798	1,506,432
1770	827,621	1799	1,271,950
1771	1,274,000	1800	904,000
1772	1,487,874	1801	1,210,350
1773	1,124,912	1802	1,559,000
1774	1,202,996	1803	931,900
1775	1,189,906	1804	1,178,526
1776	864,460	1805	898,898
1777	362,831	1806	1,262,800
1778	148,216	1807	692,700

Sources: 1750–80, PRO, Customs 3/50–80; 1781–1807, PRO, Customs 17/7–29.

over the same period. From this the average price of guns exported from England to West Africa during this period has been calculated and is shown in Table 7. This average price has been used with the real values shown in William Irving's account to compute the number of guns annually exported from England to the coast of Africa in the ten-year period, 1796 to 1805. This is shown in Table 8.

This calculation shows that between 1796 and 1805 a total of 1,615,309 guns were imported into West Africa from England, giving an annual average of 161,531. This may be compared with the statement made in 1765 by Lord Shelburne, that Birmingham alone had been

Import of firearms, 1750-1807 133

Table 7 *Prices of guns exported to West Africa, 1796-1807*

Quantity	Price		Amount
	s.	d.	£
480	6	4	152
40	8	6	17
10	9		4.5
1,870	11	6	1,075.25
200	12		120
755	12	6	471.875
350	13		227.5
680	13	6	459
300	14		210
175	14	6	126.875
100	15	6	77.5
500	16		400
320	16	6	264
200	19		190
350	20		350
100	21		105
100	22		110
Total 6,530			4,360

Average price per gun = £0.6677641.

Sources: Midland Bank Records, AE52, Ship *Earl of Liverpool* 1797; Liverpool Record Office, 387 MD 41-4, accounts of ships *Lottery* (1798; 1802), *Enterprize* (1803), and *Fortune* (1805); PRO. C.114/155, Ship *Frederick* (1805; 1806); PRO. C.114/158, Ship *Bedford* (1803; 1804; 1806).

Table 8 *Guns imported into West Africa from England, 1796-1805*

Year	(1) Value £	(2) Quantity
1796	93,588	140,151
1797	58,804	88,061
1798	82,338	123,304
1799	139,622	209,089
1800	128,901	193,034
1801	127,127	190,377
1802	145,661	218,132
1803	85,269	127,693
1804	117,131	175,408
1805	100,205	150,060

Source: *British Parliamentary Papers, Accounts & Papers 1806*, vol. XII no. 443.

Note: The source shows official value and real value separately. The real value is the one declared by the merchant exporters, and so represents price current. The latter value is the one used in this table.

The source contains only value. The quantities in column (2) have been computed by applying the average price calculated in Table 7 to the values in column (1).

sending more than 150,000 guns yearly to the African coast during the preceding twenty or twenty-five years. Taking into account quantities made in other parts of England (in particular Liverpool, Bristol and London) and sent to the African coast, Shelburne's statement could be interpreted to mean that about 200,000 guns were exported annually from England to the coast of Africa from the 1740s to 1765.[18] The apparent discrepancy between Shelburne's estimate and the figures in Table 8 can be explained in terms of the war-time demand for arms by the British government which may have made it difficult for the merchants to get sufficient supply from the manufacturers. It can therefore be said that Shelburne's estimate and the figures in Table 8 are in rough agreement. Thus, something between 200,000 and 150,000 guns were unloaded yearly on the African coast in the second half of the eighteenth century by English merchants.

The available evidence points to the fact that the other European countries who traded to the west coast of Africa expended, at least, as many guns per unit of payment for goods purchased as the English.[19] Therefore, the figures of imports from England can be used to estimate total imports from all parts, based on England's share of the total trade. This share was stated in 1775 by John Roberts[20] as shown in Table 9. While some margin of error should be expected, the share of the total trade held by English merchants suggested by these figures, about 45 per cent, may not be far from the mark, either way. Using this share with the import figures from England gives something between 444,000 and 333,000 as the total number of guns annually imported into the west

Table 9 *Slaves purchased by European nations annually*

Region	English	French	Dutch	Portuguese	Danes	Total
Port Sallee to Cape Mount	12,000	4,000	600	1,000	100	17,700
Cape Mount to Cape Palmas	7,000	2,000	1,500	—	150	10,650
Cape Palmas to Cape Appolonia	3,000	1,500	1,000	—	50	5,550
Cape Appolonia to the River Volta	3,000	1,000	2,500	150	500	7,150
River Volta to the River Lagos	2,000	4,500	1,500	2,000	—	10,000
River Lagos to the River Congo	14,000	20,000	6,000	—	—	40,000
Total	41,000	33,000	13,100	3,150	800	91,050

coast of Africa in the second half of the eighteenth century. If we take away the 50,000 estimated by Phyllis Martin as the annual import into the Loango Coast at this time,[21] we are left with a figure of 283,000 to 394,000 for West Africa proper.[22]

II

The use to which the imported firearms were put seems to be the most controversial issue relating to firearms in Africa. At one time it was suggested that the firearms were 'ostensibly for decorating the habitation of some negro chieftain'.[23] This was refuted in 1790 by Alexander Falconbridge. Asked by a committee of inquiry whether he had 'ever observed in the houses of any of the chiefs or great men, guns in a considerable number, as if kept for the purpose of show or ornament', he replied that 'I have seen a great number in their houses with different kinds of goods, which I always understood were for trade', speaking particularly of Bonny where he had been more on shore than any other place.[24]

More recently, it has been suggested that the most important use to which firearms were put in Africa was the protection of crops, the introduction of Indian corn being related to firearms.[25] Other writers argue that the introduction of firearms into Africa represented an important technical innovation in slave gathering, the imported firearms being used primarily for raids and wars directed to the acquisition of captives for sale.[26]

By examining the preference for guns by West Africans who sold different types of commodities (including slaves) to the Europeans it may be possible to get some insight into the uses to which the firearms were put. It is commonplace knowledge that in the second half of the eighteenth century captives sold as slaves represented by far the largest single item, by volume and value, exchanged for the European commodities imported into West Africa. In absolute terms, therefore, the bulk of the firearms and ammunition imported were exchanged for slaves. But the preference for guns by the people selling different commodities can still be gauged by relating the number of guns exchanged to the unit of value employed.

Some of the extant private records of the merchants give detailed information about commodities purchased on the African coast: the names of the African merchants from whom they were purchased, and the quantities of different goods expended in each purchase are carefully itemized. Appendix I shows an example of the quantity of guns and gunpowder expended in each slave purchase. All the evidence available shows that for every slave purchased some quantities of guns and gunpowder were always included in the assortment of goods employed in payment. This was never so with other commodities. For example, one of the vessels belonging to James Rogers & Co of Bristol bought slaves and foodstuff at Bonny from 1791 to 1792.[27] The slaves numbered 334 and cost 43,103 bars. For these, 198 Spanish guns, 101 blunderbusses and 1,607 Bonny guns (1906 guns in all) were included in the assortment of goods expended. This gives one gun to every 22.6 bars. This same vessel bought in the same place, 20,406 yams for 1,895 bars, 3,400 plantains for 21 bars, two puncheons of palm oil for 100 bars, 5,940 mats for 292 bars, and 400 heads of corn, 460 coconuts, 79 bundles of smoked fish, some pepper, shrimps and a few other things, all amounting to approximately 2789 bars. For all these only two Bonny guns were included in the assortment of goods expended, giving a ratio of one gun to 1394.5 bars. The foodstuffs purchased were for the slaves' use during the voyage to the Americas, so that they were as important to the ship's captain as the slaves themselves. Hence the goods employed in the purchase of the slaves and foodstuffs reflect the commodity preference of slave sellers and the sellers of foodstuffs rather than the unwillingness of the ship's captain to exchange guns for anything but slaves.

Only the ivory sellers' preference for guns comes second to that of slave sellers. Another vessel, the brig, *Sarah*, belonging to James Rogers & Co., of Bristol, traded at Old Calabar and Cameroon from 1789 to 1790.[28] The slaves bought numbered 259 and cost 26,835 copper bars. Included in the assortment of goods employed in payment are 684 guns, which gives a ratio of one gun to 39.2 copper bars of value. The same vessel purchased 128 elephant's teeth weighing 2,329 lbs and costing 2,329 copper bars. The number of guns included in the assortment of goods expended is forty-five, which gives a ratio of one gun to 51.8 copper bars.

The firm preference of the slave sellers for guns indicates very strongly the connection between firearms and the acquisition of slaves. It reinforces the slave–gun circle theory according to which the states and individual or groups of individual slave gatherers bought more firearms to capture more slaves to buy more firearms. . . . For some states the necessity may have been imposed by defence requirements.[29] But for the professional slave gatherers the firearms represented important inputs.

This is not to say, however, that the guns acquired through the sale of slaves were employed solely for the gathering of slaves. The private slave gatherer who purchased firearms for that purpose may have at the same time used his private materials in time of need to fight the wars of the state, the clan, the village, etc. – wars of aggression, retaliation or defence, unconnected or only indirectly connected with slaving. Where slave gathering was a state affair, the slave-gathering state may not only have waged offensive wars calculated for the capture of slaves. Its slave-gathering activities would of necessity provoke attack by its neighbours and so be forced to defend itself. On the other hand, the 'non-slaving' states that acquired large quantities of firearms through the sale of slaves did so in order to be able to defend themselves effectively against the onslaught of slave-gathering states and others. Because slave gathering by its very nature provoked inter-territorial wars in different ways, in addition to inter-territorial conflicts arising from other causes, firearms acquired for slave gathering or for defence against slave gatherers may have been employed in a host of operations not directly connected with slave gathering. And, for that matter, firearms purchased for slave gathering and/or military purposes may also have been put to peaceful uses at the same time by the possessors, particularly for hunting and firing during ceremonial occasions. From the foregoing, it should be clear why we cannot explain the number of guns exchanged for each slave on the coast directly in terms of the economist's input–output analysis – relating directly the number of guns expended in the purchase of a slave by European merchants on the coast to the number of guns needed, on the basis of economic calculations, to capture a slave and take him to the coast.[30]

The desire of ivory sellers to have some guns in exchange is easy to explain, since the elephants had to be hunted in order to obtain ivory. But the commodity preference of foodstuff sellers fails to support the thesis that firearms were used primarily for crop protection. If this were true one should find sellers of yams, corn, plantain, etc., demanding firearms in payment. This is not borne out by the evidence.

III

The quantities of guns and ammunition annually imported into West Africa in the second half of the eighteenth century were not evenly distributed over the whole region. Since slaves were the commodity for which by far the largest number of firearms were exchanged, the proportionate contribution of the different sub-regions to the total number of slaves annually exported, as shown by John Roberts's estimate in Table 9, should provide a fair measure of the regional distribution of the firearms imported. From this piece of evidence, it should be clear that the bulk of the firearms imported went to the region between the 'River Lagos' and the River Congo.

138 *Inikori*

Table 10 *Regional distribution of imported firearms*

Region	Number of voyages	Number of guns	Number of guns per voyage
Senegambia	5	4,320	864
Sierra Leone and Windward Coast	13	12,896	992
Gold Coast	4	3,496	874
Bight of Benin	4	865	216
Bonny	8	10,285	1,286
Calabar and Cameroon	60	25,628	427
Congo–Loango	9	4,080	453
Unspecified	8	6,167	771
Total	111	67,737	5,883

However, the number of slaves exported from different parts of West Africa is not enough to determine the regional distribution of the firearms imported, since some regions received more guns than others for every slave sold. Appendix II shows 111 trading voyages made from England to different parts of West Africa between 1757 and 1806, with the number of guns carried in each voyage. A regional breakdown of the information contained in the appendix is shown in Table 10.[31] It must be pointed out that there is some bias in the information shown in Appendix II from which the regional breakdown has been extracted. Out of the 111 ventures shown, 59 belong to some groups of small Liverpool slave traders, whose link was William Davenport. The survival of the records of William Davenport provides a considerable amount of information about these small-sized ventures. However, the individual ventures of the Davenport groups are generally very much smaller, in terms of the total outward cost and the tonnage of ships employed, than those of the large firms that dominated the trade in the second half of the eighteenth century. It has been shown that from 1783 to 1793, ten large firms employing very large ships, carried about two-thirds of the total number of slaves exported from the West African coast to the West Indies by Liverpool merchants.[32] These were the firms of Baker & Dawson (later John Dawson), William Boates & Co., Parke & Heywood, Francis Ingram & Co., Thomas Leyland & Co., etc. Since the number of guns carried per venture will be affected by the size of the ventures, the inclusion of a large number of atypical small-sized ventures in the appendix distorts the true situation to that effect. On the other hand, because the Davenport groups traded largely to Old Calabar and Cameroon the trade of these places is over-represented in the appendix. So, too, the small-sized nature of the ventures of the

Davenport groups may distort the number of guns carried per venture, shown against these places, much more than is the case for the other places.

While these qualifications are necessary, the regional breakdown shown above can still be used to demonstrate the proportionate number of guns expended on the slaves and goods purchased in the different parts of the West African coast in the second half of the eighteenth century. It can be seen that ventures to Bonny carried more guns proportionately than those to other places. Sierra Leone and the Windward Coast come next to Bonny in this respect. The pattern shown here may be compared with some other pieces of evidence.

The information contained in Appendix I shows that 1942 guns were expended on the 379 slaves bought at Bonny for the ship, *Jupiter*, between 1792 and 1793. This gives 5.1 guns per slave. Another vessel[33] which bought 334 slaves (164 male and 170 female) at Bonny from 1791 to 1792, expended 1906 guns as part of the assortment of goods employed in payment. This amounts to 5.7 guns per slave. As a general indication of the ratio of guns to slaves sold at Bonny at this time, the views of the ship captains are important. In preparation for a trading voyage to Bonny in 1792, Captain John Simmons submitted to James Rogers & Co. of Bristol an abstract of a cargo for 550 slaves at Bonny.[34] Included in the abstract are 500 French guns and 2900 Bonny guns, making a total of 3400 guns. This gives 6.2 guns per slave. Thus, it can be said that on average over five guns were expended on every slave bought at Bonny by English traders in the second half of the eighteenth century.

For the Windward Coast, 53 slaves were bought for the *Fly*[35] in 1787, for which 245 guns were expended. This gives 4.6 guns per slave. For the Gold Coast, the captain of the ship, *Frederick*,[36] expended 853 guns for the purchase of 343 slaves in 1806, giving 2.5 guns per slave. Finally, the captain of the *Sarah*[37] bought at Old Calabar and Cameroon 259 slaves (162 male and 97 female), from 1789 to 1790, for which he expended 684 guns. This gives 2.6 guns per slave.

From the foregoing it can be seen that the two sets of evidence are largely in agreement. Far more guns per slave were expended at Bonny and the area around Sierra Leone and the Windward Coast than in other places where the number of guns exchanged per slave purchased was just under three. Phyllis Martin's evidence, further on in this book, also shows that about three guns per slave were expended by the Europeans on the slaves purchased on the Loango coast in the second half of the eighteenth century.[38] The evidence thus makes it clear that the Bonny trading area not only dominated the export of slaves in West Africa in the late eighteenth century, but also received more firearms for every slave sold than other places. This means that a very large proportion of the firearms imported into West Africa in the second half of the eighteenth century went to the Bonny trading area.

IV

The firearms imported into West Africa during the period of this study were of various types. The types preferred varied from one part of the coast to another. Table 11 shows an analysis of the information relating to 64,828 firearms[39] imported into West Africa from 1757 to 1806. The table shows the price range for the different types, the quantities of each type imported into different parts of the coast, and the total quantities of each type imported into all parts. The information in the table is a fair indication of the types of firearms preferred in the different parts of the coast during the second half of the eighteenth century. But, in connection with the proportionate share of the different types in the total numbers of firearms annually imported into West Africa during this period, we cannot draw any direct inference from the table. This is because, as mentioned earlier, the trade of Old Calabar and Cameroon is over-represented in Appendix II upon which the table is based. Consequently, the preference of Old Calabar and Cameroon has an undue influence on the proportionate share of the different types as indicated in the table. The proportionate share of the different types can be inferred only indirectly from what we have already said about the regional distribution of the firearms imported into West Africa during our period.

For Senegambia, Sierra Leone, and the Windward Coast Table 11 shows that Danish guns[40] were the most popular. For the Gold Coast and the Bight of Benin the quantities are rather small, which may be due to the bias in the evidence. It is therefore doubtful whether the pattern shown sufficiently reflects the preferences of these places. However, for what it is worth, the square musket seems to be the most popular in the Gold Coast, and Danish guns in the Bight of Benin. There is not a single Danish gun among the 10,815 firearms indicating Bonny preference. The most popular here is a very cheap type called Bonny musket, sold in England for between six and seven shillings, very often for six shillings and eight pence. Spanish pattern and French pattern guns were next to Bonny muskets in popularity, at Bonny. In Calabar and Cameroon by far the most popular type was the Tower gun.[41] Round muskets, musketoons, ship-store pattern guns and Danish guns come next, in that order. For the Congo–Loango region a type described as Angola musket was the most popular.

Import of firearms, 1750–1807 141

Considering the conclusion we reached earlier, that a very large proportion of the firearms imported into West Africa during our period went to the Bonny trading area, it will follow that Bonny muskets were imported in greater quantities than any other type during this period. Apparently because of their cheapness the workers were not paid much apiece for finishing Bonny guns. This seems to have imposed some limit on the quantities produced in the last decade of the eighteenth century, as can be inferred from a letter of Samuel Galton to James Rogers & Co. in 1792:

We have repeatedly written you that the difficulty we find with the workmen in regard to finishing Bonny musquets is insurmountable for that they will not finish them unless with a double quantity of walnut guns which seems to be generally the proportion of the orders from Liverpool & we have sent many of the Bonny musqts. made for them, which disqualifies us from sending the quantity you require but by the next and the following springs we will send all we possibly can.[42]

The analysis of the types of firearms imported provides some basis for a comment on the issue of the quality of those firearms. On this issue contemporary observers seem to have spoken with one voice. In his statement of 1765 referred to earlier, Lord Shelburne added that 'what is shocking to humanity, above half of them [the firearms] from the manner they are finished in are sure to burst in the first hand that fires them'.[43] Another contemporary observer wrote in 1829:

We have shewn the imperfect manner in which the barrels for fowling-pieces were proved. But it will hardly be believed in the present day, had we not sufficient knowledge that is the fact, that firearms, if we may so call them, were made, the barrels of which neither underwent, nor were intended to undergo, any proof whatever; that immense numbers of guns were made, with the knowledge and certainty, that if they were ever fired out of, they were certain to burst in the discharge. These guns were made for one market – that of the coast of Africa. These guns – the common term by which they were designated, *slave guns*, will shew the purpose of trade to which they were applied – were called sham musquets, Dutch guns, etc. and were made the article of barter for human flesh.[44]

It will be argued later that the contemporary observers greatly exaggerated the poor quality of the firearms imported into West Africa from England in the eighteenth century. But some credence is given to their observations by a complaint made in 1750 by the Incorporated Company of Gunmakers in London to the Committee of the Company of Merchants Trading to Africa.[45] In this document, it is stated that the London gunmakers under the incorporated company had always been

Table 11 An analysis of 64,828 guns imported into West Africa from 1757 to 1806, showing the distribution among different types and regions in West Africa into which imported

Types of guns	Price range British Shillings	Senegambia	Sierra Leone Windward Coast	Gold Coast	Bight of Benin	Bonny	Calabar Cameroon	Congo- Loango	Unspecified regions	Total
Tower guns	8–16	320	1,165	120	110	—	9,880	950	891	13,466
Round muskets	6–7	500	1,965	434	200	—	5,482	—	770	9,351
Danish guns	8–20	735	3,603	476	265	—	1,182	—	1,001	7,262
Bonny muskets	6–7	—	100	—	—	5,430	—	—	270	5,800
Musketoons	8–15	—	124	—	14	630	2,930	—	234	3,932
French pattern guns	9–13	470	898	—	50	1,350	223	150	283	3,424
Spanish pattern guns	8–14	25	300	—	—	2,945	—	10	—	3,280
Trading guns	6–8	420	1,437	—	—	—	498	—	330	2,685
Angola muskets	7–8	—	50	—	—	—	—	2,455	—	2,505
Ship-store pattern guns	6–8	—	50	40	—	10	1,495	—	500	2,095
Square muskets	6–7	—	900	605	—	—	45	—	200	1,750
Buccaneers	9–22	266	1,005	150	—	—	—	—	200	1,621
Riononas	7–10	60	1,030	—	—	—	—	—	87	1,177

Import of firearms, 1750–1807 143

Type	Range									Total
Fuzee guns	10–25	550	—	300	—	—	—	—	164	1,014
Soldiers muskets	12–16	300	—	—	—	400	—	300	—	1,000
Pistols	10–84	122	221	—	160	—	309	—	20	832
Calabar guns	9	—	—	—	—	—	800	—	—	800
Birding guns	9–20	85	176	290	—	—	—	30	—	581
Flat muskets	7–8	—	520	—	—	—	—	—	—	520
Militia guns	13–14	15	82	250	—	—	12	—	—	359
Dutch guns	13–14	—	—	—	—	—	—	—	330	330
Fowling pieces	14–20	130	65	—	—	—	—	—	125	320
London muskets	7–8	—	180	20	—	—	40	—	—	240
Blunderbuss	8–24	—	—	—	6	—	40	32	70	158
Cornigian guns	14	100	—	—	—	50	—	—	—	100
Senegals	13	30	40	—	—	—	—	—	—	70
Carbines	—	—	—	—	—	—	50	—	—	50
Bundie guns	13	—	33	—	—	—	—	—	—	33
Gambia guns	12–13	10	20	—	—	—	—	—	—	30
Double barrel guns	55–84	2	6	—	—	—	4	—	—	12
Marman guns	22	—	25	—	—	—	—	—	—	25
Swivel muskets	32	—	—	—	—	—	4	—	—	4
Cannon	42	—	—	—	—	—	—	—	2	2
Total		4,140	14,295	2,385	805	10,815	22,986	3,895	5,477	64,828

Note: See Appendix II for sources.

obliged to prove all Firearms made and vended by us for Home and Foreign Trade under severe penalties, by which means the Trade and credit of that manufacture have been considerably advanced and confirmed in Foreign Parts and especially on the coast of Africa in favour of London made guns preferable to those of any other nation, principally on account of the Proof, which was the chief reason on which the grant of the charter was founded, the lives of those who use them immediately depending thereon. But of late years persons not members, nor subject to the obligations of the corporation, have made and vended great quantities of unproved guns, to the great discredit of that valuable branch of the British manufacture, which, if continued must end in the total loss thereof to this nation.

While the complaint by the Incorporated Company of London Gunmakers may have been prompted by the adverse effects of competition from other gunmakers, especially those in Birmingham, there is certainly some element of truth in their complaint. It therefore seems that the quality of firearms exported from England to the African coast deteriorated somewhat in the second half of the eighteenth century. But, for more information, we must turn to the letters of the Birmingham gunmakers which throw some light on the issue, in relation both to the resistance of the African buyers to take poor quality guns and to the competition among the producers, which ought to have ensured some level of good quality.

In February 1788, John Whately, one of the largest gunmakers in Birmingham, wrote to a Bristol slave-trading firm:

What you write regarding Mr Parr of Liverpool has, we must own, some foundation, who has lately had some degree of preference in the Old Calabar trade owing to a timely purchase of a qty. of soldiers barrels etc. in Ireland & which a short time back he made up into Plain Tower Guns the sort taken to that part of the coast. But with respect to Birmingham we cannot accuse ourselves of wanting ingenuousness in saying that we are not reckoned inferior to anybody & are not perhaps exceeded in quantity in that line. . . . I conclude with assuring you that the guns we have the pleasure of supplying you at all times (but now we speak more particularly of the present instance) shall be undeniable in their quality such as are deemed proper for the trade & we flatter ourselves in no respect inferior to the workmanship of any other manufacturer in the business.[46]

The impression one gets from this letter is that the African buyers had ample opportunity to choose from among guns of varying quality and were capable of differentiating between good and poor quality guns. On the other hand, the phrase, 'such as are deemed proper for the trade', is worthy of note. It suggests that there was a quality standard generally accepted as good enough for the African market. It is not clear what determined that standard, the profit motives of the European merchants or the uses to which the African buyers put the guns. From the competitive situation on the African coast at this time, it can be inferred that both factors were important in determining the quality standard 'deemed proper for the trade'.

The letter of Samuel Galton & Son of Birmingham to Rogers & Co. of Bristol, in August 1789, gives some additional information. Commenting on the price specified by Rogers and Co. for an order for guns, the former wrote:

> We observe in your favour of the 6th you mention 9/- for the long guns which we overlooked, but to prevent misconception we beg leave to inform you that we cannot make them with *real Tower barrels* & the *better furniture* for less than 9/6. . . . The barrels are *all real proof* & will establish a reputation on the coast, & the locks of a superior kind. If you will take common unproved barrels & an inferior lock we will supply such at 9/- but ultimately they wd. not tend to your advantage or our credit. Presuming you would prefer those at 9/6 which is the price we mentioned we are proceeding with them.[47]

Much of what is said in this letter may reflect the efforts of an entrepreneur trying to convince his customer to accept a somewhat higher price. Nevertheless, the quality indicated at the price level of between nine shillings and nine shillings and six pence, is instructive. Taken as a quality gauge, this would mean that the quality of materials employed in making those guns sold in England for less than eight shillings must have been very low. On the other hand, guns of nine shillings and above should be of some fairly high quality. If we apply this measure to the information presented in Table 11 above, it can be seen that round muskets, Bonny muskets, trading guns, Angola muskets, ship-store pattern guns, square muskets, flat muskets and London muskets belong to the low-quality group. These together amount to 24,946, being 38.5 per cent of the total number of guns in the table. This low percentage, however, is due to the over-representation of Old Calabar imports which were more of the fairly high quality type. What is worthy of note is that Bonny muskets which were imported in very large quantities into the Bonny trading area belong to the low-quality group. This may have pushed the balance of guns imported into West Africa in the second half of the eighteenth century to the low-quality group.

On the whole, Senegambia, Sierra Leone, the Windward Coast, the Bight of Benin, Old Calabar and Cameroon tended to import rather more of the fairly high-quality types of firearms – Danish guns and Tower muskets. But Bonny and the Congo–Loango region imported more of the low-quality types.

V

The evidence presented above should enable us to draw some general conclusions on the issue of firearms in West Africa in the second half of the eighteenth century. On the question of quantities, although it has not been possible to present a complete time series of guns imported into West Africa from all parts during this period, the evidence assembled makes it sufficiently clear that large quantities were annually imported. Taking out imports into the Congo–Loango area, the numbers yearly imported from Europe into West Africa proper, may be put at something between 283,000 and 394,000. These imports were due very largely to the strong preference for firearms by slave sellers and gatherers. The preference of ivory sellers for guns came a distant second to that of slave sellers. Sellers of other commodities, particularly foodstuffs, do not seem to have had any strong demand for firearms. The implication of all this is that the firearms imported into West Africa in the second half of the eighteenth century were used mainly for slave gathering and the wars largely stimulated by the latter. This is why the most important slave-exporting areas of the time, in particular, the Bonny trading area, were also the largest firearms importers in West Africa during this period. Not only did the Bonny trading area import more guns absolutely than other parts of West Africa, but also, it imported far more guns for every slave exported. Whereas the observations of contemporaries on the low quality of the firearms imported into West Africa are generally supported by the evidence, they contain a great deal of exaggeration. A large proportion of the firearms were very much better than the contemporary observers would want us to believe. What is important, however, is that the firearms seem largely to have served the purpose for which the African buyers purchased them. If this were not the case, firearms which were more efficient in meeting slave sellers' needs would have been brought to the coast in the face of the keen competition for slaves by the European merchants in the second half of the eighteenth century. It is remarkable, indeed, that the most important slave-exporting area of this period, Bonny, tended to import more of the cheaper and low-quality types of guns. Finally, it seems likely that the use to which firearms imported were put in West Africa changed over time. It is most likely that hunting became the most important employment of firearms after 1900.

Summary

A series of articles on firearms in Africa published in the *Journal of*

African History in 1971 raised a number of questions which have not been given adequate attention since those articles appeared. In the present paper an attempt is therefore made to shed some light on some of these questions in relation to West Africa in the second half of the eighteenth century. On the basis of import figures from England total imports during this period were estimated to be between 283,000 and 394,000 guns per annum, excluding imports into the Congo-Loango area which Phyllis Martin estimated to be about 50,000 yearly at this time. These guns went largely to the major slave exporting regions of West Africa, especially the Bonny trading area. The sellers of slaves showed a very strong preference for firearms, which is an indication of a strong connection between guns and the acquisition of slaves. This reinforces the gun-slave circle thesis. The evidence fails to support the idea that firearms were used primarily for crop protection in West Africa in the eighteenth century. If this were so it should have been reflected in the European goods demanded by sellers of agricultural commodities. It is likely, however, that the use to which firearms were put in West Africa changed after 1900. While the quality of firearms imported into West Africa during the period of this study was generally low, it would seem that those firearms largely served the purposes for which the African buyers purchased them.

Appendix I *Quantity of firearms in the assortment of goods expended in the purchase of ship* Jupiter's *cargo of slaves at Bonny, 1792/3*

Slave purchases					Firearms expended	
Men	Women	Boys	Girls	Total	No. guns	Kegs powder
1	—	—	—	1	4	26
1	—	1	—	2	8	52
1	—	—	—	1	4	26
—	—	3	—	3	12	78
2	2	—	1	5	20	124
1	—	—	1	2	9	50
1	1	—	1	3	12	74
5	1	—	—	6	29	154
2	—	1	1	4	16	102
1	1	2	1	5	22	126
—	—	1	—	1	4	24
—	1	—	1	2	8	48
3	2	—	—	5	20	130
1	3	—	1	5	23	122
—	—	1	—	1	4	26

Appendix I *(continued)*

Slave purchases					Firearms expended	
Men	Women	Boys	Girls	Total	No. guns	Kegs powder
3	7	4	1	15	64	296
—	1	—	—	1	4	24
2	7	—	—	9	38	220
3	2	—	—	5	23	125
1	—	—	2	3	13	74
—	1	—	—	1	4	26
—	1	—	—	1	4	24
1	—	—	—	1	5	26
—	—	1	—	1	5	26
—	2	1	1	4	21	122
—	2	—	—	2	8	52
—	—	1	—	1	4	24
1	—	—	—	1	5	26
1	—	—	—	1	5	26
1	—	—	—	1	5	26
1	—	—	—	1	5	28
2	—	—	—	2	10	56
—	—	—	1	1	4	28
—	1	—	—	1	4	28
1	—	—	—	1	5	28
1	—	—	—	1	5	28
1	—	—	—	1	5	28
—	1	—	—	1	4	28
—	1	—	—	1	4	28
—	1	—	—	1	4	28
1	1	—	—	2	9	58
1	—	—	—	1	5	28
1	—	—	—	1	5	28
1	—	—	1	2	9	44
—	1	—	—	1	4	28
—	—	—	1	1	4	18
1	—	—	—	1	5	28
—	—	—	4	4	12	84
1	—	—	1	2	9	56
1	—	—	—	1	5	28
—	—	2	—	2	8	56
—	—	—	2	2	8	56
1	1	—	—	2	9	56
—	—	—	1	1	4	30
1	—	—	—	1	5	28
1	—	—	—	1	5	28
1	—	—	—	1	5	28
—	1	—	—	1	4	28
1	—	—	—	1	5	28
4	—	—	—	4	24	120
—	5	—	—	5	25	150

Import of firearms, 1750–1807 149

Appendix I *(continued)*

| | Slave purchases | | | | Firearms expended | |
Men	Women	Boys	Girls	Total	No. guns	Kegs powder
—	2	—	—	2	10	60
—	—	—	3	3	15	60
5	—	5	—	10	60	300
—	0	—	7	17	85	510
2	—	—	—	2	10	56
2	1	—	—	3	17	90
4	—	—	—	4	24	120
—	2	1	2	5	25	150
1	3	—	3	7	31	180
4	2	1	3	10	52	300
8	—	—	—	8	48	240
—	2	—	—	2	10	60
7	—	8	—	15	90	450
—	1	—	9	20	120	600
2	—	—	—	2	12	60
—	1	—	2	3	15	90
2	—	—	2	4	22	120
—	1	—	—	1	5	30
—	1	—	—	1	5	30
7	—	—	—	7	42	210
—	2	—	4	6	30	180
6	—	—	—	6	36	180
—	3	—	2	5	25	150
5	1	—	2	8	45	240
5	4	1	—	10	56	300
3	2	3	3	11	61	330
—	1	—	—	1	5	30
3	—	1	2	6	34	180
1	—	1	6	8	42	240
2	2	1	—	5	28	150
—	1	1	—	2	11	60
—	—	1	—	1	6	30
—	1	—	1	2	10	54
1	—	1	—	2	12	60
—	—	—	1	1	3	30
1	—	—	—	1	6	27
1	—	—	1	2	11	60
—	1	—	—	1	5	27
—	—	—	1	1	5	30
1	—	—	—	1	6	30
1	—	—	—	1	6	27
3	—	—	—	3	18	81
1	—	—	—	1	6	27
—	1	—	—	1	5	27
1	—	—	—	1	6	27
—	2	—	—	2	10	54

Appendix I *(continued)*

	Slave purchases				Firearms expended	
Men	Women	Boys	Girls	Total	No. guns	Kegs powder
3	—	2	—	5	30	100
—	2	—	—	2	12	40
1	—	2	—	3	18	81
1	—	—	—	1	6	27
—	—	1	—	1	6	27
—	1	1	—	2	11	54
—	—	1	—	1	6	27
1	1	—	—	2	11	54
—	2	—	—	2	10	54
1	—	—	—	1	6	27
1	—	—	—	1	6	27
1	—	—	—	1	6	27
1	—	—	—	1	6	27
Total						
143	110	50	76	379	1942	10,514

Source and note: PRO. C.107/59, Ship *Jupiter*'s Old Wages Book. This ship was owned by James Rogers & Co of Bristol. The names of the African traders at Bonny from whom the slaves were purchased are stated. The guns and gunpowder extracted form only a part of a long list of goods expended in each purchase. The quantity of the other goods is carefully itemized in each purchase. The total number of slaves purchased was 389, including three 'dash slaves'. But complete information is available only for the purchase of 379. The voyage lasted from 19 October 1792, to 19 July 1793.

Appendix II *An analysis of 111 trading voyages made from England to West Africa between 1757 and 1806, showing names of the vessels, year of voyage, destination in West Africa and the quantity of guns carried*

Source reference	Name of vessel	Year of voyage	Destination in West Africa	Quantity of guns carried
C.109/401	*Saville*	1771	Senegambia	1608
Davenport	*William*	1764	Gambia	272
L. Museum	*Aston*	1771	Gambia	650
L. Museum	*Aston*	—	Gambia	830
C.107/5	*Mermaid*	1792	Gambia	960
Davenport	*Plumper*	1762	Windward Coast	1780
C.109/401	*Barbadoes Packet*	1771	Windward Coast	1300
C.107/1	*Fly*	1787	Windward Coast	305
L. Museum	*Eadith*	1760	Windward Coast	920
L. Museum	*Eadith*	1761	Windward Coast	1061
C.109/401	*Meredith*	1771	Sierra Leone	1511
C.109/401	*Juno*	1771	Sierra Leone	371

Import of firearms, 1750–1807   151

Appendix II *(continued)*

Source reference	Name of vessel	Year of voyage	Destination in West Africa	Quantity of guns carried
C.109/401	Cavendish	1771	Isles De Loss	856
C.107/3	Fanny	1792	Banana Islands	1084
C.107/13	Fame	1790	Bence Island	1120
C.107/14	Ruby	1788	Bence Island	1218
C.107/14	Ruby	1790	Bence Island	990
C.107/59	Morning Star	1793	Bence Island	380
380TUO.4/3	Sally	1768	Gold Coast	1876
380TUO.4/4	Corsican Hero	1771	Gold Coast	400
C.114/157	Frederick	1806	Gold Coast	570
C.114/158	Bedford	1806	Gold Coast	650
Davenport	Little Brittain	1764	Ardrah	90
Davenport	Plumper	1768	Benin	130
380TUO.4/9	Blayds	1782	Lagos	220
380TUO.4/10	Ingram	1783	Porto Novo	425
Davenport	Plumper	1771	Bonny	1080
AE 52	Earl of Liverpool	1797	Bonny	880
387MD.41	Lottery	1798	Bonny	1000
387MD.42	Lottery	1802	Bonny	550
387MD.43	Enterprize	1803	Bonny	800
C.107/6	Rodney	1791	Bonny	2475
C.107/6	Sarah	1791	Bonny	1300
C.107/13	Trelawney	1791	Bonny	2200
Davenport	Tyrrell	1761	Old Calabar	350
Davenport	Dalrymple	1768	Old Calabar	793
Davenport	Neptune	1768	Old Calabar	56
Davenport	Dalrymple	1770	Old Calabar	600
Davenport	Swift	1770	Old Calabar	111
Davenport	Dalrymple	1771	Old Calabar	760
Davenport	Swift	1771	Old Calabar	200
Davenport	Swift	1772	Old Calabar	231
Davenport	Dalrymple	1772	Old Calabar	650
Davenport	Dreadnaught	1772	Old Calabar	325
Davenport	Dalrymple	1773	Old Calabar	650
Davenport	Swift	1773	Old Calabar	200
Davenport	Dalrymple	1775	Old Calabar	900
Davenport	Swift	1775	Old Calabar	100
Davenport	Dalrymple	1777	Old Calabar	800
Davenport	Swift	1777	Old Calabar	400
Davenport	Lord Cassilis	1771	Old Calabar	672
Davenport	May	1771	Old Calabar	200
Davenport	May	1772	Old Calabar	560
Davenport	Lord Cassilis	1774	Old Calabar	625
Davenport	Dreadnaught	1774	Old Calabar	752
Davenport	Dreadnaught	1776	Old Calabar	550
Davenport	Quixote	1783	Old Calabar	823

Appendix II *(continued)*

Source reference	Name of vessel	Year of voyage	Destination in West Africa	Quantity of guns carried
Davenport	*Quixote*	1784	Old Calabar	800
Davenport	*King of Prussia*	1772	Old Calabar	120
Davenport	*Hector*	1769	Old Calabar	505
Davenport	*Hector*	1771	Old Calabar	700
Davenport	*Andromache*	1771	Old Calabar	120
Davenport	*Hector*	1773	Old Calabar	670
Davenport	*Andromache*	1773	Old Calabar	250
Davenport	*Hector*	1776	Old Calabar	800
Davenport	*Swift*	1776	Old Calabar	300
Davenport	*Dobson*	1769	Old Calabar	770
Davenport	*Dobson*	1770	Old Calabar	800
C.107/13	*African Queen*	1791	Old Calabar	800
C.107/12	*Pearl*	1787	Old Calabar	625
C.107/12	*Pearl*	1790	Old Calabar	870
L. Museum	*Chesterfield*	1757	Old Calabar	580
L. Museum	*Chesterfield*	1759	Old Calabar	446
Davenport	*May*	1774	Old Calabar	322
B. Museum	*Snow Africa*	1774	New Calabar	1230
C.107/5	*Fame*	1792	Old Calabar	400
Davenport	*Hawke*	1779	Cameroon	200
Davenport	*Hawke*	1780	Cameroon	320
Davenport	*Hawke*	1781	Cameroon	460
Davenport	*Preston*	1780	Cameroon	140
Davenport	*Preston*	1781	Cameroon	150
Davenport	*Preston*	1783	Cameroon	500
Davenport	*Badger*	1772	Cameroon	125
Davenport	*Badger*	1774	Cameroon	142
Davenport	*Badger*	1775	Cameroon	228
Davenport	*Badger*	1776	Cameroon	350
Davenport	*Henry*	1765	Cameroon	86
Davenport	*William*	1766	Cameroon	50
Davenport	*William*	1768	Cameroon	50
Davenport	*William*	1769	Cameroon	52
Davenport	*Henry*	1769	Cameroon	80
Davenport	*King of Prussia*	1767	Cameroon	40
Davenport	*King of Prussia*	1771	Cameroon	160
L. Museum	*Calveley*	1758	Cameroon	79
380TUO.4/2	*Ranger*	1767	Cabenda	440
380TUO.4/7	*Nancy*	1774	Angola	300
AE 52	*Kitty*	1789	Angola	410
387MD.44	*Fortune*	1805	River Congo	650
Lloyd's	*Hector*	1770	Angola	500
Lloyd's	*Hector*	1771	Angola	500
Lloyd's	*Hector*	1773	Angola	530

Source reference	Name of vessel	Year of voyage	Destination in West Africa	Quantity of guns carried
C.114/158	*Bedford*	1803	River Congo	450
C.114/158	*Bedford*	1804	Angola	300
380TUO.4/4	*Tom*	1771	Unspecified	1620
C.107/5	*Crescent*	1792	Unspecified	1793
C.107/5	*Sarah*	1792	Unspecified	460
Davenport	*Henry*	1767	Unspecified	160
Davenport	*King of Prussia*	1769	Unspecified	130
C.107/13	*Morning Star*	1792	Unspecified	380
C.114/155	*Frederick*	1805	Unspecified	680
C.107/5	*Pearl*	1792	Unspecified	944

Note: The location of the sources referred to above are as follows:
Davenport   Papers of William Davenport of Liverpool in the Raymond Richards Collection, University of Keele Library. I am grateful to the archivist, Mr Ian H. C. Fraser, who was very helpful during my inspection of these records from 26 October to 5 November 1970.
C.   Chancery Masters' Exhibits, PRO, London
L. Museum   Liverpool City Museum
B. Museum   Bristol City Museum
AE   Midland Bank Records, London
Lloyd's   Lloyd's Corporation Archives, London
380TUO   Liverpool Record Office
387MD   Liverpool Record Office

5 Slavery and the slave trade in the context of West African history
J. D. Fage

Editor's comments

As in Chapters 1 and 2, the present chapter examines the relationship between the export slave trade and slavery in Africa. The author holds that slavery was part and parcel of economic and political development in West Africa, to which the Atlantic slave trade was merely incidental. The author further argues that the numbers of people exported could not have caused any serious damage to the populations and economies of West African societies. These arguments have been developed in further detail in a book, *A History of Africa*, published in 1978. It would appear that the author deliberately developed these arguments in order to provoke a debate on the subject.

There have been at least three widely held and influential views about slavery and the slave trade in West Africa, and also about their relation to its society in respect both of their origins and of their effects on it.

The first is that the institution of slavery was natural and endemic in West African society, so that the coming of foreign traders with a demand for labour, whether from Muslim North Africa or from the countries of maritime Europe, led swiftly and automatically to the development by West Africans of an organized trade in slaves for export.

The second is a contrary view, that it was rather these external demands for labour which led to a great growth of both slavery and slave trading in West Africa, and so corrupted its indigenous society.

The third view, which may or may not be associated with the second, is that the external demand for West African labour, especially in the period *c.* 1650 to *c.* 1850, was so great that the export of slaves to meet it had a disastrous effect on the peoples of West Africa, disrupting not

This paper was first published in the *Journal of African History*, vol. X (1969), pp. 393–404. It has been reprinted here by permission of the author and the publishers.

only their natural demographic development but their social and moral development as well.

In this paper it is proposed to examine and reassess these views in the light of recent research and thinking, and, as a result, to offer an interpretation of the roles of slavery and the slave trade in the history of West Africa which may be more in accord with its economic and social realities.

The first view, namely that the export slave trade was possible because both slavery and trading in slaves were already deeply rooted in West African society, was of course a view propagated by the European slave traders, especially perhaps when the morality of their business was being questioned. Norris's and Dalzel's books on Dahomey towards the close of the eighteenth century are developed examples of this attitude;[1] Dalzel, for example, quite seriously argues that greater good was done by exporting slaves to American plantations than by leaving them in West Africa, where they were likely to become victims of the practice of human sacrifice. But the slave traders' view in effect persisted into the abolitionist atmosphere of the nineteenth century and was, in fact, put forward as a principal moral justification for European colonization. To stamp out the evils of slavery and slave trading in West Africa, occupation of its territories was thought essential; indeed, it was specifically imposed as a duty on the European powers following the Brussels Act of 1890. The view that West Africans left to themselves were inherently prone to own and trade in slaves became in fact one of the received myths of the conquering colonizers.

Analysis and criticism of this view are complicated by the problem of deciding what institution or institutions in West African societies corresponded to the European idea of slavery. Many people will be familiar with Rattray's analysis of slavery in Ashanti society, in which he defined at least five separate terms to describe the various conditions or degrees of voluntary or involuntary servitude in Ashanti.[2] Only two of these, *odonko*, a foreigner who had been purchased with the express purpose of making him or her a slave, and *domum*, a man or woman received in tribute from a subjugated foreign state, might seem to correspond more or less to what an eighteenth-century European or white American might understand by 'slave'. But Rattray then goes on to consider the rights of such slaves in Ashanti society, and these were far in advance of the rights of any slaves in any colony in the Americas. He concludes that the rights of an Ashanti slave were not so very different from 'the ordinary privileges of any Ashanti free man, with whom, in these respects, his position did not seem to compare so unfavourably'. He also states that 'a condition of voluntary servitude was, in a very literal sense, the heritage of every Ashanti', and that to be masterless in that society was an open invitation to involuntary servitude. Similarly, Dalzel reports of the neighbouring, somewhat more authoritarian society of eighteenth-century Dahomey, which he knew at first hand, that its inhabitants were '*all* slaves to the king'.[3]

But it is not necessary here to enter into the arguments as to whether various forms of unfreedom in various West African societies should be called by the name of 'slave', or by such other terms as 'subject', 'servant', 'serf' or 'pawn'. It would seem possible to produce a straightforward definition of slavery that is perfectly adequate for the purposes of this present inquiry: namely that a slave was a man or woman who was owned by some other person, whose labour was regarded as having economic value, and whose person had a commercial value.

It is obvious enough that slaves as so defined existed in many West African societies during the heyday of the Atlantic slave trade from the seventeenth to the nineteenth century, though possibly not in stateless societies or in societies that were little or not touched by the major routes of trade. The question is, then, whether such slavery existed in West African societies before the impingement on them of external trade.

It is impossible to answer this question with respect to those parts of West Africa in the Sudan to which external trade came across the Sahara. The only considerable body of evidence which is really relevant is the accounts of the Arabic writers who were the first to describe the West African Sudan either from their personal knowledge or on the basis of others' first-hand experience, together with early local written histories such as the Timbuktu *Tarikhs* or the Kano Chronicle. This evidence has been reviewed by Mauny.[4] It may be said that both its quantity and its quality are disappointing. The Arab authors take the existence of both slavery and trading in slaves very much for granted, and neither seems to them to call for very much comment. It is thus apparent that both institutions were well established in the major states and empires of the West African Sudan from the eleventh to the sixteenth century. We cannot tell whether these institutions were indigenous, or whether they have evolved following the growth of trans-Saharan trade, because, of course, Arab traders had preceded Arabic scholarship across the Sahara by about four centuries. Furthermore, traffic of some kind across the Sahara between North and West Africa had been in existence for something like a thousand years at least before the Arab conquests began in the seventh century AD. It has been shown, in fact, that a trans-Saharan trade in Negro slaves must have existed, though perhaps in little volume, as early as about the second century AD.[5] However, we have no means of knowing what relation this may

Slavery in the context of history 157

have had to slavery and the slave trade within West Africa itself.

In default of evidence of the relation between the existence of an external demand for slaves and of slavery and an internal trade in slaves for the West African Sudan, we must turn to the Guinea area, where commonly the first truly external traders were the European sea-traders, who first arrived on the coasts in the fifteenth century. The evidence for Upper Guinea, from the Gambia to modern Liberia, has already been analysed here by Dr Walter Rodney.[6]

The ethnographic picture that can be built up for this part of the coastlands from sixteenth- and seventeenth-century European, especially Portuguese, accounts would seem to be good and detailed, but the references to slaves are few and far between. They indicate little more, Rodney says, than that the kings and chiefs of the area had a small number of 'political clients' in their households. There is no evidence for the existence of 'chattel slaves, agricultural serfs, or even household servants' in any numbers, or in any condition to differentiate them from ordinary citizens. He concludes, therefore, that there was no sizeable class of men, and no indigenous trade in men, which could serve as a launching-pad for the Atlantic slave trade. In this part of West Africa at least, a class society involving slaves and trade in them was a consequence of the European demand for slaves for the Americas, and not an indigenous feature upon which an export trade could be built up.

Rodney contrasts this picture, not only with the eighteenth- and nineteenth-century situation in his area, when specialized traders, mainly Mandingo and Fula, possessed and dealt in large numbers of slaves, but also with the sixteenth- and seventeenth-century situation farther north, in the Senegal, and also farther east, in Lower Guinea. In the latter case, he does not do very much more than refer to the fact that, as early as about 1500, the Portuguese were *selling* slaves on the Gold Coast, which of course presupposes a society knowing of the value of slaves and having a demand for them.[7] But the whole context in which the Portuguese first traded in Lower Guinea seems to have been very different from that in which they sought to trade in Upper Guinea.

We might begin by remarking that the ethnographic picture that can be built up from early Portuguese accounts of Lower Guinea is slighter, less complete and less detailed than that which can be built up for Upper Guinea. It is sometimes suggested that this is so because, after the Portuguese Crown had asserted its control over the Gold Coast trade in the 1480s, it required that its own and its subjects' doings in Guinea should be kept as secret as possible to place their foreign competitors in the Guinea trade at a disadvantage. But in fact most of the information used by Rodney is later than 1500, and it seems possible that the relative dearth of Portuguese ethnographic material for Lower Guinea may have other explanations. It seems possible that one of these may be that on the coasts of Lower Guinea, especially on the Gold Coast and in and around Benin, the Portuguese were in contact with organized kingdoms which had developed trading systems of their own and which were already engaged in long-distance trade or in trading with long-distance traders (like the Mande merchants on the Gold Coast). Whereas in the Upper Guinea coastlands the Portuguese had to deal with societies which were politically and commercially less well developed, and which therefore had to be thoroughly examined to see what prospects of profitable trade they might offer, no such exploration was necessary for the kingdoms of Lower Guinea, which already knew what commodities they had to offer to strangers and on what terms they would deal in them.

In these circumstances, for Lower Guinea it is necessary to infer local attitudes to slavery and trading in slaves from the trade which the Portuguese conducted there. It is immediately apparent not only that there was a market for slaves on the Gold Coast, but that there were communities farther east which both had slaves and knew the conditions on which they could be offered for sale. Thus as early as c. 1500, Pacheco Pereira could write of Benin that the kingdom was 'usually at war with its neighbours and takes many captives, whom we buy at 12 or 15 brass bracelets each, or for copper bracelets which they prize more; from there the slaves are taken to [the Gold Coast] where they are sold for gold'.[8] It is interesting that Pacheco says nothing about the royal ban on the export from Benin of male slaves which Professor Ryder says was 'imposed at the beginning of the sixteenth century'. Presumably it was not yet in force when Pacheco wrote. Conceivably it may have been instituted in the belief that it was more beneficial to the kingdom to maintain than to export its manpower. Conversely, and more probably perhaps, the subsequent decline of European trade at Benin as the trans-Atlantic slave trade developed, and the need to reverse this decline when neighbouring kingdoms were gaining strength through growing trade with Europeans, may well explain why the ban was rescinded in the 1690s.[9]

In general, we can be confident that what the Portuguese sought to do in Lower Guinea from about 1480 was to profit by imposing themselves (as later they were to do in East Africa and Asia) on already existing patterns of trade, and that they found there organized kingdoms in which the idea of foreign trade, carried on under royal control and in accordance with state policy by established merchant classes or guilds, was already well established. Such a system involved the use of slaves –

Slavery in the context of history 159

and an appreciation of their economic value – in a number of ways: as cultivators of crops for market on the estates of kings or nobles; as miners, or as artisans in craft workshops; as carriers on the trade roads, and even as traders themselves; as soldiers, retainers, servants, officials even, in the employ of kings or principal men in the kingdom. A similar but, one suspects, less well developed pattern was evident, as Rodney admits, in the Senegal region on the western fringes of the Sudan, and it was undoubtedly from the Western and Central Sudan that it had spread into Lower Guinea some time before the arrival of the Portuguese. In this sense the area of Upper Guinea, where in the sixteenth and seventeenth centuries there was no organized slavery, was an economically little developed and backward region.

There seems in fact to be a close correlation in West Africa between economic development (and political development, because indigenous commercial activity was largely king- or state-directed) and the growth of the institution of slavery as here defined. This growth was already well advanced before European sea trade with West Africa began in the fifteenth century, and certainly before the main commercial demand of Europeans on West Africa was one for slaves – which was not really until the middle or the second half of the seventeenth century. Neither the first nor the second of the commonly held views about the relationship between the Atlantic slave trade and slavery and slave-trading within West African society is really satisfactory. Slavery and the commercial valuation of slaves were not natural features of West African society, nor was their development and growth simply a consequence of the European demand for slaves for American plantations. This last may well have been the case in Upper Guinea, but elsewhere, for example, in Lower Guinea, all the coming of European slave-buyers meant in principle was that African kings and merchants were increasingly presented with a new element of choice – fundamentally, it would seem, an economic choice: whether it was more advantageous to them to keep their slave labourers at home, as farmers, artisans, porters, retainers, soldiers, etc., or to exchange them or some of them for other forms of wealth (or of power, for example, guns and powder).

We arrive then at a first conclusion, that slavery and the making, buying and selling of slaves were means by which certain privileged individuals in West African society, or persons who wished to gain or to extend positions of privilege in that society, sought to mobilize the wealth inherent in the land and the people on it, and that this process had already gone some distance before the Europeans arrived. In so far as it seems to have started in the Sudan, rather than in Guinea, it is of course still possible, even perhaps likely, that the process was sparked off by the demands of visitors coming to West Africa from across the Sahara, from North Africa. On the other hand, such evidence as there is suggests that it is *un*likely that these first external demands were primarily or even essentially demands for labour. The prime North African demand was probably for gold and exotic produce, and the first basis of the trans-Saharan trade the exchange of salt for gold. It would thus be a demand for *commodities* which provoked the vital change by which some West Africans began to view some others not as kin or non-kin but as a means by which to obtain wealth and power.

We are still left, however, with the questions whether, and, if so, to what extent, the external demands for West African labour, especially the great European demands for labour for the Americas, may have distorted the natural economic development of West Africa, and have produced socially, economically, and even politically disastrous consequences.

Clearly we should begin by assessing, first, the actual size of this demand for labour exports and, secondly, its possible demographic effects in West Africa. Thanks to the recent researches of Professor Philip D. Curtin,[10] it is now possible to do this with rather more confidence than before in respect of the export of slaves to the Americas. The numbers of slaves reaching the Americas and so, allowing for losses *en route*, the numbers leaving Africa seem likely to have been appreciably smaller than has been commonly supposed. For the whole four centuries of the trade, Curtin's evaluation of the evidence available points to the conclusion that the number of slaves reaching the Americas cannot have been more than about 9 millions, and may well have been rather less. Furthermore, he doubts whether it would have been technically possible for the shipping resources available to Europe to have transported more. He also has evidence that suggests, too, that the losses *en route* from sickness, starvation and revolt, not more than 16% on average, were significantly less than the figures commonly accepted, which derive – like the earlier estimates for total volume – from the exaggerated pleadings of the abolitionist campaigners. On this basis, the total number of men and women exported from Africa during the whole period of the slave trade is unlikely to have been much more than about 11 millions. Of these, a considerable and growing proportion came from south of the Cameroons, and so from outside West Africa as commonly understood. The *West* African contribution to the Atlantic slave trade is in fact unlikely to have been much more than about 6 millions.

It would be helpful if we could compare this estimate with a figure for the number of slaves exported northwards from West Africa across the Sahara. This, frankly, is impossible: the available data are exiguous and unreliable in the extreme, as is admitted by Mauny, who, however, offers a guess of a minimum of 20,000 a year, or 2 million a century.[11] Something like the first of these figures might be reasonable for the annual capacity of the trans-Saharan caravan roads, but it would seem totally unreasonable to suppose that anything like this number crossed the Sahara every year during the seventeen centuries in which we know the northern slave trade to have existed, or even during the twelve centuries following the Arab conquest of North Africa. Thirty-four or twenty-four million Negroes would have made an impact on the population of North Africa and the Middle East quite as great as 9 million Negroes on that of the Americas, and really there is little evidence of this. It seems safer to conclude that, extending over a very much longer period, the trans-Saharan trade removed fewer Negroes than the Atlantic trade, and that its effect on the West African population during the time the Atlantic trade was operating was relatively minor.

Prior to the middle of the seventeenth century, the Atlantic slave trade was on a small scale; Curtin's figures suggest a loss of population to West Africa before 1600 of only about 200,000. The seventeenth-century figure would be nearly a million, but it was in the years from 1701 to 1810, when something like $4\frac{1}{2}$ million slaves were removed, that the effect of the trade was most serious, averaging a loss of 41,000 men and women a year. The nineteenth-century loss, in so far as West Africa was concerned, was much lighter, probably of the order of only about 11,000 a year on average.

We do not, of course, know the size of West Africa's population in the eighteenth century. But extrapolation backwards from twentieth-century censuses and estimates and rates of increase suggests that the population of West Africa may have been at least 25 million at the beginning of the eighteenth century, with a rate of natural increase of about 15 per 1000 at the beginning of the century and of about 19 per 1000 at the end. If these estimates[12] are anything like right, then at first sight the effect of the export slave trade in the eighteenth century may have been more or less to check population growth, the rates of slave exports and of natural increase being of the same order. For other centuries, the effect of the slave trade would have been slight.

Various refinements can be made to such a crude calculation. For example, some allowance should be made for deaths caused directly or indirectly by the operations of the slave trade within West Africa itself. On the other hand, such a factor might be more than offset by the fact that only a third of the slaves exported were women, so that in a polygamous society the rate of natural increase by new births may not have been as much affected as would otherwise have been the case.

It is probably more important to appreciate that the incidence of the slave trade, both in time and space, was by no means even. Thus in the 1780s, for instance, about 80 per cent of all slaves exported from West Africa (and nearly half of the slaves taken from *all* Africa) were taken from the coast from the Gold Coast to the Cameroons inclusive. Thus if there were serious depopulation and other destructive effects caused by the Atlantic slave trade, they might be expected to show most clearly in this region. In point of fact, they do not appear to show at all. This, by and large, remains the most densely populated part of West Africa, and the Ibo country is as thickly settled as any part of the whole continent. Moreover, this was the part of Guinea, including the Akan states, Dahomey, the Yoruba and Benin kingdoms, which was politically and economically best organized.

The conclusion to which one is led, therefore, is that whereas in East and Central Africa the slave trade, sometimes conducted in the interior by raiding and warring strangers, could be extremely destructive of economic, political and social life, in West Africa it was part of a sustained process of economic and political development. Probably because, by and large, in West Africa land was always more abundant than labour,[13] the institution of slavery played an essential role in this development; without it there were really few effective means of mobilizing labour for the economic and political needs of the state. (One may recall Charles Monteil's dictum that 'a Sudanic empire is in essence an association of individuals aiming to dominate the generality for profit'.[14]) But in this process the *trade* in slaves, certainly the export trade, was essentially incidental, only one of a number of ways of increasing a kingdom's wealth and power, and in the Guinea coastlands only during the eighteenth century the most important way. Whether or not to export slaves and, if so, in what quantities, seems to have been increasingly an economic choice.

It has already been suggested that this choice was exercised at Benin. Here, shortly after 1500, the authorities seem to have concluded that the kingdom and its economy would be weakened if the export of male labour were permitted. Later on, the view seems to have been taken that the resultant loss of trade with Europeans (*inter alia* the vendors of firearms), and the consequent gain to the trade and strength of neighbouring African rivals, was more dangerous than the loss of manpower. Dr Akinjogbin has suggested a similar argument in eighteenth-century Dahomey: first a refusal to export slaves (lest the kingdom be weakened), then a realization that it was only through selling slaves that the kingdom could buy the guns and powder necessary to maintain its power.[15] It may also be significant that, although the European demand for slaves for the Americas was continually growing and the price of slaves steadily increasing from about 1650 to about 1810, the numbers of slaves exported from the well-organized Gold Coast states remained more or less constant throughout the period, never really exceeding about 10,000 a year. It may be argued, then, that economic and political logic had in effect persuaded the Gold Coast authorities that this was about the number of slaves they could afford to export, in order to obtain the guns and other imports their states required, without weakening their societies. The numbers of slaves exported through the Niger delta ports did greatly increase during this period, but this too could have been a more or less conscious economic response to a different set of circumstances. In the Ibo hinterland of the delta, where, although political authority was diffuse, economic life seems to have been well developed, it may well have been that there was already an unusual growth of population in relation to the productivity of the land, so that men of enterprise may have concluded that it was becoming more profitable to export labour for sale than to employ it at home.

But the balance should not be struck exclusively in economic terms (even if it may be suggested that at the time the economic arguments were becoming increasingly important in the minds of the ruling segments in West African societies). There is not space here to enter into a discussion of the host of moral and social issues involved in the slave trade, but there is one politico-social point that should be briefly touched upon. It has been seen that European slave-traders like Dalzel justified their activities on the ground that they were rescuing Africans from oppression and exploitation by their own rulers, and that likewise the abolitionists argued that their campaigning was needed to redeem African society from the degradations brought by the slave trade. It is therefore worth asking whether the ever-increasing American demand for slaves from West Africa from the middle of the seventeenth to the beginning of the nineteenth century led to increased slave-raiding and to more wars being fought for the express purpose of securing slaves, and so to a growing political instability which was destructive of economic and social progress.

This is a very large question, and one to which there may well be no single answer applicable to all parts of West Africa and to all kinds of West African societies. It might, however, be argued – as, for example, Professor Flint has argued[16] – that the stereotyping of such polities as the emirates of Nupe and Ilorin as 'slave-raiding' was part of the apologetics by which the European colonizers justified their conquests. For one area, and for one type of West African society, namely the kingdoms of Lower Guinea, there is, however, some interesting evidence on record. Both King Kpengla of Dahomey (1774-89) and King Osei Bonsu of Ashanti (c. 1801-24) were specifically asked by European visitors whether they engaged in warfare with the express purpose of capturing slaves for trade.[17] Both are reported as saying that they did not, that their wars were fought for political reasons, to protect, maintain or promote the power and prestige of their nations relative to their neighbours.

If it is argued that their replies may not have been properly reported by their inquisitors, who may well have had their own motives for distorting them, then attention should be drawn to the strong similarities between their reported arguments, and to the fact that their reporters had opposing biases, Absom and Dalzel (in the case of Kpengla) being partisans of the slave trade, and Dupuis (in the case of Osei Bonsu) being an opponent of it. In these circumstances, Kepengla's and Osei Bonsu's statements have the ring of truth: their own opinion was that their wars were not fought to secure slaves for sale to the Atlantic slave-traders. But the existence of the Atlantic trade did give such kings a new choice; whether it was more profitable for them to sell their war captives abroad, or keep them at home, employed as soldiers, or as labourers on their and their generals' estates or on their trading enterprises, or, perhaps, whether they might best be used for the traditional sacrifices to their and the nation's ancestors (sacrifices whose scale may have been growing as the scale of royal and national power was itself growing). A similar choice was also intruding into more domestic spheres, whether criminal and civil malefactors should be punished by such traditional penalties as fines or execution, or whether they might best be dealt with by selling them to the Atlantic traders – in effect, by deportation. Here analogies from seventeenth- and eighteenth-century English history might suggest that the latter remedy was on the increase (but this might be thought a social good rather than an evil).

On the whole it is probably true to say that the operation of the slave trade may have tended to integrate, strengthen and develop unitary, territorial political authority, but to weaken or destroy more segmentary societies. Whether this was good or evil may be a nice point; historically it may be seen as purposive and perhaps as more or less inevitable.

One may perhaps conclude with the reflection that, in the context of the times in West Africa, by stopping the slave trade and by attacking slavery, Europeans did much to impoverish and weaken its monarchies.

This was so because, on the African side, the slave trade was conducted on a large scale by a relatively small number of major entrepreneurs under state patronage or, indeed, direction. Thus, when the export slave trade was ended, the African monarchies lost a major source of revenue and a large part of the economic structure which supported them. This might not have been the case had the slaves available been put to plantation production for export – an expedient which certainly seems to have been considered, for example by King Gezo of Dahomey in the 1850s.[18] But in practice the so-called 'legitimate' trades which replaced the slave trade as the staple of West African foreign commerce tended to be based rather on production by large numbers of small-scale 'peasant' farmers. The major kingdoms found difficulty in adapting their fiscal, economic and political systems so as to profit from this change in the economic structure. For this reason, as the nineteenth century progressed, they seem to have become at once less efficient in securing revenue from, and less able to provide the order needed by, their peoples' producers and traders.[19]

The steps taken by Europeans against the slave trade and slavery therefore hastened the day when, in their own economic interest, they thought it necessary first to conquer the West African kingdoms, and then to continue the process, initiated by African kings and entrepreneurs, of conquering the segmentary societies and absorbing them into unitary political structures.

Summary

This paper examines three views which have been widely held about slavery and the slave trade in West Africa, and which have tended to mould interpretations of its history, especially for the period from the fifteenth to the nineteenth century. These are:

(1) That the institution of slavery was endemic in, and a natural feature of, indigenous West African society, so that when foreigners arrived in West Africa with a demand for slaves, West Africans were able immediately to organize an export trade in slaves on an ever-increasing scale.

(2) A contrary view, that it was the external demands for labour which led to a great growth of the institution of slavery in West Africa, and so corrupted its indigenous society.

(3) A view which may or may not be combined with (2), namely that the external demand for slaves became so considerable that there was a disastrous effect on its population.

Relevant evidence is touched upon from about the eleventh century onwards, and a fourth interpretation is developed which seems better to fit the economic and social realities which can be ascertained.

In essence this is that economic and commercial slavery and slave-trading were not natural features of West African society, but that they developed, along with the growth of states, as a form of labour mobilization to meet the needs of a growing system of foreign trade in which, initially, the demand for slaves as trade goods was relatively insignificant. What might be termed a 'slave economy' was generally established in the Western and Central Sudan by about the fourteenth century at least, and had certainly spread to the coasts around the Senegal and in Lower Guinea by the fifteenth century.

The European demand for slaves for the Americas, which reached its peak from about 1650 to about 1850, accentuated and expanded the internal growth of both slavery and the slave trade. But this was essentially only one aspect of a very wide process of economic and political development and social change, in West Africa. The data recently assembled and analysed by Curtin for the volume and distribution of the export slave trade do not suggest that the loss of population and other effects of the export of labour to the Americas need have had universally damaging effects on the development of West Africa. Rather, it is suggested, West African rulers and merchants reacted to the demand with economic reasoning, and used it to strengthen streams of economic and political development that were already current before the Atlantic slave trade began.

6 The Oyo Yoruba and the Atlantic trade, 1670 to 1830

Peter Morton-Williams

Editor's comments

Some hold the view that the Yoruba people of south-western Nigeria were not seriously affected by the export slave trade until after the 1820s, following the collapse of the Old Oyo empire. In this chapter Professor Morton-Williams provides detailed information about the involvement of Old Oyo in the Atlantic slave trade. He argues that the north-eastern savanna of the Yoruba territories, occupied by the northern Ekiti, Akoko and Yagba, was a slave catchment area for the Oyo Yoruba. He suggests that other parts of the eastern Yoruba region constituted a slave catchment area for the Benin warriors. The pattern of settlement in good defensive territories of the eastern Yoruba, which contrasts the pattern of the western savanna of Yorubaland, is shown by Morton-Williams as one of the consequences of slaving operations in this part of Yorubaland. Similarly, he demonstrates that the light population of the fertile lands that became Egbado and Awori territories from the late eighteenth century was due to slave raids from the Ewe-speaking states, the Ijebu, and the Benin colonies, in the late seventeenth and early eighteenth centuries. Another slave catchment area indicated by Morton-Williams is the area to the north and west of the Oyo territory, a once densely populated territory, but now almost a wilderness, the former population having been captured or driven out in slaving wars. Like Chapter 3, the paper is based on detailed field work, oral tradition and contemporary accounts of European visitors to Africa.

The Oyo are the most northerly of the Yoruba peoples and Old Oyo (which they call Oyole) lay in the extreme north of their territory, some 30 miles from the Niger crossing at Rabba in Nupe, 180 miles from the coast and about eighty-five miles north of the present town of Oyo,

This paper was first published in the *Journal of the Historical Society of Nigeria*, vol. 3 no. 1 (December 1964), pp. 25–45. It has been reprinted here by permission of the author and the publishers.

which the Yoruba also know as Ago d'Oyo. It rose to military power, so my research in the newer town suggests, in the fifteenth century and through warfare during the next 100 to 150 years both secured its frontiers against the Bariba and Nupe and also dominated the northern and central Yoruba kingdoms, bringing the large area which extended south to the forest, south-westwards to Ketu tribal territory and east and south-eastwards to the frontiers with the Ijesa and Ife tribes, under close political control in a system of vassalage. At this time it was presumably able to control trade between a sector of the forest and the states to the north – Bariba, Bussa, Nupe and some of the Hausa. Kola would have been one important item of commerce, as it is today; but whether the northern markets were also supplied with slaves we do not know.[1] By 1650, the flow of European trade goods was well under way from the coast; as early as 1635, indeed, reputedly Yoruba artefacts, including textiles, collected on the coast for a German merchant had been bequeathed to the city of Ulm – though it does not follow that the Oyo were involved in the trade that early. What is certain is that before 1670 the Oyo had begun to supply a proportion of the slaves exported through Little Ardra (near modern Porto Novo).[2] What they got in return, apart from salt and luxuries, is less certain. Luxuries are today important as signs of prestige and of the privileges of rank and seniority and there are reliable indications that this is an ancient Yoruba trait. Imported firearms were a necessary state monopoly in Ashanti and Dahomey; but there is little evidence that this was true of Oyo. As late as the nineteenth century, they seemed to have relied on archery: Robertson[3] found the Oyo feared as archers armed with poisoned arrows and Lander[4] wrote: 'The Yaribeans have the reputation of being the best bowmen in Africa. . . . Quantities of muskets are procured from the coast, but they are of comparatively little use to the people, who do not know how to handle them with effect'. Nevertheless, even the unskilled use of firearms may have helped them to appear more formidable, increasing their security against their northern neighbours, their hold over their vassals, and their success as slave raiders.[5] It is not known precisely whom they raided; the early history of Dahomey shows that the Fon were among their victims, but it may be inferred from Johnson[6] that they preyed on the eastern, especially the north-eastern, Yoruba. Dapper[7] recorded (I use Ogilby's translation): 'The Kingdom of Ulkami or Ulkuma'.

Ulkami, or *Ulkuma*, a mighty Country, spreads Eastward of *Arder* between that and *Bynyn*, to the North-East. From hence they send many slaves, partly taken in the wars, and partly made such as punishment for their offences, to Little Arder, and there sold to the Portuguese to be transported to the *West Indies*.

Ulkami is beyond doubt Oyo – this is evident from the geographical indications in the early writers and from a passage in Barbot:

That remote inland nation, which I suppose to be the *Oyeo* and *Ulkami*, strikes such a terror at *Ardra*, and all the adjacent countries, that they can scarce hear them mentioned without trembling. . . .[8]

The name Oyeo, with its variants Io, J-oe, Ayo and Eyo, only became current towards the middle of the eighteenth century.

But in spite of its power no one before Clapperton[9] was able to give any worthwhile information about the Oyo; the following extract from Barbot is typical (and not only beause it says so little and some of that little hardly credible – the second half is paraphrased without acknowledgement from Olfert Dapper,[10] a practice which has persisted among writers about the Yoruba to the present day, making the quality of many authors suspect).

Before I proceed to the description of . . . *Benin*. . . , it will be proper to say something of the kingdom or country of *Ulkami*, situated betwixt *Ardra* and *Benin*. . . .

It [Benin] borders at east, south and west, and at north, on an unknown potent nation: the natives call it *Alkomi*, and represent it as a mighty state, whence the *Ardrasians* get most of the slaves they sell to us, whom the *Alkomi Blacks* take prisoners in their excursions on their neighbours; but are a sort of people who have little communication with them: and therefore can say no more of their manners and religion, than [here the copy of Dapper begins] that they circumcise men and women, when young; the daughters at ten or eleven years of age, which they say is done by means of large ants or pismires, of a yellow colour, fastened to a stick, and thus applied to the part, and left there, till they have bit in many parts so that the blood gushes out of it, which is a very painful operation to the patient; and then the insects are removed.[11]

It is curious that, with this lack of communication, Barbot should report 'The *Adrasians* use rather than their own, the Ulkami language'.[12]

The question of where these slaves 'taken in the Wars' came from is of some significance, both from the broader point of view of the relations of Oyo with its neighbouring states, and as we shall see later, from the narrower one of the history of the coastal trade routes. There are a few hints, no certainties.

Ulkami may be a word of Gun (an Ewe-group language) origin and be cognate with Lucumi, which Bascom (1952, and personal communication) found to be the Cuban name for the Yoruba. Bascom suggests that Lucumi may be derived from an Ijesha salutation (*oluku-mi!* – my friend!) and dates from the mid nineteenth century, when it was given by their fellow slaves to Ijesha slaves captured by raiders from the newly founded Oyo town of Ibadan and shipped at the very end of the slave trading period to Cuba, one of the last importers of slaves. If Ijesha captives were being sent down to the coast by the Oyo in the seventeenth century and not only in the nineteenth, then it can be argued that dealers on the coast gave this name to the slaves from the source Bascom suggests and also attached it by extension to the Oyo, who not only spoke a dialect of the same language and, as Dapper reported, enslaved some of their own countrymen but also claimed that all other Yoruba were their subjects. The foundation of Ede from Oyo probably (to judge from Oyo traditions),[13] at the beginning of the seventeenth century and then the building of the westernmost Ijesha town of Oshogbo as a stronghold confronting Ede suggests that some of the Oyo 'wars' were raids on the Ijesha and on the neighbouring Ekiti, Akoko, etc. Their frontier guarded by Oshogbo and shielded also by the forest, the Ijesha were able to retain the characteristic Yoruba way of life in large towns as opposed to life in farm-villages; not so with their north-eastern neighbours. While the demographic pattern in the western part of the savanna region occupied by the Yoruba tribes shows that settlements are sited not with an eye to ease of defence but to make communications between them as easy as possible, hill-tops and the most broken country being avoided (except during the nineteenth century wars), the opposite is found in the eastern Yoruba savanna. There, among the northern Ekiti, Akoko and Yagba, sites are usually in good defensive positions and their location in relation to natural obstacles makes settlements inaccessible at the cost of ease of communications or even good building sites; a pattern that, so the evidence of tradition shows, antedates the nineteenth century.

That eastern and north-eastern Yoruba tribes do not have those political and religious institutions which distinguish Oyo cultural influences throughout the western and southern parts of the Oyo empire supports the view that the eastern area was rather a slave reservoir than under Oyo administration. Further support comes from traditions that local kings east of Ede did not, like those in the west, attend the *bere* festival in Oyo, the occasion when the Alafin (king) of Oyo received the homage of his vassals (Johnson[14] says that the Ijesha and Ekiti sent token gifts, but it is not clear whether he regarded their kings as vassals. They certainly deny today that they were). If this was the case it would have been an agreement on raiding areas that led to the acknowledgement of a frontier between Oyo and Benin.[15] (Territories dependent on Benin also marched with Oyo in the neighbourhood of Ado, thirteen miles to the north of Badagri and only a few miles east of the Oyo route to the coast; oral traditions confirm and amplify eighteenth century reports on this.) West and south of Oyo lay other Yoruba tribes and kingdoms, some as old as Oyo, others founded more recently. They all have parts in our story.

The consensus of Yoruba traditions describes the peoples of the middle and south of Egbado Division in the extreme south-west of Nigeria as late offshoots of other branches of the Yoruba peoples. The Ketu in the north, their northern neighbours the Sha, and the Alake section of the Egba, are said to have left the legendary place of origin of the Yoruba, Ile Ife, as a single group at the same time that the Oyo, the Bini, the Egun (Popo), and variously listed others, went on their separate migrations.[16]

The king-lists of Oyo and Ketu (and, incidentally, of Benin) are so nearly of the same length that they may be held to give some support to the tradition. The forty-first Alafin was installed at Oyo in 1957 (Johnson's list and my informants agree on this number); the forty-eighth Alaketu since the legendary departure from Ife (but the forty-second to reign at Ketu) succeeded in 1937. We can be sure that the foundation of these kingdoms was considerably earlier than 1600, that is, long before the Dutch shipped the first slaves from the Slave Coast.

The Dutch had established themselves as the principal carriers of slaves in the West African trade with the foundation of the Dutch West Indies Company in 1621.[17] This was the stimulus for the opening of the new slaving ports along the coast between the Volta and the Oil Rivers (sixteenth century maps, such as one in Ramusio, 1956, show no stations east of El Mina); although it was not, according to Fage, until after the Spaniards had lost command of the sea and the Dutch conquest of part of Brazil had started, that is, not until the 1630s, that large-scale shipments from the Slave Coast began. As we have seen, the Oyo were playing their part in the commerce before 1670.

The early slave stations were Ouidah ('Fida, by the English called Whidah and by the French Juyda',[18] Jacquin (Jakkin, Jaqueen, etc.) and Little Ardra 'or Offra, as most of the Europeans call it',[19] the two latter being outlets for the state of Ardra (Assem). These states were small and depended on their powerful neighbours for the supply of slaves. Parrinder,[20] on the authority of Bowen[21] and Crowther,[22] considers it unlikely that Ketu was ever of any prominence as a slaving state. Perhaps it was on a trade route nevertheless. It is hardly possible to infer what route to the coast Oyo used during this early period. Until the rise to power of Dahomey under Agaja Trudo, who sacked Ardra in November 1724,[23] there is no reason to believe Oyo needed to establish a closely-administered trade route, and whether slaves passed to the west or the east of the barrier of the Kumi swamp is uncertain, though they perhaps went through Ketu on their way to the sea. There are, though, a number of small kingdoms south-east of Ketu fringing the east of the swamp in Egbado Division, whose inhabitants say they are of mixed Ketu and Ohori origin. These kingdoms derive their rights to crowns from the Alaketu (king) of Ketu. The king-lists of one of these towns, Ijoun, numbered, in 1951, twenty-four, and that of another, Ijale, twenty-two. Matching the number of reigns against dated periods in those Yoruba kingdoms for which information is available, the average length of reign lies, I find, between twelve and fifteen years, with a bias towards twelve or thirteen. This gives a date between 1675 and 1650, or at the very earliest 1605, for the foundation of these kingdoms and may therefore indicate an extension of Ketu territory along a trade route leading to Ketu and then to Oyo. Farther south, there is no evidence that at the beginning of this trading era the Oyo were in any but friendly relations with the coastal states, though the Alafin did have to tame the king of Ardra-Allada in 1698.[24] The Oyo apparently were content to leave the handling of the European shippers to the coastal states.[25] Dahomey on the other hand, under Agaja Trudo sought to monopolize the trade.[26]

According to Snelgrave,[27] the first warlike encounter between Dahomey and Oyo was in 1719/20 (and not in 1727, as Parrinder,[28] supposes, following Dalzel, whose earlier dates seem to be unreliable). A Dahomey army ravaged Weme, a small state to the south-east and 'the King of Weemey's Sons'[29] fled to Oyo for help. Oyo, presumably wishing to check the growth of Dahomey's power, sent a strong force of cavalry. On this occasion, the Dahomeans buried their treasures and fled into the forest, and the Oyo razed their towns. But by 1730, Dahomey had not only taken Ouidah and Ardra with its ports Little Ardra and Jacquin, but had also by a ruse defeated the King 'of J-oe's horses',[30] though rather than risk a counter-attack it had bought off Oyo retaliation. Oyo invaded again in 1738[31] and plundered and burnt Abomey after a desperate battle; and following this there were frequent Oyo raids until 1747, after which Dahomey paid more or less regular tribute to Oyo until Gezo's victory over an Oyo army in 1827.[32]

Another power that interested itself in this area (but seems to have been ignored by recent historians) was Benin. Benin founded colonies along the shore – of these, Lagos is of course best known, but the town of Ado (the Yoruba form of *Edo*, i.e. Benin) north of Badagri was, so its traditions imply, also a Bini foundation or at least got its crown from it; and Ipokia, west of the River Yewa and only thirteen miles ENE of Porto Novo, claims to have been founded from *Opo Bini* (the Benin colonies), though it was at the beginning of the nineteenth century, if not

The Atlantic trade, 1670–1830   173

earlier (Clapperton), subject to Oyo. I am unable at present even tentatively to assign dates to this penetration by Benin, but Snelgrave seems to have been aware of it, and the passage quoted from Barbot[33] remarking the possibility that Allada marched with Benin might encourage the view that the expansion had taken place before 1700.[34] Dr R. E. Bradbury has kindly informed me that, on the basis of his unpublished research, he thinks it might have been as early as the late sixteenth century.

Oyo founded a kingdom, Ifonyin (sometimes called Anago), marching with Ketu and Pobe in the north and Ipokia in the south (its present territory straddles the Dahomey frontier some 25 miles from the coastline). Ipokia traditions (cf. Newington, 1941) and those of the Ifonyin agree that Ipokia was at some periods tributary to Ifonyin. The title of the Ifonyin king was Elehin Odo (sometimes abbreviated to Elewi) 'King of Behind the River'. The traditions of the Anago people of Ifonyintedo, given to me by descendants of the royal lineages of the Elehin Odo (recorded also in Hatch),[35] are that he ruled the territory beyond the Agidi, a river flowing south-west through southern Ketu territory. By agreement with the Alaketu, the Elehin Odo, who was an Oyo and was given his crown by the Alafin, was allowed to lead his people through Ketu territory and was granted the land to the immediate south (in what is now Ohori territory) and his successors moved further south again until they reached the present town of Ifonyin (Ifanhim on the Dahomey maps) at the fourth stage of their journey in, so they informed Hatch, 1807. Eventually the Alaketu set a boundary between Ifonyin and Ohori territory at Oke Ita, near Pobe.

Questions concerning the relationship between Ketu and Oyo are raised, though not answered, by this agreement and by the tradition[36] that, while the Alafin's sanction was required for the choice of an Elehin Odo, he was crowned by the Alaketu. With the Alafin's permission, the Elehin Odo granted crowns to the heads of two towns in the south of his territory (each of them adjoining Ipokia territory), first, Ihumbo and, much later, Ikolaje. The king-list of Ihumbo is, oddly, longer than that of Ifonyin: The sixteenth Elehin Odo was deposed by the French in 1900; while Ihumbo has had twenty-one kings, and Hatch was told that the sixteenth Onihumbo was ruling when Ihumbo was destroyed together with Oke Odan by Dahomey (in 1848),[37] and was told, too, that Oke Odan had been founded on land granted by the twelfth Onihumbo to refugees from Ilobi, which had itself been destroyed by the Egba c. 1834–40. Our formula gives us somewhere between 1660 and 1708 for the first Elehin Odo, but 1720 to 1776 for the first in approximately their present territory (the bias being towards the later dates); yet for the first

Onihumbo we have, if we count from the installation of the twenty-first in 1930, between 1630 and 1690, or, if we reckon the twelfth to have been crowned about 1830, between 1670 and 1700.

I am inclined to regard these dates, pointing to around 1700 for the beginning of these kingdoms, as suggesting that the rise of Dahomey and the westward push of the Bini impressed upon Oyo the need to organize and defend its command of its access to the coast and that the founding of the Ifonyin-Anago kingdoms was a means to this end, and, further, that the trade route led from the ports along the eastern fringes of the Kumi Swamp and through the east of Ketu territory. Johnson,[38] who calls the Elehin Odo a Popo king, records the Oyo tradition that the wealth of this king was proverbial and that one Elehin when on a visit to Oyo (I estimate, in the middle of the eighteenth century) rivalled the Alafin in splendour. This wealth it is more plausible to regard as the reward of trade rather than of military prowess, otherwise we might have expected to have heard something about the latter even if it had been exercised only in operations to the eastward, in the area later organized into the Egbado kingdoms. Dalzel[39] is the only person to mention the Anago before the nineteenth century: he calls them Nagoes and describes them as 'inland merchants' (p. 214).[40]

Ifonyin-Anago culture differs significantly from that of Oyo and from that of the Egbado, which is in most respects closer to Oyo culture; the differences concern both important religious conceptions and also the institutions of government. These Ifonyin features generally diverge towards those of Ketu, but some of them towards the Fon, and point towards the conclusion that, as one would expect, although a ruling group may have moved from Oyo territory into this area some 250 years ago, they did not enter an uninhabited land (though they now believe they did). They more probably dominated an earlier population, which may have been mainly Ohori but might have included Fon, Gun, or perhaps some outlying Ketu groups. Of the population to the east of this area, that is, beyond the River Yewa, at the beginning of the eighteenth century, nothing can be said.

Ardra (Assem) had, by 1770 if not earlier, regained its independence of Dahomey and some of Oyo's trade still flowed through it;[41] but much of this trade had moved eastwards to Badagri, which does not appear on the maps of Snelgrave or Labat.[42] Refugees from Grewhe (Ouidah) in 1724[43] and, a little later, from Jacquin had fled in that direction and, according to Snelgrave, been received by the 'king of Appah' which was at that time probably the most easterly kingdom of the Ewe-speaking people, adjoining Yoruba-speaking groups subject to Benin. Possibly Badagri owed its entry into the trade to these refugees from Jacquin.[44]

This inference rests on more than the assumption that the refugees would have wished to resume trading activities. Fage[45] concludes that Dahomey had needed to reinstate local traders in the recently conquered sea-board states to keep trade with the Europeans going, because the Dahomeans did not know the trading conventions; the Jacquin refugees perhaps brought the technique and skills of trading to Badagri.

Badagri, protected on the west by the broad Yewa estuary with its fringe of creeks and mangrove swamp, and on the north and east sheltered by forest from cavalry, seems to have been too independent for the Alafin's pleasure. We do not know if it purposely offended him; the more readily argued hypothesis, as we shall see, is that the Alafin was reorganizing his whole system of communication with the coast.

In 1777, the King of Dahomey had planned attacks on the ports of Apee, Porto Novo, and Badagri, in order to divert trade to his own port of Ouidah; but he was warned against these adventures by the Alafin.[46] Then in 1784, the Alafin decided to reduce Badagri, and to use Dahomey as his tool for this. The Dahomey army was 'joined by a numerous body of auxiliaries from the inland countries of *Mahee* and *Nago* . . . and marched in great force towards Badagree, conducted by guides, which had been provided by the King of Eyeo.' The Dahomey commander, the Agaow,[47] laid waste the whole country in this progress, making many prisoners, which were immediately sent to Eyeo, according to a treaty which had been previously entered into with that Prince. . . .

'*Sessu*, an Adrah caboceer, gave the Agaow assurances of a plentiful supply of provisions . . . as did likewise *Kossu*, a Nago chief, belonging to Eyeo. The operations of the Dahomean army were directed by the Eyeo messengers . . . and nothing of importance was undertaken without their concurrence.

'The powerful King of *Lagos* was prevailed upon, by bribes and promises, to join this formidable confederacy; and he undertook to prevent the Badagrees from receiving supplies of corn from his dominions.'

In due course the Badagri army was defeated in a fierce battle, though through a tactical error many of the inhabitants escaped.[48]

The next events illuminate the quality of politics in this area.

The most distinguished of the prisoners were sent by the Agaow to Adahoonzou (King of Dahomey), with a message, intimating, that he waited for orders. The king soon returned an answer, instructing him to make the Ardras paddle the army across the river, and to pursue his way homewards by the beach. The reason for this manoeuvre was for some time kept a secret; but it was afterwards known that the King of Eyeo, expecting the Agaow's return by the same path by which his messengers had conducted him to Badagree, had sent a strong force to intercept him, and bring the Dahomeans, with all their plunder, to Eyeo. The messengers, therefore, who had hitherto been their conductors, were extremely astonished when the Agaow dismissed them, and bid them make the best of their way homewards.'[49]

In May, 1786, at a word from Oyo, Dahomey took Weme, a few miles to the west of Porto Novo. The King of Dahomey planned to follow up this victory with an attack on Ardra (Assem) and Porto Novo, and was chagrined to find this enterprise forbidden by the Alafin: 'Ardrah was Eyeo's calabash out of which nobody should be permitted to eat but himself'.[50] King Adahoonzou, having now declared royal monopolies in many goods, also arbitrarily fixed the price of slaves to suit himself. All he now needed was to confine trade to his own port, Ouidah; but Oyo, after the overthrow of Badagri and Weme, was obviously keeping another port free – and that the one nearest to Ifonyin territory. Dalzel contrasts the statecraft of the Alafin with that of Adahoonzou:[51] 'Adahoonzou was extremely exasperated at having been made the dupe of the people of Ardrah, and left no method untried to set the King of Eyeo against them; but they were too rich, and constantly defeated Dahomey's designs, by heaping a profusion of presents on the King of Eyeo. Porto Novo was seldom without seven or eight large French ships, and the richest European commodities were continually passing from thence, to be presented to the King of Eyeo, a very close-fisted and shrewd Monarch.'[52] 'Although Adahoonzou possessed a great store of personal courage, he appears to have been remarkably deficient in every other endowment requisite for the government of a great kingdom. His bravery, and enterprising spirit, served only to point him out as the fit instrument for accomplishing the wishes of his more politic and formidable neighbour and master, the King of Eyeo.

'This remark will account for the conquests which the King of Dahomey had been permitted to make, without the interruption or interference of Eyeo. Ardrah had been the intermediate tool, by whose instigation Adahoonzou had been prompted to harass his neighbours; and Eyeo got the major part of the spoil that had been acquired by Adahoonzou's victories.'[53]

In 1789, Dahomey made its first assault on a Yoruba town for many years, an attack on Ketu.[54] This invasion seems not to have brought about any reprisal from Oyo, so it may have coincided with the heavy defeat of an expedition from Oyo against Nupe recorded at the end of Dalzel,[55] a defeat which, so it has been surmised by others,[56] heralded the decline of Old Oyo.

Dahomey made another bid to end its tribute to Oyo about the year

The Atlantic trade, 1670–1830   177

1797, under Adahoonzou's (d. 1789) successor,[57] but Oyo was still powerful enough to invade Dahomey, destroy part of Abomey, and reimpose the tribute. But this was the last time an Oyo force invaded Dahomey. About ten years after Adahoonzou, Abiodun, the last powerful Alafin to reign at Old Oyo, died (the exact year is uncertain) and within the next twenty years or so four Alafin succeeded one another in conditions of increasing disorganization – Ilorin had declared itself independent of the Alafin, and then, in the early 1820s, fell to the Fulani. Dahomey ceased to pay tribute, and in about the year 1821 Gezo, who had become King of Dahomey in 1818, defeated an Oyo force between Sabe and Ketu.[58]

Meanwhile Badagri had been rebuilt and had again become a busy port. It is uncertain when it recovered from the sack of 1784; but it is established that the notorious slaver F. da Souza had already made a fortune in Badagri and another in Anecho, before establishing himself in Ouidah in 1818.[59] This time, it survived as an independent kingdom until it was annexed by the British in 1863.

We have no certain dates for political developments, nor do we know the economic conditions in the hinterland north of Badagri – that is, in the Egbado area – until December 1825, when Clapperton led his expedition through it to Sokoto. At that time, Badagri served Egbado and Oyo, so we may surmise that the growth of trade through Egbado favoured its re-establishment. A brief review of Clapperton's notes on the route through Egbado and of the Lander brothers' in 1829, will help us in the piecing together of historical change here from the late eighteenth century until the 1830s.

Clapperton often wrote his notes under difficulties – Lander[60] said that the suspicions of their hosts commonly prevented them making them on the spot; we can, nevertheless, as Philip Allison, who makes this point, says, 'trace the general line on the road taken by the Landers on a modern map, assisted by a certain amount of local knowledge of the names of villages and towns which have now disappeared but whose situation is still remembered by local people.'[61]

It will be most convenient to collate the names of places travelled through by Clapperton's party, as recorded by Clapperton, with the forms given in Richard Lander's account of the same journey; then with names given in the journal of Lander's second journey to the Niger (that part of the route which lay through Egbado was reported from John Lander's notes, as Richard Lander's were lost); and finally with the modern names of settlements as I construe them. This is done in the following table, and the route shown on the map.

Table 12 *Clapperton's and the Landerses' route through Egbado to Oyo*

1 Clapperton, 1825/6	2 Lander, 1825	3 Lander, 1829	4 Reconstrued
BABAGRY BAWIE market	BADAGRY	BADAGRY BAWIE (passed by)	BADAGRI IBAWE
PUKA 'a district of Eyeo'	BOOKHAR		IPOKIA
		WOW	OWO, still a busy canoe landing-place and market
ISAKO village	ISAKO		
DAGMOO village	DAGNO		not identified
		SAGBU 8 miles north	ISHAGBO?
		BASHA village	not identified
HUMBA	HUMBA town in ruins		IHUMBO not Ohumbe as in Allison
AKALOU village			not identified
	AKONGUJIE		n. i.
ETO	ETO		ITORO?
ISADO	SATTOO		n. i.
BIDGIE crossed river	BIDGIE	BIDGIE close to River Yow (first regaining of 1825 route)	IGBEJI on R. YEWA; no longer an important crossing place.
ATALIOBOLO vill.	ATULABORA vill.		n. i.
	FUNNIE small town		n. i.
		LATOO	OLUTE?
LABOO (LALOO on his map)	LABOO	LARRO	ILARO
JANNAH seat of Alafin's slave	JANNAH	JENNA	IJANNA. Present town 2 miles from ruins of old.
BACHY	BEECHY	BIDGIE	IBESHE; tradition that 4th King reigning when exped. passed through.

The Atlantic trade, 1670–1830 179

1 *Clapperton, 1825/6*	2 *Lander, 1825*	3 *Lander, 1829*	4 *Reconstrued*
TSHOW	TSHOW	CHOW	SHAWON; now scattered farming villages.
EGA (death of Dawson)	EGBO	EGGA principal market town	IGAN (KOTO), large village. (Big market now at Aiyetoro.)
EMADO			ERINMADO = EEMADO; now a ward in new town of Aiyetoro. Presumably was on Erinmado Stream 5 miles south of Aiyetoro.
LIABO village surrounded by mud wall; others had wooden stockades.			n. i.
EKWA			ERIPA? Egbado pronounce it Eekpa. Now a village near Aiyetoro.
		JADOO	n. i.
ENGWA death of Pearce. (News that Morrison had died and was buried in Ijanna)	ENGWA bare and rocky	ENGUA	n. i. (unless EWON, pron. Ewo), once most northerly Egbado town (Allison's identification with Eggua unacceptable).
	R. AKKENI crossed	CHAKKA where R. AKEENY crossed	n. i.; but a R. ISHAKA
AFOORA Now crossing tributaries of River OGUN – e.g. Oyan.	AFOORA	AFOORA	n. i. (ABURU?)
ASSULA	ASSULA	ASSINARA	ASUNORA; vill. in Ibadan Div., 33 miles north of Aiyetoro.

Table 12 – continued

1 Clapperton 1825/6	2 Lander, 1825	3 Lander, 1829	4 Reconstrued
ITALLIA vill.			n. i.
ASSOUDO walled town. Popn. c. 10,000	ASSOUDO 'first walled town' – but cf. Liabo.	ACCODOO	n. i.
	TEDI Village	ETUDY	nr. TUDI Hill?
CHOCHO	CHOKO	CHOUGHOU	P. Allison reports ruins of walled town at foot of Tudi Hill.

Column 1 in Table 12 lists the names of settlements passed through on Clapperton's expedition (December 1825 to January 1826) as they appear in Clapperton's journal;[62] column 2 the names in Lander's notes of the same journey;[63] column 3 John Lander's record of the second expedition;[64] and column 4 the present Yoruba forms for these names, according to my investigations.

Thence both expeditions went by way of Irawo, Saki, and Kisi to Old Oyo. Richard Lander, returning from Sokoto as sole survivor of Clapperton's expedition, gives no new information (he left Old Oyo 22 October 1826, arrived 'Engwa' 8 November, 'Tschow' on the 10th, Ijanna on the 11th and Badgari on the 21st – where he was obliged to undergo a poison ordeal through jealousy of the Portuguese slavers there). From Ipokia, the southern limit of the Alafin's territory, it will be noticed that a route could easily lead south-west to Porto Novo. Traffic from either Badagri or the ports south of Dahomey, therefore, could with equal convenience pass along the same roads from Ipokia to Old Oyo. The Landers noted the many toll stations:

Turnpikes are as common from Badagri to this place [Bidgie, that is, Igbeji, at the Yewa crossing] as on any public road in England. Instead of horses, carriages, &c, people carrying loads are taxed, but as we are under the protection of the Government, no duty has been exacted on any of our things.[65]

Just north of Ipokia, a village still exists at the site of one of these 'turnpikes' (Bode-Ase – *bode* is the Yoruba for gate). The tradition is that the toll-stations were set up by the Alafin, whose agents transmitted the tolls to him; the local inhabitants benefited from increased activities in the local markets.

Not only did the local rulers not receive an income from the tolls, they furthermore paid tribute at the annual *bere* festival in Oyo. Traditions relate that at first they paid it themselves, led by the Olu of Ilaro as the most prominent Egbado king[66] (the pre-eminence of the Olu of Ilaro was denied only in Ilobi, a town south-west of Ilaro, but when I was in the area there was a lively political interest involved); later the tribute was collected by the Onisare of Ijanna, the Alafin's representative.

We have, therefore, a closely administered tract of territory from Ipokia through the Egbado towns and thence to Saki and Igboho forming the corridor along which trade flowed to Old Oyo – and through which Clapperton and the Landers travelled. We have already had some indication that the trade route had moved eastwards in the second half of the eighteenth century. We shall now examine further evidence leading to the conclusion that this realignment can only have taken place late in the century, though the process of colonizing the area may have begun a few decades earlier.

All the Egbado towns, with three exceptions, claimed to have been founded from Old Oyo. These three towns, Iboro, Ibara and Ilewa, are in the north-east of Egbado tribal territory. Their traditions[67] relate that they were founded from Ife, not from Oyo. Their ancestors, it is said, migrated from Ife with the Ketu, from whom they separated only after journeying into the land that later became Ketu tribal territory. Their legends of origin, that is to say are the same as those of the Egba, though it is denied in Iboro that they are the same people as the Egba. T. S. Adewale, a member of one of the royal lineages of Ilaro, who has made some inquiries into Egbado history, cites 'an unpublished *History of Ijanna* dictated by Salu Balogun Ijanna in 1932, which is among the records of the District Office at Ilaro'.[68] According to Adewale:

Salu Balogun stated that originally Ijanna was merely a Ketu farm-village and only became important when settled by Adegbiyi, Balogun, and his war-boys from Oyo-Oro (Old Oyo). Adegbiyi, he says was descended from a previous owner of the land. This is not surprising, as the Egbado settlements were on sparsely-utilised Ketu land, and there was always a close connection between the Egbado settlers and their relatives at home. Salu says that Adegbiyi and his army soon obtained the submission of all the other Egbado towns, and that he and the Onishare Akuko Oba Ijanna [that is, The Onisare the first king of Ijanna] created the great rampart and ditch which surrounded the old town of Ijanna, and which can still be seen a couple of miles north of the present village.

The legends of most other Egbado towns state that they were either settled from Old Oyo, or from towns in Oyo territory subordinate to the Alafin, or else are offshoots of other Egbado towns, themselves founded from Oyo. As in the version of the Ijanna legend given to me, they typically assert that the sites were first settled by a hunter who penetrated from Oyo country and that subsequently the communities were created kingdoms by the Alafin. The crown was bestowed usually not upon the hunter but on another man, a son of an Alafin, most frequently of Alafin Abiodun, the son having accompanied, or soon joined, the hunter. The traditions all give the impression that the land was previously uninhabited; nevertheless, Adewale's belief 'that the Egbado settlements were on sparsely-utilised Ketu land' is indeed plausible, especially when considered together with the assertion of Iboro, Ibara and Ilewo that their founding ancestors had travelled with the Ketu people from Ife.

The question arises, in passing, of why this area was 'sparsely utilised'. That it was not densely inhabited is made the more likely by the fact that all the heads of compounds whom I interviewed in the Egbado towns of Ilaro, Ijanna and Jiga, and informants in other Egbado settlements as well, asserted that their ancestors came from Old Oyo, or from its territory. The land further eastwards may have been just as lightly populated, at least as far as the west bank of the River Ogun, if not as far as the present limits of Ijebu territory. Both the Awori, now in the neighbourhood of Otta (and further south), and the Egba, appear, on the basis of their own and Oyo legends, to have occupied land much to the north of their present territory. The territory of the Egba, according to Biobaku,[69] was formerly in the area between New Oyo, or a few miles south of it, and a line running east-west from Ibadan to Abeokuta, Abeokuta having been founded in the extreme south-west of their land. The Owu, who have been merged with the Egba since the early nineteenth century, were between the Egba (to their west) and the Ife (to their east), with the Ijebu to their south. The first phase of the southwards thrust of the Egba, which perhaps displaced the Awori, cannot have been earlier than the populating of Egbadoland.

Since Egbadoland is a fertile area on the fringe of the rain forest, not naturally forbidding, the only reasonable conclusion to be drawn from all this evidence is that the area was lightly populated for the same reason that the once densely populated northern and western Oyo territory is almost a wilderness today – the former population had been captured or driven out in slaving wars, in which the agressors might have been Oyo but perhaps more probably Ijebu, the Benin colonies, and the Ewe-speaking states.

Ijebu (Ciudad da Jaboo) is shown on seventeenth century maps (Yoruba traditions place its founding in the same era as Ketu and Oyo) and may have been in contact with the Portuguese through Lagos, and before Lagos was founded, through 'Caran' (Isherin?), a port shown on the mouth of the Rio Lagos.[70] Phillips,[71] who was at Ouidah in 1694,

The Atlantic trade, 1670–1830 183

describes vividly the widely ranging slave raids of the coastal kingdoms of that period, indicating, therefore, that much of the depopulating of the land (that was later to become Egbado and Awori territories) may have taken place in the seventeenth century. If it continued into the first half of the eighteenth, then the traffic in slaves taken from this area may have been another factor to add to that of the rapacity of Dahomey in accounting for the rise of Badagri to prominence as a slave port.

Accepting the traditions that some of the Egbado towns were founded by sons of Alafin Abiodun, who was beyond reasonable doubt the Alafin described by Dalzel, and the traditions that some other towns were founded by sons of his successor Aole (sometimes written Awole), the last Alafin to have a grip on Dahomey and Porto Novo, we cannot date this colonization to any period other than about 1760 to 1800. According to tradition, Aole did not reign long (seven years, according to Johnson),[72] and it was during his reign that Afonja became Kakanfo at Ilorin – Afonja was the man who later opened the way for the Fulani conquest of Ilorin and Oyo.

The argument so far may be summarized. Oyo had become engaged in the Atlantic slave trade before 1670. It has been argued that the earliest trade routes from Old Oyo to the coast passing through Allada to Ouidah, lay through Sa and Ketu territory and then through the Fon-speaking areas, to the west of the Kumi Swamps. At about the end of the seventeenth century, a route was organized through Ifonyin (Anago) kingdoms south of Ketu territory, these kingdoms then being ruled by vassals of the Alafin. In the eighteenth century, trade was mainly through the ports south of Little Ardra (Assem) the southern neighbour of the Ifonyin. Allada had been absorbed (1724) into the territories of the rising kingdom of Dahomey, itself intermittently tributary to Oyo. The land eastwards of the Ifonyin was lightly populated, having perhaps been depopulated in slave wars conducted by the coastal kingdoms, including the Benin colonies, and also perhaps by raiding parties dispatched by the Alafin himself. Late in the eighteenth century, Alafin Abiodun, in whose reign the power of Oyo reached its greatest extent, founded a chain of kingdoms in what is now Egbado territory. These Egbado states were ruled over, and probably mostly inhabited, by colonists from the Oyo territories to the north. Trade was now rerouted through these kingdoms, which were permitted less autonomy than the Anago kingdoms had been; and the new trade route, which led to Badagri as well as Porto Novo, was more rigorously controlled by the Alafin.

Some question still remains about the Alafin's motives in moving the trade route eastwards again. It may be taken for granted that a strong and prosperous state will be likely, sooner or later, to repopulate an area as fertile as the Egbado; but it has been established that the repopulation is linked with a displacement eastwards of the highway to Oyo, away from the still prosperous Anago territory. It might, of course, have been a move purely to benefit the new settlers, who were ruled by descendants of the royal lineage of Oyo, and at the same time to facilitate some control by the central government and perhaps increase revenues from tolls; but the principle of economy in explanation does not apply to history and there are other possibilities to explore. In spite of Abiodun's grip on the south-west, the pattern of life of the frontier (and perhaps inland) was warfare and raiding.[73] Even Abiodun might have been apprehensive about the safety of his south-western frontier. He could have felt uncertain that he would always be able to rely on the stupidity of the king of Dahomey. Tradition narrates that he stationed near Porto Novo his Kakanfo (the Oyo war-lord of highest rank) Oyabi, a man still of legendary fame, to make periodic raids on the Weme Valley and on the coast. It is possible that Abiodun sent Oyabi at the time when he decided to move his channel of communications eastwards. It must be remembered, too, that it was not only important to the Oyo to keep their frontiers secure against their most powerful neighbours; they needed also (cf. the passages quoted above) to engage in warfare for slaves. Slaves were needed not only to exchange for European goods but also as porters and labourers, and as craftsmen.

In short, the Egbado tribal territory was colonized at the desire of the Alafin at a time when Dahomey was growing more powerful, the Atlantic slave trade was still at its height, and some distance was advisable between Dahomey and the road to Oyo.

The presumption is, then, that during a period that may have been as brief as twenty years but was perhaps twice that, a set of young kingdoms flourished on or near the new trade route, independent of one another but all vassals of the parent state, Old Oyo. Economic considerations (whether in relation to geography, or to social factors such as kinship links to successful men) no doubt led to some towns, among them Ilaro, being favoured by the southward moving population settling the newly colonized land. Then, whatever the stimulus was – the attempt, perhaps, of Ilaro to dominate its neighbours, or of many of the kings to enrich themselves at the expense of travellers and of the Alafin's dues, or merely dilatoriness in the transmission of tolls and tribute – about 1820 the Alafin strengthened his hold on the area by placing a political agent, one of his *ilari* (a high grade of titled slaves) in the town of Ijanna, four miles from Ilaro. The agent, with the title Onisare ('One with the work of envoy'), was given many royal prerogatives and rated

The Atlantic trade, 1670–1830 185

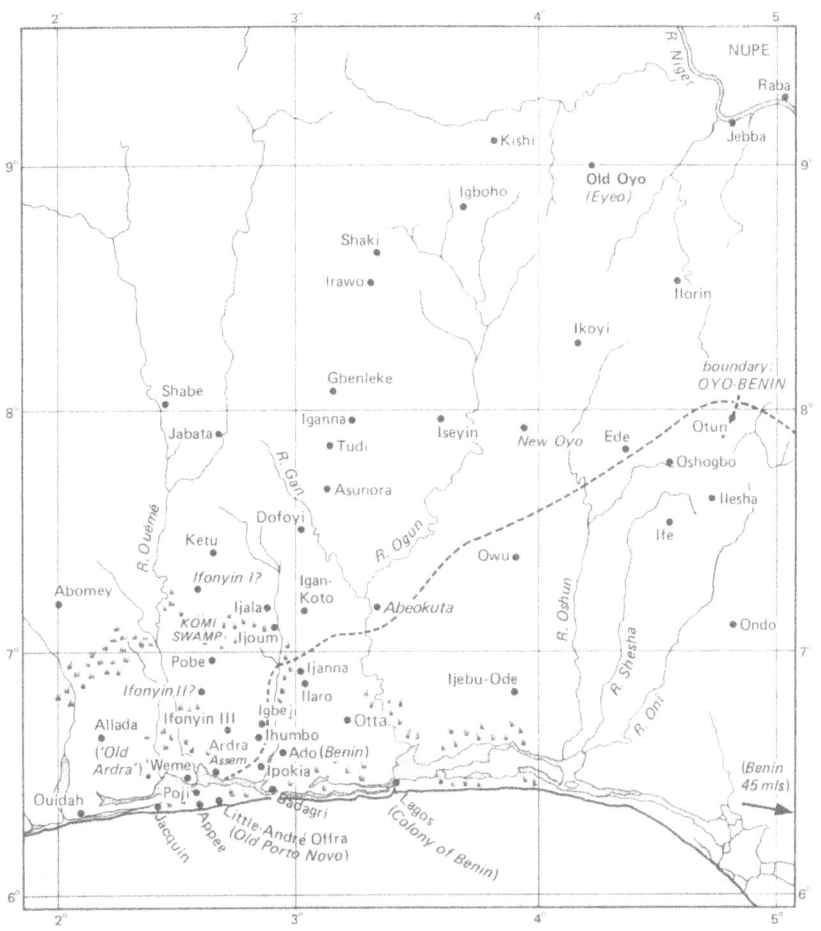

---------- approximate inland limit of coastal forest

Note: the direction of the frontier between Oyo and Benin at Otun is not known.

0   100
            miles

The main towns between Old Oyo and the Atlantic ports before 1830 locally as the equal in rank of the Olu (king) of Ilaro.[74] A tradition current in Ilaro and Ijanna[75] states that the two rulers met once a year on a hill-top marking the boundary between their territories; but, since kings might not come face to face with each other, they sat back to back.[76] The Onisare was also made one of the few exalted *abobaku* ('One dying with the king') – that is, he was obliged to kill himself at the news of the death of the Alafin.[77]

The vassal kings no longer had direct access to the Alafin; the Onisare at Ijanna was the Alafin's representative in their midst, his officials collected the tolls (eunuchs seem to have been assigned this work), he led the procession to the New Year celebrations in Oyo, and my impression is that he alone had any cavalrymen at his command, or indeed, any regular forces at all. Yet as a slave, of non-Yoruba origin (the three successive Onisare were of Hausa or Nupe stock), and *abobaku*, keeping a numerous court (cf. the accounts of Clapperton and the Landers) that probably included other servants of the Alafin,[78] the Onisare's authority was as dependent as possible upon the Alafin's sanction. We can see how effectively they held the country when it is remembered that neither Clapperton's expedition nor the two Landers could leave Badagry and enter the Alafin's dominions without the permission of the Onisare. Once that was given (presupposing the Alafin's approval), they were able to move quickly and safely, exempted from paying tolls.[79]

These efficient arrangements endured only for a few years, perhaps only for a few months, after Richard Lander's last visit to Oyo in 1830; the power of Oyo was quickly broken by the consequences of intrigues with Fulani of, first, Afonja and, later, Atiba, the future first Alafin of New Oyo. The Egba from their new metropolis of Abeokuta and also the Dahomeans overran the Egbado-Ifonyin trade corridor, destroying these south-western Yoruba settlements and killing, enslaving or scattering their inhabitants, so that by 1880 the area was becoming lightly populated as it had been a century or so earlier; and Oyo was cut off from the Atlantic more effectually than at any time since the beginning of the trading era.

7 Effects of the Atlantic slave trade on some West African societies
Albert van Dantzig

Editor's comments

One common feature in the literature on the impact of the export slave trade on African societies is the concentration of studies, at the micro level, on powerful states that captured and sold prisoners-of-war, such as Benin, Oyo, Dahomey, Ashanti, etc., and those that traded in slaves with the Europeans on the coast, such as Calabar, Bonny, etc. At the macro level of analysis, generalizations are often made for all Africa on the basis of such micro studies. This has helped to obscure the retardative effects of the export slave trade for African economic development. In the present chapter Albert van Dantzig distinguishes three types of African societies which the export slave trade affected: societies that were mainly the object of slave raids (by far the largest group); societies that were mainly engaged in the practice of capturing captives for sale; societies that were mainly engaged in the buying and selling of slaves. This is an important distinction which makes possible a more satisfactory macro analysis of the impact of the export slave trade on Black Africa as a whole. The paper is centred on the Gold Coast and the 'slave coast'. The author provides some detailed account of political developments connected with the operation of the slave trade in different parts of these two regions.

The Atlantic slave trade has for a long time been the object of elaborate studies and academic controversies. One of the last of these controversies is based on what is sometimes labelled 'the numbers game', the use of available trade figures in an attempt to work out the sum total of the number of Africans shipped as slaves across the Atlantic. Philip Curtin has become the outstanding protagonist for a

This paper was first published in *Revue française d'histoire d' outre-mer*, Tome LXII nos. 226–7 (1975), pp. 252–69. It has been reprinted here by permission of the author and the publishers.

scientific analysis and computerized processing of these figures, and his *The Atlantic Slave Trade*[1] has become a standard work on that subject. Whilst Curtin tries to get to the truth of the total number of slaves transported on ships of all nations, others, like Johannes Postma, have made elaborate studies on the participation of an individual nation in that trade.[2] These studies are generally limited to the subject of the 'middle passage', the voyage between the African ports of trade and the slaves' destination in the Americas. Only rather superficial attempts have so far been made to apply these data to Africa, and insofar as such attempts were made they have led to new controversies, in particular about the extent of the negative effect of the Atlantic slave trade on African society.

It is not so much my intention to discuss in this paper the merits or demerits of these studies, as to suggest a more differentiated approach to the subject and to gather out of the discussion new information and suggestions.

Not only has the Atlantic slave trade had different effects on different areas of Africa, within those areas themselves this trade has affected various groups of people in different ways. Even the suggested subject of this paper is a very wide one, and I want to limit the present discussion to the 'Gold Coast' and the 'slave coast' in the late seventeenth and early eighteenth centuries. Even then it remains a subject which can of course not be exhaustively treated in the framework of a simple seminar paper. The greatest problem is that of the unevenness of available evidence: whilst there is a great fund of archival and secondary material on some restricted coastal areas, there is hardly anything, documentary or not, on those areas from which the majority of the slaves sold to the Europeans are generally believed to have been taken; yet, it is in those areas that one may presume that the effects of the trade were (and to some extent still are) most severely felt. Among the peoples affected by the Atlantic slave trade we may distinguish three main groups:

(a) Societies which were mainly the object of slave raids, or 'slave producing' societies, which are generally found in the distant interior, but occasionally also near to the coast;

(b) Societies which were mainly engaged in the practice of capturing slaves in order to supply the markets, not only those on the coast but also those of the interior;

(c) Societies which were mainly engaged in the sale of slaves, either in the function of middle men or of retailers who sold straight to the Europeans.

Although none of these groups could be regarded as a uniform unit – we may find groups of slave raiders and merchants in those societies which were generally the object of raids, whilst on the other hand many members of the coastal slave selling societies fell themselves victim to slavery and transportation – we may assume that the first, and doubtlessly the largest group, was most negatively affected, whilst the two other groups made at least material gains.[3]

If geographically speaking the above mentioned groups could be found in belts parallel to the coast, one may also recognize, at least in the early eighteenth century, a 'vertical' division:
(1) to the west of Elmina an area where slaves were occasionally sold, but where the mainstay of the trade was in other products, particularly gold;
(2) between Elmina and the mouth of the Volta an area of a 'mixed economy' in which the slave trade took ever growing importance and sometimes even replaced the gold trade;
(3) east of the Volta the real slave coast where slaves constituted the mainstay of the trade with Europeans, but which exported also other commodities like palm oil, cotton cloth and ivory. It is however interesting to note that in matters of currency the middle area remained faithful to the old gold currency, although occasionally Europeans expressed their fear that it might join the cowrie zone of the slave coast.[4]

There is little doubt that slavery and slave trade existed in West Africa, as in most other parts of the world, before the fifteenth century, and that much earlier slaves were already transported far from their place of origin, for instance in caravans going across the Sahara. There is also the well known story that the Portuguese in the early sixteenth century bought slaves in Benin in order to sell them on the Gold Coast, where rich gold traders from the interior needed carriers for the goods they bought with their gold from the Portuguese.[5] The Portuguese, in the sixteenth and seventeenth centuries carried on a considerable slave trade to supply the Spanish asiento and their own fast growing sugar plantations in Brazil; but their reliance on the Gold Coast for this purpose was minimal, as they quickly realized that the purchase of slaves, mostly war-captives, would encourage warfare, which would negatively affect the gold trade. The Dutch attack on Elmina, in 1637, was launched by John Maurice of Nassau from Brazil, where he needed slaves for the sugar planters then under Dutch authority. But the attack on Elmina was made because it was the Portuguese headquarters in Africa, not because it was a centre for the supply of slaves; as a result of the fall of Elmina the main slave-supplying area for the Brazilian plantations, Angola, fell into Dutch hands three years afterwards. It is significant to note that in 1646 Elmina Castle could not even house a number of forty slaves as was requested by a captain who, contrary to usage, had gone to 'Ardra' before passing Elmina; the Commander of the castle had to ask him not to land the slaves before some barracoons had been set up outside the castle.[6]

There is not much known about the early Portuguese activities on the slave coast, but their trade on that coast was probably less important than that in the Congo-Angola area. With the spread of the technique of sugar planting and processing into the British, Dutch and French West Indian colonies, in the 1640s, trade on the slave coast steadily increased, and soon we find British, Dutch and French, later also Portuguese and Brandenburg factories in Popo, Ardra and Whydah. In the last quarter of the seventeenth century there was a kind of boom in the slave trade on the Guinea Coast, and the Gold Coast was no longer excluded from slave-trading activities. The turn of the century was also a period of immense political change in the area, and although the influence of the rise in the demand for slaves on these changes is another matter of controversy among historians, we may assume that these changes did not occur entirely in isolation of this boom.

The sudden increase in the demand for slaves cannot but have brought about considerable changes in the economic, social and therefore political structures of society. As it is rightly pointed out by Hopkins,[7] 'there was no servile class simply waiting to be shipped'. Yet, by the end of the seventeenth century a place like Whydah was estimated to be able to 'produce' over 1000 slaves per month.[8] I do not think that it would be correct to regard the rise of Ashanti as the direct result of the increased demand for slaves, but it could be argued that it has much to do with the suddenly increased supply of firearms on the Gold Coast, which in its turn was justified in European eyes because of the decline in the supply of gold and the increase of that of slaves. At the same time we see east of Cape Coast a growing concentration of power in a few states, especially those with a big stake in the slave trade: Fanti, Akwamu and Whydah. Fanti and Akwamu had risen as gold-trading rather than gold-producing states, and had the aggressiveness of middle men eager to control the market.

By 1700 Akwamu was ruled by 'upper-king' Basua and 'under-king' Ado; the former favoured expansion into the interior to get control of the gold-mining areas of Akim, whilst the latter preferred eastward expansion along the coast to turn the state into a major slave-trading power. Under Ado's successors the latter policy was pursued with vigour, and soon Akwamu influence was felt beyond the Volta, up to Whydah.[9] A settlement of Ga refugees who had migrated in several groups to Little Popo after each Akwamu attack on Accra, had by 1700 become an aggressive power in its own right, actively engaging in the slave trade and offering its mercenary services to the highest bidder.

The rise of the Whydah kingdom is even more striking; when Henry Caerlof, then in the service of the French Guinea Company, established in 1671 his factory 'Pillau' in the Houeda kingdom, that state was hardly known and thought to be part of the Allada kingdom. Caerlof built his factory at Gléhoué, a hamlet which within a quarter of a century was to grow into the greatest slave port of the Guinea Coast. By 1700 Whydah had submitted the Pla state to the west and reduced the formerly much more powerful kingdom of Allada to the position of a middle man in the slave trade. Allada got its slaves chiefly from Oyo, but may also have engaged in slave raiding itself. Bosman noted that at the time that he was in Whydah (1698) ambassadors from a powerful inland state had come to convey to the king of Allada the message that many 'Ardrasian Negroes' were coming to their master's court complaining about the 'tyrannical rule of Ardra', and that he would feel compelled to take them under his protection if the king of Allada did not censure his viceroys. The ruler of Allada had these ambassadors however killed, and consequently his country was invaded by a huge army on horseback, which caused a 'horrible massacre'.[10] Bosman noted elsewhere that Allada 'with its subject states' was at least twenty times as big and powerful as Whydah, which cannot but signify that in Bosman's time Dahomey was still regarded as a subject state of Allada. The inland kingdom with a cavalry must be Oyo. The passage could be interpreted in this sense: Allada, which by that time functioned mainly as a middle man between slave-raiding Oyo and slave-selling Whydah, at times of shortages in the supply of slaves resorted itself to slave raiding expeditions into neighbouring states like Weme and Dahomey. These states which have a tradition of having emerged from the Allada state in the early seventeenth century and could be regarded as 'sons' of Allada, appealed to a power more senior than Allada, Oyo, for protection.[11]

Allada's decline had set in during the last quarter of the seventeenth century, when it was no longer able to control even the king's 'fidalgo' or viceroy at its port of trade, Offra, which was soon abandoned by the European traders who began to prefer the relative safety and well regulated trade at Whydah. In 1682 the English extended their activities from Offra to Whydah, in spite of the strong objections of the fidalgo who tried to keep them at Offra. Their first factor at Whydah, John Winder, was *panyarred* (*panyar* – seize a person or his next of kin on account of a claim) for not having 'studied ye humour and dispositions of these people whoe will neither be slighted by a high and lofty carridge or abused by bad language, in both of which hee gave too much liberty to his selfe'.[12] Another factor, Arthur Windover, decided to try his luck farther east at Appa, where he got without much trouble 'a great many slaves, some coming by land, others by sea'. This Appa, he reported, was situated about thirty to forty leagues to the east of Whydah. The 'Phidalgoe', whom he supplied at once with a St George's flag, had his residence at a town 3 miles from the coast, a town 'incompassed around with water', near 'a very famous river yt goes to Beneen', and it was also 'ye chiefest place for slaves . . . from where ye people of Guidah and Ophra are furnisht'. The fidalgo is described as 'a very good man . . . and ye trade is wholly with him and noe men elce, hee takeing charge of all, so ye trouble is but small'. Shortly after his arrival at Appa Windover had 'two devious fitts of sickness', but the fidalgo offered his personal services as a successful physician, making him take every day one medicine or another.[13] It is interesting to note that this ruler, like those of Allada and Whydah, had full control of the slave trade. Appa got its slaves not only by land, but also by sea; this may be an indication that Benin, which refused to sell slaves directly to the Europeans, did sell slaves to African middle men. Yet, in spite of the disarming friendliness of the fidalgo and the apparent advantages of the trade at Appa, the English continued, like most other European traders, to concentrate their commercial activities on Whydah.

In 1689 the Dutch factor at Offra, Van Hoolwerff, was assassinated, and the Dutch West India Company (WIC) could not get satisfaction from the king of Allada who had to cope with a civil war.[14] The fidalgo of Offra seems to have made an alliance with Whydah and his insubordination caused the first of a series of wars between Allada and Whydah in which both states relied on mercenary armies from Akwamu, Little Popo and Keta. Bosman expressed some surprise at this habit of relying on mercenaries, as he estimated that Whydah could for instance easily mobilize 200,000 men; he offers a rather unsatisfactory explanation of the inability or unwillingness of Whydah and Allada to rely on their own armed forces: their cowardice and lack of military leadership. He noted that very few firearms were to be seen at Whydah, and that the most common and effective weapon there was a heavy $1\frac{1}{2}$ yard wooden club, which, if thrown with force and precision, could disable any enemy.[15] The Whydah kingdom was relatively small, but very densely populated. Bosman admired the flat, intensely cultivated countryside which must have reminded him of home. Government was highly centralized under a monarch with absolute powers; yet the person of the king seems not to have mattered so much, and European traders were even allowed to interfere with his appointment. But everyone in Whydah, indigenous as well as foreign, was totally subjected to the will of the king. In Bosman's time the European traders were even kept under such strict control of the monarch, that they were only allowed to establish their factories within the premises of the royal palace at Savi. In 1703 the king was even in a position to enforce on the French, Dutch and English a peaceful co-existence, in spite of the war they were then having 'in the Christian Empire'.[16] Before they could proceed with the purchase of the bulk of their slaves, the European traders were compelled to buy first a number of the king's slaves at an inflated price. All prices were fixed by the king. Although most of the slaves sold at Whydah were captives supplied by 'middle man' Allada, Whydah society was organized in such a way that it could supply a considerable number of 'criminals' as slaves, if need be. All sorts of misdemeanours were punishable by slavery and transportation. King and aristocracy had taken to an extreme form of polygamy, which must have left a large section of the male population without wives. Although there was a form of organized state prostitution, the least suspicion of adultery, in particular with one of the many wives of king or elders, could be punished with sale into slavery.

There is very little known about the early history of the Houeda state. The population traces its origin, like that of Allada, from Adja-Tado, but it is believed to have constituted an independent state in the early sixteenth century, probably before the Allada kingdom was founded, and of which it was probably not a tributary, as several seventeenth and eighteenth century authors assumed. Although the first transactions between Houedas and Europeans are said to have taken place in the 1580s,[17] European factories were only established there after those in Popo and Allada. Could it be that the great density of population of Whydah and the absolute monarchy were a reaction of the local population to the slave raiding activities of Allada and Popo? The soil of the Whydah area is not known to be more fertile than that of neighbouring areas. Another indication may be that Grand Popo, after it was conquered by Whydah in the late seventeenth century, ceased for a long time to be a slave port. To the new centralistic monarchy, which as a result of booming trade had plenty of capital to spend, the maintenance of a standing army may not have been felt and even have been considered a danger to the unity of the state, and the occasional use of mercenaries a safer bet. The same may have applied to Allada. In 1724 to 28 Allada and Whydah paid however dearly for this policy: Allada was unable to drive out the Dahomeans who had been invited to settle a succession dispute, and Whydah, counting on mercenary help from Akwamu which was not forthcoming, was quickly overrun by the militant Dahomeans.

Akwamu, at that time, was in a state of confusion and decline. Wilks has pointed out that the slave capturing policy of the Akwamuhene with his royal prostitutes and 'siccadingers' (slave hunters) within his own empire was one of the main causes of the revolts which took place during the reign of Ansah Kwao, and which in the end weakened the empire so much that it virtually eclipsed.[18] Whether Ashanti and Dahomey 'learnt their lesson' from the experience of Akwamu is difficult to say, but certain is, that both had a fixed rule that no true subjects of their kings could be sold as slaves for export.

Dahomey, of course, became after the conquest of Allada and Whydah West Africa's slave-trading power *par excellence*. Yet, there are several indications that King Agadja's conquest of the coastal states was not so much inspired by a desire to trade directly with the Europeans in that 'commodity' of which the slave coast derived its name, as rather by the need to defend his kingdom. Just before the conquest the slave trade at Whydah and Jaquin (the new port of trade of Allada) was brisker than ever. But Akwamu, which had been an important slave supplier to Whydah,[19] was at that time in turmoil on account of the way in which these slaves were acquired, so that there must have been a marked decline in the supply from that side. Allada and Whydah had again to rely entirely on their old Oyo suppliers, and may have resorted to slave-raiding expeditions into the immediate interior themselves; the victim of these raids must have been Dahomey[20] which by that time had extended its authority already South of the Abomey plateau.[21] Reference is often made to a letter by the English factor, Bulfinch Lambe, who spent some time as prisoner of Agadja at Abomey, from which it appears that Agadja suggested that the Europeans would do better by starting plantations in Dahomey – for which he would supply the labour – rather than continuing to bring all their slaves to the other side of the ocean.[22]

Immediately after the Dahomean invasion of Whydah, Oyo nearly destroyed the Dahomey kingdom in a series of savage attacks, during which Agadja – like Frederick II during the Seven Years War did in Prussia – left his capital to the mercy of his enemies, tenaciously holding on to his new conquests; he knew that Oyo relied on them for the export of its captives. For eight years a lonely Dutch factor, Hertogh, fought a losing battle against Agadja, moving from Jaquin (where he supported the fidalgo's rebellion against the conqueror) to Ekpe, and eventually to Badagri in an attempt to monopolize the purchase of Oyo slaves, but in 1738 Agadja caught up with him and had him murdered.[23] By that time Dahomey had negotiated a truce with Oyo, by which it obliged itself to pay the latter an annual tribute, implicitly recognizing it as its superior; it also meant that Dahomey would continue to sell the bulk of Oyo captives to the Europeans at Whydah.

Much has been written about the social structure and the economic system of the Dahomey kingdom after the conquest. Much of the Dahomean civilization was borrowed from neighbouring civilizations: the centralistic system of government and economy and much of its religion from Whydah, the system of the 'annual slave wars' from Oyo,[24] etc. In the Spartan Dahomean state there was no room for personal profit; most of the captives were used to cultivate the ubiquitous royal farms, which in their turn fed the huge army and court; many slaves were every year killed as human sacrifices (which, in the late eighteenth century would be used by the defenders of the slave trade as an argument for continuing it, as if the kings of Dahomey only sacrificed those slaves whom he did not manage to sell) and a large number, but probably not the majority, was sold on the coast.

Little or nothing can be said with certainty about the peoples who were the victims of these annual slave raids. One area which is sometimes mentioned in this connection, is Mahi, to the north-west of the Abomey plateau; but the same state is also sometimes mentioned as a mercenary in the service of Dahomey. At present one finds signs of natural or man-made defence works around Mahi villages, but the area is relatively densely populated, especially when compared to the area to the north and east of it, which forms part of the great 'empty belt' running through the sub-sahelian zones of Ghana, Togo, Dahomey and Nigeria, and which is often said to have constituted the main slave-raiding area of West Africa. In some regions much nearer to the coast, however, we also find large stretches of empty land and other signs of regular slave raiding; there are the wide open spaces of virtually empty land in south-eastern Ghana and south-western Togo which are by no means infertile, but from which people probably have fled, either to the coastal towns or to the safety of the hills, which are quite densely populated. Much of Yoruba land has remained densely populated, but there many towns and villages are surrounded by defence works, sometimes consisting of not less than three concentric walls and moats.[25]

At first sight it may seem somewhat surprising that powerful war-like states like Dahomey and Oyo were no great customers for firearms; Dahomey only bought them in limited numbers, and Oyo did not introduce firearms until the nineteenth century.[26] Both Ashanti and Dahomey strictly controlled the export of firearms to the North, and only in the late eighteenth century allowed some of their most faithful client states (like Dagomba and Bariba) to use some,[27] probably in order to increase their capacity for supplying slaves to the coast. Firearms were important for regular strategic (political) warfare, but less for slave wars: the slave raiders used a large infantry or cavalry to surround villages by surprise, after which it was a matter of capturing as many inhabitants as possible, *alive*. Small slaving-states along the coast, on the other hand, were great buyers of firearms; as they did not have the large armies needed for raids as described above, they had to encourage regular wars, paying for the war-captives with firearms to the contending parties. A typical example of such a state is the Ga state of Little Popo; Anecho (or Little Popo) became one of the most important slave ports beyond the reach of Dahomey. Isert remarked in the late eighteenth century that the people there 'knew better how to use firearms than the stupid Krepis whose masters they became'.[28] The name 'Krepi' was applied to a wide variety of Ewe groups which never developed strong central political leadership and to which some of the slave-selling coastal states probably applied the principle of 'divide and rule' in order to assure themselves of a regular supply of captives. Little Popo seems from its inception to have had a military tradition, and was in the 1680s already able to supply Allada with a powerful mercenary army. In the 1730s a member of its royal clan, Ashangmo, had become one of the most able generals of Agadja; but he mutinied, and after having fled across the Volta before a pursuing Dahomean army, he routed that same army near Little Popo, overtaking it on its return,[29] and remained one of the great heroes of Popo history. Bosman noted that the traders of Little Popo were able to supply 200 slaves in three days' time, but that it was a matter of chance; sometimes one had to wait for months before the warriors returned with their prisoners. At that time the warriors of Little Popo apparently still went on slave raids themselves, but later Little Popo must have left warfare to others, limiting itself to the business of selling slaves. Westermann was told at Glidji, the 'inland capital' of Little Popo, that the slaves sold on the coast were brought from the interior to the markets at Togodo and Sagada on the Mono river, where they were bartered for salt, gunpowder, cloth and money. His informants also told him that most of the slaves they bought there were used to work on the fields of Little Popo, that buying slaves was 'just like putting your money in the bank, because when they get children it is like interest', and that the ones who were sold to whites were only 'unworthy people, thieves and highwaymen'.[30] Glidji seems to have been an important agricultural area: Isert called it 'the nursing mother of all the Popo villages, down to Whydah'. With its relatively small autochthonous population of traders and military men it may well have left much of the farming to slaves. It is not very likely that the traders only sold 'unworthy people' to the Europeans. The slave trade at Little Popo had a more occasional character than at the Dahomean ports of trade, but it was sufficiently organized to have a special chiefly family for the slave trade, the later highly Europeanized family of the Late or Lawsons, who at Little Popo must have fulfilled much the same function as the *Yevogan* at Whydah.

In many densely populated coastal areas bad harvests could lead to an increased offer of slaves for sale. Many instances of this phenomenon have been described, but in some areas, such as Calabar, slave-trading captains would even make it a rule to go there in August and September 'when slaves are cheap because yams are scarce', whilst in January and February they went there to load yams, which were then plentiful and cheap, leaving the slaves till the next year's famine.[31] One of the most neglected subjects in the well documented history of Ghana is that of the slave trade. Very little is really known about how it was carried on. We do know some trade figures; in most of the minor forts not more than a 50 to 100 slaves were bought per year. Even Cape Coast and Elmina Castle, which had dungeons which could contain several thousands of slaves, were slave entrepôts rather than slave markets. Only Anomabu is sometimes mentioned as a major slave port, and, in connection with the Fanti slave trade, the inland market of Manso, where Fanti middle men may have bought slaves from Ashanti, many of whom were paid as tribute by subject states. I assume that wars fought purely for the purpose of capturing slaves were rare in the south – perhaps more common north of Ashanti, particularly in the second half of the eighteenth century – and that most of the slaves sold on the Gold Coast were rather the 'by-product' of many wars between coastal states and states of the immediate interior, or criminals explicitly condemned to slavery and transportation. The European traders sometimes got into trouble about sending on board slave ships people who had been condemned or sold themselves into slavery on account of a debt. I think one could safely say that nowhere on the Gold Coast, at least west of Accra, was society ever organized specifically to serve the interests of slave traders. It is certain that the number of slaves sold on the Gold Coast was always far inferior to that of the much shorter stretch of slave coast.

On the African as well as on the European side the slave trade was a speculative and capital-intensive business. The Europeans on the coast met generally only the richest among the African slave dealers, the wholesalers.[32] But the value of one slave was always considerable, and a slave, unlike most other commodities offered for sale, could not be divided in smaller units; the slave trade often involved the granting of credit, and this applied to middle men as well as to those who sold to the ships. African slave dealers, whether they were traditional chiefs, like those on the slave coast, or private traders, developed an expensive taste for European luxury goods, in particular for silks, velvets and gold-embroidered cloth. One might say that the slave trade prevented or suppressed the development of an African industry of refined luxury goods; but there are various accounts of the existence, for instance, of an important cottage industry for the production of coarse cotton cloth on the slave coast. Some of this cloth was produced for export and bought by European traders who sold it again on other parts of the coast and even in the West Indies. In the densely populated lands around the main slave ports only a small section of the population was directly involved in the slave trade; those who were not engaged in agriculture had to find other occupations. On the Gold Coast the increase in the sale of slaves was accompanied by a diminished export of gold. Increased insecurity not only caused a decline in the gold trade, but probably also in the production of gold. As gold continued to be the Gold Coast's currency, and money buys safety, the Gold Coast became even a gold-importing area: there are for instance several cases known of the Dutch and English using Brazilian gold to buy slaves.

The coastal slave dealers, some of them mulattoes, were often highly Europeanized. Isert was much impressed by the palatial three-storeyed mansions of some rich slave dealers at Little Popo.[33] Even former slaves sometimes became quite successful in the slave trade: there is the example of 'Hannibal', the slave from Assini, who as a result of a misunderstanding was believed to be the heir to the stool of Assini and who was brought to France where he was greatly honoured by Louis XIV. After the truth had become known and his disgrace in Assini where he had returned,[34] he embarked on a French slave ship in the hope of returning to France. The captain of that ship abandoned him however at Keta, and about 15 years later a Dutch factor, travelling on land from Whydah to Accra met him there and described him as one of the richest and most successful members of the community.[35]

The former slave Johannes Eliza Capiteyn, although not a slave trader himself, would later in the eighteenth century as Reverend Minister in Holland write a passionate religious–philosophical tract to justify the slave trade. In the nineteenth century a whole community of former Brazilian slaves was actively engaged in most towns between Accra and Lagos in the slave trade, also after it had been declared illegal.

One aspect of the Atlantic slave trade to which very little attention has been paid is that of what one could term 'ancillary services': some places along the coast were great producers of maize, yam, beans, pepper, etc. specifically intended to feed the slaves during the middle passage. There was the class of the *bombas*, the supervisors of the barracoons or dungeons, sometimes slaves themselves, the canoe-men who had to bring the slaves from the beach to the ships on the roads. There was on the slave coast no indigenous seafaring population, and the Europeans always had to rely on Gold Coasters for this purpose. A large section of the Anecho community consists of descendants of these canoe-men, many of whom were Fantis, and one quarter of the town still goes by the name of Fantexome. Finally, at regular intervals the chartered companies bought slaves on the slave coast for maintenance work at the forts and castles ('castle slaves'), who became experienced craftsmen. Those who have written on the development of education in Ghana, have, as far as I know, paid little attention to the practical education which the training of these craftsmen must have involved; they mostly start with the story of Philip Quaque and the castle schools, but I should say that those who trained these castle slaves played a role at least as important as those who spread 'book knowledge', the more as most of these castle slaves were eventually freed, and are likely to have imparted their knowledge to other members for the coastal community. European attempts to make plantations on the Guinea Coast were invariably unsuccessful, but there were instances where expert slaves were brought from the West Indies to train Africans in such crafts as cotton ginning.[36]

Conclusions

Even having restricted myself to a limited area and period, I can only conclude that an enormous amount of research is still to be done before one can make some valid statements on 'the effects of the Atlantic slave trade on some West African societies', let alone on the whole of Africa. It is also very difficult to distinguish cause and effect in some cases. For instance: did Dahomey invade the coast and develop its particular system of government and economy because it was situated in an important slave-raiding area, or did it develop in the way it did with the purpose of extending its own slave trade?

At any rate, the often mentioned negative effects of the slave trade, such as depopulation, decay of agricultural and general civilization and general insecurity must have been felt chiefly in those areas which were regularly the object of slave raids. Depopulation was not only caused by the actual capture of thousands of people who were to be sold as slaves – mainly able-bodied young men and fewer women – but by the disruption of community life after a raid. Many villages must simply have ceased to exist after one or two of such attacks; if those who were not carried off as slaves were not killed on the spot, many of them would seek refuge for instance in nearby hills, where they might set up new communities. If village life was not entirely disrupted, the community had at least to face a serious labour shortage, and surrounding agricultural land tended to turn into bush, leaving a disproportionate population of either very old or very young people without sufficient food. The slave trade not only led to the depopulation of certain areas, it led also to the concentration of population in others; this made some observers make the misleading statement that the slave trade was often carried on in densely populated areas, and may therefore have had a palliative effect on over-population. It is true that people in those areas sometimes sold their private slaves or even themselves to the Europeans in order to provide food for their relatives, but in better agricultural years such families or communities would consequently be faced with labour shortages. The simple truth that it was better to sell than to be sold may have driven many people to the coast.

There seems to be little evidence for the existence of a real desire to stop the slave trade out of moral or political considerations, either among the Africans or among the Europeans in the period under consideration. Agadja's conquest of the coastal states is sometimes seen in this light, but if ever he thought along these lines, he seems to have changed his ideas very quickly; it seems more likely that under the pressure of contemporary Oyo attacks he could not afford to sell captives he badly needed for his own farms whilst the entire male Dahomean population was under arms. There is of course the case of Benin, which after a brief stint of slave trade with the Portuguese, prohibited the sale of slaves to the Europeans. The rulers of Benin may have realized at an early stage the dangers connected to a large-scale slave trade and accompanying importation of firearms for the preservation of national unity in a great coastal kingdom. The other example of a major coastal power, Akwamu, which did not have such a rule, shows how real such dangers were.

As soon as a state became predatory or engaged in the sale of slaves, its future seemed assured. By the time that the Abomey plateau became the object of intensive slave raiding, a sufficiently strong state, Dahomey, had already developed there to prevent political and social disruption; Dahomey's most effective weapon was extreme centralism and its ability to turn its defence mechanism into one of aggression. Most other areas which fell victim to slave raiders failed to pool their forces together, and there the people sought defence in isolation, often retreating into areas which offered natural defence. Mutual distrust and fear among these people, suspecting other communities of planning raids or individual 'panyarring' on their own people prevented political unification. These communities were in fact caught in a kind of vicious circle: because they were regularly submitted to slave raids, they were always short of labour, and preyed on their neighbours in order to make up for their loss. Because of their constant mutual distrust they did not unite, and therefore remained an easy prey to the slave raiders.

In the coastal, slave-selling societies, the trade led to a concentration of capital and power in the hands of a few chiefs and traders, and to a certain extent to specialization in certain crafts. There was a mixing of African, European, and later (South) American culture, but the intense contact with Europeans and the importation of European manufactures to some extent also destroyed a former authentic African civilization in those areas.

Summary

So far, little research has been done on the effect of the Atlantic slave trade on the social and political constitution of the African societies which were involved in that trade, whether as slave-selling or as slave-raiding communities, or as the objects of such raids. Still, we find concentrations of population near the former slave ports – it was better to sell than to be sold – or in areas where nature, for instance in the form of mountains, offered a kind of refuge or barricade against raids. We know least of those societies which formed the objects of slave raids: as a result of these raids and general insecurity, their lands remain thinly populated.

Concentrating on the Gold and slave coasts and their immediate interior, we may offer a few generalizations based on the considerable documentary evidence available for this area. The Gold Coast west of Elmina remained relatively unaffected by the slave trade, as that trade continued to have there a rather occasional character; but about the region east of the Volta, in particular, one could say that the trade became the central element in the development of social and political organization. As a result of the fast increase in the European demand for slaves by the end of the seventeenth century, Akwamu, on the eastern Gold Coast, emerged suddenly as a major empire, but a few decades later collapsed as rapidly, not having been able to adapt itself to the inherent dangers of slave-raiding and selling. Whydah, on the slave coast, acted for a short time successfully as a 'middle man' for Allada, but both were overrun by Dahomey. Dahomey may have learnt from the mistakes of others; it successfully turned its defence mechanism against Oyo and Allada raids into one of aggression, and prevented internal decay by an elaborate and highly centralized system of government.

8 The trade of Loango in the seventeenth and eighteenth centuries
Phyllis Martin

Editor's comments

One major question in the analysis of the impact of the export slave trade on African economies is the extent to which that trade prevented the growth of commodity trade between Africa and the rest of the world during the several centuries it lasted. In the present chapter Phyllis Martin describes in detail both the pre-European and the early trade of the Loango coast with Europeans in commodities such as copper, palm-cloth, skins, redwood, ivory and elephants' tails. The Vili people on the Loango coast obtained these products from the interior of West Central Africa and organized their sale both to African consumers and to the Europeans on the coast. The trade expanded from the first contact with the Portuguese in the 1570s to the middle decades of the seventeenth century. But from the 1630s, the Dutch switched from commodity trade to develop the slave trade on the Loango coast, in order to meet the labour needs of their newly acquired sugar territories in Brazil. By 1670, the Dutch West India Company was exporting 3,000 slaves annually from Loango. By this time, the French and the English had also come to boost European demand for slaves on the Loango coast. And so, the slave trade of Loango expanded from the 1670s. With the change in European demand, the Vili traders switched from the trade in commodities to the privately more profitable supply of slaves from the interior. The author's detailed account shows that the efforts of the Europeans took some time to yield large supplies of slaves from the Loango coast. This indicates that there were no large stocks of slaves in the possession of rulers in the Vili trading area waiting to be exported. On the contrary, it took some time for the political, social and economic organization of the area to be restructured for the regular supply of large quantities of slaves. As the slaves sold on the Loango coast came from

This paper was first published by Richard Gray and David Birmingham (eds.), *Pre-Colonial African Trade: Essays on Trade in Central and Eastern Africa before 1900* (London: Oxford University Press 1970), pp. 139–61. It has been reprinted here by permission of the author and the publishers.

far in the interior, Loango operated mainly as a slave-selling territory. This is reflected in the impact of the trade as shown by the author.

The Vili of Loango began their first regular trade with the Portuguese in the 1570s. Although Portuguese traders must have visited Loango before this time, they seem to have confined their main activities to the Kongo and Ndongo kingdoms, south of the Congo river. A regular trade was started between Loango and Luanda after the founding of the latter in 1576.[1] Portuguese ships sailed to the Loango coast with cargoes of European manufactured goods – cloths, rugs, mirrors, and beads. These the Vili exchanged for ivory, elephants' tails, palm-cloth, redwood, and skins.[2] These products, together with copper, remained the staple export of Loango in the first half of the seventeenth century.

Ivory, the most important Portuguese export from Loango, was sent first to Luanda and then to Europe. The trade in the high-quality Vili palm-cloth, redwood, and elephants' tails, was the result of African tastes. In order to obtain slaves from the Mbundu states east of Luanda, local trade goods as well as European products were necessary. Among African products the redwood of Mayumba and the cloth of Loango seem to have been in great demand.[3] Palm-cloth, in particular, was the means used by the Portuguese to pay their soldiers in inland forts such as Massangano; there the soldiers were able to exchange the cloths locally for food and supplies.[4] Every year two or three ships were sent from Luanda to Loango to fetch cargoes of 6–7000 pieces of palm-cloth.[5] The main source of supply for the trade in redwood was the two northern provinces of Loango, Sette-Cama and Mayumba. Redwood, called *tacula* by the Portuguese, was in great demand along the whole coast from Cape Saint Catherine to Benguela. For example, it could be exchanged in Ngoyo for palm-cloth, in the Congo river for ivory, or taken to Luanda and exchanged for slaves.[6]

An important extension of Loango's external trading contacts came with the arrival of the Dutch in the area in the closing years of the sixteenth century. In the first decade of the seventeenth century, they set up factories at Loango Bay and at Mayumba, the two principal ports of the kingdom. Dutch traders were also active in the kingdoms of Kakongo and Ngoyo, Loango's southern neighbours on the Atlantic coast north of the Congo river.[7] Whereas Portuguese trade in Loango remained secondary to their interests in Kongo and Angola, Loango became the centre for Dutch interests in West Central Africa.

The Dutch, like the Portuguese, participated in the local trade in palm-cloth and redwood, but their main trade in Loango was in ivory. Pieter van den Broecke, who made three visits to Loango between 1608

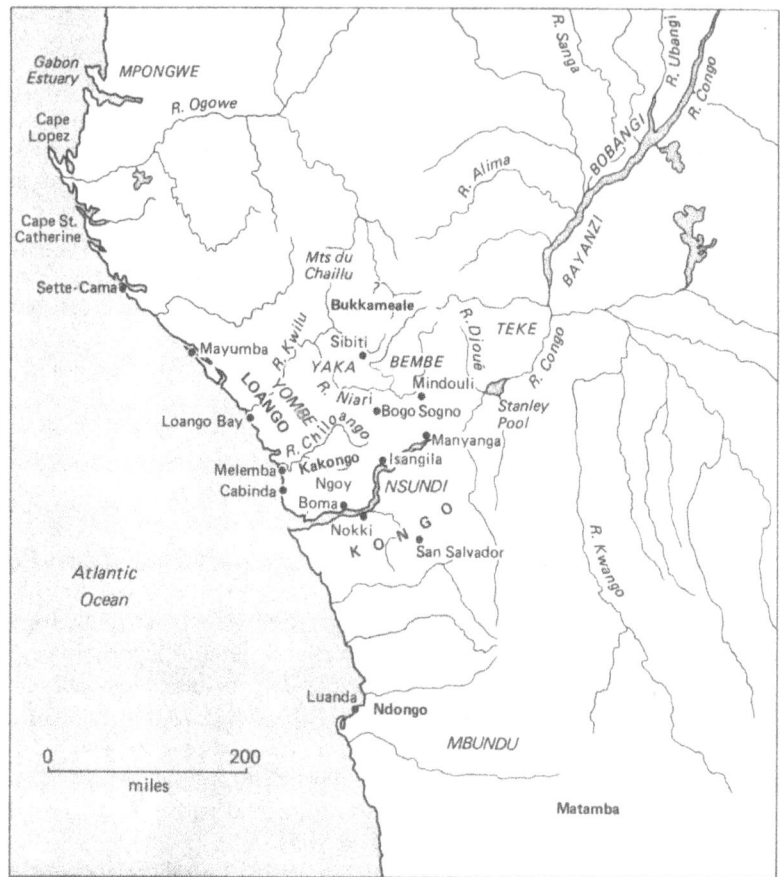

West Central Africa

and 1612, reckoned that during these years the Dutch alone were exporting 50,000 lbs of ivory annually. At the same time he was much impressed by the fine red copper that he saw in Loango,[8] although the Dutch do not seem to have discovered the commercial possibilities of exporting Loango copper to Europe until a decade later; by the 1620s copper had become one of Loango's main exports.[9]

These new trade contacts of Loango, starting with the Portuguese in the last decades of the sixteenth century and expanding with the Dutch in the first half of the seventeenth century, brought a great stimulus to the Vili economy. It seems, however, that the trade expansion brought an intensification of the existing trade activities of the Vili, rather than a completely new pattern of trade.

In the first place, Europeans were dealing in Loango products that were already part of traditional commerce and were in local circulation. Andrew Battell, writing towards the end of the sixteenth century, described the market of Buali, the Loango capital, as follows:

and there is a great market every day, and it doth begin at twelve of the clock. Here there is a great store of palm-cloths of sundry sorts, which is their merchandizes; and a great store of victuals, flesh, hens, wine, oil and corn. Here is also very fine logwood, which they use to dye withall . . . and molangos [bracelets] of copper. Here is likewise a great store of elephants' teeth, but they sell none in the market place. . . .[10]

Although this account was written some twenty years after regular trade was started by the Portuguese at Loango, it seems reasonable to suppose that such a market flourished before there was much European contact. The palm-cloth industry was essential for clothing and currency. Cloth was traditionally standardized according to quality and pattern and four different varieties could be distinguished.[11] The hairs from elephants' tails and copper rings were much prized as jewellery. Copper was a sign of wealth and Vili women could be seen wearing rings up to fourteen pounds in weight.[12] Ivory was used for personal ornamentation, for musical instruments, for knives at table, and in religious ritual.[13] Redwood was essential in Vili life as a dye and a cosmetic.[14]

Although farming remained the basis of economic activity, the Vili of Loango had clearly developed, by the end of the sixteenth century, a commercial system which had advanced from a subsistence-oriented economy. The first Vili, according to some traditions, were farmers who broke away from other Kongo groups on account of a land shortage in the interior. They passed through the Mayombe region and settled in the coastal plain between the Kwilu and Chiloango rivers. This almost certainly took place in the thirteenth or fourteenth centuries.[15] The growth and consolidation of the Vili kingdom of Loango which had taken place by the sixteenth century, must have been accompanied by considerable economic expansion and specialization. This specialization seems to have been possible both in terms of regional production and in terms of occupation. Certain Loango provinces were famous for their special products and the description of Buali market suggests that some form of organization had developed to allow the transport and exchange of products at central markets – redwood and ivory from Sette-Cama and Mayumba, palm-oil from Loangomongo (a province probably situated in the Mayombe foothills), fish and salt from the coastal province of Loangeri.[16] At the same time copper was imported from beyond Loango's boundaries and salt was carried to the interior.

Specialized occupations such as those of palm-cloth weavers and coppersmiths were highly respected.[17]

The development of a palm-cloth currency also seems indicative of an economy of some sophistication. P. Bohannan suggests that money may be the most important single item in the changing of an economy. A general-purpose money, such as the Loango palm-cloth, might do at least three things. It could be a method of evaluating and comparing goods of different kinds; in the Loango context, by the end of the sixteenth century, these goods would include copper, ivory, and redwood as well as salt and the produce of farming, hunting, and fishing. It could be a means of payment; this factor would be increasingly important in an economy where there was specialization of occupations such as those of an ivory porter or a smith's helper. It could be a means of facilitating exchange.[18]

Palm-cloth, like cowries or *nzimbu* shells, had the additional advantage of being a comparatively non-perishable substance which could be stored. At his court at Buali, the king had houses full of palm-cloth, ivory, and copper.[19] This suggests firstly that palm-cloth was a means of storing wealth, and, secondly, that the Maloango, who presumably only kept the finest palm-cloth in the kingdom, could control its current value. The Loango ruler was probably the chief guarantor of the value of the palm-cloth. The wide circulation of this indigenous money has already been referred to.[20] It was current in Loango, Kakongo, and Ngoyo (where it was also manufactured), and also in the coastal regions of Kongo such as Bemba province, and among the Mbundu.[21] Considering the greater accessibility of the Luanda island *nzimbu* shells, it is remarkable to find Loango palm-cloth so widely used. The fine quality of the cloth was probably an important element in its popularity. It may not be going too far, however, to deduce that at the beginning of the seventeenth century this was a 'hard currency'; that the strength of Loango palm-cloth reflected the status of the Maloango, not only internally, but among other peoples of West Central Africa.

Perhaps the best example of a developed pre-European trade organization was the trade in copper. Europeans remarked on the quantities of fine copper jewellery worn by the Vili, long before they themselves began to export the mineral. Dutch traders in the Gabon estuary in the last decade of the sixteenth century also remarked on the quantities of copper jewellery worn by the Mpongwe peoples.[22] The source of Vili copper was the great metalliferous region between Boko Songo and Mindouli in the Niari basin. This area at the beginning of the seventeenth century was in Teke hands, but later in the century it was occupied by the Kongo Nsundi who crossed into the region from the south bank of the Congo river.[23] It seems likely that the copper seen in Gabon was also from this area. There is no important local source of copper in the Gabon region, and it could have reached the Mpongwe via the Teke and traders on the Ogowe river, or, more likely, via the Vili who carried it to Loango whence it could be transported north along the coast.

By the 1660s the mining, smelting, and transporting of the copper on sale at Loango was a highly organized operation and in Vili hands. Large caravans of smiths and traders, with their slaves, left Loango for the mining regions in September. There the slaves brought the copper from the mines to centres where it was moulded by the smiths into the shapes in which it was brought to the coast. They remained until May when the dry season began and wars often broke out. Then they returned to the coast with the smelted copper.[24] The whole operation had doubtless grown in size by the 1660s under the impetus given to trade by European demand. Yet it seems probable that the organization of the copper trade may have been similar at a much earlier period, although on a smaller scale. The Teke who occupied the region may have allowed the Vili to work the mines in return for some arrangement over mining rights. The Vili could also offer the Teke goods such as salt and redwood.

The European demand for ivory caused a considerable extension in the external trade contacts of the Vili. While caravans probably continued to be organized in the traditional manner, they must have increased in number. The need to equip a caravan to cover distances of over a hundred miles must also have demanded greater organization. Unfortunately the contemporary sources have little to say on how this was done in the seventeenth century; but by 1642 the Vili traders had won a reputation among the Dutch as being skilled men of business who always remained calm in a situation where there was a profit to be made.[25]

As long as the demand was limited to local needs, the elephant population, for example in the Mayombe region to the east of the coastal plain, would have supplied Vili requirements. Following the great increase in demand, stimulated by the Portuguese and the Dutch, it was necessary for the Vili to go further inland as the more accessible sources of ivory became exhausted. At the end of the sixteenth century, Mayumba, Sette-Cama, and regions in the Mayombe remained the main sources of supply.[26] By 1642, however, ivory was being bought by the Vili from Teke markets at what is now Stanley Pool, and Vili caravans were crossing the Congo river into the Kongo kingdom, going as far as Luanda itself. The Teke markets were reached by a trade-route that left the Loango capital, passed through the difficult Mayombe mountains and forests, and then had a relatively easy passage along the Niari and

Djoué valleys to Stanley Pool. Tusks weighing between eighty and ninety pounds were carried back to the coast in caravans that might number fifty men and more.[27]

By the 1660s, Bukkameale, a region also known as 'the Mountains of Ivory', had become the main source for the Loango ivory trade. The province was situated on the borders of the Vili and Teke kingdoms, possibly in the region of the present-day du Chaillu Mountains between the upper Ogowe and Niari rivers. The journey from the Loango coast was long and arduous; it took three months to go and return. The Vili carried baskets of salt, palm-oil, locally made knives, cloth, and trinkets. These they exchanged for ivory which the people of Bukkameale obtained from pygmy hunters who killed elephants with poisonous darts. The Maloango seems to have concluded some sort of agreement with the Bukkameale ruler, perhaps as a result of his trading interests there. Bukkameale provided soldiers for the Maloango's army, thus being a useful ally on the eastern boundaries of the Loango kingdom.[28] On the other hand, Bukkameale also benefited from the association since the Vili were prepared to come the long distance from the coast with salt and carry back Bukkameale ivory.

The Maloango seems to have maintained a considerable degree of control over the economic affairs of his kingdom, through a hierarchy of royal officials. Administration of the six coastal states was in the hands of officials appointed by the king in villages, towns, and provinces. These were responsible for justice and the collection of tribute.[29] This tribute may have been in the form of redwood, ivory, or food, depending on the region. One example of a royal tax was the 10 per cent duty which the people of Sette-Cama had to pay to the Governor of Mayumba province when they brought their redwood to sell at Mayumba.[30] The fact that there was no ivory for sale at Buali market, and yet houses full of ivory at the royal palace, suggests the possibility of a royal monopoly or at least some limitations on its general marketing.[31] The Maloango himself and his nobles were apparently the main beneficiaries of Loango's thriving economy.[32]

The extent of the royal authority was also exemplified in the experience of early Europeans on the coast. It was necessary to have royal assent to open trade at Loango Bay or at Mayumba.[33] The fact that the Maloango lived only a few miles from the main trading point at Loango Bay must have aided him in controlling trade. In this respect, he was much better placed than the Manikongo at his inland capital of San Salvador. The Maloango early established the principle of free trade for all Europeans and this made possible the establishment of Dutch interests in face of Portuguese opposition. There were obvious reasons why the Maloango should welcome Dutch traders. In the first place, they brought European goods which were denied the Vili in large quantities as long as the Portuguese traded mainly with Luanda. Also, he was doubtless aware of the fate of the rulers of Kongo and Ndongo under Portuguese domination. Two incidents serve to illustrate the Maloango's attitude.

Shortly before 1608, some Portuguese captains plotted the death of some of the leading Dutch traders in Loango harbour. The Vili traders were infuriated by the plot and with the approval of the Maloango beat one of the Portuguese to death with ivory tusks and made the others pay a large fine.[34] In 1624, the Portuguese governor of Luanda again tried to counter Dutch influence at Loango by writing to the Maloango exhorting him to close the Dutch factories and only to trade with the Portuguese. He also offered to send missionaries to Loango. The Maloango refused the missionaries and replied that he intended to trade with the Dutch and the Portuguese on equal terms.[35]

A striking feature of the trade of Loango until about 1670, especially when compared with the trade of Luanda in the same period and with that of Loango in the eighteenth century, was the small volume of the slave trade. At first the Portuguese seem to have concentrated on exploiting their Angola sources, while the Dutch, before 1630, had no territories which demanded a supply of slaves. In the 1630s, however, the situation changed. Between 1630 and 1636, the Dutch captured Pernambuco and Paraibo in north-eastern Brazil where the expanding sugar industry created a huge demand for labour. Loango was now viewed as a potential source of slaves. A Dutch factor was appointed to the Loango factory in 1637 with special responsibility for increasing the slave trade there.[36] Portugal also seems to have become interested in the possibilities of opening up a trade in slaves at Loango. From 1636 to 1644, an asiento contract was issued for the slave trade in 'Angola, Congo and Loango'.[37]

These efforts met with little success. In 1639, the Dutch agent reported to the West India Company directors that only about 200 slaves could be acquired annually at Loango, and about one hundred in Kakongo.[38] Since the Dutch were in a much stronger position than the Portuguese in Loango, it is unlikely that the Portuguese did any better. Records of Dutch cargoes in the 1640s and 1650s suggest that the slave trade continued to be sluggish, and that ivory and copper remained important items in Dutch trade from Loango.[39]

Given the strength of Dutch demand and the fact that the Vili had a considerable reputation as astute traders, one is led to ask why so few slaves were available at Loango in this period. Clearly the Loango situation seems to disprove any theory that it was sufficient for European traders to appear on the African coast with cheap manufactured goods, in order to obtain a plentiful supply of slaves. The African response was by no means automatic, and in Loango, at least, the initiative in the trading situation was apparently on the African side. To be certain of the attitudes and motives of the Loango government is, however, difficult, due to the lack of source material for this crucial period.

It is possible that the sources that the Vili tapped for ivory and copper could not supply slaves. The hinterland of Loango was probably not thickly populated before about the middle of the seventeenth century, and slave raids in the Mayombe region and in the Niari valley beyond would not have proved very fruitful. It was only in the course of the seventeenth century that Kongo groups started to move into the area of the Niari valley and occupy the borderlands between the Vili and Teke kingdoms.[40] It may have been necessary for the Vili to forge new trade links in order to acquire slaves; this would take time. This may have been especially true of areas south of the Congo river, which were a major source of slaves in the eighteenth century. In terms of extending trade, slaves were a 'commodity' akin to ivory.

Another possible explanation for the paucity of Loango slaves was that the Maloango may have resisted the introduction of the slave trade with Europeans; and in this period his power was probably strong enough to maintain the policy. There were close contacts, both traditional and commercial, between the kingdoms of Kongo peoples north and south of the Congo river. The ruler of Loango must have been well aware of the adverse effects of the slave trade in the kingdom of the Manikongo. Reports of a Capuchin missionary who worked in Loango in 1663 suggest that the Maloango still had considerable influence internally in enforcing his will on his subjects.[41] In relation to European traders the Loango government also seems to have retained the initiative. The Dutch factory at Loango in 1670 was only allowed to exist 'subject to the African government', which contrasted with the more secure tenure of the Gold Coast forts.[42]

Gradually, however, the slave trade at Loango grew in volume. By the 1660s, Vili traders were finding it was more profitable to trade in slaves than in ivory and were bringing ivory to the coast in smaller quantities.[43] They may also have consolidated their contacts south of the Congo river. By 1651 they were regular visitors in San Salvador.[44] Besides, by the 1670s, the Dutch at Loango had been joined by the English and the French, whose primary interest was the trade in slaves for their New World colonies. The Maloango may have either bowed to these pressures or found it politic not to resist them.

By 1670, the Dutch West India Company factory at Loango was exporting three thousand slaves annually.[45] In 1680, the Directors of the new Royal Africa Company were sufficiently interested in the prospects of the Loango Coast trade,[46] to discuss the possibilities of setting up a factory there.[47] In 1686, a French report estimated that the king of Loango could provide five hundred slaves per month.[48] A new phase in the development of the trade of Loango and her southern neighbours had begun. Although slave ships continued to trade in small quantities of ivory, copper, and redwood, especially at the northern port of Mayumba, the trade in slaves began to dominate all other activities.

By the 1740s, competition had reached considerable proportions. The French ship the *Flore* arrived on the Loango Coast in 1742 and found fourteen other ships. It took four months to collect a cargo of 362 slaves at Loango Bay.[49] A Dutch ship from Middelburg, arriving at Malemba in 1749, found eighteen competitors, seven at Malemba, six at Cabinda, and five at Loango. After nine months it had bought 348 slaves, and already eighty-three had died before it set sail for Surinam.[50] Apart from a lull during the Seven Years' War (1756-63), this competition seems to have continued and increased.

In the years 1765-75, it was normal to find about twenty ships trading on the Loango Coast. Taking as an average a cargo of four hundred slaves and an average trading time of six months, the number of slaves obtained per year on the Coast would be in the region of 16,000.[51] This if anything would be a conservative estimate, since many of the French ships could carry more than four hundred slaves. A French report of the trade of the Loango Coast for the years 1762-78 estimated the French trade at 10,000 slaves per year, the English trade at 1000, and the Dutch trade at 1500.[52] While the estimate for French trade may be accurate, the figures for the trade of their rivals seem very low, especially when compared with Dutch reports on the number of ships to be found on the Coast. In 1786-7, Degranpré estimated French trade alone at 15,000 slaves annually, this being the lowest estimate he thought possible.[53] A Portuguese report of the 1770s put the Loango Coast trade at 20,000 slaves per year,[54] while reports to the Committee of Inquiry into the Slave Trade which met in England in 1789 suggested a figure of 13,000 to 14,000 for the slave trade at Loango Bay, Malemba, and Cabinda.[55] Taking these figures together, a figure in the region of 14,000 to 18,000 may be suggested as an average for the export of slaves from the Loango Coast in the years 1765-90.

Most of those slaves were brought in caravans to the coast from long distances in the interior. One of the best contemporary sources on the

Loango Coast slave trade is the book written by the Frenchman Degranpré, who himself traded in slaves in the area for thirty years. He suggests that the traders of Loango, Kakongo, and Ngoyo were both exploiting old trade-routes used in the copper and ivory trade in the sixteenth and seventeenth centuries, and also developing new trade-routes.

There were different categories of slaves on sale at the three ports. At Loango Bay were to be found *Monteques, Mayombes,* and *Quibangues*; at Malemba were *Mayombes* and *Congues*; at Cabinda were *Congues, Sognes,* and *Mondongues*.[56] These names did not, however, indicate the exact source of the slaves; rather they derived from the peoples who supplied the slaves or across whose territory the slaves had passed en route to the Loango Coast.[57] This would explain, for example, why Mayombe slaves figured prominently at Loango Bay and Malemba. These were not necessarily the Yombe inhabitants of the Mayombe region. They were rather given this name since the caravans going to Loango Bay or Malemba would pass through this region. The same would be true of the many *Congues* on sale at Malemba and Cabinda. This would be a general term for all slaves provided by the Kongo south of the river Congo, or for slaves which passed through Kongo territory on the long journey to the Atlantic coast.

Many Loango caravans continued to follow the old caravan route to the Teke markets at Stanley Pool. A quarter of the slaves on sale at Loango Bay were Teke (*Monteques*) while a sixth were known as Boubangui (*Quibangues*).[58] The latter name is particularly significant since it suggests how far inland the trade contacts from the coast had been extended by the second half of the eighteenth century. French explorers who went up the Congo river beyond Stanley Pool in the nineteenth century, found that the term Boubangui was a very broad one; it was used to designate different peoples who lived along the banks of the Congo, Alima, Sanga, and lower Ubangi rivers. Peoples who were individually referred to as Bayanzi, Apfourou, and Bobangi were all part of a larger Boubangui group. They had many common characteristics, including the same language, customs, and tribal marks. The Boubangui originated on the upper Ubangi river, and according to their traditions were pushed down the river by new arrivals. They were also attracted to the Congo river by the European goods arriving in the area from the Teke at Stanley Pool. They continued their advance to Stanley Pool and were only stopped by the Teke after they had reached the stretch of the Congo river immediately upstream from Stanley Pool. This seems to have happened about the year 1840.[59] From Degranpré's comments, it seems that by the second half of the eighteenth century, the

Teke already had contacts with the Boubangui. Pechuel-Loesche also found confirmation that the slaves who reached Loango included Teke and Yanzi.[60]

Another trade-route led from Loango in a north-easterly direction, crossing the Niari river and climbing the Sibiti plateau to the Yaka. These were probably descendants of the Jaga who had ravaged the Kongo kingdom in the sixteenth century.[61] From there routes communicated with peoples on the upper Ogowe and the upper Alima, bypassing the Teke plateau to the south-east. De Brazza, who crossed from the upper Ogowe to the Alima river in the 1870s, found that the people of that area received salt, guns, and cloth from the Loango Coast. In return they sent slaves to the coast.[62] A trade-route may also have reached the coast at Mayumba, having followed the Nyanga river. From Mayumba, slave caravans went south to the three main ports.[63] Although these connections between the upper Ogowe regions and the Loango Coast were not documented before the nineteenth century, they probably existed from a long time previously. Bukkameale, the seventeenth-century source of ivory, was probably situated in the same area.

By the second half of the eighteenth century, Loango had lost the initiative in the slave trade to her rivals, Kakongo and Ngoyo. Degranprés states that the best-quality slaves, and also the greatest quantity, were to be had at Malemba.[64] The two attempts that were made to monopolize trade on the Loango Coast in the eighteenth century were made at Cabinda, where first the English and then the Portuguese attempted to erect forts.[65] Not only did Cabinda have the best harbour on the coast, but its position near the mouth of the Congo river gave it a favourable situation in the slave trade to the south; it was also within easy reach of Malemba, only a few miles along the coast. The thriving trade of Malemba and Cabinda was due to the fact that the trade-routes from the south crossed Kakongo and Ngoyo, and their rulers could simply prevent the caravans going further north to Loango. An important route led to San Salvador from Nokki, which could be easily reached from Boma on the north side of the Congo river. Another possibility was upstream beyond the Yellala cataracts at Isangila where the river becomes navigable as far as Manyanga. The *Mayombes, Congues, Sognes*, and *Mondongues* may all be references to slaves who arrived at Malemba and Cabinda from a southerly direction. Although the situation was much regretted by the king of Loango, he lacked the power to gain trade by force and had to watch the lucrative Kongo trade passing to his rivals.[66] By 1683, traders who crossed the Kongo kingdom from the Loango Coast had reached the Mbundu state of Matamba on the west side of the upper Kwango river. They aroused the attention of the Portuguese since they offered firearms and gunpowder in exchange for slaves.[67] In the eighteenth century, the Portuguese became even more alarmed by the activities of these traders from the north since they were siphoning off trade that might otherwise have reached Luanda. It is probable that some of the slaves reaching Malemba and Cabinda from the south had come from places as distant as the Lunda empire.

These traders from the Loango Coast had a formidable advantage over their Luanda rivals, for the English, French, and Dutch on the Loango Coast attracted trade by offering higher prices than the Portuguese in Angola and by selling firearms without restriction.[68] Comparing the number of guns contained in each slave ship's cargo on the outward voyage with the number of slaves bought, one finds that about two or three guns were unloaded by the Dutch for every slave acquired.[69] Since the French were offering better prices than the Dutch, it is probable that at least three guns changed hands for every slave sold. If one takes the figures of 14,000 to 18,000 as the number of slaves sold on the coast per year, it would mean that something in the region of 50,000 guns may have arrived on the Loango Coast each year in the second half of the eighteenth century. From there they were probably widely dispersed through West Central Africa.

The organization of the slave caravans was a highly specialized business. The dry season saw the peak of caravan activity. The main problem was to ensure an easy passage through the various small chieftaincies through which the caravans passed, especially in the Mayombe region after Loango power had shrunk, among the various Kongo groups who had settled between the Yombe and the Teke, and in the old Kongo kingdom which had disintegrated into many small chieftaincies by the eighteenth century.

Supplies of slaves at the coast could dry up completely if chiefs in the interior decided to close the roads to the passage of caravans. Although there were no fixed duties that a caravan had to pay for such privileges as the right to pass through a chief's land, or the use of bridges, the rate was generally calculated according to the worth of goods in the caravan. Ivory incurred the heaviest tax.[70] Chiefs were, however, strongly placed to exploit their position by raising duties, or even, on some pretext, seizing the trade-goods carried by a caravan. There were certain points where a chief could extort special terms from a vulnerable caravan leader. For example, the roads from Loango to the interior had to pass through the treacherous Mayombe region where the good paths were few and the routes passed along the sides of mountain slopes, by deep precipices, and through dense tropical forest. Here, there was little choice of route, and chiefs had a strong hand in levying customs. They erected barriers across the path and appointed watchmen to keep a lookout for caravans that could be stopped to pay duties. Ferry-places were other lucrative points which chiefs put in the hands of their most trusted followers so that tolls would be collected. Usually the position of ferryman was passed down in certain families.[71]

The caravans that left the Loango Coast were accompanied by guards armed with guns. These seem to have been more to prevent rebellious slaves from running away than to deal with opposition en route.[72] The Loango Coast caravans do not seem to have depended on gunpowder to force a passage through the lands of unco-operative chiefs. If guns were widely spread through West Central Africa, they would probably have been foolish to attempt to do so, especially when they were not on their home ground. The safe-passage of caravans was due, rather, to the skill of the caravan leader who was usually a far-travelled and intelligent man from the coast.[73]

The caravan leaders were, above all, specialists in the art of negotiation; men who knew the customs and duties that had grown up round the passage of caravans in the course of years in the various regions. They had to be able to negotiate prices with difficult chiefs although this might take days to achieve; they had to know when to call a chief's bluff by threatening to turn back, when to give in and pay, and the possibilities of alternative routes. Chiefs always had the fear that if they abused the traders too much, the caravans might stop using the route through their territory and the revenue from customs might dry up. Clearly, a skilled caravan leader had some cards to play, too. Another problem for the leader was that of inexperienced porters and guards. He must be able to discipline them and prevent them from being enticed off the road by the comforts of a village or from being frightened by the fear of some fetish on the road.[74]

Once the duties had been paid to a chief or his representative, he would send one of his officials before the caravan. This man would sound the chief's bell and escort the traders as far as the next district, so that they were not molested; and so the caravan progressed from region to region.[75] As trade expanded, the occupation of a caravan leader must have become both lucrative and a highly skilled profession.

Once the slaves had arrived on the coast, their sale was also a highly organized affair. In each of the three ports of Loango Bay, Malemba, and Cabinda, a similar system of administration was evolved to deal with the great volume of the eighteenth-century slave trade. The chief official at the port was the Mafouk. He was appointed by the king as a sort of Minister of Commerce and was one of the most important members of the royal council. No trade, either on the European or on the African side, could be commenced without his consent. On arrival in port, the European captain had to go ashore to arrange for the building of a temporary trading-house and to discuss the terms of trade. The latter included such matters as the price of slaves, the duty that must be paid to the king and the royal officials, and the fees for the brokers who were the middle men between the caravan merchants and the European buyers.[76] On the African side, no merchant could trade directly with a European captain, but only through the brokers appointed by the Mafouk. All trade regulations laid down by the king and the Mafouk had to be obeyed.[77]

In this situation, the Africans of Loango and her neighbours seem to have retained the initiative on most occasions, especially in the second half of the eighteenth century when trade reached its peak. For demand seems generally to have outstripped supply in this period, and no European nation was able to build a permanent base and gain a trade monopoly on the Loango Coast. The attempt by the Portuguese to fortify the port of Cabinda (1783–4) and monopolize trade, failed, not only because of the hostile reactions of the French but also because of the African response to their efforts.

The French version of the incident, which claimed that the Mambouk[78] of Cabinda had agreed to the building of a Portuguese fort only after he was taken on board a Portuguese frigate and put under considerable pressure, seems verified by the events that followed.[79] When the Portuguese soldiers started to build their fort, the Cabindans adopted a policy of passive resistance. The brokers, merchants, and those who generally worked as servants of European traders, ran away into the interior and refused to co-operate.[80] Trade almost ceased, and any Portuguese who ventured from the fort did so in danger of his life. When a French expedition arrived the following year to destroy the fort, the Mambouk of Cabinda promised 800 African soldiers to help the French eject the Portuguese and declared that the Cabindans favoured free trade.[81]

It seems likely that if a similar situation had arisen at Loango and Malemba, the African response would have been the same. The lack of a permanent base certainly made the work of European captains more difficult. Time was a vital factor in their trade negotiations. The outward voyage to the Loango Coast could take from two to six months, and if competition was severe, a captain must reckon another six months or more on the coast in order to acquire a cargo of slaves. Yet trade had to be concluded in the shortest possible time, if the crew and slaves were to survive the Atlantic crossing. In this situation concessions often had to be made to African brokers. The few attempts at price-fixing agreements among European captains were abortive because of the degree of competition. European merchants were generally prepared to work within the trading system which was essentially an African-initiated one.

European competition was reflected in the rise of Loango's rivals, and by the end of the eighteenth century the external authority of Loango had shrunk drastically. At the beginning of the seventeenth century, the Loango kingdom had dominated the whole area of West Central Africa from the Congo river to Cape Saint Catherine. Ngoyo and Kakongo recognized Loango's superior military strength and accepted the Maloango's mediation in their disputes.[82] A very different picture was presented just under two centuries later. Loango had declined so much that the kingdom was smaller than that of Kakongo or Ngoyo. Since Loango continued to have a longer coastline than Kakongo or Ngoyo, the inference is that she had lost territories in the Mayombe region. Although the Maloango was still recognized as suzerain over her two southern neighbours, their kings did not go in person to pay tribute to the Maloango but sent princes of the royal blood.[83] In the north, Mayumba, once a province of Loango, had its own ruler by the end of the eighteenth century; like Kakongo and Ngoyo, the Mayumba ruler sent an envoy to pay homage to the Maloango.[84]

Loango, therefore, had shrunk, in terms of real power, to a coastal strip from the Chiloango river in the south to just north of the Kwilu river. It seems certain that this was due to the effects of the slave trade. It has already been suggested that Kakongo and Ngoyo won a bigger share in the eighteenth-century slave trade than did Loango.[85] This must have led to a greater confidence on the part of the southern kingdoms and affected their dealings with their traditional overlord. At the same time, Loango itself was shrinking. The temptation to try and dominate the caravan routes through the Mayombe may have caused the Yombe chiefs to end their allegiance to the Maloango. Although Mayumba was not much concerned in the slave trade, English and Portuguese ships continued to call for ivory and redwood. The Mayumba ruler may have felt strong enough to follow the example of other break-away states. All this, the Maloango was powerless to resist because of domestic problems, also in part brought by the slave trade. At the same time, the weakening of external authority may have created a loss of respect for the Maloango's political authority at home, and exacerbated existing internal tensions.

The slave trade caused fundamental changes in the political and social structure within the Loango kingdom. Its main effect was to undermine the traditional system by creating new opportunities for advancement quite independent of it. Those with a vested interest in preserving the traditional structure were unable to resist the new pressures.

Power in seventeenth-century Loango society seems to have rested firmly in the hands of the king and nobles. These 'nobles' or 'princes', who figure prominently in most seventeenth-century accounts, probably originated in certain families who were the leaders of Vili clans which united to form the Loango kingdom. The privilege of belonging to the class was passed on by matrilineal inheritance.[86] Only those whose mothers were princesses or who had married a princess could claim the traditional prerogatives that belonged to the princely class.[87]

Since the Maloango appointed his royal officials in provinces and districts from this same class, they were able to exploit both their traditional and administrative positions in Vili society.[88] Traditionally, the common people were bound to work in the fields of the nobles at certain times of the year, just as they worked in the fields of the king.[89] The nobles meted out justice and collected tribute on behalf of the Maloango. As has already been suggested, the early European trade in ivory, redwood, copper, and palm-cloth, may have been administered through this same system.[90] Thus it was the king and nobles who most benefited from the early trade contacts with Europeans. This was indeed evidenced by their enormous wealth; the nobles imitated the king in the details of their daily life, living in splendour, dressing finely, possessing quantities of servants and slaves, and receiving the great respect traditionally shown to them by the common people.[91] At the other end of the social scale were the freemen and slaves, with little to distinguish them except that the former could move freely about the country.[92]

The main effect of the great volume of the eighteenth-century slave trade was to broaden the base of political, economic, and social power. Vili society became more open, and men outside the class of nobles could find opportunity for advancement. In the first place, the system that evolved to deal with the slave trade involved a greater number of people than under previous trading conditions – brokers, merchants, caravan leaders, interpreters, surf-boatmen, water-carriers, personal servants for Europeans, and so on. Power came to be measured less in terms of traditional rights and more in terms of a man's place in the slave-trading system and the wealth he amassed from his position. Those new opportunities cut across the traditional distinction of noble or commoner. In many cases nobles became involved in the slave trade as brokers and merchants. At the same time, common people found new opportunities open to those with business acumen.[93] Even slaves were able to enrich themselves, perhaps at first as the servants of a rich broker and, later, for the personal reputation they had acquired. Technically, a man might remain a slave but he was protected by his new wealth.[94]

The Maloango himself may have initiated changes in the administrative system to deal with the demands of the slave trade. In the seventeenth century, the most important members of the royal council were provincial governors.[95] By the eighteenth century, however, these seem to have been less important. The principal members of the royal council were officials who had direct dealings with Europeans, for example, the Mafouk, and the Mangova and Manpoutou who were responsible for foreign affairs and the introduction of strangers at court.[96] The Maloango retained the power to appoint these officials, but instead of appointing those of noble birth, he tended to sell these lucrative offices to the highest bidder.[97] This may have been an attempt to bolster up his own economic position in relation to those of his subjects who were benefiting from their role in the slave trade. Yet he was merely exalting the status of these 'nouveaux riches' further, for they were the very ones who were able to pay large sums and take over office. Once in an important administrative post, this same class was able to exploit their office by extorting tribute from the common people in proportion to their land, cattle, and slaves.[98]

The king, however, was not a pauper in relation to the 'nouveaux riches'. Not only did he continue to retain traditional powers that went with his office, but also he was able to benefit financially from the slave trade. The captain or officers of every ship that traded at Loango visited the Maloango at his capital and gave him considerable presents.[99] More important was the sum of money paid by every ship for the right to trade freely. The combined value of this duty and the presents gave the Maloango an income equal to that of most of the brokers, although he seldom made as much as the Mafouk.[100] Yet although not poor, he was now economically one among his equals.

One of the most striking changes in the system of government in Loango by the end of the eighteenth century concerned arrangements for the succession of a new Maloango. In the seventeenth century, the succession was based on the hereditary principle. When the king died he was succeeded by his sister's son. The king's nephews were appointed in his lifetime to four lordships with the titles of Manikaye, Manibock, Manisalag, and Manicabango. When the Maloango died the Manikaye became the new ruler, the others were promoted, and a new Manicabango was appointed.[101] At the same time, there was by the 1660s some friction among the claimants to the throne and possibly the issue was not as cut-and-dried as the description makes it seem.[102]

By the end of the eighteenth century there was a definite deterioration in the working of the system. The king nominated his successor, the

Manikaye, but almost always the appointment was disputed. In this case a Regency Council consisting of the chief ministers took over power and elected a successor.[103] This council, with full political authority in its hands, sought to perpetuate the interregnum in its own interests.[104] Since the chief ministers were generally those that had bought their offices, one can see the important role that the slave trade had in influencing the system of Loango government. The new Maloango usually bribed his way into office. Still, once in power, his traditional authority remained, and he was in the position of having powers of life and death over those who had just elevated him to the throne.[105]

In conclusion, one can agree with Jan Vansina's view that the changes in Loango society brought about by the trade contacts of the seventeenth and eighteenth centuries should be viewed, not in terms of decay, but in terms of mutation, an adaptation to a new set of circumstances.[106] Seventeenth-century Loango was apparently a vigorous kingdom which had the ability to adapt to the new trade contacts. The result was a greater diversification in the means of climbing the economic and social ladder. Politically, there was a sharing of power between the traditional repositories, the Maloango and the nobles, and the new-type politicians who had gained their position through trading connections.

The real fragmentation of central authority in Loango seems rather to have been associated with events in the first half of the nineteenth century. During the Napoleonic wars and with the influence of the anti-slave trade movement, the slave trade of Loango declined.[107] This was a blow which the already weakened central authority could hardly adapt to. When the slave trade at Loango partially recovered after the war, due to the influence of Portuguese, Spanish, Brazilian and American traders, it was organized in a different fashion. The whole object was to escape the surveillance of anti-slave trade cruisers; this demanded many small trading-points along the coast.[108] By this period, the slave trade was practically the only means of making a living known to the coastal merchants. Mafouks sprouted all along the coast. It seems that this new generation of mafouks were recognized as having political authority, and not just as the chief commercial agents of the king, as had previously been the case.[109] Elaboration of this point, however, must await further research on nineteenth-century Loango history.

9 The Portuguese slave trade from Angola in the eighteenth century

Herbert S. Klein

Editor's comments

The export of slaves from Angola by the Portuguese was a very early development in the history of the Atlantic slave trade. In the sixteenth century slave exports from Angola formed a large proportion of total slave exports from Africa by way of the Atlantic trade. The proportion remained large through the seventeenth to the eighteenth century. And by the nineteenth century that proportion further increased. In the present chapter Herbert Klein examines various issues relating to the eighteenth-century volume and organization of this important segment of the export slave trade from Africa. While not specifically concerned with the impact of the trade on the Angolan trading area, much of the information and analyses in the paper can be used for that purpose. The paper shows that the Angolan slave trade was different from the West African one in some important respects. As a Portuguese colony from the sixteenth century, the Portuguese had direct control of the access into the Angolan interior for export slaves, something very different from the situation in West Africa. Again, in the Angolan ports, the aspect of the slave trade usually handled by African traders was in the hands of Portuguese traders resident in Angola. This is reflected in the population of Luanda in 1773, with only 147 free Africans (of which only four were women, indicating the low class of the free Africans, being largely unmarried) owning only 9 slaves, as compared with 251 whites owning 787 slaves, and 138 free mulattoes, owning 187 slaves. (See author's endnote 24.) As to the volume of the trade, the author points out that the Angolan official export figures, based on tax records, understated the numbers actually exported. But the month by month variation of the volume of slave exports shown by the author is of some interest. The months of largest exports were July to December (both

This paper was first published in the *Journal of Economic History*, vol. XXXII no. 4 (1972), pp. 894–918. It has been reprinted here by permission of the author and the publishers.

inclusive), which are usually months of harvest and farm clearing in tropical Africa. The large food imports of Luanda in the nineteenth century (see endnotes 25 and 46) indicate the state of agriculture in the Angolan trading area at the time. The extent to which the slave trade dominated the external trade of Angola is shown by the fact that in 1815 slave exports accounted for 94 per cent of Angola's total export by value. (See endnote 46.) The evidence in the paper does suggest that while the large numbers of people exported annually over a period of about 400 years had the usual negative effects on the Angola trading area, even the minimal short-term private profits which African traders obtained in West Africa, went largely to Portuguese traders resident in Angola, rather than to indigenous Angolan middle men.

Recently the Atlantic slave trade has received scholarly attention through the work of European and American historians. Account books of European merchants engaged in the slave trade, studies of the exports of given continental ports, and analyses of special trade routes have all led to a greater understanding of the dynamics of the trade. Also, the important work of Philip Curtin on the volume and direction of the entire Atlantic slave trade has finally provided us with the rough parameters of the trade in terms of total numbers.

Even with this increasingly quantitative and detailed literature, however, there still remains much to be done. Large funds of unexamined primary materials exist in all the major European and American archives on all aspects of the trade. These statistical sources can begin to answer some of the very basic questions about the trade which still have not been fully analysed. Aside from total volume, little is known about the relation of exports and imports to season, to local and international economic conditions, and to conditions of supply in the interior. The very questions of the size and productivity of ships and crews, and the sex and age of the slaves shipped, for example, are unknown for most routes during most of the period of the trade. Finally, the differences among the major slave-trading nations, and/or major routes in terms of financing, shipping, and selling of the African slaves have yet to be studied.

The aim of this article is to attempt to answer some of the basic questions about the organization, rhythm, direction and volume of the operations of the least studied of the major Atlantic slave trading nations, Portugal. Within the Portuguese trading area, I have selected

Angola for detailed study because of the excellent quality and quantity of its records (especially when compared with the other major Portuguese zones of Guinea and Mozambique) and also because of its prime importance within the Portuguese slave-trading zone.

My concern will be with the detailed Angolan records of the eighteenth century. From port records and government reports I have tried to estimate the number of slaves shipped in this century and the relative importance of the various contributing African ports within Angola. Using detailed mid century shipping registers, I attempt to answer basic questions about destination, seasonal variations, ship's capacity and tonnage, vessel types and frequency of voyages. Though data on the demographic makeup of the transported slave population are relatively poor, there is enough material available to determine the relative numbers of adults and children in this forced Atlantic migration. The last part of the study will concentrate on the economic organization of the trade. Using hitherto unused merchant records and those of the Pombaline trading companies, I hope to make a first approximation as to the investments, costs and returns in the eighteenth-century Portuguese trade.

From the early decades of the sixteenth century until the middle of the nineteenth century, Angola produced a steady supply of African slaves. This enormous human migration was unique by slave trade standards both for the long-term stability in numbers and because of the almost exclusive monopoly maintained over this trade by Portugal. Although the Loango coast remained a free trade area for most of this period, the dominant trade of Angola was under Portuguese control, and a majority of the forced migration went to Brazil. The Dutch, of course, did temporarily seize Angola from the Portuguese in the early seventeenth century, but even then, the trade continued to flow into the ports of Brazil.

By the eighteenth century, the boom in the gold fields of central Brazil brought even further demands for slave labour from African sources and Angola met the demand over the next century, along with the traditional sources on the Upper and Lower Guinean coast. If the estimates of Curtin are accepted, then Angola accounted for 70 per cent of the Brazilian-bound slaves.[1] Within the Angolan region itself, the primary exporting centre remained Luanda, until 1800. From early in the sixteenth century and until well into the eighteenth century, Luanda overwhelmingly dominated the trade.[2] But Luanda's supremacy was beginning to be challenged by the previously minor port of Benguela by the end of the period. Benguelan trade had been quite small until the middle decades of the century, when its exports began averaging between 1000 and 2000 slaves per annum. After 1760, however, its exports expanded greatly, and by the 1780s accounted for one quarter of the trade, a percentage it would maintain until the end of the century.[3] As for the period from 1741 to 1780 (see Table 13), Luanda itself accounted for 69 per cent of the total Portuguese slave exports from Angola. The third leading slaving-zone of Angola, Cabinda, was a free-trade area until the end of the century, where French, British, and Dutch, as well as Portuguese slavers, traded.[4]

The eighteenth century Portuguese trade from Luanda was a rather steady trade in terms of volume. While there was a fairly rapid growth in

Table 13 *Estimates of the African slave exports from Angola in the eighteenth century*

Decades	Luanda exports	Benguela exports	Total Angolan exports	Curtin's estimates*
1701–10	—	—	—	70,000
1711–20	77,093	—	—	55,300
1721–30	73,572	—	—	67,100
1731–40	88,621	—	—	109,300
1741–50	106,637	13,180	119,817	130,100
1751–60	96,590	24,265	120,855	130,100
1761–70	76,377	49,753	126,130	123,500
1771–80	94,505	67,667	162,172	131,500
1781–90	—	—	—	153,900
1791–1800	—	—	—	168,000

*Philip D. Curtin, *The Atlantic Slave Trade, A Census* (Madison: University of Wisconsin Press 1969), p. 207, table 62. Curtin's estimates are based on the works of Birmingham, Correia Lopes and Goulart. Correia Lopes, upon whom Goulart bases his own estimates, used only manuscript summary tables, often made a dozen or more years after the recorded year and therefore subject to greater error than individual contemporary year recordings. The latter have been the prime source of my own estimates and therefore are more accurate than Curtin's less complete and more summary sources.

Note: I have adopted two basic methods in reaching my estimates when no export figures were available in either the archival sources or in the statistics provided by David Birmingham, *Trade and Conflict in Angola: The Mbundu and Their Neighbours Under the Influence of the Portuguese, 1483–1790* (Oxford: Oxford University Press 1966), which are also based on sources in the Arquivo Histórico Ultramarino in Lisbon. The first method was to adopt the highest given total slave figure within the decade and round it to the next highest hundred for all unknown years. I justify this procedure on the assumption that official figures, based as they are on tax records, underestimate actual exports of adult slaves. My resulting upper limit figures are thus probably closer to actual exports than would be the case if I used either lowest export year, or took the average of all given years and used this as the multiplier. The second method involved an estimator for children when this figure was not given. Based on the available statistics for children, I adopted a 6 per cent addition for Luanda (see Appendix Table I for justification) and a 3 per cent addition for Benguela (see Appendix Table II for justification).

Table 14 *Slave trade from Luanda, Angola, 1723-71*

Year	No. of ships	No. of adults	Total slaves (adults and children)	Average cargo size
1723	18	6,704	—	(372)
1724	17	6,108	—	(359)
1725	22	6,726	—	(305)
1726	21	8,321	8,440	401
1727	20	7,539	7,663	381
1728	21	8,418	8,532	406
1731	16	5,715	5,808	363
1734	25	8,713	10,109	404
1738	19	7,623	8,810	463
1740	22	8,075	8,484	385
1741	23	8,268	9,158	398
1742	24	10,207	10,591	441
1744	20	8,256	8,848	442
1747	25*	8,328	9,869	394
1748	30	10,815	11,810	393
1749	25	8,895	9,776	391
1758	24	9,799	9,938	414
1762	22	8,268	8,415	365
1763	21	7,525	7,634	363
1764	18	7,500	7,648	424
1765	27	10,394	10,672	395
1766	25	9,237	9,420	376
1767	26	9,228	9,318	358
1769	17	5,651	5,733	337
1771	21	7,591	...	(361)
Totals	549* [471]	203,904	[186,646]	(371) [396]†

*Plus 1 ship unknown as to slaves shipped, which makes the total for 1747 26 ships, and a grand total of 550 ships recorded. I have eliminated from these totals several ships which paid taxes on only 1 or 2 slaves and were thus not really slavers. Most of these ships did not go to Brazil.

†Thus when children data were given, for 471 ships, the total export of slaves was 186,646, for an average cargo size of 396.

Sources: For 1723-4 see original tables (or *mappas*) in Arquivo Histórico Ultramarino, Angola, caixa 16 [Hereafter AHU; Angola will be understood before the caixa designation, with latter shortened to standard cx. abbreviation]; for 1725-7 mappas see cx. 17; 1728 in cx. 18; 1731 in cx. 19; 1734 in cx. 20; 1738 in cx. 21; 1740, 1743 and 1744 in cx. 23; 1741 in cx. 22; 1747-8 in cx. 24; 1749 in cx. 25; 1758 in cx. 27; 1762 in cx. 29; 1763-4 in cx. 30; 1765-6 in cx. 31; 1767 in AHU, Angola, maço 9; 1769 in cx. 32; and 1771 in cx. 33.

the early years of the century, from the 1730s to the 1770s the trade remained at about 8000 to 10,000 slaves per annum. Fortunately for the historian, there is preserved in the Arquivo Histórico Ultramarino in Lisbon detailed annual export statistics for Luanda for some twenty-seven non-consecutive years which range from 1723 to 1771. This fortuitous sample covers not only the most stable period of the eighteenth-century trade, but also the pre-Pombal and Pombal Companies eras. It thus gives evidence of one of the major structural changes in the eighteenth-century Portuguese trade, that of the temporary introduction of private monopoly companies alongside the free traders. As indicated in Table 14, there was no secular trend either upward or downward in slave exports during the period for which the detailed annual records were available. Average cargo sizes, as well as total slave export figures, fluctuated from year to year, and in the case of the former, were considerably lower than end-of-century estimates. Thus in the trade to Rio de Janeiro from Angola in the period 1795-1811, the average cargo size was 496 slaves per ship.[5] As for total volume, it would appear that by the last two decades of the century there was a clear secular movement upward in Angolan exports (Table 13).

Based on the evidence relating to the 549 ships during the period 1723 to 1771 generalizations can be made about the structure of the African slave trade from Angola and the impact of a number of variables on the trade. As can be seen in Tables 15 and 16, the months of July through November were heavier, in terms of shipping and volume of adults exported, than were the other months of the year. When proper allowance for voyage time is made, this very roughly matches the seasonal data for importation of slaves into Brazil.[6] However, the cause

Table 15 *Slave exports from Luanda, Angola, by month, 1723-71*

Month	No. of adults	No. of ships	Average cargo size
January	15,284	43	355
February	14,103	39	361
March	15,209	43	353
April	16,953	44	385
May	13,876	37	375
June	12,694	36	352
July	20,165	54 [55]*	373
August	22,319	60	371
September	17,764	48	370
October	18,452	47	392
November	18,525	50	370
December	18,388	47	391
Unknown	172	1	—
Totals	203,904	549	371

*Plus 1 ship unknown as to adults transported.
Source: Same as Table 14.

Table 16 Slave exports from Luanda, Angola, by season 1723-71

Season	No. of adults	No. of ships	Average cargo size
Summer (Dec., Jan., Feb.)	47,775	129	370
Autumn (Mar., Apr., May)	46,038	124	371
Winter (June, July, Aug.)	55,178	150 [151]*	367
Spring (Sept., Oct., Nov.)	54,741	145	378
Unknown	172	1	—
Totals	203,904	549	371

*Plus 1 ship unknown as to number of adults.
Source: Same as Table 14.

for these seasonal variations is still difficult to explain on the basis of current economic and climatic data. Moreover, there is no really close relationship between high months of exports and high months of imports.

Whatever the specific cause of the marked seasonality in total volume, it was clearly due to an increase in the number of ships employed in the trade, rather than any significant change in the carrying capacity of individual ships. An analysis of variance based on average cargo size shows that there is no significance to cargo size and its relationship to season. There is, however, a high correlation between the number of ships employed (and therefore the total number of slaves shipped) and months.

If the seasonal variation exhibited by Angolan exports in the eighteenth century is valid, then it could prove a very useful index. In many routes, the slave trade to the Americas was not a direct African trade. It often involved seasoning in certain West Indian entrepôt islands, as well as a lively inter-regional American trade, at least for the West Indies and continental North America. It appears that the inter-regional or even intra-regional trade, as in the Cuban case, was of sufficient importance to suppress any significant seasonal variation in the slave trade due to direct African importation. The lack of seasonality thus indicated the relative weakness of the direct African source for Cuban supplies of slaves. Thus, seasonality in importation, as a reflection of seasonal variation in exportation, can provide an index of the relative importance of direct contact with African exporting ports of the particular importing zone when other sources of information are lacking.

In terms of the direction of the trade, the sample mid century data fully support all previous assumptions about the intake of the Brazilian

Table 17 *Slave exports from Luanda, Angola, by port of destination, 1723-71*

Brazilian port	No. of adults	%	No. of ships	Average cargo size
Rio de Janeiro	104,170	(51.0)	281 [282]*	370
Bahia	55,696	(27.3)	158	352
Pernambuco	37,092	(18.2)	95	390
Maranhão	2,570	(1.2)	5	514
Pará	2,161	(1.0)	4	540
Colonia de Sacramento	1,569	(0.7)	4	392
Santos	474	(0.2)	1	474
Unknown	172	(. . .)†	1	172
Totals	203,904	(99.5)	549	371

*Plus 1 ship unknown as to adult passengers.
†Less than 0.1 per cent.
Source: Same as Table 14.

ports. Rio de Janeiro accounted for over 50 per cent of the total slaves shipped from Angola in the period 1723 to 1771 (see Table 17). Together with Bahia, Rio de Janeiro handled over two thirds of the mid century trade. Pernambuco, Maranhão and Pará received a quarter of the trade, due to the deliberate encouragement of the two Pombaline Companies (the Companhia Geral do C rão-Pará e Maranhão, and the Companhia Geral de Pernambuco e Paraíba). With the abolition of the trading monopolies, starting in the 1770s, these centres seem to have expanded their trade to Luanda and by the early decades of the nineteenth century they (above all, Recife in Pernambuco) had increased their share in the Angolan slave trade.[7] It should also be stressed that for most of the regions of the Brazilian northeast, the prime source of slaves remained the Guinea coast, with Angola being only a secondary supplier,[8] while, for Rio de Janeiro, the primary supplier remained Angola until the end of the slave trade.[9]

In the mid eighteenth century, just as in the late eighteenth and early nineteenth centuries, a few vessel types dominated the slave trade. Whereas eighteen types of vessels were employed, just two, the *Galera* (Galley) and *Curveta* (Corvette), together accounted for 302 vessels, or 55 per cent of the total employed in the twenty-seven years. These two vessels were extremely important in the Rio de Janeiro trade in the 1795 to 1811 period, but were equalled then by the *Bergantim*.[10] In mid century the *Bergantim* was a rarely used vessel and its average cargo size was quite small.[11] Of these leading vessel types, the *Galera* was clearly the largest in capacity. While vessel designation primarily concerned the arrangement of sails and masts, it also seems to have roughly reflected volume capacity as well.

Crown treasury officials collected statistics of the legal slave capacity of some eighty-eight ships. This capacity, called the *arqueação*, was a measure based on the actual tonnage of the ship. By the law of 1684 the crown determined that each vessel was to have its tonnage legally recorded in its papers and that the slave ships were to express tonnage as the maximum capacity to carry slaves. The ratio, involving different measures for different areas of the vessel, worked out to between 2.5 and 3.5 slaves per ton, depending on the construction of the ship.[12] Table 18 gives the breakdown of the *arqueação* and number of slaves actually carried on these eighty-eight ships.

While there may be some serious question as to the accuracy of the figures of slaves carried, the capacity data seem worthy of being treated as valid. Since these figures were part of the legal ship's papers and did not vary from voyage to voyage, they were probably not tampered with. If figures were deliberately distorted, it would be in the actual carried column. If then, we take 420 as the average carrying capacity, and accept the 2.5 to 3.5 tons ratio for below deck capacity allowed by Portuguese law, then it is evident that the average tonnage of mid eighteenth century ships was between 120 and 168 tons.[13]

One of the most difficult items to determine properly is the counting of children. Unlike adults, there seems to have been no stability in their exportation rates, as Table 19 indicates. The annual variation could be due to any number of factors.

Table 18 *Legal carrying capacity of ships and number of slaves actually carried, 1762–5*

Legal capacity	No. of ships	Total legal capacity	Total actually carried
200–299	13	3,286 (252)*	3,270 (251)
300–399	27	9,220 (341)	9,274 (343)
400–499	22	9,459 (429)	9,067 (412)
500–599	17	8,821 (518)	7,846 (461)
600–699	6	3,792 (632)	3,321 (553)
700–799	1	720 (720)	488 (488)
800–899	1	800 (800)	705 (705)
900–999	1	940 (940)	706 (706)
Totals	88	37,038 (420)	34,677 (394)

*The figures in parentheses represent the average per category.

Source: Same as Table 14.

Table 19 Children, by category, shipped from Luanda, 1726-69

Year	Taxed children*	Half-taxed children (crias de pé)	Untaxed children at the breast (crias de peito)	Total children	Total slaves
1726	—	—	119	—	8,440
1727	—	—	94	—	7,633
1728	—	—	114	—	8,532
1731	—	—	93	—	5,808
1734	—	—	—	1,396	10,109
1738	—	—	—	1,187	8,810
1740	—	311	98	409	8,484
1741	—	736	154	890	9,158
1742	—	249	135	384	10,591
1744	—	426	166	592	8,848
1747	—	1,442	99	1,541	9,869
1748	—	894	101	995	11,810
1749	—	782	99	881	9,776
1758	—	—	—	139	9,938
1762	45	22	80	147	8,415
1763	31	17	61	109	7,634
1764	54	18	76	148	7,648
1765	16	62	200	278	10,672
1766	72	14	97	183	9,420
1767	13	8	69	90	9,318
1769	—	36	46	82	5,733

*This seems to have been a special term only used in the decade of the 1760s. Thereafter such children, since they were fully taxed, must have been placed in the adult (cabeça) category.

Source: Same as Table 14.

The most obvious possibility is that there were gross errors in counting children. Since infants at the breast (crias de peito) went free of any export tax, and children up to a certain height (crias de pé) went only half taxed, there might have been a tendency to count more adults in these categories. This especially would have been the case when there was a problem over the legal capacity of a ship. As one Treasury official of Angola candidly admitted, local officials tended to consider the capacity, or arqueação figure, as referring to adults alone.[14] Thus the desire to avoid taxes and/or to avoid action against illegal overcrowding would have led officials consistently to overstate the number of children. However, as Table 19 indicates, the number of

Table 20 *Income and expenditures of seven slaves shipped to Rio de Janeiro in 1762 by Captain João Xavier de Proença e Sylva (in reis)*

	Portuguese reis
I *Income:*	
Two young girl slaves who died at sea	—
1 *negro*[1] sold to Ignacio Martins on 30 May	90$000
1 *molecão*[2] sold to Manoel Francisco dos Santos on 4 June	64$000
1 *molecão* sold to Francisco Lobo on 14 June	70$000
1 *moleque*[3] died, after landing, on 14 June	—
1 *moleque* sold to Manoel Machado Borges on 30 June	51$600
Total income	275$600
II *Expenditures:*	
For shipment by sea and costs to Sea Captain	100$295
For the services of a priest (for baptising 5 slaves at 1$500 rs. per slave)	7$500
For medicinal foods and medicine for one slave who was sick after landing	2$120
For a total of 76 days of maintenance at 60 rs. per diem	4$560
For sales commission of 6 percent	16$536
Partial Costs[4]	131$011
Excess Revenues[5]	144$589

[1] *negro* here refers to an adult male (*cabeça*).
[2] *molecão* a youth, male.
[3] *moleque* a child, male. Both these terms are fairly common to both the Spanish and Portuguese slave trade. The former distinguishes a youth from c. 7 to 10 years of age, and *molecão* defines a teenager from c. 11 to 17 years.
[4] Includes all costs except original purchase price of slaves.
[5] Excess revenues over all costs except purchase price.

Note: Portuguese currency in the eighteenth century was expressed in units of *reis*. The dollar sign was the standard sign used to distinguish *milreis*, or units of a thousand *reis* and thus stands where modern usage would put the comma. Finally, there was the *conto* which was equivalent to 1 million reis and was expressed as follows: 1:000$000. In this case the colon stands for the second comma. Since all documents and published works in Portuguese use these conventional signs for commas, this usage has been adopted by most works in English as standard and I have thus used them in this paper instead of the comma sign.

Source: BNL, Colecção Pombalina, Codice 617, folio 222.

children reported shipped to Brazil was quite low. On the other hand, it could also be that there was little serious effort made to record the children since they were unimportant to royal officials in terms of taxation. Officials did not all record their observations in an identical manner, and thus entries often differed from person to person. Also, at various times children were carefully recorded, and at other times ignored, and it is often difficult to determine if no children in a given instance were shipped, or if they were simply not recorded. Thus it is probable that many more children were shipped than were recorded by the port officials.

Nevertheless, I am still of the belief that children were not shipped in any large quantities in the slave trade. In the Luanda data, only 6 per cent of the 156,638 slaves shipped between 1734 and 1769 were children. In the Benguela listings (see Appendix Table II) only 3.1 per cent of the 57,689 slaves shipped between 1738 and 1784 were children. Nor were these low figures particularly unusual. In fact, if anything, they were a bit on the high side. In the Dutch slave trade the number of children under 15 years of age shipped in the eighteenth century was anywhere from 8 per cent to 13 per cent of the total slaves shipped,[15] while the Pernambuco Company figures indicated children accounted for only 1 per cent of total cargoes.[16] Finally, the registers for the port of Rio de Janeiro between 1795 and 1811 report the shipping from Africa of only 923 children out of 170,651 Africans, or 0.5 per cent. One explanation for the low number of children involved in the slave trade could be their higher mortality in the 'middle passage.' But an analysis of the Rio de Janeiro data shows that the children suffered less than adults, with their overall mortality at sea being 6.2 per cent of those shipped from Africa, as opposed to 9.5 per cent for the adults.[17] The question remains, then, why so few children were shipped. At this stage it is difficult to determine if Africans were extremely reluctant to supply children to the slave trade, or if planters were reluctant to purchase them.

While the quantitative data in the Arquivo Histórico Ultramarino give some rough ideas of the general volume, direction, and components of the trade, other documents available in Lisbon's archives provide a glimpse into the economic organization of the trade. From the accounts left by the Luanda merchant Capitão João Xavier de Proença e Sylva, some initial statements can be made about the trade itself.[18] It seems evident from the papers of this merchant and other related documents that an important fraction of the slaves shipped from Angola were shipped to the account of Angolan merchants. Proença e Sylva himself shipped only a few slaves with each voyage, but other merchants shipped a dozen or more, either for themselves or for the account of other Luandans. Thus, the *Galera* 'Santo Antonio, Santa Anna e Almas' which left Luanda on 26 October 1727 and landed in Bahia a short time later, listed 90 owners of the 385 adults and 77 children who were shipped. This would mean an average of 5.1 slaves per owner. Actually the captain of the vessel, João de Tavora, was listed, along with an undesignated Company ('Capitão João de Tavora, e Companhia') as owner of 101 adults and 22 children, and the captain alone possessed another 10 adults on his own account exclusive of the company.

Presumably the captain and his company represented Bahian merchant and planter capital, which both owned the vessel and probably also purchased part of the cargo on its own account. If these 133 slaves are subtracted, the other 88 owners of slaves, all of whom appear to be residents of Luanda, would thus have averaged 3.7 slaves per owner.[19]

How representative this particular voyage was of the whole eighteenth-century trade is impossible to say. As of the moment no other such detailed listings of owners of slaves aboard a slave vessel have come to light. From the accounts of Captain Proença e Sylva, however, some corroborative evidence to support some of the data is available. Captain Proença e Sylva was involved in the trade at a much later date, his papers covering the late 1750s and early 1760s. As a resident of Luanda he shipped a large number of slaves from that port to Brazil, both on his own account and for the account of other Luandans. Though he obviously had a thriving trade, most of his shipments were in lots of only a few slaves. On the average he sent one or two slaves per vessel, his biggest recorded shipment being seven slaves aboard one *Galera* which went to Rio de Janeiro in 1762.[20]

Not only were the shipments quite small, but it appears that Captain Proença e Sylva retained ownership of the slaves from the time they were purchased in the interior of Africa to their final sale to a Brazilian planter. Thus he was required to pay not only the initial purchase price and transportation to the coast, but the sea transportation and the maintenance of the slaves in Brazil as well. Additional to the account in Table 20, he had to pay the cost of clothing the slaves in new Brazilian clothes, as well as medical expenses, and even funeral expenses, should the slave die before sale. Finally he was required to pay his factor in the Brazilian city a sales commission, and even to pay for the purchase of a letter of credit so as to remit his profits back to either Luanda or to his representative in Lisbon.[21]

Since I could not obtain the costs to Captain Proença e Sylva of his purchases in Portugal and Angola of goods which he used to buy slaves in the interior, nor do I have any idea of the costs to him of employing *pombeiros* and/or their commission, and finally the varying costs to him of maintaining the slaves in Luanda until the arrival of a slave ship, I cannot estimate net profits.[22] What the Captain's papers do reveal is that he had a trusted network of traders in the two major Brazilian ports, Rio de Janeiro and Bahia, and that his commercial connections also extended to Portugal. Thus while Portugal was not a shipping base for the trade, as was England or France, it played an important role in financing the trade. It would also appear that from time to time ships were built and outfitted in Portugal for the African slave trade, but that once launched they never returned to Portugal, at least not from Africa.[23]

Thus the African slave trade from Angola, at least for the free traders, was primarily a two-way trade, rather than the more common triangular trade that most of the other European slave trading nations developed. Because of wind and current conditions in the South Atlantic, it was far too difficult for a ship to sail directly from Angola to Portugal, and even the trip from Brazil took from two to four months. So it was Brazilian-made ships, by and large, and Brazilian crews that maintained the Angolan slave trade. It was also Brazilian-produced goods that supplied most of the imports for the 2000 persons who inhabited the town of Luanda in the mid eighteenth century.[24] The chief imports from Brazil were alcohol, European and Asian cloths and textiles, and basic foodstuffs to help feed the Luanda community.[25] It was, above all, alcohol and cloth which were used by the Luanda merchants in the purchase of slaves in the interior. *Geribita*, a special type of alcoholic beverage, seems to have been a highly prized Brazilian import in the Angolan hinterland.[26] But these Brazilian goods were only a part of the products used in the interior slave trade, and it seems that many African products, especially salt and palm-cloth, still played a major part in the trade.[27]

It would also seem apparent, from the important role played by Luanda merchants, that the actual movement of slaves was closely regulated. Since the merchants could anticipate ships' arrivals, they could control local supplies so that there was little waiting at Luanda itself, which would have been an added cost.[28] Also, given the fact that Portugal remained neutral during almost the entire eighteenth century, through the famous series of imperial wars, the regularity of shipment gave to the trade a predictable quality.

Although the bulk of the trade was in the hands of independent merchants, there were other aspects to the trade in which either the government or its representatives took an active part. In the eighteenth century, for example, the crown farmed out its taxes on slave exports to private entrepreneurs. Often these men engaged in direct trading themselves, and usually they maintained a monopoly on the small ivory trade leaving Luanda.[29] Until the middle of the eighteenth century the crown tended to rent out its taxes, and then as need for more funds arose, it would set up a new tax independent of the already rented royal taxes. These new taxes were collected by royal tax officials, and from all the evidence I have seen so far, it appears that the crown never rented out all of its pre-1758 taxes to a private entrepreneur at any one time. Thus the royal tax officials were always employed, and while the data are unclear, many of them may have also collected the taxes for the private tax farmer as well.[30] By the middle of the century some four different taxes were being collected on the export of slaves.[31] By this time, even the crown realized the excessive complexity of its tax structure. Thus in 1758 it abolished all the outstanding taxes and instituted a single head tax of 8$700 reis per adult slave (*cabeça*), and 3$400 for every walking child (*crias de pé*) exported from Angola.[32] This tax, however, it also farmed out.[33]

Another area in which the government intervened as an active economic agent in the slave trade had to do with the establishment during the time of Pombal of the monopoly trade companies for Maranhão and Pernambuco. These two companies were set up in 1755 and 1759 respectively and their object was to promote the development of these respective regions.[34] Both companies were given the exclusive rights to import slaves into these Brazilian areas. Of the two companies, the most important as far as Angola was concerned was the Pernambuco & Paraíba Company. Of the grand total of 49,344 slaves which this company shipped to Brazil between 1761 and 1786, 41,777 (or 85 per cent) came from the port of Luanda.[35] As for the Grão-Pará & Maranhão Company, only 6235 (or 22 per cent) of its total of 28,083 slaves came from this same port. The bulk of its slaves (19,666) came from the Upper Guinean ports of Cacheu and Bissau.[36] In the overall trade between 1723 and 1771 (see Table 21), the Luanda slave exports to Pará, Maranhão and Pernambuco totalled 41,823 slaves or 20 per cent of the total slaves exported from Luanda in this period. Of this total, the monopoly companies had an extremely important share, though their disappearance, as will be seen, did not alter the pattern of the flow of slaves to all Brazilian ports.

In his exhaustive study of the Pombaline companies during this period, António Carreira has provided data on a whole range of topics which complement the free trade materials. His data, for example, provide complete runs for a period of thirty-two and twenty-seven consecutive years for slave voyages made by the Maranhão and Pernambuco Company ships respectively. From these well-preserved materials frequency of voyage patterns can be constructed. The result shows an unusually high average for the number of sailings per ship engaged in the slave trade, being 4.0 (or 43 ships having 175 voyages in 32 years), and 5.0 (or 25 ships making 125 trips in 27 years) respectively. Over half the Maranhão company vessels made two voyages or less, and the median was three sailings per vessel for the Pernambuco company ships. For the free traders, I have only been able to compile complete returns for two separate six-year periods: 13 February 1723 to 18 December 1728 and 25 January 1762 to 23 December 1767. For the 1720s the mean voyage

Table 21 *Slave exports from Luanda of the Pombaline slave trade companies and Brazilian ports of destination, 1756–88*

Company	Pará	Maran-hão	Pernam-buco	Rio de Janeiro	Total
'Pernambuco e Paraíba'	—	—	41,557	220	41,777
'Grão Pará e Maranhão'	5,318	808	—	109	6,235
Totals	5,318	808	41,557	329	48,012
Luanda Exports (1723–1771)	(2,161)	(2,570)*	(37,092)	(104,170)	

*Of this total, 996 slaves were carried to Maranhão in 1758 by two ships that were not listed as Company vessels, and are therefore presumed to be free traders. The other three ships are, however, listed as Company vessels and were all from the export year of 1762. Checking Carreira's detailed list of ships (contained in his Appendix, Document 'S', pp. 454–61) against my own records, it is evident that two of these 1762 ships he has listed as destination Pará (ships 1 and 3 on his list, which carried a total of 1150 slaves), the AHU documents list as leaving for Maranhão. He is, moreover, missing one voyage completely, that of the Galera 'São João Baptist' (his ship no. 35) which also made a trip from Luanda to Maranhão in 1762 and carried 424 slaves. Of the two ships which make up Carreira's 808 total, one sailed from Luanda in 1756, for which no port records survive in the AHU, and the other sailed in 1765 (no. 4 vessel on his list), the AHU documents giving its port of destination Pará instead of Maranhão as listed in his company records.

Sources: Carreira, *As companhias pombalinas*, pp. 91, 261; and Table 17 above.

frequency was 1.9 (61 ships for 118 voyages) and 2.2 (or 63 ships for 140 trips) for the 1760s, with the median being two voyages in the first case and three in the latter one. Though there is a serious bias in the free trade data,[37] and they are for much shorter periods than the company records, they do seem to agree with the figures for the free-trade slavers working out of Rio de Janeiro in 1795 to 1811, and the Bahian free-trade slavers in the century before 1815. In the former, covering some seventeen years, the average was 2.9 sailings per ship and the median frequency was two voyages. In the latter case, covering over a century of shipping, with 626 ships making 1736 sailings, the average was 2.7 and the median frequency two sailings per ship.[38] It would thus seem that the 1760s listings are probably a more accurate reflection of the norm for free traders than were the 1730s recordings. Also, it would seem from the Bahian, Luandan, and Rio de Janeiro data, that the monopoly company ships had a much higher than average frequency of voyage pattern than free traders. This differential frequency appears to be a direct result of the monopoly contracts of the companies. The entrance of private traders into the trade was based on relative rates of return, whereas the monopoly companies were constrained to deliver a given number of slaves per annum to preserve their lucrative monopolies over the export trade of the slave plantation colonies.

In terms of cargoes carried, the Pernambuco Company came quite close to the overall Luanda trade average of 397 slaves (adults and children) carried per vessel. It carried 49,344 African adults and children to Brazil in 125 voyages, for an average of 394 persons per vessel.[39] The Maranhão company, however, has a much smaller capacity for its ships, since in its 175 voyages it shipped only 28,083 slaves, for an average cargo size of only 160 Africans.[40]

This very rapid survey of the port registers of Luanda from 1723 to 1771 and the books of the monopoly companies reveals certain basic features of the Angolan slave trade which place it in harmony with the growing knowledge of the Portuguese and European slave trade in general. The regularity of the trade and the very high volume of shipments and large carrying capacity in rather small vessels are well revealed by the Luanda data. There is also the clear response to changes in season, and the surprisingly low number of children. Though sexual breakdowns of slave cargoes are not provided by Angolan sources, it can probably be assumed that here as well, the Angola trade duplicated the Dutch, English, and French trades.[41] What is probably unique about the Angolan trade was the very important role played by African-based merchants – in this case the Portuguese Luandans – in the carrying trade, if our rather small sample of data is correct, as well as the unusually steady quality of that trade. The fact that Portugal abstained from most of the international conflicts which so disrupted the Dutch and French trades[42] and that it controlled access to the interior and successfully defended its local monopoly against European competitors helps to explain the steady volume of the trade. Equally important was the seemingly inexhaustible Brazilian demand for slaves, coupled with a thriving and largely Brazilian based merchant fleet well supported by planter and miner capital.[43]

There were, of course, changes within the trade from Angola during the course of the century. The major development in this respect was the steady increase in both total volume and size of cargoes by the end of the eighteenth century. This new trend continued into the next century, and also saw the increasing importance of the older port of Benguela and the opening up of Cabinda to systematic Portuguese exploitation.[44] Reflecting this growing volume of trade by the end of the century, there was also a decline in the number of children being shipped from Angolan ports. If these numbers are not simply due to recording errors, they may reflect the better supply of adults available to the slave trade. Since children were considered an undesirable element by most slave traders, their diminution in the trade may be considered as an indicator of a steadier supply of the more highly priced *cabeças*, or adult slaves.

While the data presented in this paper have resolved some of the broader questions of volume, direction, rhythm and vessel types employed in the trade, there are many problems which the data leave unresolved. The lack of sexual breakdowns, at least for the Luanda free trading vessels in the eighteenth century, makes it difficult to calculate this very important factor with any degree of certitude. The existence of seasonal variations, while marked, still remains a puzzling problem in terms of cause. Though the papers of Captain Proenca e Sylva give a hitherto unsuspected picture of an extremely vital Luanda merchant community, the data are still too fragmentary to detail the importance of this community in the financing and maintenance of the slave trade over time.[45] Nor are there any detailed archival sources in the eighteenth century to show the balance of trade between Brazil and Angola. Though the balance of trade was unfavourable to Angola by the early nineteenth century,[46] this pattern may not have existed in the previous century. Finally, the role played by European and Portuguese merchants in the supply of textiles, trade goods, and capital is a subject as little studied as the financial arrangements made by the Luanda merchants with their own trading agents, the *pombeiros*. The costs of transportation to and from the interior, of commissions paid to the *pombeiros*, along with actual costs of imported goods, remain to be determined before profit figures can be fully ascertained. While the unanswered questions thus remain formidable, the systematic exploitation of the port registers of Luanda and Rio de Janeiro, along with the detailed records of the Pombaline slave trading companies, have at least provided the broad outlines of the eighteenth-century Portuguese slave trade from Angola to Brazil.

Appendix Table I *Slave exports from Luanda in the eighteenth century, exclusive of complete return years.*[1]

Year	Adults	Children	Infants	Total slaves	Number of ships	Average cargo size[5]
1710	3,549	n.a.	n.a.	n.a.	n.a.	
1711	4,158	n.a.	n.a.	n.a.	n.a.	
1712	4,188	n.a.	n.a.	n.a.	n.a.	
1713	5,617	n.a.	n.a.	n.a.	n.a.	
1714	5,581	n.a.	n.a.	n.a.	n.a.	
1718	6,747	n.a.	n.a.	n.a.	n.a.	
1719	6,886	n.a.	n.a.	n.a.	n.a.	
1720	7,213	n.a.	n.a.	n.a.	n.a.	
1721	5,378	n.a.	n.a.	n.a.	n.a.	
1722	5,062	n.a.	n.a.	n.a.	n.a.	
1735	8,059	1,198[2]		9,257	n.a.	
1736	10,961	1,290[2]		12,251	n.a.	
1737	8,946	967[2]		9,913	n.a.	
1739	8,169	1,329[2]		9,498	n.a.	
1743	12,130	355[2]		12,485	n.a.	
1745	11,122	824[2]		11,946	n.a.	
1746	9,397	1,147[2]		10,544	n.a.	
1750	10,253	1,149	146	11,548	27	427
1751	8,323	476	70	8,869	23	385
1752	9,196	878	112	10,186	27	377
1753	9,043	973	136	10,152	25	406
1754	7,820	860	127	8,807	20	440
1755	9,077	35	108	9,220	22	419
1756	9,988	36	127	10,151	26	390
1757	10,653	31	80	10,764	27	398
1760	8,211	n.a.	n.a.	n.a.	n.a.	
1761	7,911	n.a.	n.a.	n.a.	n.a.	
1768	7,214	n.a.	n.a.	n.a.	n.a.	
1776	10,194	n.a.	n.a.	n.a.	n.a.	
1784	8,974	n.a.	n.a.	n.a.	20	(448)
1797	8,938[3]	n.a.	n.a.	n.a.	n.a.	
1798	10,271	1	...[4]	10,272	16	641
1799	7,661[3]	n.a.	n.a.	n.a.	17	(450)

[1] These are given, with sources, in Table 14.
[2] This is an infant-children total which does not distinguish between *crias de pé* and *crias de peito* (infants).
[3] This is an estimated total which I obtained by dividing the total royal tax by 8$700 reis.
[4] This indicates a zero sum; n.a. is not available.
[5] Average cargo size is given only when full information is available. Parentheses indicate partial figures.

Sources: For 1710 to 1714, see Birmingham, *Trade and Conflict*, p. 137; 1718–1722 in AHU, Angola, cx. 16; 1735–1737, 1739, 1743, 1745–1746 are all found in cx. 32; 1750–1753 in cx. 26; 1754–1757 in cx. 27; 1760–1761, and 1768 in cx. 32; 1776 in AHU, Codice 409, folio 111v; 1784 in AHU, Angola, maço 13; 1797 in AHU, Angola maço 1a; 1798 in cx. 46; 1799 in cx. 47.

Appendix Table II Slave exports from Benguela in the eighteenth century

Year	Adults	Children	Infants	Total slaves	Number of ships	Average cargo size[4]
1738	1,515	206	72	1,793	5	303
1740	834	64	...	898	3	299
1741	593	176	5	774	2	387
1744	1,212	80	3	1,295	4	323
1747	856	99	8	963	3	321
1748	328	...[1]	...	328	1	328
1749	807	99	10	916	3	304
1750	1,687	...	17	1,704	5	340
1751	1,371	...	7	1,378	6	229
1752	1,897	...	24	1,921	7	274
1753	2,495	297	27	2,819	9	313
1754	2,787	n.a.[2]	n.a.	n.a.	9	(309)
1755	2,173	n.a.	n.a.	n.a.	8	(271)
1756	2,541	n.a.	n.a.	n.a.	8	(317)
1757	1,461	n.a.	n.a.	n.a.	5	(292)
1758	2,419	n.a.	n.a.	n.a.	7	(345)
1759	3,192	n.a.	n.a.	n.a.	n.a.	
1760	2,506	n.a.	n.a.	n.a.	n.a.	
1761	3,889	n.a.	n.a.	n.a.	n.a.	
1762	4,124	20	36	4,180	12	348
1763	3,423	5	17	3,445	10	344
1764	3,821	8	38	3,867	11	351
1765	6,081	22	80	6,183	18	343
1766	5,084	11	65	5,160	14	368
1767	6,583	12	40	6,635	18	365
1768	5,643	n.a.	n.a.	n.a.	n.a.	
1769	5,531	15	52	5,598	15	373
1770	4,726	n.a.	n.a.	n.a.	n.a.	
1771	5,293	n.a.	n.a.	n.a.	13	(407)
1772	5,021	n.a.	n.a.	n.a.	n.a.	
1773	5,363	n.a.	n.a.	n.a.	n.a.	
1774	4,321	n.a.	n.a.	n.a.	n.a.	
1775	5,739	n.a.	n.a.	n.a.	n.a.	
1776	8,115	n.a.	n.a.	n.a.	n.a.	
1784	7,608	42	182	7,832	20	391
1798	5,610[3]	n.a.	n.a.	n.a.	12	(467)

[1]This indicates a zero sum.
[2]n.a. is not available.
[3]This is an estimate since only the tax figure was available. I simply divided by 8$700 to obtain the above figure, even though this slights children and special *subsidio* tax, if collected.
[4]Average cargo size is given only when full information is available. Parentheses indicate partial figures.

Sources: 1738 was taken from AHU, Angola cx. 21 [Hereafter, AHU, Angola, will be understood before each caixa citation]; 1740, 1744 in cx. 23; 1741 in cx. 22; 1747 in cx. 24;

1748-1753 in cx. 26; 1754-1758 in cx. 27; 1760-61, 1768-1769 in cx. 32; 1762 in cx. 29; 1763-1764 in cx. 30; 1765-1766 in cx. 31; 1767 in AHU, Angola, maço 9; 1771 in cx. 33; 1776 in AHU, Codice 409, folio 112; 1784 in AHU, maço 13; 1798 in cx. 47; 1759, 1770, and 1772-1775 are taken from Birmingham, *Trade and Conflict*, pp. 151-152. I have only used Birmingham's figures when I could not obtain original documents, since they refer generally to adults only and are often drawn from later general lists, therefore making them sometimes less accurate.

10 The impact of the slave trade on East Central Africa in the nineteenth century
Edward A. Alpers

Editor's comments

For several centuries slaves were exported from East Africa to the Muslim world through the Red Sea and the Indian Ocean. Exports to the Indian Ocean islands held by the Europeans were later added to the Muslim trade. But, unlike the west coast of Africa, exports from East Africa by way of the Atlantic trade became significant only from the late eighteenth century onward. It was in the first half of the nineteenth century that the Atlantic slave trade from East Africa greatly expanded. The impact of this great expansion on the economies and societies of East Africa has been little studied. Edward Alpers is one of the few authorities in this aspect of East African history. The present chapter is an extract from his book on the East African slave trade, covering the nineteenth and earlier centuries. Alpers shows that the available records, especially British consular figures for Brazil, greatly understate the numbers of slaves actually exported. This is so because there were a great deal of illicit slave imports into Brazil, particularly after 1830. The author gives an example in 1821 when British consular officials reported only 2941 slaves exported from Mozambique in Brazilian ships, while it was shown that export duties were collected on 12,272 slaves at Mozambique in the same year. Yet, even the Mozambique customs figures are conservative, since large numbers were smuggled to avoid the payment of export duties on the slaves. From the point of view of the opportunity cost of the slave trade, the author shows how the export trade of East Africa in gold and other commodities declined as slave exports expanded. This was the more so for the trade of Quelimane, where in 1821 slave exports accounted for 85 per cent of total exports by value. As the author shows, the main African slave dealers in East Africa

This chapter is an extract from Edward Alpers, *Ivory and Slaves in East Central Africa: changing patterns of international trade to the later nineteenth century* (London: Heinemann 1975), pp. 209–43. It has been reprinted here by permission of the author and the publishers.

were the Yao and the Makua. Among the Makua, the Matibane and the Uticulo predominated. But, as was the case in Angola, resident Portuguese traders were directly involved in the acquisition of slaves from the interior. This gave them ample opportunity to ferment political conflicts among the hinterland states. In the Mozambique trading area the impact of the trade was very much felt by the Makua who inhabited the immediate hinterland. But in the Kilwa trading area, the thinly populated hinterland was quickly exhausted, and the centre of supply moved farther inland to the best endowed and thickly populated region around Lake Nyasa – an example of the export slave trade attacking parts of Africa with the greatest potential for modern economic development.

The Mozambique Coast

The first half of the nineteenth century in East Africa was marked by the continued rapid growth of the slave trade. All along the coast the demand for slaves steadily mounted, as Arabs, Brazilians, French, Spanish slavers from Cuba, and Americans discovered East Africa in the wake of the British anti-slave trade campaign in West Africa. East Africa was not completely ignored in the British campaign to abolish the slave trade, but it clearly was considered to be of secondary importance until the successful eradication of the West African traffic. Treaties were sought and sometimes secured with the Portuguese, the French, 'Uman, and the Hova rulers of Madagascar, but severe limitations on the rights of the British navy to seize and search suspected offending vessels, the inadequate size of the anti-slave trade patrol in the Indian Ocean, and the desire of virtually no body of traders in East Africa to abandon a most lucrative business rendered the campaign largely ineffective until the second half of the century.[1] Thus there were no serious obstacles to the unprecedented expansion of the exportation of slaves from East Africa for the half century after 1810.

At Mozambique Island slaves were already established as the most important item of commerce. In 1809 ivory exports had declined to about 7300 *arrobas*; in 1817 they had sunk to less than 4000 *arrobas*.[2] By the following year revenue collected on the exportation of slaves (52:815$600 *reis*) was more than five times that accruing from exportations of ivory and other goods (10:089$215 *reis*), alone accounting for 32.26 per cent of the total revenue of the customs-house (163:673$288 *reis*).[3] And in 1819 the Governor-General of Mozambique, João da Costa de Brito Sanches. observed that 'the present commerce of the

Colony only consists of the principal article of slaves, and some ivory, which is exported to the North in two, or three vessels'.[4] A few years later, this impression was substantiated by the visiting Captain Owen, who observed that 'the commerce of Mozambique has much decreased, and at present it is little more than a mart for slaves, together with a small quantity of ivory, gold dust, and a few articles of minor value'.[5]

According to Governor-General Sebastião Xavier Botelho, whose memoirs on the colony are often fanciful and unreliable, there was a marked revival of the ivory trade of Macuana during his administration in the late 1820s. But Botelho's figures are undoubtedly inflated, and his description of this trade looks suspiciously derivative from several later eighteenth-century accounts of this trade during its heyday.[6] Perhaps there was a temporary increase in the ivory trade of Macuana in those years – it was never abandoned completely – but official customs-house figures for 1829 demonstrate convincingly the commanding position of the slave trade at Mozambique. Slaves (110:667$790 *rèis*) produced some 55 per cent of the revenue received from total exports (201:909$792 *réis*) in that year, with coinage accounting for slightly less than 3 per cent and 'diverse goods' among which ivory must have been included, accounting for the remaining 42 per cent.[7] Since 1818 revenue from the slave trade had more than doubled, while that of the colony as a whole had increased by not quite 24 per cent. The export economy gradually ceased to be dominated by the slave trade in the 1850s, when the colonial encyclopedist, Francisco Maria Bordalo, wrote of the customs-house at Mozambique: 'For a long time the duties from this customs-house were the principal revenue of the colony: almost exhausted by the extinction of the slave trade, a new expansion is today promised with the gradual development of legitimate commerce'.[8]

Most of the demand for slaves at Mozambique came from Brazil. Following Great Britain's abolition of the slave trade by British subjects in 1807, much pressure was brought to bear on the Portuguese crown first to restrict and then to abolish the slave trade carried on by Portuguese subjects and in Portuguese territories. These measures did not achieve their purpose until the second half of the century; but by legally limiting, in 1815 and 1817, the Portuguese slave trade to Portuguese possessions in Africa lying south of the equator, they encouraged the diversion of much of the Brazilian traffic from West Africa to Portuguese East Africa. The achievement of Brazilian independence in 1822 further frustrated Britain's attempts to abolish the slave trade south of the equator.[9] Thus, although slaves from Mozambique were less in demand than those coming from the Congo region and Angola – in Maranhão they simply did not flourish – this

Impact of slave trade on East Central Africa: 19th century 245

trans-Atlantic trade was pursued vigorously.[10]

As usual, quantification of the slave trade is a risky undertaking, especially after 1830, when the trade at Brazil was declared illegal. Milburn's estimate that some 10,000 slaves annually were exported from Mozambique at the beginning of the second decade of the nineteenth century seems to be exaggerated; but by the end of that decade this was probably a minimal figure.[11] In 1818 export duties were collected on 8164 slaves, but in order to appreciate the significance of that figure it is necessary to recognize that these were not the only slaves brought to the market at Mozambique.[12] Generally, some fifteen to eighteen Brazilian vessels arrived at Mozambique between July and October to trade for slaves in return for money. According to D. Fr. Bartolomeu dos Mártires, Prelate of Mozambique from 1819 to his death in 1828, in 1819 sixteen Brazilian ships embarked from that port with cargoes of slaves. Fr. Bartolomeu recorded that the Brazilians bought 9242 slaves, 1804 of whom died at Mozambique; and of the 7920 who were embarked, 2196 died on the voyage to Brazil, so that only 5234 were landed there, at Rio de Janeiro, Bahia, and Pernambuco, a mortality rate of 27.7 per cent on the sea passage alone. Furthermore, some 1200 slaves who were awaiting sale at Mozambique died before they could be purchased. In 1819, then, at least 10,442 slaves were known to have been carried to Mozambique for sale to Brazilian slavers alone. Of these, only half ever reached their intended destination.[13]

Figures compiled by British consulate officials in Brazil, in particular Rio de Janeiro, reflect the increasing volume of the Mozambique slave trade during the 1820s, but they are undoubtedly incomplete. Many slaves were disembarked in Brazil without paying duties at Rio de Janeiro, just as untold numbers were taken on illegally along the coast running north and south from Mozambique Island. In 1821, for example, the first year for which these detailed figures exist, only 2941 slaves were reported by the British as having been embarked at Mozambique aboard Brazilian vessels. In the same year, dos Mártires, who was by then a member of the Revolutionary Provisional Government, reports that export duties were collected on 12,272 slaves at Mozambique.[14] However, even official figures from Mozambique tended to be conservative. In 1826, the Captain of a British cruiser anchored at Mozambique wrote:

> Between eight and ten thousand [slaves] are entered at the Custom house annually as being exported from the Port of Mozambique to the Brazils – however I consider that about $\frac{1}{4}$ or more may be added to that number as being shipped off to the Brazils in these vessels. This additional fourth is smuggled on board to cheat the Custom house.[15]

Table 22 *Slaves exported from Mozambique, 1818-30*

Year	Number of slaves
1818	8,164[1]
1819	7,920[2]
1820	—
1821	12,272[1] (2,941[3])
1822	4,973[4]
1823	4,204[5]
1824	3,173[3]
1825	3,753[3]
1826	—
1827	2,810[3]
1828	6,655[3]
1829	7,789[6]
1830	6,350[3]
Total	68,063

Sources: ACL., Azul Ms. 648, no. 17; Mártires, 'Memoria', fo. 35; PRO., FO84/17, Hayne to Earl of Clanwilliam, Rio de Janeiro, 15 May 1822, enclosure, and 21 August 1822, enclosure; PRO., FO 84/24. H. Chamberlain to George Canning, Rio de Janeiro, 25 January 1823, enclosure, and 15 August 1823, enclosure; PRO., FO 84/31, same to same, Rio de Janeiro, 5 January 1824, enclosure, and 31 March 1824, enclosure; PRO., FO 84/42, same to same, Rio de Janeiro, 4 January 1825, enclosure; PRO., FO 84/55, same to same, Rio de Janeiro, 4 January 1826, enclosure; PRO., FO 84/71, A. McCarthy to John Bidwell, Rio de Janeiro, 10 November 1827, enclosure; PRO., FO84/84, A. J. Heatherly to same, Rio de Janeiro, 15 January 1828; ibid., McCarthy to same, Rio de Janeiro, 26 April 1828, enclosure, and 9 August 1828, enclosure; PRO., FO 84/95, same to same, Rio de Janeiro, 26 February 1829, enclosure, and 30 April 1829, enclosure; ibid., same to Earl of Aberdeen, Rio de Janeiro, 11 July 1829, enclosure; PRO., FO 84/112, William Pennell to same, Rio de Janeiro, 25 January 1830, enclosure, and 15 July 1830, enclosure; ibid., Charles G. Weiss to same, Bahia, 6 February 1830, enclosure; ibid., John Parkinson to same, Pernambuco, 13 February 1830, enclosure; PRO., FO 84/112, Pennell to same, Rio de Janeiro, 8 January 1831, enclosure; see also, PRO., FO 84/95, Arthur Aston to same, Rio de Janeiro, 30 September 1829, enclosure no. 3. 'List of National Vessels to which Passports have been granted for the Slave Trade to Moçambique', Secretary of State's Office, 15 September 1829.

[1] Based upon customs-house duties.
[2] Exports to Brazil only.
[3] Exports to Rio de Janeiro only.
[4] Exports to Rio and Maranhão.
[5] Exports to Rio and Bahia.
[6] Exports to Rio, Bahia, and Pernambuco.

Portuguese objections to this contraband trade from Quitangonha to Brazilian vessels anchored in Mozambique harbour became particularly vocal in 1830.[16] Accordingly, although they are better than no index at all, the figures reproduced in Table 22 primarily from British consular dispatches in Brazil for the 1820s, the last decade of the legal slave trade

Impact of slave trade on East Central Africa: 19th century   247

in Brazil, must be recognized for what they are – seriously deficient, especially when the primary consideration is not how many slaves were landed in Brazil, but how many were brought to the Mozambique coast as a result of the increased demand for slaves to be exported. Nevertheless, they do indicate that at least more than 4950 slaves each year were being shipped from Mozambique Island to Brazil.[17]

After 1830–1, it is impossible to match even this level of quantification for the slave trade from Mozambique to Brazil. In the absence of official Brazilian records, British consuls were reduced to an exercise in intelligent guesswork. In most cases they greatly underestimated the volume of the illicit trade. Bethell's compilation of British Foreign Office statistics for the last two decades of the Brazilian slave trade indicate that at least 500,000 slaves were illegally imported into Brazil during this period.[18] How many of these came from Portuguese East Africa, let alone Mozambique Island, is impossible to establish. Nevertheless, it seems reasonable to assume that the proportion for Portuguese East Africa of nearly one quarter of all slaves imported at Rio de Janeiro in the flush years of 1828–30 immediately preceding the end of the legal traffic continued unabated in the 1830s and 1840s.[19]

Throughout this half century, however, Brazil was not the only source of demand for slaves at Mozambique. Though less important now, a considerable business in slaves continued to be carried on by the French at the island-capital. Operating from the Seychelles and Comoro Islands, ships from Bourbon and Mauritius boldly traded there despite British efforts to end this particularly localized trade and renewed Portuguese efforts to prohibit foreign trading in their East African empire. Mozambique slaves were also carried on Arab and Swahili vessels to the Comoros, where French traders purchased and then transported them to the Seychelles, before introducing them to the Mascarenes. The key to this system was the period of *francisation* which the slaves experienced at the Seychelles. After acquiring a smattering of French, they were imported to Bourbon and Mauritius under the pretext that they were already the slaves of French residents of the islands, not new slaves being brought in for sale there.[20] In 1826, Captain Acland remarked that

I have been given to understand that 35 Cargoes of Slaves have been shipped off in French vessels within the last 2 years from the Portuguese settlements. These vessels are not large perhaps averaging about 200 Slaves each Cargo.[21]

Many of these vessels operated outside Mozambique – at Ibo, Quelimane, Inhambane, and Delagoa Bay – but there is no doubt that some of them did their business at the capital, where the District Judge observed in 1829 that the French were the most frequent foreign traders.[22] French traders continued to ply their trade there in the next two decades, but they appear to have shifted their attention away from Mozambique during these years. Not until the extension to Mozambique of the thinly disguised system of slave trading which was known as the 'free labour emigration scheme' in the early 1850s did the French traders again become a major factor in the slave trade of the island.

Even less is known about the slave trade to Cuba, but in 1819 four or five Spanish vessels from Havana entered Mozambique harbour, certainly to take on slaves, before continuing on to Zanzibar to complete their cargoes.[23] Cuban slavers, and even a few American slavers, continued to put in occasional appearances at Mozambique right through the 1840s. Mention should also be made of the Arab and Swahili slave trade to Madagascar, much of which was supplied from the coast adjacent to Mozambique. These slaves were transported to several ports on the north-west shore of Madagascar, the most important of which was Bombetoka. Most of these slaves, the majority of whom were Makua, were absorbed by the Sakalava, but as time wore on some of them were also traded by the Sakalava to the Hova in the interior of the island.[24] Wholly beyond the control of the Portuguese, this trade dragged on unabated into the last quarter of the nineteenth century (see below, p. 259 and n. 73).

Considering all this activity, then, the frequently expressed estimate that at least 15,000 slaves were exported each year from Mozambique Island during the 1820s and 1830s seems quite reasonable.[25] The abolition of slave trading in Portuguese territory in 1836 was fiercely resisted in Portuguese East Africa and was certainly unenforceable by the Governor-General, the Marquês de Aracaty. However, a British blockade of Mozambique harbour in 1840, which was a preamble to the Anglo-Portuguese Slave Trade Treaty of 1842, does appear to have brought about a temporary abatement in the level of slave trading at the capital.[26] But by mid century the last fling of the Brazilian trade probably stimulated the renewed demand for slaves which produced a surplus of slaves being held for export at the coast in the early 1850s (see below, p. 257). Indeed, despite yearly fluctuations in the volume of the export trade from Mozambique, it seems unlikely that African slave traders were able to adjust their supplies on a seasonal basis, for fear of being caught empty handed when the port was full of vessels ready to take on cargoes. Thus, there was probably less seasonal variation in the numbers of slaves carried to the coast than in the numbers actually purchased there for export. Furthermore, Bishop Mártires's evidence that large numbers of slaves brought to Mozambique for export died before being purchased suggests that perhaps nearly 20,000 slaves were gathered each year in the vicinity of Mozambique during this period. Clearly, the slave trade from Mozambique in the first half of the nineteenth century imposed an unprecedented demand on the peoples of the coastal hinterland and the farther interior.

Until the nineteenth century, no direct trade had been allowed between the subordinate ports of Portuguese East Africa and the metropole. But in a very few years after the transferral of the Royal Court to Rio de Janeiro in 1808, Brazilian slave traders were clamouring for permission to open up other East African ports besides Mozambique for direct commerce. As early as 1807, a Brazilian slaver had been granted permission by the Provisional Government to carry a cargo of slaves directly from Quelimane to Ile de France, but this was an unusual exception.[27] The Governors-General of Mozambique were violently opposed to this trade, some because it hurt Mozambique and the Crown's finances, others more probably because it affected their own pockets. Their pleas were not successful, however, and on 4 February 1811, a royal decree was promulgated which opened the subordinate ports of Portuguese East Africa to direct trading by Brazilian vessels, without requiring them to call at the capital.[28] In no time at all Quelimane became a thriving slave port. Official figures compiled at Quelimane in 1820 show that in the previous six years, 15,055 slaves were exported from that port to Rio de Janeiro, Bahia, and Pernambuco. A third of these were accounted for in 1819.[29] In 1823, Lieutenant Thomas Boteler estimated that the town yielded 10,000 slaves annually and considered it to be 'now the greatest mart for slaves on the east coast'. Three years later another British naval officer observed that many French slavers from Bourbon also traded there.[30] His impressions were verified in the next year by a notorious French slave trader named Charles Letord, better known as Dorval, who testified before the British Commission of Enquiry at Mauritius in exchange for personal amnesty. Dorval told the Commissioners that he thought that perhaps 12,000 to 15,000 slaves were taken away from Quelimane each year by 1827.[31] How many of these slaves were carried to Brazil and how many to the Mascarenes is difficult to ascertain. The statistics compiled by the British at Rio de Janeiro for slaves shipped from Quelimane for the period 1820–32, plus the lone Portuguese set of statistics from 1821, total 45,205, an annual average of slightly more than 4100 individuals during each of the eleven years for which statistics are available.[32] The incompleteness of these consular figures for the Mozambique trade has already been noted, but nevertheless they provide a useful base line for the Brazilian trade against which to weigh the estimates of British naval officials and men like Dorval. In fact, by this time the transformation of Quelimane and the Rivers of Sena to a slave-trading economy was virtually complete, and even more stunning than that of Mozambique. In 1806 ivory and gold accounted for 57 per cent of the total value of exports from Quelimane, with slaves taking only 17 per cent. In 1821 slaves yielded 85 per cent of export revenue, while ivory and gold brought in only 7 per cent.

After 1832, knowledge of the slave trade at Quelimane again depends entirely upon the observations of occasional visitors. In general, these random reports suggest the same level of trading which existed at Mozambique, a continued brisk trade in the 1830s and a slight decline during the 1840s. In 1838, Texugo condemned Quelimane as a place wholly committed to the slave trade and noted that 'during the whole year the harbour was never without some slavers'.[34] If Quelimane prospered somewhat less in the 1840s, like at Mozambique its slave trade was revitalized in the following decade by the French *engagé* system.

Ibo, too, enjoyed a marked revival as a result of the slave trade during the first half of the nineteenth century. Until 1820, the continual threat and realization of Sakalava raids, as well as attacks from the neighbouring Makua, completely paralysed the trade of the Kerimba Islands. The low point for the Portuguese was probably reached in 1811, when the Makua routed an expedition sent against them on the mainland and killed the Governor of the Kerimba Islands.[35] By the end of the decade, however, the Portuguese had finally reorganized themselves at Ibo, and the power of the Sakalava raiders was being broken at its root by the imperial expansion of the Hova. During these desperate years, only a few bold Swahili continued to ply their coastal trade. Soon after an end had been put to the Sakalava threat, French slave traders began to return to the islands, which had been one of their favourite haunts in the eighteenth century. In 1827, Dorval gave evidence that there were nearly always slaves ready for purchase there, a statement which conforms to the impression of the responses of African suppliers at Mozambique. According to Dorval, the export slave trade at Ibo was exclusively French, as Brazilian vessels never went there. A man named Fortuné Bataille (Batalha), who was a friend of the Governor of the Kerimba Islands, was the principal supplier to the French slavers at Ibo.[36] In 1829, Governor-General Botelho warned the new Governor of the islands against admitting any foreign vessels to trade there, indicating that the majority of the 'fantastic arrivals' were French ships from Bourbon. Botelho's admonishment had about as much effect as similar warnings had in the past, and this traffic continued to flourish. After

Impact of slave trade on East Central Africa: 19th century 251

1830 Brazilian traders seem to have put in at Ibo occasionally, and in the late 1850s Cuban slavers took on cargoes there.[37] In 1858, H. Lyons McLeod, the first British Consul at Mozambique, reported that Ibo had acquired a reputation as 'the great Warehouse for Slaves'.[38]

As Mozambique and Quelimane were the principal markets for the Brazilian slave traders, and Ibo served in a similar capacity for the French in Portuguese East Africa, the independent Sultanate of Angoche provided perhaps the most important outlet for the Swahili traders on the Mozambique coast. Angoche had been marking time since the first half of the sixteenth century, when it served as a major way-station for Swahili traders who were operating in Zambesia. Although it was theoretically subject to Portuguese rule, Angoche continued to survive under the leadership of its own Swahili dynasty, trading on a small scale with the hinterland of the northern lower Zambesi. The growing demand for slaves all along the coast of East Africa in the nineteenth century elevated Angoche to a position of renewed importance, however, as Arab and Swahili dhows took port there in search of slaves for the growing markets in Madagascar and the Comoro Islands. They very likely also transported some of their cargoes to the subordinate ports flanking Mozambique, like Sanculo and Quitangonha, so that some of the slaves taken on at Angoche probably found their way to Brazil eventually. In 1823, Captain Owen reported sighting

a small schooner in the River Angozha, where much traffic is carried on by the Arabs, which the Portuguese term contraband, though the country is subject to independent Regulos [chiefs], and no Portuguese dare approach it.[39]

Fifteen years later, Texugo heard news at Mozambique of two French slavers at Angoche, where they could deal openly.[40]

In the 1840s Angoche increasingly became an embarrassment for the Portuguese, whom the British held responsible for the slave trade carried on there because of their empty claims to political authority over the town. In 1846, the intrusion of a British vessel at Angoche prompted the mounting of a joint Anglo-Portuguese expedition later in the year. Typically, the Portuguese regarded this assault as a success, but in spite of a second joint mission four years later, Angoche remained quite independent right through the next decade.[41] McLeod reckoned its population at about 1000 inhabitants, and noted that it drove a thriving trade with the towns of the Swahili coast. The Sultan controlled ninety miles of the coast, from twenty miles north of Angoche to some seventy miles south. His political authority was reputed to be recognized by thirty to forty chiefs on the mainland.[42] McLeod also reported to the Cape Station that Angoche's prosperity arose from its recent abandonment of the slave trade, but when the Portuguese succeeded in forcing the submission of Angoche in 1861, the town was described as 'the focus of an immense contraband in cloths and in slaves'.[43]

The Makua of Macuana

The volume of the slave trade at Angoche and at Ibo was not guessed at even by contemporary observers, but taken together with the trade to Quelimane and Mozambique, there can be no doubt that an immense demand for slaves was imposed upon the peoples of what is now northern Mozambique during the first half of the nineteenth century. How was the impact of the slave trade felt by these peoples? By their proximity to the coast, the Makua continued to suffer most from the slave trade to the Mozambique coast. It is, of course, important to recognize that the rise of the slave trade and the eclipse of the ivory trade provided Makua chiefs near the coast with an unprecedented opportunity to build up their own power at the expense of their neighbours farther inland, both Makua and Yao. But the advantages of slaving for these chiefs operated only in the short run, and in any case did not alter the basic political configuration of Macuana. Such was the nature of the slave trade that in the long run it worked to weaken the economic, social, and political structure of the Makua who inhabited the coastal hinterland of Mozambique.

Following a Portuguese expedition against the Uticulo chiefs in 1811, there appears to have been nearly a full decade of peaceful relations between the Makua and the Portuguese of Mozambique.[44] During these years, there is no way of ascertaining the adjustments which were being made by the Makua in response to the rapidly growing demand for slaves at the coast. By 1819, however, rivalry over control of the slave trade had clearly become the main bone of contention among the major powers in Macuana. The chief contestants against the Portuguese were the Mauruça, chief of Uticulo, and the Impahiamuno, chief of Mutipa. A decade earlier, the Impahiamuno had been closely allied with the Portuguese against the Mauruça. Now the Makua chiefs were allies. The cause of the strife in Macuana were the robberies to which coastal traders had been subjected in the hinterland.[45] According to Mártires, most of the slaves who were sent to Brazil came from this part of Macuana, a fact which surely accounts for the willingness of the Portuguese to forget the long history of surprise attacks and humiliating defeats which they had suffered at the hands of the Makua of Uticulo, so that the Bishop could write of their present '*boa inteligencia*' – 'amiable understanding' or 'harmony of interests' – with the state.[46] But the Portuguese were not content to depend on this arrangement, so that one of the features of the heyday of the slave trade in Portuguese East Africa was the more active participation of the local Portuguese (and, to a lesser extent, Indian) traders in actually procuring slaves for themselves in the interior.

During the eighteenth century, when ivory had dominated the trade of the colony, the carrying trade was exclusively in the hands of the Africans, especially those of the Yao. Banyan merchants used to send out *patamares* to negotiate with the Yao caravan leaders on their march to the coast, but the Banyans did not themselves organize trading or hunting expeditions on their own account. Nor did the Portuguese, who used *patamares* only on a limited scale in connection with the petty trade of the immediate hinterland. But so great was the demand for slaves along the coast after 1810, and so rapidly were the leading Portuguese traders able to amass their fortunes and to command large retinues of personal slaves, that they soon began to send their own parties into the interior in search of slaves at the source. This development posed a serious challenge to the control which the African traders of the interior, in this case those of Matibane and Uticulo, exercised over the carrying trade in slaves. The '*boa inteligencia*' of which Fr. Bartolomeu spoke could not long survive such a threat. Similarly, it must have been clear to the Portuguese that this conflict involved a fundamental problem in the economics of the slave trade, particularly since Matibane and the Impahiamuno were supposed to be subject to the authority of the crown.[47] Despite the urging of the crown to seek a peaceful conciliation with the Impahiamuno and the Mauruça, then, the local interests at stake were too great to let their robberies pass without censure. Prudence and political reality argued against an attack on the Mauruça, but towards the end of 1820 the Portuguese waged a campaign against the Impahiamuno in Mutipa. Notwithstanding the usual glowing reports of a crushing defeat of the rebel, the problem persisted for at least the next few years.[48]

By 1830, relations with the Makua of Mutipa and Uticulo were good,[49] but now a new conflict erupted in Matibane with the ambitious Sheikh of Quitangonha, Selimane bin Agy. It, too, was rooted deep in the struggle for control of the slave trade in the vicinity of Mozambique Island. In this case, the problem focused on the contraband export trade in slaves from Quitangonha itself and from Fernão Veloso Bay, at the north end of Matibane. Quitangonha had for years carried on a desultory contraband trade with the Swahili, although its sheikhs were nominally subordinate to the Portuguese Government at Mozambique, but in 1829 both French and Portuguese vessels put in there to make up cargoes of slaves.[50] This the Portuguese could not tolerate. When they started to investigate the matter more carefully, however, they discovered that Sheikh Selimane was already in the process of developing a lucrative slave trade at Fernão Veloso Bay with the Swahili and the French.[51] Repeated warnings to the Sheikh, who guilelessly claimed no responsibility for affairs over which he had no control and proclaimed his continued loyalty to the Portuguese crown, were to no avail. As the Sheikh wrote to Governor-General Paulo José Miguel de Brito at the end of 1830, the slave trade was 'a tree with sweet fruit which all wish to eat'.[52] No less the Portuguese. Already in May of that year they had begun to attack the trade at Fernão Veloso at its source by establishing an outpost there.

The *Estabelecimento de El-Rei o Senhor D. Miguel Primeiro* was the first serious attempt by the Portuguese to bridge the gap between their outlying coastal colonies since these were first conquered in the sixteenth century.[53] Then the logic underlying the establishment of bases in the Kerimba Islands and at Quelimane was to protect against what the Portuguese considered to be the contraband trade in gold from Zambesia. Now the same mercantilist logic of imperial expansion prevailed, only the colony at Fernão Veloso was designed to protect Portuguese control of the slave trade. Almost at once it came under attack from the Sheikh of Quitangonha and his Makua allies and subordinates in Matibane.

For the next three years the Portuguese attempted to eradicate the thorn in their side which was Sheikh Selimane of Quitangonha. Elaborate overtures were made to the chiefs of Uticulo. At the end of October 1830, the Governor-General wrote to pledge his friendship to the Mauruça, and assured him that he could send his people freely to the mainland of Mozambique.[54] By the last week of November, negotiations were being conducted between the Portuguese, represented by the Captain-Major of the Mainland. Gabriel José de Sousa Ferreira, and the Makua of Uticulo, represented by Mwaviamuno Napu.[55] On 25 November 1830, Sousa Ferreira and the Mwaviamuno negotiated a five-point treaty which began by asserting that 'an inalterable peace and all the relations of friendship' would obtain between the Portuguese and Uticulo. Points two to four specified that the Mwaviamuno would immediately sever all communication with Matibane, that his forces would be at the ready to attack Matibane and that the Portuguese would supply him with gunpowder and shot to that end, and that the Portuguese would provide him with an appropriate gift in trade goods upon the fulfilment of his part of the bargain. Finally, the treaty called upon Mwaviamuno Napu to secure the assent of his 'uncles' – the other chiefs of Uticulo – to these terms. The Mwaviamuno was especially implored to gain the unfailing support of the Mauruça, who had considered his earlier agreement with a past Captain-Major of the Mainland to be a personal treaty of friendship, rather than a contract between his nation and that of the Portuguese.[56] To this end the Governor-General promised the Mauruça a special present of 'bone encrusted with gold filigree, and a pair of good pistols', as well as the items usually given in exchange for a tusk of ivory which the Makua paramount had sent to him.[57]

At the beginning of 1831, Brito was still attempting to line up African allies against the Sheikh of Quitangonha, using his understanding with the chiefs of Uticulo to dragoon those of Marezane and Simuco, immediately to the north of Fernão Veloso Bay, into the Portuguese camp.[58] Typically, alliances were tenuous, and the Portuguese never succeeded in mounting an outright assault against Quitangonha. By 1833 rumours were circulating on the mainland of an impending invasion by the Makua of Uticulo. Embassies were sent to Mozambique Island by the Mauruça and the Mwaviamuno to complain about the insufficient gift which the Mauruça had received from the now deceased Brito in exchange for the tusk of ivory which the Makua chief had sent to the former Governor-General.[59] By the end of that year, the alignments of 1830 were almost completely reversed, with the contrite, but still independent Sheikh Selimane first offering to 'clear the road to Macuana' and then launching an attack on the Makua around Fernão Veloso on his own initiative.[60] And less than two months later, the Mwaviamuno himself appeared in the Crown Lands lying between Uticulo and the coastal settlements to claim the return of two slaves belonging to him.[61]

The efforts made by the provisional government to treat the Makua chiefs of Uticulo with all due respect, and their inability to curb the rambunctious Sheikh of Quitangonha, reveal once again how little control the Portuguese were able to exercise over affairs on the mainland. The feeble establishment at Fernão Veloso was abandoned in April 1834.[62] When he visited Mozambique a decade earlier, Captain Owen had commented on this situation:

Even at Mozambique the Portuguese jurisdiction and settlements do not extend ten miles in any direction, and to the southward not at all. The natives, who are termed Makwomas [Makua] and Majowjes [Yao], form an insurmountable barrier; they will trade with them, but have a great objection to their entering the country, which often leads to wars, that only in the end impress more strongly on the minds of the Portuguese the determination of their neighbours to support themselves in their native territorial possessions.[63]

Three decades later, Bordalo tersely reiterated Owen's dismal account of the extent of Portuguese authority on the mainland at Mozambique after three and a half centuries of imperial presence in East Africa: 'Our effective dominion on this side does not extend to more than three leagues inland.'[64] To be sure, in the mid 1850s a column sent to restore order in Matibane was routed and the mainland settlements at Ampoense and Nandoa razed in retaliation, while as late as 1864 the Mauruça and the Impahiamuno were still being described as 'brigands' as a consequence of their intermittent raiding on the mainland.[65]

Yet if the Portuguese were no more able to impose order on the mainland in the middle of the nineteenth century than they had been in the previous centuries, their involvement in the slave trade had turned them into more effective agents for disruption than ever before. I have already mentioned the increased use of *patamares* and of organized slave trading expeditions mounted by coastal traders in the 1820s, as well as the resistance which these evoked from the Makua. By the 1850s these agents seem to have been used much more extensively in the hinterland, and among the Makua may well have seized the initiative in their trade with the coast. According to Jeronimo Romero, writing about the operations of these traders inland from the Cape Delgado coast, the *patamares* – some of whom may themselves have been independent small traders – were generally from the coast and they spoke Makua and other languages of the interior well. They travelled in company with anywhere from five to fifteen skilled slaves (*ladinos*), each of whom was armed with a rifle and supplied with a load of trade goods which was designed for easy travelling. They also carried beads with them for purchasing food in the hinterland. These caravans could take anywhere from two to six months going and coming, depending on how far inland they travelled. Most trips varied between thirty and ninety leagues (perhaps 170 to 450 kilometres). With their trade goods these *patamares* purchased ivory, rhinoceros horn, slaves, and malachite, as well as other products of lesser importance. Travel was not without risk, but so long as they avoided trouble and kept to themselves, they appear to have been relatively free to pursue their business. Romero also writes that these small caravans set out from the coast in every month of the year.[66] This change in the pattern of trade in the Mozambique hinterland was not by itself disruptive, of course, although it does indicate that the initiative of the trade of the interior was passing from the Makua to the people on the coast. But without this initial shift in the trade of the continent, it would not have been possible for the Portuguese to employ these coastal traders as *agents provocateurs* when the demand for slaves at the coast to supply the French 'free labour emigration scheme' met with no response from the chiefs of Macuana in the 1850s.

The source for our knowledge of this new stage in the direct intervention by the Portuguese in the affairs of the people of Macuana is the headstrong British consul at Mozambique, Lyons McLeod. McLeod never attempted to understand the Portuguese and finally came to despise them.[67] Nevertheless, and allowing for the verbal barbs which he aimed at Governor-General Vasco Guedes de Carvalho e Meneses, who seems to have been neither better nor worse than most of his predecessors, McLeod's description of this change bears careful consideration.

In the early 1850s, the slave trade at Mozambique was moribund. The sudden end of the Brazilian trade in 1851 – the result of stringent measures taken by the Brazilian Government – made it realistic for the Portuguese administration to enforce the 1836 abolition of the slave trade for the first time since it had been ordered from Lisbon. Thus, when the French free labour scheme was inaugurated in 1854,

there was a surplus of slaves in all the Portuguese settlements on the east coast of Africa; and the Governor-General of Mozambique, and his subordinates, found no difficulty in supplying the demand for the first twelve months, that is to say, from 1854 to 1855; for the Portuguese residents were only too glad to sell to the Portuguese officials those slaves whom the orders of the government of Portugal had prevented being supplied to the regular slave ships from Cuba, and the southern parts of the United States; and the effect of this trade was to rid Mozambique of a great portion of its slave population, with which it was overburdened. After the first twelve months of the traffic, the price rose, the demand still increased, but the French slave-dealers were unwilling to give the prices now demanded by the residents in Mozambique. To supply the demand, keep prices low, and secure the enormous profits which the Governor-General of Mozambique, and his partners in this nefarious traffic, were enjoying, it became necessary to send into the interior for slaves.[68]

McLeod does not mention it, but the fact that an epidemic of smallpox took the lives of more than 5000 slaves in Mozambique was a factor at play in this situation.[69]

In a wonderfully ironic turnabout, the Swahili agents of the Portuguese were refused by the chiefs whom they approached, who said that the slave trade was against the wishes of the Portuguese government. This episode provides a vivid index of how thoroughly colonized in outlook the chiefs of Macuana had become by the 1850s, even though they were still politically independent of the Portuguese. Their attitude, if McLeod is correct, was the historical outcome of the prolonged contact of Macuana with European mercantile capitalism.

To prove to the chiefs in the interior that the Moors went with the consent of the Portuguese authorities in search of slaves for the French Free Labour Emigration, some of the Portuguese soldiers, who had been living with the women of the country, and had acquired the Makua language, were despatched with the Moors into the interior, and the uniforms of the soldiers of the King of Portugal were found a sufficient guarantee to the chiefs of the interior that the slave trade was authorized by the Portuguese government, and immediately they set to work to supply the traffic in earnest; by these means the prices of slaves were kept low at Mozambique, the Portuguese officials made enormous gains, and the French Free Labour Emigration flourished.

At first, McLeod tells us that these slaves were produced from those at hand in the interior, but in a very little time the renewed demand for slaves led to extensive slave raiding among the Makua of Macuana.

At last a reaction took place: the natives found that they were destroying each other to obtain a few prisoners for the supply of the slave-trade which the Portuguese were carrying on; and for a time, they ceased from warfare, and again there was a scarcity in the slave market at Mozambique.

When the Portuguese attempted to send troops into Macuana for slaves in 1857, the Makua beat them off and threatened to attack the mainland. Only the Governor-General's expedient promise not to seek slaves from their country prevented war.[70]

Knowing very little about the way in which slaves were procured before the middle of the nineteenth century, when British abolitionists first began to examine the interior trade closely, it is difficult to determine how much of a departure the system described by McLeod represents. Although he nowhere identifies the Makua to whom the Portuguese sent their agents, the principal focus of their activity must have been Uticulo, which continued to be 'the nearest slave preserve to Mozambique' right into the 1870s.[71] The chiefs at Uticulo had almost certainly been raiding their neighbours to capture slaves for the Mozambique trade for many decades by mid century. From the 1850s, however, it would appear that a half century of intensive slaving had driven many of these victimized societies away from the immediate reach of raids launched from Uticulo and the other regions of the immediate coastal hinterland, so that the chiefs of Macuana had now to turn to raiding each other's people in order to satisfy the demand for slaves at the coast. Inexorably fettered to the international slave-trading economy, they were unable to do otherwise, since their mid century strength had been built upon the profits of the slave trade. Accordingly, the Makua reaction of the mid 1850s was only a temporary assertion of African over Western economic values. Now most of the Makua chiefs were to pay dearly.

Two decades after McLeod observed the first signs of this process, Frederic Elton, the second British consul at Mozambique and a remarkable perceptive traveller, commented upon its effects.

In the hill and forest districts of Okuso, Maridi, and Nangiri, through which I travelled [north] from Tugulu [Uticulo] to reach the neutral ground of Namoti upon the Nkomburi [Mocubúri] river, flowing into Mwendazi [Memba] Bay, narrow, tortuous ways, and thorny paths choked up with brambles and undergrowth, lead one to the villages and water, the broader paths almost invariably terminating in a *cul-de-sac*. The fear of slave-dealers' raids – their tracks are marked by many a burned and desolated settlement – has engendered a suspicious uneasiness among the villagers for so many years, that it has now become an innate feature of the Makua character, is marked upon their faces, and colours every action of their lives at the present day. No communication with a stranger or with an adjoining tribe is allowed without express permission from a 'baraza' of chiefs. The Lomwé country, lying between Makuani and the Lake Nyassa, Mosembé, and Mwendazi, may not be visited under pain of capital punishment, without the headman of the subdivision of the tribe to which the intending traveller belongs referring for leave to higher authority. Tracks of land are purposely laid waste and desolated upon the frontiers, where armed scouts, generally old elephant hunters, continually wander, their duty being to report at the earliest moment any approach of strangers, who are invariably treated as enemies.[72]

Matters were scarcely any better on the eastern marches of Uticulo.

For years past Makuani has furnished the main supply of slaves and 'libres engagés' for the Portuguese, French, and Madagascar markets. Fighting is constantly going on, dissensions being actively promoted by the unscrupulous dwellers on the coast, anxious to purchase the prisoners taken by the successful side, and utterly careless as to who is the winner. So long as the Makua held together they were formidable enemies to the Portuguese; but the breaking-up of the tribe into fragments, and faction-fighting among the chiefs for the supreme power, eventually placed them at the mercy of any Arab intriguer who chose to instigate hostilities in order to secure a slave cargo.[73]

In truth, the Makua had never been united politically, but they had almost always 'held together' in the face of Portuguese attempts to undermine their strength and to subordinate them to Portuguese rule. It was their ability to submerge petty rivalries which had served them so well since the eighteenth century in their relations with the Portuguese. That lost, the very resiliency of coastal Makua society soon succumbed to the increasing pressures emanating from the coast. When Elton met in

1876 the reigning Mauruça, who was still the most important chief in Uticulo, the consul found him unable to influence affairs beyond Uticulo, where a triple alliance with his brother and another related chief rendered him strong. Caravans travelling the short distance from Uticulo to the coast to trade provisions were always subject to raids and had to 'take the precaution of throwing out scouts and establishing nightly patrols round their bivouacs'. The country between Uticulo and the coast was thoroughly depopulated, except for a few isolated pockets, and although the Mauruça had recently concluded a peace treaty with the authorities at Mosembe, on the mainland opposite Quitangonha Island,

> putting an end to the kidnapping of the inhabitants of the flats as slaves by either side, and arranging a division of the land; yet it is still with fear and trembling that the Makuas venture down to till the soil.[74]

If, then, the Makua of Uticulo seemed to be as formidable an obstacle to the Portuguese in the 1850s as they had been for nearly three centuries of intimate commercial contact, they were much weakened within two decades as a result of changes in the pattern of the slave trade at Mozambique, which had its roots in the middle years of the century. On the threshold of the modern colonial era their reduction was complete. When Mousinho de Albuquerque opened his disputed and inconclusive operations on the mainland against the *namarrais* in 1896, Uticulo and the reigning Mauruça cooperated with the Portuguese against this upstart aggressive Makua confederacy whose chiefs were too deeply wedded to the slave-trading system to abandon it without a prolonged struggle.[75] But although the Mauruça and the *namarrais* were on oppposite sides in the wars of colonial conquest, which stretched into the twentieth century, both were the products of their historical relationship with international trade. Indeed, from the African perspective, the nature of these wars must have seemed no different from the constant struggles which had characterized the political economy of Macuana since the beginning of the slave trade in the eighteenth century.

The Yao trade to Mossuril

While there is no doubt at all that most of the slaves exported from Mozambique during the nineteenth century were Makua, it is equally clear that the Yao were the second greatest suppliers of the Mozambique slave market until about mid century.[76] In 1819, Governor-General Brito Sanches wrote that the reason Brazilian ships were leaving Mozambique laden with slaves is due to the abundance which some types of cafilas called Yao, who come from the interior near Tete, the farthest of the Rivers of Sena, bring to the Mainland of Mossuril, so that this year they brought more than 3500 slaves, and not due to those which come from the environs of this City. . . .[77]

1819 was, in fact, a bad year for Luso-Makua relations, but as more than 10,000 slaves were brought to the coast for export in that year, Brito Sanches' comments probably reflect a decline in the supply of slaves from Mutipa and Uticulo, rather than from Macuana as a whole. As for his remarks on the Yao, these are vividly borne out by the detailed observations of Bishop Mártires.

The Yao, he said, were 'a great, and numerous Nation . . . , who have always maintained a trade with the Portuguese which has been very profitable to the Colony'. Each year the Yao came to Mossuril bringing 2000 to 3000 slaves, together with only 'some ivory, and a small quantity of provisions', as well as tobacco and iron wares. Their slaves were bought at a low price, for although they were thought to be superior in many respects, many of them perished or were seriously debilitated before making the adjustment to the disease environment – what Mártires calls 'climate' – of the coast, a factor which had been mentioned by earlier sources on the Yao. Fr. Bartholomeu also provides a lengthy and fascinating description of the organization of Yao slave caravans, which in turn helps us to understand the nature of Yao slave trading in about 1820.

According to what he could learn, all the slaves were Yao. In passing through the hostile territory of the Makua, the caravan was defended by 'a few Kaffirs, their compatriots'. Mártires believed that the slaves did not know that they were to be sold at the coast, 'because the secret of their business is only confided to a few: out of 3,000, fewer than 30 return to their lands'. That they did not forcibly seize their freedom he attributed to the fact that they were outcasts in their own country and that they would surely be killed or enslaved in foreign lands. In effect, they had no alternative but to submit.

Now these Yao are certainly not prisoners of war, because they are of the same nation as their sellers: but all are victims of some crime, either real, or supposed; and among them there are some crimes which, though committed by only one individual, the onus falls upon his entire family, and most remote relatives; thus it is not rare to see the father, mother, sons, daughters, nephews, etc., being sold in the same fair.[78]

Mártires was surely mistaken in his belief that there was no internecine warfare among the Yao at this time; in any case, the Yao have never been a nation in any political sense. But he is probably correct in his analysis that the increased demand for slaves may have caused criminal liability to be more widely and arbitrarily applied in Yao law than ever before.

On a less grand scale, Bishop Mártires' account of the organization of Yao caravans was echoed a quarter-century later by Froberville. Writing about the slave trade in general, he observed that 'The caravans are usually composed of twenty or thirty persons, without counting the captives who are often as numerous as their masters, but who rarely seek to regain their liberty by force'. Kidnapping was common practice on the march to the coast, and it was this problem which forced most traders to band together in large caravans, a practice which also served to reinforce the authority of the big trading chiefs, who could employ large numbers of armed guards. However, most slaves were prisoners of war, 'because domestic slavery is absolutely unknown in East Africa'.[79]

After Mártires, there is little substantive evidence on the trade of the Yao to Mozambique.[80] According to Vasconcelos e Cirne, who was Governor at Quelimane and then in the Rivers of Sena from 1829 until his death at Tete in 1832, the Yao continued to bring 'a great number of slaves, and some ivory' to Mossuril during this period, although 'they have given up coming in the past few years owing to the robberies and wars which they have suffered at the hands of the chiefs near Mozambique'.[81] Warfare in Macuana, then, appears to have continued to obstruct Yao trade to Mozambique well into the nineteenth century. Yao slaves continued to be sold at Mozambique in the 1830s, and Yao caravans seem to have come there as well, but information for these years is very scarce.[82] Accordingly, it is impossible even to speculate about the changes which might have been taking place in the trade of the Yao to Mozambique in the years following Fr. Bartolomeu's detailed observations in 1822.

Before long, however, the rise of Ibo and Quelimane as major trading towns in their own right provided the Yao and other traders from the far interior with alternate coastal outlets to Mozambique Island along that stretch of the East African coast. According to a memoir written by the Marquis of Bemposta Subserra in December 1853, but quite possibly referring more generally to the second quarter of the nineteenth century,

each year, 'great *mangas* [caravans] of Negroes, some Bisa, who come from the lands of the Kazembe, others Yao, and of different tribes or nations, all of them traders, show up on that peninsula [Cabaceira], in order to trade their merchandise for others which they need; a makeshift fair is set up for this purpose, in which everyone cheats with the greatest expertise and perspicacity. These Negroes do not enter our territory without permission, nor do they usually commit any acts of violence there; when, however, they are unable to overcome the difficulties which they encounter in the interior on the part of other nations, they go to Quelimane or Ibo.'[83]

Whatever the exact provenance of his information, his remarks throw a valuable light on the way in which the growth of the slave trade in East Central Africa during the first half of the nineteenth century fostered the development of two major overland routes to the coast.

During the eighteenth century, when the trade in ivory dominated the foreign trade of East Central Africa, neither Ibo nor Quelimane was capable of emerging as a major outlet for this trade. Quelimane suffered from the same onerous tax structure as the rest of the Rivers of Sena, while Ibo lacked a body of merchants who could finance the credit base of the ivory trade, concentrating instead on the more localized trade in cowrie shells and slaves. The opening of the subordinate ports to direct trade from Brazil at the beginning of the second decade of the nineteenth century, the revival of the French slave trade, and the fact that the slave trade was primarily in European hands and did not depend on Indian capitalization, combined to raise both Ibo and Quelimane to the status of major trading ports. Together with Kilwa and other towns along the coast, they further undermined the once dominant position of Mozambique Island as a principal entrepôt for the trade of the far interior.

As early as about 1830, the Yao were trading slaves directly to Ibo, while by about 1844 the route linking the Lake Nyasa region to Ibo was already being plied by Swahili slave trading caravans, as John Rebman learned at Mombasa from the freed slave who served as his informant in compiling his *Kiniassa Dictionary*. This man

was an Mniassa, who in consequence of international expeditions for slave-catching was seized by a tribe called Wapogera, who sold him to the Wamaravi, and these to the Swahili slave merchants who had come from Uibu (a small island belonging to Moçambique and on the map called Ibo). At Uibu which was reached after two months' travelling at a very slow rate (in effective march only half the time is wanted), he was at last bought by slave-merchants from Mombas.[84]

Similarly, by 1859, after the beginning of the great Yao migration into the Shire valley, Yao traders were well known at Quelimane, where they traded slaves, ivory, and Maravi iron hoes.[85] During the second half of the nineteenth century, both Ibo and Quelimane, as well as Angoche, were to remain important termini of long-distance trade routes in East Central Africa. The trade of Mozambique, on the other hand, was progressively limited to its own immediate hinterland as a result of the changes in the pattern of the slave trade which were described earlier in this chapter. The increasing incidence of violence in the hinterland of Mozambique and of man-stealing at the coast probably combined with the greater accessibility of markets such as Ibo, Angoche, Quelimane, and those of the southern Swahili coast, to make the journey to the fair at Mossuril an unnecessarily risky venture. Indeed, the changes in the operation of the slave trade at the coast itself made even that once protected fair a convenient arena for man-stealing. As McLeod observed,

In 1856 many of these Natives who came down to trade, were seized by the Portuguese to supply the so-called French Free Labour Emigration, since which occurrence they have not made their appearance at Mossuril.[86]

Already by 1854, when the *pombeiros* of the important Angolan trader, António Francisco Ferreira da Silva Porto, crossed the continent to the coast of East Africa, they followed the increasingly popular route which crossed the Shire, held to the east of the Lujenda River, and debouched at the coast between Ibo and Kilwa.[87] After nearly three centuries of serving as one of the most important coastal entrepôts for the overland trade of the interior of the continent, by about 1860 Mozambique Island was reduced in all but administrative terms to a minor position in the export trade of East Central Africa.[88]

The Indians of Mozambique

The changing context of trade at Mozambique during the first half of the nineteenth century had as profound an effect on the Indian community of the island as it did on the Africans of the continent. Not only was the demand for slaves beyond the control of the Indians, but they also found their control over the importation of African trade cloths was being challenged by British and American cotton sheeting. British cottons first entered the Mozambique trade as a consequence of the Anglo-Portuguese Treaty of Commerce and Navigation, which was concluded at Rio de Janeiro on 19 February 1810. According to at least one overly pessimistic Portuguese trader, they had struck a death blow to the trade in Indian textiles by the early 1820s.[89] That this was not the case is demonstrated by the detailed accounting of a standard bale of trade cloths current in the Rivers of Sena in 1832 which A. C. P. Gamitto appended to his remarkable narrative of the Portuguese expedition to the Mwata Kazembe in 1831–32. Each bale contained ninety-eight pieces of cloth, of seven different varieties, all of Indian manufacture. But Gamitto notes that

Since the author left Mozambique, this kind of trade has altered considerably, and today [1853] good cotton cloths of English and American manufacture are preferred to the Indian weaves.[90]

At Tete, three years later, Livingstone also observed that 'English or American unbleached calico is the only currency used'.[91] Indeed, so important had American cottons become to the trade of Mozambique by this time that the Portuguese Minister of the Navy and Overseas Provinces was moved to comment upon the impact which the American Civil War had upon their availability in his annual report to the Chamber of Deputies at Lisbon in January 1864.[92] Indian traders still remained an important factor in the trade of the colony as a whole, but their influence was now exerted more in the trade with the subordinate ports than in that of the mainland opposite the island-capital. Finally, trade from East Africa to Portuguese India was depressed throughout this period. Encouraged during the second and harried during the fourth decade of the nineteenth century – though always defended by the crown – the varying fortunes of the Indian traders at Mozambique seem to have had little decisive effect on African trade during this era.[93] Only with the slow development of 'legitimate' trade, that harbinger of impending colonial conquest, for the securing of cheap raw materials from Africa, did Indian traders come forward again to dominate the trade of Mozambique.[94]

Zanzibar and the Kilwa Coast

By contrast, to the north of Portuguese jurisdiction Indian traders and Indian merchant capital were two of the most important factors in the phenomenal rise of Zanzibar in the economy of the Indian Ocean under the energetic 'Umani ruler, Seyyid Sa'id ibn Sultan al-Bu Sa'idi (1804–56). The growth and impact of Zanzibar on the trade of East Africa is a well-known story. Here it is important to stress not only the more spectacular rise in the slave trade – which was brought about by the creation of a colonial plantation economy on the islands of Zanzibar and Pemba – but also the concomitant growth of the ivory trade at Zanzibar, where American traders, in particular, augmented the long-standing demand of the Indian market.[95] The wealth produced by the industrial revolution in America and western Europe brought with it the fashion for a number of amusements and trinkets – billiards, pianos, and carved curios and jewellery – which gave rise to this new trade in ivory. In 1856, according to the French consul at Zanzibar, Western exports of ivory totalled some 242,975 pounds, with American merchants carrying more than three-quarters of the trade.[96] Three years later, his British counterpart gave the total export of ivory from Zanzibar as 488,600 pounds, with some 243,600 pounds going to Western countries and the remainder clearly destined for the Indian market.[97] Although it is impossible to break down the volume of the ivory trade to Zanzibar from the various ports on the mainland, there is no doubt that Kilwa continued to maintain a thriving ivory trade alongside its booming export trade in slaves right through the period of this study. The continued importance of ivory there was probably one of the main reasons why most Yao continued to prefer carrying their merchandise to Kilwa, instead of to Mozambique, during the first half of the nineteenth century.

But it is for the slave trade that Kilwa gained its greatest notoriety in the history of East Africa during the nineteenth century. In 1811, Captain Smee commented that the various tribes which supplied the Zanzibar slave market were 'too numerous to describe', but that the chief one was the Nyamwezi. Among the other peoples whom he identified were the Makua, the Yao and the Ngindo.[98] A year later, when HMS *Nisus* visited Kilwa, a temporary decline in the slave trade seems to have set in there as a result of the recent British seizure of the Mascarene Islands, and James Prior, the ship's surgeon, took particular note of the ivory trade. Prior also made a passing reference to the slave and ivory trade carried on at Lindi and Mongalo.[99] In both 1816 and 1817, Kilwa and the Mafia Islands were attacked by large Sakalava fleets. After suffering considerable losses during the first raid, a combined expedition of local Swahili and 'Umani forces from Zanzibar inflicted a crushing defeat on the Sakalava at Msimbati Bay, just north of the mouth of the Ruvuma River.[100] Thus, for much of the second decade of the nineteenth century conditions in the Western Indian Ocean may have been less than ideal for the successful prosecution of the slave trade from Kilwa.

Not long after the defeat of the Sakalava, the Sultan of Kilwa, Yusuf bin Hasan, died. In 1819, when the gifted French linguist and Orientalist, Fortuné Albrand, visited Kilwa, a successor to the deceased Sultan had not yet been chosen. By now, however, real political and commercial power were firmly in the hands of the 'Umani. Alluding to its medieval splendour, Albrand remarked that it was 'now only a miserable village to which the slave trade alone gives any importance'. He was nevertheless sceptical of the assurance he received at Zanzibar that 13,000 slaves were imported there from Kilwa each year. Albrand also noted that 'in addition to the traffic in blacks, Zanzibar also does as extensive a trade in ivory', although he does not specifically comment on the ivory trade at Kilwa.[101] During the next decade the Arab slave trade at Kilwa was supplemented by a renewed spurt of activity by French slavers at the several ports dotting the coast below it, where 'Umani hegemony was less than effective. Of these, Mongalo seems to have been more important than either Lindi or Mikindani, for in 1826 the 'Umani governor of Zanzibar told Captain Acland that 'Mongalo was the principal depot for the French'.[102] Indeed, article 10 of the interim agreement concluded between the ambassador of Seyyid Sa'id and Governor-General Botelho at Mozambique on 28 March 1828 recognized that the coast between Mongalo and Tungui, which lay immediately to the south of Cape Delgado, was not subject to the jurisdiction of either 'Uman or Portugal.[103]

In the 1830s, Kilwa Kisiwani finally succumbed to a combination of continuing political dissension within the Swahili community and an increasingly violent environment.[104] By the end of the decade the once insignificant mainland village of Kivinje, which was situated some twenty-seven kilometres to the north of Kilwa Kisiwani, fell heir to the mantle of the once great island-state, assuming the popular name of Kilwa Kivinje and emerging as the principal collection point for slaves on the coast of East Africa. Already the 'Umani had put a governor there by 1819.[105] But the rise of Kilwa Kivinje represents something more than the simple relocation of a townsite. As G. S. P. Freeman-Grenville pointed out a decade ago, it also stands as a symbol of the changed orientation of trade at Kilwa from the pre-Portuguese to the early modern period of East African history, the one being dominated entirely by the Indian Ocean and the sea lanes north to Western Asia and south to Sofala, the other drawing its strength as much from the overland trade of East Central Africa as from the seaborne trade of Zanzibar and the north.[106] Moreover, there can be little doubt that one of the most important factors in the rise of Kilwa Kivinje to prominence in the trade of East Africa was the contribution made by individuals from the far interior like the Masaninga Yao adventurer, Mwinyi Mkwinda, who settled at Kivinje during the late eighteenth century.[107]

By the 1840s Kilwa Kivinje had become a thriving market town. Although its fame was justifiably built on the slave trade, its export trade was not so thoroughly dependent upon slaves as was that of Mozambique Island. Even Atkins Hamerton, who served as British Consul at Zanzibar from May 1841 to his death in July 1857, and was the source of many irresoluble estimates of the slave trade, was able to comment in 1842 that Kilwa Kivinje was 'the port to which the ivory, gum copal, &c., are brought from the interior and chiefly sent to Zanzibar for sale'. His remark that the rebellious 'Umani Governor of Kilwa Kivinje had levied a special tax on ivory exported to Zanzibar also suggests that this trade may well have been at least as important as the

Table 23 *Slaves exported from Kilwa Kivinje, 1862–9*

Year	Number of slaves
1862–3	18,500[1]
1863–4	17,500[1]
1864–5	16,821[1]
1865–6	22,344[1]
1866–7	22,038[1]
1867–8	—
1868–9	14,944[2]
Total	112,147

Source: Burton, *Zanzibar*, II, p. 347.
[1] Exports through customs to Zanzibar and elsewhere.
[2] Exports for year ending 23 August 1869.

slave trade in the early 1840s.[108] The slave trade expanded even further in the following years, largely in response to the increasing need for hands to work the mature clove and coconut palm plantations on Zanzibar and Pemba. During these years perhaps an average of 13,000 to 15,000 slaves entered Zanzibar each year from the mainland, and most of these came from Kilwa.[109] In 1850, J. L. Krapf described Kilwa Kivinje as 'the most important town on the coast between Mozambique and Zanzibar', and a great trading centre. Its population he estimated to be between 12,000 and 15,000 inhabitants. He reckoned slaves to be the principal item of trade there and he was told that some 10,000 to 12,000 slaves, both from central Tanzania and from the vicinity of Lake Nyasa, passed through Kilwa Kivinje each year. At the same time, however, Krapf also observed that the town 'drives a very considerable trade in ivory, rice, copal, tobacco. . . .'[110] If slaves were the mainstay of Kilwa Kivinje's trade, this was not so to the exclusion of all other products.

Yearly fluctuations in the volume of the slave trade could be considerable. Hamerton informed Richard Burton that the average annual importation into Zanzibar was 14,000 but that the extremes varied from 9000 to 20,000.[111] In 1851 the American Consul at Zanzibar, Charles Ward, judged the annual rate of importation to be between 8000 and 10,000, 'and they mostly from Kilwa'.[112] Not all slaves exported north from Kilwa went to Zanzibar, however, as Krapf learned during his brief visit to the mainland port at mid-century.

Although the Sultan of Zanzibar has prohibited the slave-trade with Arabia, yet many slave-ships proceed there annually, starting from Kiloa and sailing round Zanzibar on the eastern side of the island, so as to evade the sultan's police; and

Impact of slave trade on East Central Africa: 19th century

slaves are often smuggled to Arabia by the aid of a declaration of the captain that they are sailors.[113]

Similarly, slaves from Kilwa had been exported to the south for many years in small numbers in order to supply the Brazilian trade at Mozambique.[114] During the late 1850s French slavers also were active in direct trading at Kilwa.[115] In fact, by the 1860s, returns from the customs-house at Kilwa Kivinje show that nearly one-fifth of all slaves exported were destined for markets other than Zanzibar.[116] This decade in all likelihood marked the apogee of the export trade from Kilwa Kivinje. The export trade from the mainland was officially abolished during the 1870s, but slaves continued to be driven to Kilwa from the interior of East Africa, and from Kilwa north to the towns of the Mrima coast, whence they could be smuggled more easily to Zanzibar, as Elton discovered during his march behind the Swahili coast in 1873, when he was Vice-Consul at Zanzibar.[117] Thereafter, although the export trade continued from the many smaller ports along the Kilwa coast, the slave trade in East Africa was largely internalized, and slaves brought down to the coast from the interior frequently ended up working on Arab or Indian plantations on the coast itself. This aspect of the slave trade does not concern us here. The question remaining is to determine the impact of a half-century of intensive slave trading to Kilwa on the peoples of the southern interior of East Africa.

The peoples of the Lake Nyasa region

Perhaps the most reliable information on this problem was compiled by Consul Rigby. In his extensive 'Report on the Zanzibar Dominions', completed on 1 July 1860, Rigby observed:

During the past year, 19,000 slaves were brought to Zanzibar from the coast of Africa. Of these, four thousand were from the 'Marima', or coast opposite to Zanzibar, and fifteen thousand were from the neighbourhood of the great lake of Nyassa, situated about forty days' journey south-west of Keelwa. The tribes which formerly furnished most of the slaves are now nearly exhausted, and this miserable traffic is being carried further into the interior every year, and is depopulating vast tracts of fertile country. . . . The majority of the slaves belong to the great tribes of M'Nyassa, Miyan, and Magindo.

Later on in his report, Rigby adds that 'many of the Manganga are now amongst the slaves brought to Zanzibar from Keelwa'.[118] Concerning the depopulation of the coastal hinterland,

Natives of India who have resided many years at Kilwa . . . state that districts near Kilwa, extending to ten or twelve days' journey, which a few years ago were thickly populated, are now entirely uninhabited; and an Arab who has lately returned from Lake Nyasa informed me that he travelled for seventeen days through a country covered with ruined towns and villages which a few years ago were inhabited by the Mijana and Mijan [Yao] tribes and where no living soul is to be seen.[119]

Rigby was not alone in his impression of the depopulation of large tracts of territory along the march to Lake Nyasa, as a reading of von der Decken and Livingstone reveals.[120] It is important, however, not to give too much weight to these accounts, as they can lead to completely erroneous statements like Burton's assumption that 'the Wahiáo tribe has been so favoured in the slave-market that it is now nearly extinct' and 'nearly annihilated by the slave-trade'.[121] Clearly this was not so. Yet it is true that by the middle of the nineteenth century, most of the slaves coming to Kilwa were from the region around the lake, rather than from the immediate hinterland. In an earlier note on the slave trade at Kilwa, when he was not defending his interpretation of East African geography against his critics, as he was in the notes to Lacerda's travels, Burton singled out the Yao and Ngindo among the various peoples exported as slaves from Kilwa to Zanzibar. A decade later he included a variety of other people from both far and near in a list of the ethnic derivation of the slave population of Kilwa Kivinje, but also noted that in the export market it was the Yao who were 'preferred to all others'.[122] Similarly, von der Decken learned during his exploration in the Kilwa hinterland in December 1860 that most of the slaves exported from Kilwa were Bisa and Yao.[123]

But it is not necessary to rely exclusively on European accounts of the sources and operation of the slave trade in East Central Africa. For the later nineteenth century there are a number of published freed-slave accounts which, although they must often be set in the context of their mission origin or in that of their British interrogators, nevertheless do represent a genuine African voice. The individuals from whom these personal accounts come include several Yao, Nyasa, Makua, two Bisa, one Ngindo, and one Bemba. Some of their stories are long, others include but a few brief details. Most of these people were enslaved when children as a result of warfare. The captors of Petro Kilekwa, a Bisa, are described as Maviti, which in the late nineteenth century was more often a euphemism for any brigand rather than an Ngoni party. In the case of another Bisa and one Nyasa child, the war was carried to their homes by Mpezeni's Ngoni, while the Bemba child was seized in a Gwangwara raid.[124] The Ngindo woman was captured in a war with the Yao, as was another Nyasa boy, while one Yao was enslaved by Ngindo. Many of the

Yao slaves interviewed by Speke in 1860 stated that they had been 'captured during wars in their own country'.[125] James Mbotela's father, a Yao, was captured in a raid on his country by a party of Arabs led by Makua from Mozambique, and one of the Makua children was seized in a raid by the Lomwe.[126] Kidnapping was another widely practised form of acquiring a slave for sale, and this was the fate of several of the Kiungani children. It was also common practice among the Chewa.[127] The Chewa also acquired slaves for their own use and for sale as a result of internal warfare, while the Nsenga traded large numbers of slaves to them for foodstuffs during periods of famine. Certain crimes, especially murder, also required payment in slaves among the Chewa, and some of these slaves found their way into the hands of Yao slave traders. One of the Makua children lost his freedom by first being pawned in this fashion in payment for his elder brother's adulterous behaviour, after which he was sold and resold to an Arab.[128] Finally, at least one Yao was apparently sold by his father (or more probably his uncle) for what was very likely the simple acquisition of trading goods.[129]

The main slave traders who emerge from these accounts are the Yao, Makua, and Arabs. Abdallah confirms and extends the sources of slaves for the Yao trade by listing Nyasa, Bisa, Senga (possibly Nsenga?), and Chikunda.[130] All of Isaacman's Chewa informants stress the importance of Yao as slave traders, whom they preferred to the Portuguese or their agents because they gave the Chewa a better price for both their slaves and their ivory. The Yao travelled among the Chewa of Makanga in small groups of from three to six men. When they reached a village they were greeted warmly by the headman, who gave them a place to sleep and food to eat. The next day they would begin to do business with their host, trading cloth and, less commonly, guns for slaves. Among the Bisa, according to Rashid bin Hasani, it was also the chief who reaped by far the largest profit from the slave trade with Yao. This same pattern was repeated by coast traders who came to trade at Yao villages.[131] All of those captives coming from the area west of Lake Nyasa passed through a number of hands, several changing owners three or four times before reaching the coast at or near Kilwa. In several instances freed slaves reported that they lived with their masters for a period of one or two years before finally being sold to the coast.[132] The same was true for those whose homes were at any distance from the coast, so that the normal pattern of the trade was clearly the passage of individual slaves, or small groups of them, from their point of origin until they reached either the coast or a major caravan town in the interior – such as those of the Yao chiefs Mponda, Makanjila, and Mataka – from whence they were assembled in large numbers and driven to the coast. By the last decades of the century this part of the trade was largely in Arab hands, although it was not so in previous years.

The obvious point about the profits to be made from the sale of slaves is that prices were lowest in the interior and highest at the point of final destination. That is not surprising. The nature of the business and the evidence makes it almost impossible to calculate the percentage of profit involved, and European observers tended to exaggerate, but it is clear that a handsome profit could be made by all parties concerned. In particular, it was more prosperous Indian merchants at Zanzibar who profited most from the trade, by virtue of their capitalization of its operation in East Africa.[133] In the interior there is no doubt that the main item involved in trading for slaves was cloth. Isaacman's Chewa informants all mention cloth, in general, and one gives the price of a slave as three *peças* or pieces of cloth. According to another Chewa elder, an important distinction was made between male and female slaves, the latter being valued more highly because of their reproductive capacity. Indeed, he also gives higher prices of one gun and five *peças* for a male, and two guns and ten *peças* for a female slave.[134] Abdallah, on the other hand, mentions a price of 'a wide piece of calico about four yards long for one slave, double that for others'. But he also mentions that coast people normally paid 'two lengths and eight yards of fringed cloth' for a slave, which at least gives a rough notion of the middleman's profits which were turned in the interior. Again, after his capture and sale to slave dealers from the coast, Petro Kilekwa was taken back to his village where his mother offered to buy him back for three yards of cloth. She was refused, the price being eight yards, and he was carried away. Similarly, when the father of one of the Makua captives attempted to ransom him for a new gun, four hoes, some beads, and some iron, he was refused because only cloth was wanted.[135] In all of these cases the only sale in the interior which did not involve cloth was that of the young Bemba, who was sold by his Gwangwara captors for seven hoes.[136]

It is apparent that most contemporary observers attributed the prominence of slaves from the lake region at Kilwa to the fact that the country lying immediately behind Kilwa had been so thoroughly depopulated by the ravages of the slave trade in previous decades that it could no longer meet the insatiable demands of the Kilwa market. How accurate an interpretation is this? In certain respects it is very likely correct. At first, most slaves were taken from the peoples living nearest to the coast, as happened at Mozambique. There, however, the coastal hinterland remained the primary region from which slaves were taken for exportation right through the nineteenth century. Perhaps one reason for the different distribution of slave supplies to Kilwa is that the

Kilwa hinterland was never as thickly populated as that of Mozambique. Turning to the historical sources, in 1616 Gaspar Bocarro found almost the entire line of march from the Ruvuma River to Kilwa to be uninhabited, while the late eighteenth-century French commentators like Crassons and Saulnier de Mondevit suggest that it was only in the more fertile river valleys of the hinterland that a significant population existed.[137] Further support for this interpretation may be found in Froberville's notes on the Ngindo, which state plainly that their settlement pattern was one of small, isolated family homesteads.[138] Finally, the large Makua population of the Kilwa hinterland seems not to have begun to enter this region from across the Ruvuma River until after the middle of the nineteenth century.[139] At Mozambique, on the other hand, the general impression which emerges from the Portuguese documentation is that the hinterland was more thickly populated. Perhaps, then, the Kilwa hinterland was exhausted as a major source of slaves for export by the middle of the nineteenth century because it began with a smaller and less dense population than that of Macuana, which remained at the centre of the Mozambique trade. Similarly, it was no accident that the Lake Nyasa region became the chief supply area for the slave trade from the middle decades of the century. The country surrounding the lake is one of the richest, most densely settled areas in all Africa, and was ideally suited to the slave trade for the simple reason that it sustained an unusually high population.[140]

Notes and references

Introduction

1 K. O. Dike, *Trade and Politics in the Niger Delta, 1830–85: An introduction to the Economic and Political History of Nigeria* (London: Oxford University Press 1956), p. 4.
2 However, Dike's work has stimulated a number of works on trade and politics in which the political consequences of the slave trade form an important part. See, for example, K. Y. Daaku, *Trade and Politics on the Gold Coast 1600–1720* (Oxford University Press 1970); J. K. Fynn, *Asante and Its Neighbours 1700–1807* (London: Longman 1971); Walter Rodney, *A History of the Upper Guinea Coast 1545–1800* (London: Oxford University Press 1970); D. Birmingham, *Trade and Conflict in Angola: The Mbundu and their Neighbours under the Influence of the Portuguese, 1483–1790* (London: Oxford University Press 1966); Phyllis M. Martin, *The External Trade of the Loango Coast 1576–1870* (London: Oxford University Press 1972); I. A. Akinjogbin, *Dahomey and its Neighbours, 1708–1818* (Cambridge University Press 1967); Edward A. Alpers, *Ivory and Slaves in East Central Africa: Changing Patterns of International Trade to the Later Nineteenth Century*, Chapter 10 in this book; A. J. H. Latham, *Old Calabar 1600–1891: The Impact of the International Economy upon a Traditional Society* (London: Oxford University Press 1973); Basil Davidson, *Black Mother: Africa, the Years of Trial* (London: Gollancz 1961), pp. 235–47.
3 Most of these seminars have been organized by American and European universities. For example, the Rochester (New York) Conference in 1972; the sessions on the history of the slave trade at the Sixth International Conference for Economic History held in Copenhagen in August 1974 (two of the papers presented during this conference dealt specifically with the impact of the slave trade on some African societies, and these are included in the present collection); Conference on the Economic History of the Trans-Atlantic Slave Trade held at Colby College, Waterville, Maine, USA, 20–2 August 1975; Conference at Columbia University on the Transition from Slave Labour to Wage Labour, to be followed by another at the State University of New York in Binghamton on the same subject; International Conference on the Economic History of the Central Savanna of West Africa, held in Kano, Nigeria, 5–10 January 1976 (one

276 *Notes and references to pages 16–20*

of the papers presented during this conference is included in the present collection); Seminar on African Historical Demography, held in the Centre of African Studies, University of Edinburgh, 29–30 April, 1977; UNESCO Meeting of Experts on the African Slave Trade held at Port-au-Prince, Haiti, 31 January – 4 February, 1978; Conference on the Population Factor in African Studies, organized by the African Studies Association of the United Kingdom, September 1972.

4 See Melvin Rader, *Marx's Interpretation of History* (New York: Oxford University Press 1979), for a stimulating discussion of this subject. Rader sees the organic totality and base-superstructure as two separate models. But whether they are regarded as separate models, or the former is seen as one version of the latter, is not very important, so long as the nature of the relationship between the factors in the model is clearly spelt out.

5 Douglass C. North and Robert P. Thomas, *The Rise of the Western World: A New Economic History* (Cambridge: Cambridge University Press 1973).

6 See Robert S. Lopez, *The Commercial Revolution of the Middle Ages 950–1350* (Cambridge: Cambridge University Press 1976) and Edward Miller and John Hatcher, *Medieval England: Rural Society and Economic Change 1086–1384* (London: Longman 1978).

7 See the contributions in D. V. Glass and D. E. C. Eversley (eds.), *Population in History: Essays in Historical Demography* (London 1965) and M. Drake (ed.), *Population in Industrialization* (London: Methuen 1969).

8 It should be noted that we are here considering only those societies that have already moved away from hunting and gathering to the cultivation of crops and the domestication of animals.

9 Lopez, *The Commercial Revolution*, p. 151.

10 Ester Boserup, *The Conditions of Agricultural Growth: The Economics of Agrarian Change Under Population Pressure* (London 1965).

11 David Levine. *Family Formation in an age of Nascent Capitalism* (New York: Academic Press 1977), p. 5.

12 ibid., p. 11.

13 ibid., p. 15.

14 Levine's main contribution is that he has reasserted the primacy of rising birth rates over declining death rates in the explanation of English demographic change in the eighteenth century. But the way the arguments are presented rests the analysis on its head rather than on its feet.

15 Philip D. Curtin, *The Atlantic Slave Trade: A Census* (Madison: University of Wisconsin Press 1969), pp. 3–13.

16 ibid.

17 Dike, *Trade and Politics*, p. 3.

18 J. E. Inikori, 'Measuring the Atlantic slave trade: an assessment of Curtin and Anstey,' *Journal of African History*, vol. XVII, no. 2 (1976), pp. 197–223. See also the discussion in *Journal of African History*, vol. XVII, no. 4 (1976): Curtin's comments, pp. 595–605; Anstey's comments, pp. 606–7; Inikori's Rejoinder, pp. 607–27.

19 Leslie B. Rout, Jr., *The African Experience in Spanish America 1502 to the*

Present Day (Cambridge University Press 1976), p. 65.
20 It should be pointed out that Professor Drescher has commented on some sections of the present writer's assessment of Curtin's and Anstey's estimates. (Seymour Drescher, *Econocide: British Slavery in the Era of Abolition*, Pittsburgh 1977, pp. 205-13.) Since these comments are relevant to our subject, it is pertinent to deal with them briefly.

Starting with imports into Spanish mainland America, Drescher accepts my own evidence as indicating large slave imports into Mexico and Peru. (Drescher, p. 205) But Drescher argues that since the imports into Spanish mainland America were largely re-exports from other territories in the New World, the omission of such imports in Curtin's estimates does not affect the accuracy of the global import estimates. This argument is wrong, because the method adopted by Curtin to estimate imports into individual New World territories took account of re-exports. Jamaica was the main centre of the re-export trade in the New World. Curtin's Jamaican import estimates were based largely on recorded *net* imports after re-exports. The Jamaican import estimates were used in various ways in the estimate of imports into other regions, especially the British and French territories. And the Jamaican *net* import figures used by Curtin for all these calculations are actually lower than the total recorded figures. (Inikori, 'Rejoinder', pp. 623 and 626) The truth is that all import estimates based on slave populations in each territory at a given point in time automatically eliminate the issue of re-exports. It is now quite clear that the slave populations of each New World territory were very much greater than those employed in Curtin's import estimates. These much greater slave populations were the result of imports that were equally much greater than those estimated by Curtin.

Drescher's comments on the Brazilian imports are rather surprising. He says, 'Regarding the Portuguese trade, Inikori cites only one secondary work which gives the Negro population of Brazil in a single year (1798).' [Drescher, pp. 205-6] But in fact, apart from the figure for 1798, we presented another set of *slave* population figures for seven years taken from the scholarly work by Professor R. B. Toplin, published in 1972, with the archival sources of the figures clearly shown. (Inikori, 'Rejoinder', pp. 622-3)

Drescher's comments on a small portion of the British export estimates contain similar surprising inaccuracies. Commenting on my application of the 1788 legal ratio of slaves per ton to the whole period, 1789-1807, Drescher says:

> Inikori accepts without demur the ratio of 1.6 slaves per ton imposed by the act of 1788. . . . Why the law of 1788 should have been totally effective, and that of 1799 only to the exact demands of the act of 1788 is unexplained. [Drescher, p. 211]

In order to show how inaccurate these comments are, we have to quote at some length just one of the relevant sections of the papers in question:

For the remaining period, 1789-1807, divided into two by Anstey, my reason for making it a single period in my original paper is the fact that the law of 1799 did not state any specific slave per ton ratio, although the new measures imposed may have had the effect of reducing the earlier ratio. The assumption upon which I used the earlier imposed legal ratio for both periods is that the unrestricted larger cargoes which went directly to non-British islands, together with the fact of evasion in the British islands would mean that using the legal ratio for 1789–99 would lead to a substantial under-estimate for that period, which could then offset any over-estimate that may arise from using the same ratio for the period 1800–7, if the law of 1799 reduced the ratio so much that the greater cargoes to non-British islands plus violations in the British islands failed to make it up. [Inikori, 'Rejoinder', p. 609]

The problem of space makes it impossible for us to deal with other weaknesses of the Drescher's comments on the British exports for 1777–1807. But it should be mentioned that Drescher's estimate of the volume of British slave shipping unrecorded in Britain (25,000 slaves in 1803, Drescher, p. 208) indicates a total volume of British exports greater than the one we presented. Only a few of these may have been included in continental estimates, particularly as much of these unrecorded exports relate to British shipping trading from Spanish ports (and using Spanish flags) whose trade is not included in any of the existing estimates. As for the small number of foreign vessels trading from British ports, including them in British export estimates does not lead to any double counting, since their clearances could not have been recorded in any other ports in Europe. It should be pointed out that in the papers in question we presented two independent estimates of British slave exports. The method and data employed in each estimate are such that it is practically impossible for one to manipulate the computation in order to make the two estimates agree. The very close agreement between the results of the two estimates is therefore an important measure of the accuracy of both estimates. (See Inikori, 'Rejoinder', pp. 611–15)

21 Raymond Mauny, *Tableau géographique de l'Ouest Africain au moyen âge* (Dakar 1961); *Les siècles obscurs de l'Afrique noire* (Paris 1971).
22 Ralph A. Austen, 'The trans-Saharan slave trade: a tentative census', in H. A. Gemery and J. S. Hogendorn (eds.), *The Uncommon Market* (New York 1979), pp. 23–76.
23 Mauny, *Les siècles obscurs*. The distribution in time of the Mauny's figures is as follows:

AD 600–700	100,000	1300–1400	1,000,000
700–800	200,000	1400–1900	10,000,000
800–900	400,000	20th century	300,000
900–1300	2,000,000		

24 Austen, 'The trans-Saharan slave trade', Table 2.8., p. 66.
25 ibid., Table 2.9., p. 68.
26 Johannes Postma, 'Mortality in the Dutch slave trade, 1675–1795' in Gemery and Hogendorn (eds.), *The Uncommon Market*, Table 9.9, p. 257. Postma does not break his figures into African regions of origin.

27 Ernst van den Boogaart and Pieter C. Emmer, 'The Dutch participation in the Atlantic slave trade, 1596–1650', in H. A. Gemery and J. S. Hogendorn (eds.), *The Uncommon Market*, Table 14.3, p. 366. These figures are broken into two broad regions, Guinea and Angola. For Guinea the ratios are 58 per cent for male slaves and 42 per cent for female slaves and for Angola, 62.3 per cent for male slaves and 37.7 per cent for female slaves.
28 Postma, 'Mortality in the Dutch slave trade', Table 9.9, p. 257.
29 This is the view suggested by Postma, 'Mortality in the Dutch slave trade', p. 256.
30 These two sets of figures are to be found in CO. 137/88, Appendix no. 4, p. 24, and T. 70/1574, respectively.
31 Also see Chapter 9, note 41, in this book, for some more information. At the moment we have no information about the sex ratios of slaves exported to the Americas from East Africa.
32 See T. 70/1574 for the data relating to 1795.
33 Gabriel Baer, 'Slavery in nineteenth-century Egypt', *Journal of African History*, vol. VIII, no. 3 (1967), p. 423.
34 J. D. Fage, *A History of Africa* (London: Hutchinson 1978), p. 260.
35 ibid., p. 260.
36 See Postma, 'Mortality in the Dutch slave trade', pp. 241–6, where mortality among slaves purchased by the Dutch before the departure of the vessels for the Americas is discussed.
37 PRO., C. 113/273, Part 2, fo. 260, RAC, officials at Cape Coast to the company in England, 25 January 1721.
38 Edward A. Alpers, *Ivory and Slaves in East Central Africa*, Chapter 10 pp. 245–8 and 257 in this book. Edward Alpers states that about 20,000 slaves were annually brought to Mozambique during this period out of which only 15,000 were exported, the others dying at Mozambique. This gives a mortality rate of 25 per cent.
39 R. W. Beachy, *The Slave Trade of Eastern Africa* (London 1976), p. 187.
40 ibid., p. 191.
41 ibid., p. 191.
42 ibid., p. 191.
43 See W. Smith, *A New Voyage to Guinea* (London 1744), pp. 166–93.
44 J. F. Ade Ajayi and Robert Smith, *Yoruba Warfare in the Nineteenth Century* (Ibadan 1964, second edition 1971), p. 51. There is an indication that the researches of C. Becker and V. Martin on some Senegalese kingdoms, soon to be published, contain some information on the subject. See Chapter 3 in this book.
45 J. D. Fage, 'The effect of the export slave trade on African populations', in R. P. Moss and R. J. A. R. Rathbone (eds.), *The Population Factor in African Studies: The Proceedings of a Conference Organised by the African Studies Association of the United Kingdom, September, 1972* (London 1975), p. 18.
46 Fage, *A History of Africa*, pp. 267–9. Fage concludes that, 'The prime motive for warfare and raiding in Africa, then, was not to secure slaves for

280 *Notes and references to pages 29–31*

sale and export, but to secure adequate quantities of this resource and to diminish the amounts available to rivals', p. 269.

47 For purposes of clear thinking the calculations involved can be reduced to the following equation:

$$Y = x + ax - b - c$$
$$\text{or} \quad Y = x(1 + a) - b - c$$

where x = total size of population at the beginning of the year;
Y = total size of population at the end of the year's warfare, raids and slave exports;
a = the annual rate of net natural increase;
b = the annual average number of slaves actually exported;
c = the annual average of the total number of persons who died in warfare and raids, in famine and epidemics due to warfare and raids, in different bulking centres, and during the march from depot to depot and to the final points of exports.

The exercise by Fage relates to the eighteenth century, the population of West Africa being put at 25 million by 1700, with net annual growth rate at 0.0015. Based on Curtin's low estimates, Fage puts average annual slave exports from West Africa by way of the Atlantic trade in the eighteenth century at 41,000. Austen puts the average number for the trans-Saharan trade in the eighteenth century at about 8900 (including 25 per cent mortality across the desert and desert edge retention). Since some of the trans-Saharan numbers may have come from territories outside West Africa proper, West African contribution can be put at 7000. From the evidence displayed earlier, a realistic view of total additional population losses, c, should put the annual average at 100 per cent of the actual numbers exported. But for a very conservative view one may wish to adopt a 50 per cent proportion, just for the sake of argument. When these figures are substituted in the equation one gets a significant deficit in the population from year to year, even with Curtin's very low estimates. When Curtin's estimates are adjusted upwards by 40 per cent the deficit increases accordingly. Because the population is declining the magnitude of the deficit increases from year to year. It should be noted that the equation does not take account of declining birth rates which the evidence strongly indicates. In addition, it is clear from our arguments that the eighteenth-century population of West Africa used by Fage is greater than the actual population. This means that x, the population of West Africa by 1700, should be less than 25 million, making the year to year deficit greater still.

48 J. C. Caldwell, 'Major questions in African demographic history', in *Proceedings of the Edinburgh Seminar on African Historical Demography* (Edinburgh 1977), p. 9.
49 ibid., p. 18.
50 Thurstan Shaw, 'Questions in the Holocene Demography of West Africa', in ibid., pp. 108–9.
51 Caldwell, 'Major questions in African demographic history', p. 15.

52 ibid., p. 15.
53 Samir Amin, trans. Francis McDonagh, *Neo-Colonialism in West Africa* (London 1973), pp. 4–6.
54 See M. J. Mortimore, 'Land and population pressure in the Kano close-settled zone, Northern Nigeria', in R. Mansell Prothero (ed.), *People and Land in Africa South of the Sahara* (London 1972), pp. 60–70. Mortimore shows that in the Kano close-settled zone the density of rural population rises to over 600 per square mile in the centre and to over 900 in places (p. 60). Even Pierre Gourou who is often associated with the idea of African soils being incapable of sustaining high population densities has changed his position on the subject. See Pierre Gourou, 'The quality of land use of tropical cultivators', in William L. Thomas (ed.), *Man's Role in Changing the Face of the Earth*, vol. 1 (Chicago: University of Chicago 1956), pp. 336–49; 'Les Conditions du développement de l'afrique tropicale', *Geneva-Africa, Acta Africana*, vol. 1 no. 1 (1962), pp. 43–52.
55 Philip D. Curtin, 'The slave trade and the Atlantic basin: intercontinental perspectives', in N. I. Huggins, M. Kilson and D. M. Fox (eds.), *Key Issues in the Afro-American Experience, I* (New York 1971), p. 92.
56 John Caldwell, 'Introduction' to John C. Caldwell (ed.), *Population Growth and Socio-Economic Change in West Africa* (New York 1975), p. 4, cited by K. David Patterson, 'The impact of modern medicine on population growth in twentieth-century Ghana: a tentative assessment', in *Proceedings of the Edinburgh Seminar 1977*, p. 438.
57 See J. E. Inikori, 'Slave trade and the Atlantic economies, 1451–1870', paper prepared at the request of UNESCO, to be published in the *Proceedings of the Meeting of Experts on the Slave Trade*, Port-au-Prince, Haiti, 31 January – 4 February, 1978, where this method of calculation was first adopted, but now slightly modified in the light of more evidence. See also J. E. Inikori, 'Slave trade: a retardative factor in West African economic development, 1451–1870', in Mahdi Adamu (ed.), *Economic History of the Central Savanna of West Africa* (Zaria, forthcoming). The latter paper was first presented at an international seminar in Kano on the economic history of the Central Savanna of West Africa, 5–10 January, 1976.
58 See Patterson, 'The impact of modern medicine', p. 447.
59 See Peter Duignan and L. H. Gann (eds.), *The Economics of Colonialism* (Cambridge University Press 1975).
60 CO. 96/94: Brew to Pope-Hennessy, 16 April, 1872, cited by Edward Reynolds, *Trade and Economic Change on the Gold Coast*, (London: Longman 1974), p. 169.
61 Ivor Wilks, *Asante in the Nineteenth Century: The Structure and Evolution of a Political Order* (Cambridge University Press 1975). Ivor Wilks shows in detail the close relationship between economic conditions and political processes in Asante leading to the economic-modernization efforts of the nineteenth century. See in particular, chapters 12, 14 and 15.
62 *Cf* CO./520/61, enclosure no. 2, cited by W. I. Ofonagoro, *Trade and*

Imperialism in Southern Nigeria 1881–1929 (New York: Nok Publishers International 1979), p. 202.
63 Lopez, *The Commercial Revolution*, p. 84.
64 Fage, 'The effect of the export slave trade', p. 17.
65 ibid., p. 17.
66 P. E. Hair, 'Ethnolinguistic Continuity on the Guinea Coast', *Journal of African History*, vol. VIII no. 2 (1967), pp. 247–68.
67 It has been shown that as a result of the Thirty Years War of 1618–48 all the urban centres in the German lands lost one-third of their population and the rural areas lost 40 per cent. The average population loss over all Germany is put at between 30 and 40 per cent. Besides, in many towns the birth rate fell below the pre-war level by as much as 48 per cent. See Henry Kamen, 'The economic and social consequences of the Thirty Years War', *Past & Present*, no. 39 (April 1968), pp. 48 and 50; T. K. Rabb, 'The effects of the Thirty Years War on the German Economy,' *Journal of Modern History*, vol. XXXIV no. 1, 1962, p. 48.
68 Fage, *A History of Africa*, p. 265.
69 Martin A. Klein, 'Social and economic factors in the Muslim revolution in Senegambia', *Journal of African History*, vol. XIII no. 3 (1972), p. 419–41; Martin A. Klein, 'Slavery, slave trade and legitimate commerce in late nineteenth-century Africa', *Etudes d'Histoire Africaine*, vol. II (1971), pp. 5–28; Ivor Wilks, 'The Mossi and Akan States 1500–1800', in J. F. A. Ajayi and Michael Crowder (eds.), *History of West Africa*, vol. I (London: Longman 1971).
70 F. D. Lugard, *The Dual Mandate in British Tropical Africa* (London 1922), p. 366, cited by Beachy, *The Slave Trade of Eastern Africa*, p. 181.
71 Walter Rodney, 'African slavery and other forms of social oppression on the Upper Guinea Coast in the context of the Atlantic slave trade', Chapter 1 in this book.
72 See Fage, 'Slavery and the slave trade in the context of West African history', Chapter 5 in this book; *A History of West Africa: An introductory Survey* (Cambridge University Press 1969); *A History of Africa*.
73 Fage, *A History of Africa*, p. 268.
74 Walter Rodney, 'Gold and slaves on the Gold Coast', *Transactions of the Historical Society of Ghana*, vol. X (1969), pp. 19–20.
75 See Chapter 2 in this book. The factual basis of Meillassoux's statement is the contributions contained in Claude Meillassoux (ed.), *L'Esclavage en Afrique Précoloniale* (Paris: Maspero 1975).
76 'Evidence of John Barnes' in *British Parliamentary Papers, Accounts and Papers, 1789*, vol. 83 no. 635, p. 24.
77 A. F. C. Ryder, *Benin and the Europeans 1485–1897* (London 1969), p. 38.
78 Dike, *Trade and Politics*, pp. 22–5.
79 Allan G. B. Fisher and Humphrey J. Fisher, *Slavery and Muslim Society in Africa: The Institution in Sudanic Africa and the Trans-Saharan Trade* (London 1970), p. 65.
80 Wilks, 'The Mossi and Akan States'; Akinjogbin, *Dahomey and its Neigh-*

bours; Fynn, *Asante and its Neighbours*.
81 Robin Law, *The Oyo Empire c. 1600–c.1836: A West African Imperialism in the Era of the Atlantic Slave Trade* (Oxford University Press 1977), pp. 38–9.
82 See Chapter 2 in this book. According to Meillassoux, the *Tarikhs el-Fattash* and *el-Sudan* show that Sudanic slavery in the sixteenth century mainly concerned the court, its supply with foodstuffs and its administration. Enslaved farm labourers were organized and supervised on plantations for subsistence production to provide for the needs of the king, his followers, his army, as well as those of the poor.
83 ibid.
84 Martin Klein and Paul E. Lovejoy, 'Slavery in West Africa', in Gemery and Hogendorn (eds.), *The Uncommon Market*, p. 201.
85 For example, see Fage, *A History of Africa*, p. 267.
86 Klein, 'Slavery, the Slave Trade and Legitimate Commerce', p. 13. See also Martin A. Klein, 'The study of slavery in Africa', *Journal of African History*, vol. XIX no. 4 (1978), pp. 599–609.
87 Klein, 'Slavery, slave trade and legitimate commerce', pp. 13–20.
88 See Douglass C. North and R. P. Thomas, 'The rise and fall of the manorial system: a theoretical model', *Journal of Economic History*, vol. XXXI no. 4 (December 1971), pp. 777–803; also D. C. North and R. P. Thomas, *The Rise of the Western World: A New Economic History* (Cambridge University Press 1973).
89 Baer, 'Slavery in nineteenth-century Egypt', pp. 438–40.
90 Klein, 'Slavery, slave trade and legitimate commerce', p. 20.
91 Philip A. Igbafe, 'Slavery and emancipation in Benin, 1897–1945', *Journal of African History*, vol. XVI no. 3 (1975), p. 410.
92 A. J. H. Latham, 'Currency, credit and capitalism on the Cross River in the pre-colonial era', *Journal of African History*, vol. XII no. 4 (1971), p. 604.
93 Igbafe, 'Slavery and emancipation in Benin', p. 424.
94 W. D. Cooley, 'The Geography of N'yassi or the Great Lake of Southern Africa, investigated', *Journal of the Royal Geographical Society*, vol. XV (1845), p. 194, cited by Helge Kjekshus, 'The population trends of East African history: a critical review', in *Proceedings of the Edinburgh Seminar 1977*, p. 355.
95 Kjeshus, ibid., p. 355.
96 Kwame Arhin, 'The structure of Greater Ashanti, (1700–1824), *Journal of African History*, vol. VIII (1967), p. 84. For another reaction to the savage Africa hypothesis, see Ajayi and Smith, *Yoruba Warfare*. The interesting debate between Professors J. F. Ade Ajayi and A. G. Hopkins brings out some of the elements in the attitude of historians to the political consequences of the slave trade. See A. G. Hopkins, 'Economic imperialism in West Africa: Lagos, 1880–92', *Economic History Review*, vol. XXI (1968), pp. 580–606; J. F. Ade Ajayi and R. A. Austen, 'Hopkins on economic imperialism in West Africa', *Economic History Review*, vol. XXV (1972);

and A. G. Hopkins, 'Economic imperialism in West Africa: a rejoinder', *Economic History Review*, vol. XXV (1972).
97 P. D. Curtin, *Economic Change in Precolonial Africa: Senegambia in the era of the Slave Trade* (Madison 1975), p. 153.
98 Fage, *A History of Africa*, p. 269.
99 Fage, 'Slavery and the slave trade,' pp. 401–2.
100 Dov Ronen, 'On the African role in the trans-Atlantic slave trade in Dahomey', *Cahiers d'Etudes Africaines*, vol. XI no. 1 (1971), p. 9.
101 Joseph Dupuis, *Journal of a Residence in Ashantee* (London, 1824), pp. 162–4. For the reported statement by King Kpengla of Dahomey, see Archibald Dalzel, *The History of Dahomey, an Inland Kingdom of Africa* (London 1793), pp. 217–21.
102 Dupuis, ibid., p. 163.
103 Akinjogbin, *Dahomey and its Neighbours*, pp. 73–81; Law, *The Oyo Empire*, p. 220; Albert van Dantzig, 'Effects of the Atlantic slave trade on some West African societies', Chapter 7 in this book; Paul E. Lovejoy and Jan S. Hogendorn, 'Slave Marketing in West Africa,' in Gemery and Hogendorn, *The Uncommon Market*, p. 223.
104 James D. Graham, 'The slave trade, depopulation and human sacrifice in Benin history', *Cahiers d'Etudes Africaines*, vol. 5 (1965), pp. 327–30. From Professor Igbafe's discussion of the numbers of persons involved in each of the occasions for human sacrifice in Benin, and the restricted number of chiefs entitled to perform ceremonies requiring human sacrifice, the indication is that the annual average number over a period of years may not have been enough to fill the smallest of the slave vessels. See Igbafe, 'Slavery and emancipation in Benin', pp. 411–12.
105 E. Phillip LeVeen, 'The African slave supply response', *African Studies Review*, vol. XVIII no. 1 (1975), p. 13.
106 Curtin, *Economic Change in Precolonial Africa*, pp. 164–5, 181–2.
107 ibid., p. 182.
108 It is said that Alexander the Great once visited Diogenes, the Greek philosopher, and offered him anything he might wish to have from the whole of his vast empire. In reply, the philosopher made a modest request: 'Stand aside that the sunshine may continue to fall upon me'. (Walter Birmingham, *Economics: An Introduction*, 2nd edn, London 1962, p. 11). This reply indicates that Diogenes at that time was above economic desires.
109 For Meillassoux, see Chapter 2 in this book; for Hopkins, see 'Economic imperialism', together with the discussion which that paper generated; for Klein, see 'Social and economic factors in the Muslim revolution', and 'Slavery, the slave trade and legitimate commerce'.
110 Law, *The Oyo Empire*, pp. 273–6.
111 For Senegal, see Charles Becker and Victor Martin, 'Kayor and Baol: Senegalese kingdoms and the slave trade in the eighteenth century', Chapter 3 in this book; for East Africa, see Edward A. Alpers, 'The impact of the slave trade on East Central Africa in the nineteenth century', Chapter 10 in this book.

112 See Dantzig, 'Effects of the slave trade', where this distinction is discussed. Dantzig refers to the victims of slave raids as slave producers. We use the term differently. By slave producers we mean those who capture slaves in wars or raids.
113 For example, see Latham, *Old Calabar*.
114 Inikori, 'Slave trade: a retardative factor'.
115 Klein, 'Slavery, the slave trade and legitimate commerce', pp. 13–14.
116 Curtin, *Economic Change in Precolonial Africa*, p. 333.
117 J. E. Inikori, 'West African import and export trade 1750–1807: volume and structure', in Obaro Ikime (ed.), *Essays in Honour of K. O. Dike* (Ibadan University Press, forthcoming).
118 Hopkins, 'Economic imperialism', p. 589. David Northrup has produced some graphs purporting to show the compatibility of the export slave trade and palm oil export production in the Bight of Biafra. What Northrup does not tell us is whether the slaves and the palm oil exported from the ports of Bonny and Calabar in the 19th century were produced in the same geographical area. It is known that the palm oil exported from the Bight of Biafra in the first half of the 19th century was produced very close to the coast. It is also known that by this time the main catchment area of the slaves exported through the Bight of Biafra had shifted very much into the hinterland. In fact, by this time, captives from the *jihad* in Northern Nigeria were being exported through the Bight of Biafra. The evidence suggests, therefore, that the export slaves and the palm oil did not come from the same geographical area. Indeed, it would have been surprising if they did. Palm oil production in south eastern Nigeria (of which the writer has personal knowledge) was highly labour intensive. An economic activity as labour intensive as palm oil production cannot be compatible with the export of slaves that depleted the labour force, even if one leaves aside the insecurity and social disruption it engendered. See David Northrup, 'The Compatibility of the Slave and Palm Oil Trades in the Bight of Biafra', *Journal of African History*, vol. XVII no. 3 (1976), pp. 353–64.
119 See Inikori, 'Slave trade: a retardative factor', where these attempts are documented with detailed arguments.
120 Say's Law had postulated a situation in which production took place without a pre-existing demand, not even anticipated demand. The very process of production was expected to create demand for the goods produced. Even in the closed economy in whose context the theory was put forward, it has long been found to be erroneous. In the context of international trade, it is even more erroneous.
121 H. A. Gemery and J. S. Hogendorn, 'Comparative disadvantage: the case of sugar cultivation in West Africa', *Journal of Interdisciplinary History*, vol. IX no. 3 (Winter 1979), pp. 429–49.
122 See Inikori, 'Slave trade: a retardative factor'.
123 See Inikori, 'West African import and export trade'.
124 Fage, *A History of Africa*, pp. 272–3.
125 A. P. Wadsworth and J. de L. Mann, *The Cotton Trade and Industrial*

Lancashire (Manchester University Press 1931), p. 141. See also J. E. Inikori, 'English trade to Guinea: a study in the impact of foreign trade on the English economy, 1750-1807' (University of Ibadan Ph.D. thesis 1973), chapter IV.

126 Paul A. David, 'Learning by doing and tariff protection: a reconsideration of the case of the ante-bellum United States cotton textile industry', *Journal of Economic History*, vol. XXX no. 3 (1970), pp. 521-601.

127 See Daaku, *Trade and Politics*, p. 24; Fynn, *Asante and its Neighbours*, pp. 11 and 12.

128 H. A. Gemery and J. S. Hogendorn, 'The economic costs of West African participation in the Atlantic slave trade: a preliminary sampling for the eighteenth century', in Gemery and Hogendorn (eds.), *The Uncommon Market*, pp. 143-61.

129 Morton-Williams, 'The Oyo Yoruba and the Atlantic Trade, 1670-1830'.

130 Fage, 'The effect of the export slave trade', p. 15.

131 Final Report of the UNESCO Meeting of Experts on the African Slave Trade, Port-au-Prince, Haiti, 31 January – 4 February, 1978, hereafter referred to as UNESCO Final Report on the Slave Trade. There were 33 participants among whom were Philip D. Curtin, J. E. Inikori, Walter Rodney, Hubert Gerveau, and others. The proceedings of the conference are in the process of publication by UNESCO.

132 ibid.

1 African slavery and other forms of social oppression on the Upper Guinea Coast in the context of the Atlantic slave trade

1 D. Rinchon, *La traite et l'esclavage des Congolais par les Européens* (Brussels 1929), p. 169.

2 D. Mannix in collaboration with M. Cowley, *Black Cargoes, a History of the Atlantic Slave Trade* (London 1963), p. 43 (pp. 44-5 are also relevant).

3 J. D. Fage, *Introduction to the History of West Africa* (London 1959), p. 78.

4 See p. 67 in this book.

5 M. McCulloch, *Peoples of Sierra Leone*, Ethnographic Survey of Africa, (ed.) D. Forde (London 1964), pp. 28, 29, 68.

6 R. S. Rattray, *Ashanti* (London 1923), pp. 40-3, 222, 230.

7 For example, Stanley Elkins, *Slavery, a Problem in American Institutional and Social Life* (New York 1963), p. 96; and Basil Davidson, *Black Mother* (London 1961), p. 40. (For a discussion of African 'slavery' and 'serfdom', see the section on pp. 33-40.)

8 Christopher Fyfe, *A History of Sierra Leone* (London 1962): see index under 'slave trade, internal'.

9 Alonso de Sanderval, *Natureleza ... de Todos Etiopes* (Seville 1623).

10 *Biblioteca de la Real Academia de la Historia* (Madrid) – 'Papeles de Jesuitas', tomo 185, no. 1346, report of P. Baltezar Barreira (Sierra Leone 1606).

11 Th. Monod, A. Texeira de Mota and R. Mauny (eds.), *Description de la côte occidentale d'Afrique (Sénégal au Cap de Monte, Archipels) par Valentim Fernandes* (1506–10) (Bissau 1951), p. 82. (To be cited subsequently as 'Valentim Fernandes'.)
12 Valentim Fernandes, p. 88; Alvares de Almada, 'Tratado Breve dos Rios de Guiné' (1594), in P. Antonio Brasio, *Monumenta missionaria africana, Africa ocidental (1570–1600)*, 2nd series, vol. III (Lisbon 1964), pp. 323, 324, 333; and Manual Alvares, 'Ethiopia Menor, o descripçao geografica da Provincia de Serra Leoa' (1616), ms. of the *Sociedade de Geografia de Lisboa*.
13 Valentim Fernandes, p. 10.
14 Alvares de Almada, 'Rios de Guiné'. pp. 234, 235.
15 ibid., pp. 344, 345, 347; and Damiao Peres (ed.), *Duas descriçoes seiscentistas da Guiné de Francisco de Lemos Coelho* (Lisbon 1953), pp. 59–61, from the description written in 1669. (To be cited subsequently as 'Lemos Coelho'.)
16 Mungo Park, *Travels in the Interior Districts of Africa in the Years 1795, 1796 and 1797* (London 1799), pp. 297, 298.
17 P. Mateo de Anguiano, *Misiones capuchinas en Africa*, (ed.) P. Buenaventura de Carrocera, vol. II (Madrid 1950), p. 136 – missionary report of 1686 on the Atlantic slave trade as pursued on the Upper Guinea Coast. *Cabo* or *Gabu* was a Mandinga province extending between the Gambia and the Corubal. The ruler was called *Farim* or 'governor', because he was ostensibly a representative of the emperor of Mali.
18 Alvares de Almada, 'Rios de Guiné', p. 275.
19 C. B. Wadstrom, *An Essay on Colonisation* (London 1795), part 2, pp. 113–7. A 'bar' originally signified an iron bar about 22½ cms long. It came to be a unit of currency in the trade of the Upper Guinea Coast with a very imprecise and fluctuating value. Wadstrom estimated it at about 3 shillings (p. 56).
20 ibid., part 2, p. 117.
21 P. Cultru, *Premier voyage de Sieur de la Courbe, fait à la Coste d'Afrique en 1685* (Paris 1913), p. 252.
22 John Mathews, *A Voyage to the River Sierra Leone* (London 1788).
23 A. G. Laing, *Travels in the Timannee, Kooranko and Soolima Countries* (London 1825), p. 221.
24 P. Marty (trans.), 'Islam in French Guinea', in *Sierra Leone Studies* no. XIX (old series, 1936), pp. 49–129.
25 L. Tauxier, *Moeurs et histoire des Peuhls* (Paris 1937), p. 9. He renders the word *rimaibe* as 'agricultural serfs'. The singular is *dimadio*.
26 Captain Canot, *The Adventures of an African Slaver* (London 1928), pp. 128, 129. (This account was actually written in 1854 by one Brantz Meyer to whom Canot related his experiences.)
27 *Public Record Office*, London (to be cited below as *PRO*), T. 70/1465; diary of agent Walter Charles, 1728. This mentions 'Cayoba, a castle slave who had been made such from a sale slave'.

28 *PRO*. T. 70/51: instructions to agent Freeman, 4 August 1702.
29 *PRO*. T. 70/51: instructions to agent Freeman, 1 December 1702.
30 *PRO*. T. 70/60: instructions from the directors, 5 October 1723.
31 *PRO*. T. 70/1465: diary of agent Walter Charles.
32 *Arquivo histórico ultramarino*, Lisbon (to be cited below as *AHU*), Guiné, caixa 11, no. 230, minute of the Conselho Ultramarino, 30 October 1694.
33 Alvares de Almada, 'Rios de Guiné', p. 326, and Fr. Francisco de Santiago, 'Chronica da Provincia Franciscana de Nossa Senhora da Soledade' (ms), extracts in A. J. Dias, 'Crenças e costumes dos indigenas da Ilha de Bissau no seculo XVIII', *Portugal em Africa*, vol. II, no. 9 (1945), 159–69.
34 Fyfe, *A History of Sierra Leone*, p. 270.
35 *PRO*, T. 70/53: instructions to agent Plunkett, 9 February 1721. (He was sent a new branding iron.)
36 *PRO*. T. 70/16: letter from agent Edmund Pierce, February 1682.
37 *PRO*. T. 70/361: Bence Island accounts, 1682.
38 *AHU*., Cabo Verde, caixa VI: Bishop of Cape Verde to the Conselho Ultramarino, 27 July 1694.
39 C. B. Wadstrom, *An Essay on Colonisation*, part 2, pp. 84, 85, 87.
40 ibid., part 2, p. 117.
41 British Museum, Add. ms. 12131: papers relating to Sierra Leone, 1792-6, journals by Mr Gray and Mr Watt, 1795.
42 Captain Canot, *The Adventures of an African Slaver*, pp. 68, 169.
43 J. J. Crooks, in his *A History of the Colony of Sierra Leone* (Dublin 1903), holds to the view of African slavery being ancient, but he makes no connection with the Atlantic slave trade.
44 See, for example, Eric McKitrick (ed.), *Slavery Defended: the Views of the Old South* (New Jersey 1963).
45 Obviously, the early records of the Portuguese in Benin and the Congo could be of vital importance here. Basil Davidson cited Pacheco Pereira to the effect that there were wars in Benin providing captives for the Europeans, and added that 'these wars provided slaves for domestic use, much as in medieval Europe'. This is a reasonable presumption, but it is nevertheless an interpolation and not the evidence of Pacheco Pereira (*Old Africa Rediscovered*, p. 124, and Mauny (ed.), *Esmeraldo de Situ Orbis*, p. 134). For the Congo (pp. 121, 122) Davidson cites a secondary work: A. Ihle, *Das alte Königreich Kongo* (1929).
46 Besides, Mungo Park was heavily influenced by the West Indian slave owner Bryan Edwards; and it was one of the pro-slavery arguments that, if the majority of Africans were already slaves in Africa, then it would be no improvement in their lot to end the Atlantic slave trade and American slavery. For a discussion of the extent to which Park was influenced by Edwards, see the introduction by John Murray to the publication of Park's second Niger journey, *The Journal of a Mission to Africa in the Year 1805*.
47 Valentim Fernandes, pp. 92, 96.
48 See, for example, the report of three Spanish Capuchin missionaries on the conduct of the Atlantic slave trade on the Upper Guinea Coast in the latter

part of the seventeenth century in P. Mateo de Anguiano, *Misiones capuchinas en Africa*, vol. II, pp. 132–46 (written in 1686).
49 M. McCulloch, *Peoples of Sierra Leone*, pp. 24, 25.
50 Raymond Mauny (ed.), *Esmeraldo de Situ Orbis, par Duarte Pacheco Pereira (vers 1506–8)* (Bissau 1956), pp. 134, 126.
51 Alvares de Almada, 'Rios de Guiné', p. 301.
52 Richard Jobson, *The Golden Trade* (London 1933), pp. 108, 109. The 'slaves' in the Gambia were owned by the Muslim *imams*.
53 See p. 65 in this book.
54 R. Oliver and J. D. Fage, *A Short History of Africa* (London 1962), 172.
55 R. K. Udo, 'The migrant tenant farmer of eastern Nigeria, in *Africa*, vol. XXXIV/no. 4 (October 1964), 333. There is a reference to the regime of household service in southern Nigeria in *Black Mother*, p. 39.
56 James Duffy, *Portugal in Africa* (London 1962), pp. 61, 62, 69.

2 The role of slavery in the economic and social history of Sahelo-Sudanic Africa

1 C. Meillassoux (ed.), *L'esclavage en Afrique pré-coloniale* (Paris: François Maspéro 1975).
2 R. Mauny, *Tableau géographique de l'Ouest Africain au Moyen Age*, (Dakar: Institut Fondamental d'Afrique Noire 1961), mém., p. 337.
3 D 114; A. Barthily, 'A discussion for the traditions of Wagadu', *Bulletin IFAN*, vol. 57, Series B, no. 1.
4 Mauny, *Tableau géographique de l'Ouest Africain au Moyen Age*, p. 337; Edrissi, trans. R. Dozy and M. J. de Goeje, *Description de l'Afrique et de l'Espagne* (Leyde: Brill 1866), p. 4 and 11.
5 ibid.
6 Mauny, *Tableau géographique de l'Ouest Africain au Moyen Age*, p. 337.
7 One need not accept the exactitude of these figures, as with those of other chroniclers. but they indicate a considerable number of effectives.
8 Al-Bakri, 'Routier de l'Afrique blanche et noire du nord-ouest' (an eleventh-century text translated by V. Monteil), *Bulletin, Institute Fondamental d'Afrique Noire*, vol. 30 no. 1, pp. 39–116.
9 ibid.
10 ibid.
11 ibid.
12 Al-Omari, *L'Afrique moins l'Eygypte* (fourteenth-century text, *Masalik el Absar*, translated by Gaudefroy-Demombynes) (Paris: P. Teuthner 1927), pp. 66–7.
13 ibid., p. 8.
14 A. Es-Sa'di, *Tarikh Es-Soudan* (Paris: Leroux 1964), p. 20.
15 ibid., p. 85.
16 ibid., p. 104.
17 J. Rouch, *Contribution à l'histoire des Songhay* (Dakar: IFAN 1953), mém. 29, p. 182.
18 M. Kati (trans., O. Houdas and M. Delafossel), *Tarikh el-Fettach* (Paris:

Adrien Maisonneuve 1964, first published 1913), p. 135.
19 ibid., p. 145.
20 ibid., p. 214.
21 Rouch, *Contribution à l'histoire des Songhay*, p. 195.
22 It is, however, known from more recent examples (J. Bazin, 1974), that the sharing out of the booty was an important and strictly codified institution.
23 Rouch, *Contribution à l'histoire des Songhay*, pp. 182–3.
24 Kati, *Tarikh el-Fettach*, p. 214.
25 Es–Sa'di, *Tarikh Es-Soudan*, p. 157.
26 To 'devour' someone is generally the synonym for exploiting him.
27 Es–Sa'di, *Tarikh Es-Soudan*, p. 223.
28 cf. note 22, above.
29 Es–Sa'di, *Tarikh Es-Soudan*, p. 275.
30 ibid., p. 171.
31 C. Meillassoux and A. C. Naire, 'Histoire et institutions du Kafo de Bamako, d'après la tradition des Niaré', *Cahiers d'Etudes Africaines*, vol. IV no. 2 (14), pp. 186–227.
32 The latter seem sometimes to have suffered in the course of expeditions in hot countries like Gurma (*Tarikh Es-Soudan*, p. 426). See also on this point C. Aubin-Sugy (forthcoming, chapter XI).
33 The Dogon compound, or the Bamana or Malinke *tatas* provide evidence of this for more recent times.
34 C. Aubin-Sugy ('Economic growth and secular trend in the pre-colonial Sudanic belt', Unpublished Ph.D thesis, Faculty of History, University of Columbia 1975, Chapter 5), believes that the employment of slaves in the cavalry contributed to a more disciplined organization of armies.
35 'In the twinkling of an eye, the Askia's troops were routed.' Thus the battle between the Askia's 30,000 horse and foot and the 1000 Moroccan invaders is summed up. (*TES*, p. 219–20).
36 On the relative efficacy of firearms see the special nos. of the *Journal of African History*, vol. XII nos. 2 and 4 (1971). See also M. Hiskett, *The Sword of Truth: the Life and Times of the Shehu Usuman Dan Fodio* (New York: Oxford University Press 1973), pp. 78–9 and footnotes 6 and 7. – *Ed.*
37 Es–Sa'di, *Tarikh Es-Soudan*, p. 217.
38 Y. Person, *Samori, une révolution dyula* (3 vols., Dakar: IFAN 1968), mém. 80.
39 ibid., pp. 34–70.
40 Es–Sa'di, *Tarikh Es-Soudan*, pp. 121–2.
41 See in Brunschvig, Abd, *Encyclopedia of Islam*, pp. 27 and 32; the permanent justification that Islam gave to the capture of slaves under cover of holy war. Such a justification betrayed the slave-holding character of the civilization which had by then developed and envisaged the incessant demand for slaves that it exercised.
42 The major importance of the capture and sale of slaves is clearly established by R. S. O'Fahey, 'Slavery and the slave trade in Dà-Fûr', *Journal of African History*, vol. XIV no. 1 (1973), pp. 29–43, for Dàr-Fûr in the eighteenth and nineteenth centuries.

43 N. Levtzion, *Ancient Ghana and Mali* (London: Methuen 1973), pp. 155–6.
44 Al-Omari, *L'Afrique moins l'Eygypte*, p. 58 and 70; As later, the conquest of the Taghaza salt deposits by the Sultan of Morocco, led to a fall-off in production.
45 A controversial explanation since the Bure and Bambuk placers have been continuously exploited up to the present day. In 1937 the production of the placers in French West Africa was three and a half tons (A. G. Hopkins, *An Economic History of West Africa*, London: Longman 1973; see also A. Barthily, 'A discussion for the traditions of Wagadu', *Bulletin IFAN*, vol. 57 series B, no. 1).
46 One can find traces for a more recent period for the flight of populations as a result of slave raids, in all the oral traditions of 'paleonigritic' populations – see in particular G. Pontie for the populations driven off by the Mandara, the Hausa, etc., into the mountains of north Cameroun. These populations generally considered as having been 'pushed back' by an invader or dispossessed of their lands by conquest, should rather be considered as having fled from zones infested by slave raiders. One can observe in fact that when a people established itself in an already inhabited place, coexistence is more often the rule than exception.
47 In similar fashion, in the eighteenth century the subjects of Dahomey could not be sold by their ruler. The fall of kingdoms often resulted from the breaking of this rule, as can be seen with several states, like for example, Wolof or Oyo.
48 I. Batuta (trans., C. Defremery and B. R. Sanguinetti), *Voyages d' Ibn Battuta*, 3 vols., (Paris: Anthropos 1854), p. 53 and 64.
49 ibid., p. 53.
50 ibid., p. 59.
51 ibid., p. 46.
52 ibid., p. 63.
53 ibid., p. 64.
54 ibid., p. 76.
55 ibid., p. 78.
56 Al-Omari, *L'Afrique moins l'Egypte*, p. 66.
57 A distinction must be made here between the data provided by the original and a later manuscript (N. Levtzion, 'A seventeenth century chronicle by Ibn al Makhtar: a critical study of Tarikh al Fattash', *Bull SOAS*, vol. XXXIV no. 3, pp. 571–93), which reflects a change in the concept of slavery.
58 Two eunuchs surrounded the king, ready to offer him their sleeves to spit on (*TEF*, p. 208). The daughters of the royal soldiers were at the disposal of the ruler, for his pleasure.
59 Kati, *Tarikh el-Fattach*, p. 191.
60 ibid., p. 109.
61 One finds an analogous development in nineteenth-century Senegal. (cf. M. Klein, 'Servitude among the Wolof and Serer of Senegambia' in I. Kopytoff and S. Miers, *Slavery in Africa*, Madison: University of Wisconsin Press 1977).

62 The African military aristocracy, like most of its counterparts, considered it derogatory to engage in money-making activity.
63 Al-Omari, *L'Afrique moins l'Egypte*, p. 75; Batuta, *Voyages d'Ibn Batuta*, p. 72; E. W. Bovill, *The Golden Trade of the Moors* (London: Oxford University Press 1968); Mauny, *Tableau géographique de l'Ouest Africain au Moyen Age*; M. Johnson, 'The cowrie currencies of West Africa', *Journal of African History*, vol. XI no. 1, pp. 17–49 and vol. XI no. 3, pp. 331–54.
64 Es-Sa'di, *Tarikh Es-Soudan*, p. 36.
65 Es-Sa'di, *Tarikh Es-Soudan*, p. 26.
66 Mauny, *Tableau géographique de l'Ouest Africain au Moyen Age*, p. 389.
67 According to Niare tradition, the first merchant families were established in Bamako around 1640 (C. Meillassoux, 'Histoire et institutions du Kafo de Bamako, d'après la tradition des Niare').
68 See J. L. Triaud, 'Quelques remarques sur l'islamisation du Mali, des origines à 1300', *Bull, IFAN*, vol. XXX no. 4 (1968), pp. 1329–53.
69 G. Doutressoule, 'Le cheval au Soudan français et ses origines', *Bull. IFAN*, vol. II no. 3–4, pp. 342–6; D. F. McCall, 'The horse in West African history', *Congrès International des Africanistes*, second session (Dakar 1963).
70 The most recent history of Africa provides some examples: the decline of the kingdom of Congo (G. Balandier, *La vie quotidienne au royaume de Kongo du XVIe au XVIIIe siècles*, Paris: François Maspéro 1965; K. Ekholm, *Power and Prestige, the Rise and Fall of the Kongo Kingdom*, Uppsala: Skriv Service AB 1972), the falling apart of the principalities in the Senegal valley (B. Barry, *Le royaume de Kongo du Waalo*, Paris: François Maspéro 1972), the collapse of the kingdoms of Senegambia (M. Klein, 'Social and economic factors in the muslim revolution in Senegambia', *Journal of African History*, vol. XIII no. 3, 1972). We have also discussed the capacity of merchants in the savanna to escape from the control of states (C. Meillassoux (ed.), *The Development of Indigenous Trade and Markets in West Africa*, London: Oxford University Press 1971).
71 The term *marke* is applied by the Bamana, Bonzon, Senufo, Minyaka peoples, etc., to the families of 'stranger' origin who are either muslims among pagans, merchants among peasants or warriors and conquerors.
72 It is also the name of a people in Upper Volta that seems to have nothing in common with the Soninke peoples.
73 C. Meillassoux (ed.), *The Development of Indigenous Trade and Markets in West Africa* (London: Oxford University Press 1971), p. 32.
74 J. Vansina has taught us the importance one should give to the silences of oral traditions.
75 C. Monteil, *Les Bambara de Segou et du Kaarta* (Paris: Larose 1924), pp. 20–1.
76 C. Binger, *Du Niger au Golfe de Guinée* (2 vols., Paris: Hachette 1892), vol. 2, p. 393.
77 The contestable correctness of dates is less important than the fact recorded, that is to say, a reinforcement of the merchant classes and their

78 The first Jula families may have been the Da'on, the Kerou, the Barou, the Toure and the Wattara, which were later joined by the Sakhanokho, the Sisse, the Kamata, the Mamakhate, the Timite and the Danokho.
79 J. Bazin, verbal communication.
80 Monteil, *Les Bambara de Segou et du Kaarta*, p. 44.
81 ibid., p. 40-4.
82 cf. the Naire tradition in C. Meillassoux, *Anthropologie économique des Gouro de Côte-d'Ivoire* (Paris: Mouton 1964).
83 ibid.
84 These Segu soldiers were therefore not similar to the royal 'janissaries' we meet in, for example, Wolof or Mossi.
85 J. Bazin, 'Commerce et predation: l'etat de Segou et ses communantés Marka', in Conference on Manding Studies (London 1972).
86 A. H. Ba and J. Daget, *L'Empire Peul du Macina* (Paris: Mouton 1962), p. 173.
87 ibid., p. 46 and 161.
88 ibid., p. 151.
89 ibid., p. 67.
90 ibid.
91 ibid., p. 67.
92 ibid., p. 151.
93 *talibe* – discipline.
94 *dolo* – beer made from millet, prohibited by Islam.
95 The reasons for these preferences arose from the modes of slave reproduction, as we will see.
96 While Samori, like Al Hajj Umar to a lesser degree, found himself caught in this vicious circle and obliged to fight perhaps more than he would have wished, the fact remains that his enterprise was founded upon slaving warfare. Yves Person's attempts (*Samori, une révolution dyula*, 3 vols., Dakar: IFAN 1968, mém. 80), in his otherwise remarkable work, to absolve Samori from the sin of slaving, do not seem to me to be well founded. Likewise, I cannot agree with P. D. Curtin (*Economic Change in Precolonial Africa*, Madison: University of Wisconsin 1975), for whom the capture of slaves was only a by-product of wars undertaken for no other reason than war itself. Klein contests this thesis but admits that wars may not have had the capture of slaves as an object until after 1870 (forthcoming).
97 Made up of distinct parts and entities closely intertwined.
98 I shall not, here, go over the analyses made on the occasion of the examination of commercial development in West Africa since the second half of the nineteenth century (Meillassoux [ed.], *The development of indigenous trade and markets in West Africa*), and which relate particularly to this critical period that coincides with the disappearance of the European slave trade.
99 cf. C. Aubin-Sugy, 'Economic growth and secular trend in the pre-colonial Sudanic belt'.

294 Notes and references to pages 91–4

100 M. Klein, 'Slavery, the slave trade and legitimate commerce in late nineteenth-century Africa', *Etudes et d'Histoire Africaine*, vol. 11 (1971), p. 8.
101 Dakar Archives, series K 14, folio 2.
102 T. G. Mollien, *L'Afrique occidentale en 1818* (Paris: Calmann-Lévy 1967), GK 23.
103 Dakar Archives, K 18, folio 20, Dagana.
104 ibid., K14; M171.
105 Dakar Archives, K4, Sokolo; M160.
106 ibid., K19, f. 6; FQ 26.
107 ibid., M189.
108 ibid., K14, Kerounane.
109 ibid., M162.
110 ibid., M156.
111 ibid., K14, Bamako.
112 ibid., K14, Kankan.
113 ibid., K14, Segu.
114 ibid., K14, Siguiri.
115 ibid., K25, f. 204.
116 ibid., K21, f. 8.
117 This conversion is particularly well illustrated by B. Barry, *Le royaume du Waalo* (Paris: François Maspéro), part 3, chapter 1.
118 The analysis of these numerous data would require additional information on dates, places and the nature of transactions (merchanting or direct exchange – see for this distinction, Meillassoux [ed.], *The development of Trade and Markets*, pp. 26 and 42), as well as the conditions in which the information was gathered (observation, reports by interested parties, reports from memory, etc.). Moreover, the exploitation of such data could only be effected within the framework of a price theory for this type of economy.
119 Dakar Archives, K14.
120 For example, in the region of Kourroussa, the following are the estimates made by the local reporter (ibid., K14, Kourroussa): a woman was worth a good captive and a cow (200 francs plus 50 francs), a horse was worth 3 captives (two good plus one average).
121 This was noted as early as 1814 by R. G. de Villeneuve. We should note also that the mercantile value reversed all the hierarchies: a recaptured slave sold dearer than a free man, a woman was dearer than a man, the young were dearer than the old, the stranger dearer than the indigene. (Dakar Archives 1904, K18, f. 14.)
122 C. Meillassoux, *Anthropologie économique des Gouro de Côte-d'Ivoire* (Paris: Mouton 1964), p. 270; Person, *Samori, une révolution dyula*.
123 Cited in A. G. B. Fisher and H. J. Fisher, *Slavery and Muslim Society in Africa* (London: C. Hurst & Co. 1970), p. 13.
124 See also J. L. Boutillier, 'Les captifs en AOF (1903–5)', *Bull. IFAN*, vol. 30, series B, p. 528; M. Diop, *Histoire des classes sociales dans l'Afrique de l'Ouest*, vol. 1, *Le Mali* (Paris: François Maspéro 1971), p. 225.
125 Boutillier, 'Les trois esclaves de Bouna', in Meillassoux (ed.), *L'esclavage en Afrique pré-coloniale*, pp. 253–280.

126 According to C. Aubin-Sugy, one should add to productive slavery, the deportation and establishment on new land of entire populations, organized by conquerors to ensure their supplies. Certain regions, such as Ojenne or Segela, whose inhabitants had been themselves massacred or carried off, may have been repopulated in this way by deported people who had been destructured and rendered more docile. Aubin-Sugy estimated that these transfers of populations who were more open to the exploitation and exactions of their conquerors, may have contributed to the growth of agricultural production.

127 While from the point of view of price, these exchanges were less disadvantageous than in the course of the colonial period (C. Coquery-Vidrovitch, 'De la traite des esclaves à l'exportation de l'huile de palme et des palmistes au Dahomey: XIXe siècle', in Meillassoux [ed.], *The Development of Indigenous Trade and Markets in West Africa*), from the point of view of the relative productivity of goods they were disastrous.

128 E. Terray, 'Long distance exchange and the formation of the state: the case of the Abron Kingdom', *Economy and Society*, vol. 3 no. 3, pp. 315–45.

129 A. Ca da Mosto, *Relations des voyages à la côte occidentale d'Afrique, 1455-7* (Paris: Leroux 1937), p. 30.

130 Ruler of Jolof in present-day Senegal.

131 C. Meillassoux, 'Ostentation, destruction, reproduction', *Economies et Sociétés*, vol. 2 no. 4, pp. 760–72.

132 The extent to which the slave trade in Dahomey was monopolized by the king and the state officials has recently been examined by R. C. C. Law. The evidence produced by Law indicates that while the trade was dominated by the king and his officials, independent private traders in Dahomey also had some share. See R. C. C. Law, 'Royal monopoly and private enterprise in the Atlantic trade: the case of Dahomey', *Journal of African History*, vol. XVIII no. 4 (1977), pp. 555–77. In general, however, the Atlantic slave trade was largely dominated in Africa by kings and state officials. – *Ed.*

133 Terray, 'Long distance exchange and the formation of the state'.

134 K. Polanyi (*Dahomey and the Slave Trade*, University of Washington Press 1966), justly characterized this procedure as administrative trade, but wrongly interpreted it as characterizing a phase of historical development and not the result of a conjuncture.

135 P. P. Rey, *Colonialisme, néo-colonialisme et transition au capitalisme* (Paris: François Maspéro 1971), p. 273.

136 An important distinction since because of this the mercantile circuit was not completed in such a system and without that, the creation of a profit capable of starting off the accumulation and eventual establishment of capital, was not allowed for.

137 By contrast with states in the savanna which, it would seem, never directly controlled the production of gold. This always remained in the hands of independent populations, with whom contact was maintained by merchants.

138 P. Bonnafe, 'Les formes d'asservissement chez les Kukuya d'Afrique Centrale', in Meillassoux (ed.), *L'esclavage en Afrique pré-coloniale*.

139 C. Perrot, 'Les captifs dans le royaume Anyi du Ndenye', and Bonnafe, 'Les formes d'asservissement chez les Kukuya d'Afrique Centrale', in ibid.: Rey, *Colonialisme, néo-colonialisme et transition au capitalisme.*
140 Perrot, 'Les captifs dans le royaume Anyi du Ndenye'.
141 Bonnafe, 'Les formes d'asservissement chez les Kukuya d'Afrique Centrale'.
142 Rey, *Colonialisme.*
143 Terray, 'Long distance exchange and the formation of the state', p. 10.
144 Bonnafe, 'Les formes d'asservissement chez les Kukuya d'Afrique Centrale'.

3 Kayor and Baol: Senegalese kingdoms and the slave trade in the eighteenth century

1 This research has been led by V. Martin, as part of a CNRS research programme. A more detailed study will shortly be undertaken of the history of Kayor and Baol between 1695 and 1809. It will include a chronology of sovereigns and a more complete presentation of the facts given here. It will be accompanied by several unpublished archive documents which confirm and rectify traditional chronology, and which explain the machinations and methods of European trade. The complete bibliography of the subject – which has been used in this present article – will be examined in detail.
   As we explain in this study, political history, which brings the solution to chronological problems, is a necessary stage in the understanding of peoples and societies.
2 L. A. G. Colvin's important work on the history of Kayor (*Kayor and its Diplomatic Relations with Saint-Louis of Senegal, 1763–1861*, New York: Columbia University Press 1972) puts forward an interesting interpretation, but makes almost no mention of the internal effects in Kayor or the slave trade. Despite pertinent analysis of the policies of European administrators and useful questioning of several traditional ideas, the impact of the slave trade seems to have been grossly underestimated. The conclusions of our study are very different and are closer to those of Boubacar Barry on the history of Walo (*Le royaume du Walo. Le Sénégal avant la conquête*, Paris: François Maspéro 1972).
3 The Senegalese historian, Yoro Dyao, established a chronology of Damels in the middle of the nineteenth century which was used unquestioningly by subsequent authors. Yoro Dyao's knowledge of Senegalese history was extremely detailed. The extent and accuracy of his knowledge is confirmed by the date available to us at present, and it seems plausible to accuse Yoro Dyao of collaboration with the French, and to suspect historical falsification, as Colvin seems to suggest (*Kayor and its Diplomatic Relations*, p. 6). Dyao's history of Damels could have been used to propagate the colonial theme of 'chronic political instability'. However, a detailed examination of written sources suggests that the Senegalese historian rather minimized the extent of conflicts and wars that took place in the eighteenth century.

4 The maternal families from which Damels were descended before the Gedj were the following:
   Moyoy, Wagadu, Sonyo, Gelwar, Dorobé and Bey. In the eighteenth and nineteenth centuries, only the Dorobé and the Gelwar managed to replace the Gedj for brief intervals.
5 T. L. Fall, 'Recueil sur le vie des Damel', *Bulletin, IFAN*, vol. XXXVI series B no. 1 (1974) p. 112–5.
6 The three branches of the Fall royal family, designated by the Wolof word *keur* (house, line) were descendants of Madior Fatina Gologn (*Keur* Madior), the Tegn Tye Ndela (*Keur* Tye Ndela) and the Tegn Tye Yasin Demba Nudji (*Keur* Tye Yasin).
7 Nasir Al-Din's message, as reported by a European observer, Chambonneau, announced that 'God does not allow Kings to pillage, kill or enslave their people; on the contrary, they are to watch over and protect them from enemies; people were not made for Kings, but Kings for people'; C. I. Ritchie, *Two texts on Senegal*, 1763–7, *Bulleton IFAN*, vol. XXX series B no. 1 (1968), p. 339. The same text explains that, in all countries obedient to the Muslims:

   ever since they [the Muslims] have been masters of the country, not one [slave] has entered our landing-boats; unless we can involve the leaders themselves it is impossible for us to carry on much trade, whatever the commodity. For if a (private) individual slaughters an ox, he will consume its hide too; if he has a slave, he will keep him for his labour; if he is from the gum-producing region, as he has few people [to work for him] he will not collect it from the trees - whereas a King will part with anything he has when he sees a boat-load of good merchandise like canvas, brandy, coral, silver, iron, glass-ware, and all the other things usually conveyed there.... The fact is, too, that since there is peace everywhere (now), there is no great prospect of slaves from these four kingdoms.

   ibid, p. 352–3. The gum would be gum arabic, in this instance probably from a grey-barked tree in those parts, called *Acacia Senegal*.
8 B. Barry, *Le royaume du Walo*, p. 138.
9 J. Mettas's work on the movement of French ships on the African coast illuminates the question of the number of slaves who embarked at Saint-Louis and at Gorée. Figures on the Senegambian slave trade in the eighteenth century are given in our commentary on Doumet's essay 'Mémoire inédit de Doumet', published and commented on by C. Becker and V. Martin, *Bull. IFAN* vol. XXXVI series B, no. 1, n. 64 (1974), pp. 63–83.
10 See 'Mémoire inédit de Doumet', n. 9, p. 43 and n. 75, p. 85, in ibid. The French tried to use brokers too. Thus Rocheblave's *Observations on the Isle of Gorée*, to his successor, Boniface, in 1772 emphasize that inhabitants of Gorée are needed 'to hunt for captives like hares' and to prevent the Moors delivering them to the English at Saint-Louis; Archives, nat., col., C⁶ 16.
11 See the third section of this article. Detailed surveys of over a hundred villages in Kayor and Baol, and investigations in other areas, all stress the indisputable importance of captives in the rural societies of these two countries.

12 Arch. nat., col., C⁶ 16; documents s.d.
13 Note here the divergence between these conclusions and those of L. A. G. Colvin (*Kayor and its Diplomatic Relations, n. 2*), who considers that 'the tyranny of Kings towards their subjects and the permanent political instability' were myths invented by the colonizers in the nineteenth century.
14 French methods were centralizing, with rigid directorship of the companies and fixed tariffing, whilst the English left room for initiative and private competition in Senegambia. Throughout the eighteenth century the French complained of their rivals and of unauthorized dealers in particular, accusing them of overpaying for slaves and causing a rise in tariffs.
15 These texts are numerous and will be analysed in more detail in our forthcoming study.
16 Bibliothèque nationale, ms franç. 21690 'Rellation tres fidelle de ce quy s'est passe dans le voyage que le Sr François Directeur general . . . a fait au dt lieu du Senegal, Gorée et lieux dépendens de la concession de la de Compagnie', par le Sieur Mathelot, 1687, f138.
17 Arch. nat., col., C⁶.6, Saint-Robert à la Compagnie, 26 August, 1720.
18 Arch. nat., C⁶.8, Dubellay à MM. les Directeurs de la Compagnie, 28 March, 1724.
19 Arch. nat., copy of Dubellay's letter to Lafore, 26 August, 1724.
20 Arch. nat., col., C⁶.10, 'Suite de Journal historique depuis le premier septembre 1730 jusqu'au premier septembre 1731'.
21 Arch. nat., col., C⁶.11. Gorée Council to the company, 31 May 1737.
22 ibid., C⁶.14. letter from the High Senegal Council to the company, 20 June 1753.
23 Bibl. nat., ms franç. 8993, 'Mémoire sur le Sénégal', by Capitain Godeheu, f3 r⁰.
24 Arch. nat., col., C⁶ 15, extract of Poncet's letter to the Minister, 25 May 1764.
25 ibid.
26 ibid., C⁶16 Boniface to the Minister, 22 March 1773.
27 Having set out the Moorish project against Kayor and Baol, and the request for arms, Le Brasseur notes his neutrality: 'As I do not feel it is my duty to enter into a conspiracy, I do feel it would be useful, but I have not listened to any of the Moors' propositions, and will never do so unless you order me to'. (Arch. nat., col. 17, Le Brasseur's letter to the Minister, 29 April, 1777). After the year-long trade blockade imposed by the Damel-Tegn Makodu Kumba Diaring, Le Brasseur resolutely took the part of the Moors and sent his 'Plan for revolution in the kingdoms of Kayor and Baol' to break the Damel-Tegn. However, the reconciliation with Makodu, a few days before his death and the partition of Kayor and Baol between two kings, prevented the realization of the project, which nonetheless remained a threat.
28 Arch. nat., col., 17, Armeny to the minister, 5 March 1778.
29 The effects of the European slave trade on Kayor and Baol cannot be minimized by invoking the Arab trade. Right up until 1778 the French consistently barred the Moors from access to the two kingdoms, sometimes by

force. The settling of some Moorish groups in Kayor and Baol and their continued links with Mauritania was favourable to the export of slaves towards the north, but this was very small in number and far inferior to the European trade. It is essential to stress that Nasir Al-Din's movement, of Moorish origin, protested at the end of the seventeenth century against different forms of enslavement, but in particular against the selling of slaves to Europeans.

The development of the Arab–Moorish slave trade, which is referred to in European documents of the time as 'Moorish incursions into Negro lands', took place in the eighteenth century, and was more a consequence of than a parallel phenomenon to the Atlantic slave trade. In fact, the Moors traded rubber and bought arms, on the whole. The frequent Moorish attacks on the riverside settlements in Senegal may have been for political and religious motives, but these were secondary to economic causes. The demand created by European trade and especially by the sale of arms were the major reasons which led to the rise of the Arab–Moorish slave trade. Abundant written evidence confirms this: in particular, the direct participation of the English Governor of Saint-Louis, O'Hara, in the Moorish ravage of Walo and Fouta (of B. Barry, *Le royaume du Walo*, p. 208–11), and Le Brasseur's proposal of a 'Plan for revolution in the kingdoms of Kayor and Baol', which aimed to provide maximum profit for the European slave trade by acquiring the slaves captured by the Moors in Kayor and Baol. As Le Brasseur's letter of 29 April 1777 points out, 'it seems that the French would be able to buy more than 3000 slaves in less than 2 years, and the English twice that amount', after the Moorish invasion of the two kingdoms – the continuation of the Arab–Moorish slave trade in the nineteenth century and the preponderance of slave trading in the north at this time are an attested phenomenon. In order to understand this objectively, it is essential to take the eighteenth century historical background into account, and to remember that the European slave trade continued clandestinely. The European abolitionist movement had its limits.

30 J. Suret-Canale, 'Contextes et conséquences sociales de la traite africaine', *Présence africaine*, no. 50 (1964), p. 142–3.
31 A study of peasant resistance, from tradition and written sources, demonstrates that rebellion was not merely a result of internal political problems, but a specific reaction to the consequences of the chiefs' participation in the Atlantic slave trade. The aim of the revolts was to put a stop to the pillaging and capture of slaves.
32 See our forthcoming publication for further detail.
33 Right until the eighteenth century, the capitals of Kayor and Baol were at Mboul and Lambaye, respectively. The frequent unification of the two kingdoms in the eighteenth century led the sovereigns to reside at frontier villages in the south of Kayor, for example Maka and Khandan. See n. 35 on the Tyedo.
34 It is not possible here to examine in detail the link between famines in the

eighteenth century, the slave trade, and climatic conditions. Our conclusions are dealt with in more detail in our forthcoming publication.
35 According to A. B. Diop ('Lat Dior et le problème musulman', *Bull. IFAN* vol. XXVIII series B. nos 1-2, 1966, p. 497-9), who sets out a traditional interpretation of the role of Islam in the history of Kayor, the word *tyedo* 'denotes a man who holds political power. It contrasts with the word *badolo* which denotes a man who has no power at all at any level'. According to this author, the *tyedo* could be of noble origin as well as of caste descent (captives, *griots*, craftsmen). There were a substantial number of captives who were *tyedo*.
36 See the example of the ruin of Damel Daou Demba by the laman Diamatil, Kotya Barma, in 1640, which is commented on in detail by Yoro Dyao (in Colvin, *Kayor and its Diplomatic Relations*). Kotya Barma, descendant of the maternal Khagan family, enjoyed immense popularity amongst the Wolof peoples, and his maxims remain famous: he was a scholar and a shrewd politician who defended the rights of the people against the king and brought about the king's downfall.
37 There is much that can be said about the captive group and its internal hierarchy. The Wolof system contained several categories of *dyami*, whose role in social and political life was very unequal.
38 We shall not have time in this article to elaborate on the change in status of the *griots* and craftsmen.
39 On the question of relations with the Moors, see note 27 and 29.
40 See A. B. Diop, 'Lat Dior', passim, p. 493-539 and L. A. G. Colvin, '*Kayor*', passim, in particular, p. 32-7.
41 Despite the importance and interest of the conflict between Islam and Wolof earth worship, it is secondary in comparison to the deep-rooted influence of the religion of the Prophet in the Wolof world and its culture.
42 It would be interesting to examine the role played by the traditional Serer religion in the resistance against the raids by political leaders. Written sources inform us that accusation of sorcery was often used by leaders to enslave the opposition and the wealthy. This use of the traditional religion for political ends deserves further study.
43 G. Thilmans and N. I. de Moraes have made a detailed study of competition between different European nations for trade in *Bull. IFAN*.
44 We are indeed talking about 'gradual' abolition, as the work of S. Daget shows, cf. 'L'abolition de la traite des Noirs en France de 1814 à 1831', *Cahiers d'Etudes Africaines*, no. 41 (1971), pp. 14-58.

4 The import of firearms into West Africa 1750-1807: a quantitative analysis

1 *Journal of African History* vol. XII nos. 2 and 4 (1971). These articles were the outcome of seminars on firearms in Africa held at the University of London from 1967 to 1970.
2 Public Record Office, Literary Search Room, *Acts of the Privy Council Colonial, Series IV (1745-66)*, p. 18.

3   PRO. C.O. 267/6, Petition of Henry Hardware to Pitt. The ship mentioned in the petition had been seized by government officials and Hardware was asking for its release. In the same source, there is another petition dated 20 March 1759, by 'Mr Henry Hardware and other merchants trading to Africa', asking for permission to export arms and ammunition 'as usual' to Africa, together with an Order in Council to that effect.
4   David Tuohy's Papers, Liverpool Record Office, 380 TUO. 2/4, David Tuohy to Messrs Ryan and Begone, Liverpool, 5 Oct. 1775. Messrs Ryan and Begone had written to Tuohy on 24 August and 30 September 1775, asking him if he would agree to sell corn spirit at Liverpool on behalf of a friend of theirs on a commission basis. Corn spirit, often described as British brandy, was also exported to West Africa in large quantities at this time.
5   PRO. C.107/1, Cargo invoice of the sloop *Fly*, Richard Rogers, master, and the account of trade with James Cleveland on the Windward Coast, 1787. James Cleveland was a European merchant resident on the coast. The *Fly* belonged to James Rogers & Co., slave merchants in Bristol.
6   The extant private records of this firm are in the Birmingham Reference Library. The firm was heavily involved in the production of guns for the West African trade. The correspondence between the partners from 1748 to 1754 shows that the firm supplied guns not only to British merchants trading to West Africa but also to Portuguese, French and other European merchants in the trade. In fact, the firm was also directly concerned in the trade to West Africa, some of the letters containing references to guns sent to the coast by the firm for sale. The firm also held shares in slave trading ventures. One of the documents, Galton 564, shows a detailed account of one such venture made from Liverpool *c.* 1800, selling 527 slaves in the West Indies and returning a net profit of £6430. Later in the eighteenth century, the firm changed from Farmer & Galton to Galton & Son. Although the firm benefited from war-time government demands, demand from the West African trade remained the main support of the firm and this is borne out by the firm's documents. For a general history of the firm and of the Galton family, see B. M. D. Smith, 'The Galtons of Birmingham: Quaker gun merchants and bankers, 1702-1831', *Business History*, vol. 9 no. 2 (1967). Samuel Galton had a lot of problems with his fellow Quakers for making guns for the African trade as they encouraged wars and slaving in Africa, pp. 144–5.
7   Galton 405/1, Samuel Galton to Mr Farmer, 9 March 1754.
8   ibid. Samuel Galton to Mr Farmer, 3 June 1754.
9   ibid. Samuel Galton to Mr Farmer, Birmingham 9 December 1754. The reference to Manchester relates to the city's cotton textile industry, another important industry connected with the West African trade. The Hadley mentioned in the letter was a major rival of Farmer and Galton in the supply of guns for the West African trade. He played a major role in the workmen's riots against Farmer and Galton in 1772. See below.
10 Galton 550, Case against Thomas Hadley and others, Evidence of Samuel Galton, and witnesses.

11 PRO. C.107/10, John Goodrich to James Rogers, 11 July 1792.
12 ibid. Samuel Galton & Son to James Rogers & Co., Birmingham, 27 June 1792. The Mr Whately referred to in the letter is John Whately who was also heavily involved in the manufacture of guns for the West African trade in our period. See PRO., BT.6/10, pp. 354-7, 'Representation of Mr John Whately dated Birmingham, 27 March 1788, on the importance of the manufacture of guns carried on there, which in times of peace is chiefly supported by the African Trade, to the Lords of the Committee of the Council of Trade'.
13 PRO. C.107/10, Joseph Grice to James Rogers & Co., Birmingham, 27 June 1792.
14 ibid. Henry P. Whately to James Rogers & Co, Birmingham, 27 June 1792. Henry Whately was the son of John Whately mentioned earlier. See n. 12 above.
15 British Museum, *House of Commons Journals*, vol. LX (15 January 1805 to 7 January 1806), 28 February 1805, Petition of Birmingham Gun-Manufacturers, p. 100.
16 Lord Edmond Fitzmaurice, *Life of William, Earl of Shelbourne* (1875), vol. I, pp. 400 and 404, quoted by Smith, 'The Galtons of Birmingham', p. 139.
17 PRO. Customs 3 and 17, for the eighteenth century.
18 At the time when English trade to West Africa was under the Royal African Company's monopoly the guns for the trade were produced mainly by London gunsmiths. It was after the trade had been thrown open to all English merchants in 1698 that Birmingham gradually became the main centre of supply. But tenders made to the Company of Merchants Trading to Africa for the supply of guns show that many London gun-makers continued to produce guns for the West African trade throughout the second half of the eighteenth century. (For these tenders, see T.70/1516-86.) The growth of trade to Africa in the outports, particularly Bristol and Liverpool, also attracted the gun-making industry to these ports. In Liverpool, the scale of operation of at least two of the producers can be gauged from the available evidence. One of them is John Parr, who stated in his will, dated 19 June 1794, that he had been 'largely concerned in the Gun Trade for a great number of years and for the greater convenience and more extensively carrying on the same [I] have erected very large and commodious workshops and warehouses adjoining and contiguous to my messuage or Dwelling house in Argyle Street and extending also to Pitt Street upon ground held by me under lease from the Corporation of Liverpool for three lives and twenty-one years which workshops and warehouses with the messuage of appurtenance I compute and value at three thousand pounds' (Lancashire Record Office, Preston, Will of John Parr of Liverpool, Gunsmith). The other Liverpool gun-maker is Thomas Falkner (or Faulkner). Between August and December 1771, he supplied 4991 guns to a single slave-trading firm, Samuel Sandys & Co. of Liverpool, for five of their vessels, the *Barbadoes Packet, Meredith, Snow Juno, Saville*, and the *Cavendish* (PRO. C.109/401).

It is on the basis of this type of evidence that we made the very conservative guess that sources of supply in England, other than Birmingham, must have produced for the West African trade at least 50,000 guns per annum, on average, during our period.

19 See R. A. Kea, 'Firearms and warfare on the Gold and slave Coasts from the sixteenth to the nineteenth centuries', *Journal of African History*, vol. XII (1971), p. 200, n. 97; William Bosman, *A New and Accurate Description of the Coast of Guinea* (London 1705), pp. 184–5; Phyllis Martin, 'The trade of Loango in the seventeenth and eighteenth centuries', in this book.

20 PRO. T.70/1538, 'A calculation on the supposed number of negroes purchased annually on the coast of Africa between the Port of Sallee in South Barbary and the River Congo', by John Roberts. John Roberts was formerly the governor, treasurer and one of the chief agents of the Royal African Company at Cape Coast Castle. Thomas Melvil succeeded him at Cape Coast Castle on 20 June 1751. Roberts then became a private merchant in partnership with Husband and Boteler. See T.70/1525 and T.70/1526.

21 Phyllis Martin, 'The trade of Loango in the seventeenth and eighteenth centuries', pp. 214 in this book.

22 Since the British Customs records and other evidence relating to English import and export trade to West Africa during our period often refer generally to Africa without specifying regions, some doubts may arise as to whether English merchants were not also trading guns to areas outside West Africa proper, other than the quantity going to the Loango region. However, there is sufficient evidence to dispel such doubts. The term, 'African trade', was usually used interchangeably with the term, 'slave trade', in England in the eighteenth century. This was because, apart from the trade to Mediterranean Africa, which was recorded with the trade to the Mediterranean region generally, English trade to Africa so recorded was overwhelmingly in slaves during the century. In a forthcoming paper I have shown that the trade in slaves made up about 91 per cent of the total, by value. Apart from the slaves purchased from the Loango region, broadly defined, all the other slaves purchased by English merchants during our period came from West Africa proper. The remaining 9 per cent of the trade was in Senegal gum, redwood, ivory, gold dust, palm oil, and some other very minor products. Again, apart from those that came from the Loango region, these products were purchased from West Africa proper. Furthermore, we shall show later in this paper that the guns were employed almost entirely to pay for slaves purchased. It is, therefore, very certain that apart from the quantity going to the Loango region the guns stated here were all going to West Africa proper.

23 D. W. Young, 'History of the Birmingham gun trade' (Master of Commerce thesis, University of Birmingham 1936), p. 39.

24 *British Parliamentary Papers, Accounts and Papers*, vol. 87 no. 698 (9) 1790, p. 586. Evidence of Alexander Falconbridge, 8 March 1790, who made four trading voyages to the coast of Africa as a surgeon from 1780 to 1787.

25 Gavin White, 'Firearms in Africa: an introduction', *Journal of African History*, vol. XII (1971), pp. 178-9. Some of the papers in the 1971 volume of this *Journal* also mention firing of salutes on ceremonial occasions as another important use to which the firearms were put.
26 H. A. Gemery and J. S. Hogendorn, 'Technological change, slavery, and the slave trade', in C. J. Dewey and A. H. Hopkins (eds.), *Studies in the Economic History of India and Africa* (London 1978).
27 PRO. C.107/15.
28 PRO. C.107/5, Brig. *Sarah*, Captain John Goodrich, Master. Trade Book Commencing from 18 December 1789.
29 See Basil Davidson, 'Slaves or captives?: some notes on fantasy and fact', in N. I. Huggins, M. Kilson and D. M. Fox (eds.), *Key Issues in the Afro-American Experience*, vol. I (New York 1971), p. 69.
30 It should also be noted that there was no automatic relationship between the quantity of firearms acquired by a territory or state and its intentions or capability of building an empire. As we shall show later, the Bonny trading area was one of the largest areas importing firearms in West Africa during our period. Yet Bonny was not the centre of a large empire at this time. However, the slaves sold in the Bonny trading area were actually supplied mainly by the Aro Chuku people, so that the guns obtained through the sale of the slaves were simply passing through Bonny to these people who were feared for their military might and their famous oracle.

While there was no automatic relationship between the quantity of firearms and state-building, there can be no doubt that the proliferation of firearms on the West African coast and its hinterland in the eighteenth century, connected with slaving as it was, helped powerfully to create unpeaceful conditions generally in the African regions affected. See Patrick Manning, 'Slaves, Palm Oil, and Political Power on the West African Coast', *African Historical Studies*, vol. II no. 2 (1969), p. 288, n. 19, where the point about the quantity of firearms and political power is briefly discussed. Manning's argument is open to criticism, even as a model. The fact that the state which imported the largest number of firearms was not also the largest or most 'powerful' state only shows that other factors were also important, without disproving the point that firearms were critical to the security of some states and/or to their expansion. One has to take into account what the political conditions of the states in question would have been without firearms. On the other hand, the port of arrival may be different from the final destination of the firearms. Hence, the quantity of firearms imported into the Delta ports is not an accurate index of the number of firearms the Delta states actually retained and used.
31 See Appendix II for sources.
32 *A General and Descriptive History of the Ancient and Present state of the Town of Liverpool* (Liverpool 1795), pp. 230-1.
33 PRO. C.107/15. This vessel was earlier referred to above.
34 PRO. C.107/10, John Simmons to Captain John Fitz Henry of Bristol, Liverpool, 9 January 1792.

35 PRO. C. 107/1. The vessel belonged to James Rogers & Co. of Bristol.
36 PRO. C.114/157. This vessel belonged to Thomas Lumley & Co. of London.
37 PRO. C.107/5. The vessel belonged to Rogers & Co. of Bristol.
38 Martin, 'The trade of Loango', p. 214 in this book.
39 The firearms included in the cargoes of ships sailing to West Africa in the second half of the eighteenth century are usually described in some detail in the merchants' private records. See Appendix II for references to these records. The difference between Appendix II and Table 11 totals is due to the fact that a few of the guns in Appendix II are not described in the records.
40 Apparently these were guns made to Danish pattern. In November 1791, Galton & Son, a large gun-making firm in Birmingham, wrote to Rogers & Co., of Bristol, that 'the African captains are apt to confound Danes with Danish. By Danes we understand Dutch guns with black stocks, and barrels 4 feet 3 or 4 inches long, narrow bore'. But what Danish guns are is not stated. C.107/7 Part I, Galton & Son to Rogers & Co., Birmingham, 17 November 1791.
41 See Gavin White, 'Firearms in Africa', p. 177, for a description. Some of the other types included in the table are also described by White.
42 PRO. C.107/10, Samuel Galton to James Rogers & Co., Birmingham, 23 January 1792. Apart from some special guns, such as those specially referred to as elephant guns and those sent to the rulers as presents, of which very small numbers were brought to the coast by the merchants, the main difference between the major types of guns imported into West Africa during our period seems to have been the quality of the materials used in making them. The relatively more expensive ones were made with walnut and better iron, while the cheaper ones were made with beech wood and probably inferior iron. On present evidence it is not possible to relate different types to different uses. But it is very unlikely that the major types imported – the Tower guns imported into Calabar, the Bonny muskets imported into Bonny, the Danish guns imported into Senegambia, Sierra Leone and the Windward Coast, etc. – were put to significantly differing uses.
43 Smith, 'The Galtons of Birmingham', p. 139.
44 *Observations on the Manufacture of Firearms for Military Purposes, on the number supplied from Birmingham to British Government* (1829), pp. 45–6. Birmingham Reference Library L65.52.
45 PRO. T.70/1516, Incorporated Company of Gun-makers to the Committee of the Company of Merchants Trading to Africa, London 8 March 1750.
46 PRO. C.107/7 Part 2, John Whately to James Rogers & Co, Birmingham, 25 February 1788. The Mr Parr mentioned in this letter is John Parr, a large gun-maker in Liverpool in the late eighteenth century. This letter indirectly confirms our earlier conclusion that Tower guns were the most popular in Old Calabar.

47 PRO. C.107/9, Samuel Galton & Son to James Rogers & Co., Birmingham, 10 August 1789.

5 Slavery and the slave trade in the context of West African history

1 Robert Norris, *Memoirs of the Reign of Bossa Ahadee, King of Dahomy* (London 1789), and Archibald Dalzel, *The History of Dahomy* (London 1793).
2 R. S. Rattray, *Ashanti Law and Constitution* (1929), ch. 5.
3 Dalzel, *History of Dahomy*, 124.
4 Raymond Mauny, *Tableau géographique de l'ouest africain* (Dakar: Institut Fondamental d'Afrique Noire 1961), mém. pp. 336–43, 377–9, 422–4.
5 R. C. C. Law, 'The Garamantes and trans-Saharan enterprise in classical times', *Journal of African History*, vol. VIII no. 2 (Oxford 1967), p. 196.
6 Walter Rodney, 'African slavery and other forms of social oppression on the Upper Guinea Coast in the context of the Atlantic slave-trade', Chapter 1 in this book.
7 Barbot in 1682 also reported that the Dutch sometimes *sold* slaves on the Gaboon in A. and J. Churchill's, *A Collection of Voyages and Travels* (6 vols., London 1732), vol. 5, p. 390.
8 D. Pacheco Pereira, *Esmeraldo de Situ Orbis* (ed.) Raymond Mauny (1956), p. 134.
9 A. F. C. Ryder, 'The Benin missions', *Journal of the Historic Society of Nigeria*, vol. II no. 2 (1961), p. 237, and 'Dutch trade on the Nigerian coast during the seventeenth century', *JHNS* vol. III no. 2 (1965), p. 203. To Professor Ryder, the Benin refusal to supply male slaves to the Portuguese seems to be associated with the Portuguese refusal to sell firearms to the pagan Benin kingdom. But this does not seem to invalidate the argument about the economic, and therefore (in a state-directed economy) the political, appreciation of the value of slaves. By the later seventeenth century, with the growing and competitive European arms trade, Benin's rulers must have concluded that the acquisition of firearms was more vital to the strength and wealth of the kingdom than the conservation of its manpower.
10 P. D. Curtin, *The Atlantic Slave Trade: A Census* (Madison 1969).
11 Mauny, *Tableau géographique*, p. 379. A. Adu Boahen estimates the volume for the first half of the nineteenth century at about 10,000 slaves a year: *Britain, the Sahara, and the Western Sudan, 1788–1861* (1964), p. 127.
12 In which I have been guided by the experience and calculations of my colleague Dr P. K. Mitchell.
13 As was pointed out to me by my colleagues Mr D. Rimmer and Dr A. G. Hopkins.
14 Charles Monteil, 'Les empires du Mali', *Bull. Com. et Sc. de l'AOF.* vol. XII (1929), p. 312 (p. 22 in the separate (1968) reprint).

15 I. A. Akinjogbin, *Dahomey and its Neighbours, 1708-1818* (Cambridge 1967), pp. 73-80, 90-5.
16 John E. Flint, *Sir George Goldie and the Making of Nigeria* (1960), p. 246.
17 Dalzel, *History of Dahomy*, pp. 217-21; Joseph Dupuis, *Journal of a Residence in Ashantee* (1824), pp. 163-4.
18 D. A. Ross, 'The autonomous kingdom of Dahomey, 1818-94' (Unpublished London Ph.D. thesis, 1967), chapter 2.
19 The only place in which this argument seems to have been developed is, with reference to Yorubaland, in an article by A. G. Hopkins, 'Economic imperialism in West Africa: Lagos, 1880-92', *Economic History Review*, vol. XXI no. 3 (1968), pp. 587-92.

6 The Oyo Yoruba and the Atlantic trade, 1670 to 1830

1 R. C. Law suggests that the highly expensive importation of horses into Old Oyo was financed in the 16th century by the northward export of slaves by Oyo. See Law, *The Oyo Empire c. 1600 - c. 1836* (Oxford 1977), p. 217. *Ed.*
2 The town called Ardra in the seventeenth century is now Allada, about 25 miles north of Ouidah on the road to Abomey. To be distinguished from it are *(i)* Little Ardra (or Offra), on the coast, which was then the port of *(ii)* Great Ardra, otherwise Assem (or Azem). Allada was absorbed into the kingdom of Dahomey in 1724 (Smith, 1745, 169). Barbot (1732, 346), evidently using sources antedating its fall, wrote 'that it is of great length and breadth up inland, some making it border on the West upon the *Rio da Volta*, and at the Last on Benin . . . and will have it to reach at north and north-west to *Oyeo*, a large populous country, and to other potent kingdoms situated towards the *Niger*.' Ardra-Assem, though taken by Dahomey 1734-7, flourished under the protection of the Oyo during the second half of the century (J. Barbot, *A Description of the Coasts of North and South Guinea; and of Ethiopia Inferior* (London 1737), Book 4, chap. 4; A. Dalzel, *A History of Dahomey an inland kingdom of Africa, compiled from authentic memoirs, with an introduction and notes* (London 1793), esp. fn. to p. 31).
3 G. A. Robertson, *Notes on Africa; particularly those parts which are situated between Cape Verd and the River Congo* (London 1819), pp. 269, 282.
4 R. L. Lander, *Records of Captain Clapperton's last expedition* (2 vols., London 1830), vol. 2, p. 222.
5 The Alafin's historians in Oyo today say Oyo never fought with Nupe or Bariba – 'they have the same mother'. S. Johnson, in O. Johnson (ed.), *A History of the Yorubas* (Lagos 1921) was informed that the Nupe took Old Oyo in the reign of the eighth Alafin and that was why the capital was moved to Igboho for the duration of four reigns, when the Alafin had become strong enough to return to the old site. R. Norris (*Memoirs of the Reign of Bossa Ahadee, King of Dahomey an inland Country of Guiney, to which are added the author's journey to Abomey*, London 1789, p. 139) and A. Dalzel (*A History of Dahomey*, p. 229) say Oyo was tributary to 'Tappah',

308 Notes and references to pages 168-72

      which is the Yoruba name for Nupe. Just as Oyo strove to control the route to the sea, so may Nupe have striven, constantly threatening the northern frontier of Oyo.

6 S. Johnson, in O. Johnson (ed.), *A History of the Yorubas* (Lagos 1921), p. 174.
7 O. Dapper, *Umstandliche und eigentliche Beschreibung von Africa* (Amsterdam 1670).
8 Barbot, *A Description of the Coasts*, p. 352.
9 H. Clapperton, *Journal of a Second Expedition into the Interior of Africa from the Bight of Benin to Soccato* (Philadelphia 1929).
10 Dapper, *Umstandliche und eigentliche Beschreibung von Africa* (French edition 1670).
11 Barbot, *A Description of the Coasts*, p. 356.
12 ibid., p. 345.
13 cf. Johnson, *A History of the Yorubas*, p. 156.
14 ibid., p. 50.
15 Robin Law disputes the point that the Ekiti and Yagba area formed a major 'slave reservoir' for Oyo slave raids. Law thinks that Oyo slave raids were directed primarily against their northern and western neighbours. However, Law's evidence for the Ekiti and Yagba area is not conclusive, and his argument does not seem to take account of Morton-Williams's point that the forest areas of eastern Yorubaland, including Ijesa, were protected against the Oyo raids. See Law, *The Oyo Empire*, p. 226. Ed.
16 For an Oyo version of this myth substantially the same as the version I have heard, see Johnson, *A History of the Yorubas*; for Ketu, E. G. Parrinder, *The Story of Ketu an Ancient Yoruba Kingdom* (Ibadan 1956) and E. Dunglas, 'Contributions à l'histoire du Moyen-Dahomey' (Royaumes d'Abomey, de Ketou et de Ouidah), *Etudes Dahoméennes*, pp. 19, 20, 21; for the Egba, S. A. Crowther, *Church Missionary Intelligencer*, (London 1956), J. O. George, *Historical notes on the Yoruba Country and its Tribes* (Lagos 1895), A. K. Ajisafe, *History of Abeokuta* (Suffolk 1924), J. B. O. Losi, *History of Lagos* (Lagos 1914), S. O. Biobaku, 'An historical sketch of the Egba traditional authorities', in *Africa*, no. 22 and *The Egba and their Neighbours 1842-72* (London 1957), and Parrinder, *The Story of Ketu*.
17 H. A. Wyndham, *The Atlantic and Slavery* (London 1935); J. D. Fage, *An Introduction to the History of West Africa* (Cambridge 1955).
18 Barbot, *A Description of the Coasts*, p. 453.
19 ibid., p. 345.
20 Parrinder, *The Story of Ketu*.
21 T. J. Bowen, *Central Africa: Adventures and Missionary Labours in Several Countries in the Interior of Africa* (London 1927), pp. 148-9.
22 Crowther, *Church Missionary Intelligencer*, p. 246.
23 See Bullfinch Lamb(e)'s eyewitness account in F. E. Forbes, *Dahomey and the Dahomans* (2 vols., London 1851).
24 W. Bosman, *A New and Accurate Description of the Coast of Guinea* (London 1705, 1721), p. 396-8. Bosman's 'Great Ardra' is almost certainly

Allada. Dalzel, *The History of Dahomey*, p. 12, gives the page reference in Bosman as 374, presumably having used a different printing.
25 There may have been an attempt to find a 'charter' for this economic expedient in the taboo noticed by W. Snelgrave (*A new account of some parts of Guinea*, London 1734, p. 58), that the Eyeo were forbidden to see the sea, 'their natural *fétiche*'.
26 This is clear enough from the accounts in Snelgrave, in ibid., J. Atkins, *A Voyage to Guinea, Brazil, and the West Indies* (London 1735), and Norris, *Memoirs of the Reign of Bossa Ahadee*; but the king of Dahomey's motives are still debated. Rosemary Arnold (in K. Polyani, C. M. Arensberg and H. W. Pearson (eds.), *Trade and Markets in the Early Empires: Economics in History and Theory*, Illinois 1957, ch. 7) has argued that his trade and military policies were forced on him in self-defence. But the precise aims of the policies as he saw them at the beginning are not known. Norris reported: 'I knew many of the old *Whydasians* as well as *Dahomans* who were present when Trudo attacked that kingdom. They attributed his enterprise *solely* to the desire of extending his dominions, and of enjoying at *first hand* those commodities which he had been used to purchase of the Whydasians, who were in possession of the Coast.' But the accounts of the events preceding the conquest of Ardra make this interpretation improbable (Norris wrote) his book in 1773 and his informants may have been too young at the time of the conquest to realise the issues involved). Atkins thought that Agaja Trudo's motives for 'turning things topsy-turvy, and entirely destroying out Slave-Trade' were *(i)* to end the wars and slavery 'continually imposed upon' Dahomey by Ouidah and Ardra; *(ii)* by going on to destroy the slave trade at Jaqueen, to leave it only 'at *Appah*, a place beyond the bounds of his conquest. Yet in all this, could we separate our Idea of the sufferers, and the temporary views of the Traders; the King's actions carry great reputation, for by the destruction of this Trade, he relinquished his own private interests for the sake of public Justice and Humanity.' And, as evidence that Agaja's motive was to end the trade, he cites Snelgrave on his character and his proposals to Lambe that the British should start plantations on the coast, employing the slaves there, and stop carrying them away (Atkins, *A voyage to Guinea, Brazil and the West Indies*, p. 119-20) Be it noted that Norris was a professional slaver and Atkins, a surgeon, was on his own testimony (pp. 176-9) antipathetic to the trade.

Additional note: Robin Law who has written more recently on Dahomey holds that the Dahomean conquest of the coastal states was made to ensure direct participation in the Atlantic slave trade by Dahomey. This seems to be the more fashionable view at present. See Law, *The Oyo Empire* p. 220. Ed.
27 W. Snelgrave, *A New Account of Some Parts of Guinea* (London 1734), p. 121.
28 Parrinder, *The Story of Ketu*, p. 27.
29 Snelgrave, *A New Account*.
30 ibid.

31 Norris, *Memoirs*, p. 13–14.
32 Dalzel, *The History of Dahomey*; A. Le Hérissé, *L'ancien royaume du Dahomey* (Paris 1911).
33 Barbot, *A Description of the Coasts*, p. 346.
34 R. L. Buell's (*The Native Problem in Africa*, New York 1928) date, 1630, for the conquest of Lagos by Benin is taken from Losi (*A History of Lagos*, p. 11), and is unsupported by any evidence. Losi also put the foundation of Isheri, of which Lagos was an offshoot, at about 1699!
35 W. R. Hatch, Intelligence report upon the people of Ifonyin in the Ilaro Division of the Abeokuta Province (Unpublished typescript 1936).
36 ibid.
37 According to Forbes, *Dahomey and the Dahomans*, vol. 1, p. 15–16.
38 Johnson, *A History of the Yorubas*, p. 179.
39 Dalzel, *The History of Dahomey*, p. 214.
40 G. A. Robertson (*Notes on Africa; particularly those parts which are situated between Cape Verd and the River Congo*, London 1819, p. 286) does talk of wild, red-painted nagoes coming down to Badagri, but the description sounds more likely of the men of the Ohori swamps. All their Yoruba-speaking neighbours from the Ifonyin to Atakpame are called Nago by the Fon and Gun. (Compare the map in Bowdich, 1819, which puts 'Anagoo' west of Abomey, in the region of Atakpame.)
41 Dalzel, *The History of Dahomey*, p. 166.
42 Snelgrave, *A New Account*, and J. B. Labat, *Voyage du Chevalier Des Marchais* (Paris 1730).
43 Robertson, *Notes on Africa*, p. 285.
44 Once again, doubt is cast on the accuracy of Norris's (*Memoirs*) testimony. He writes (1789, p. 34 and fn.) that when Jacquin was destroyed, 'Dahomey extirpated the whole nation, not leaving a single inhabitant alive in the whole country. Adaunzou II sent a few families to re-establish a settlement there in the year 1777.' Writing later still, Robertson (*Notes on Africa*, p. 285) asserts: 'The people of Badaghe are the descendants of some of the refugees who were driven from Grewhe [sc. Ouidah] by the Dahomians, and settled here. . . .'
45 J. D. Fage, *An Introduction to the History of West Africa*.
46 Dalzel, *The History of Dahomey*, p. 166.
47 The 'Agaow', or Gau, was one of the four principal officers of state and commander of the right wing of the army. P. Labarthe (*Voyage à la Côte de Guinée*, Paris 1803, p. 104) reported from Ouidah in 1788 that the Mahis (although Fon) were the enemies of Dahomey and under the yoke of Oyo.
48 Robertson (*Notes on Africa*, p. 283) heard of this destruction as an achievement of the Lagos forces: 'Badaghe . . . was destroyed by a numerous army which was sent from Lagos. Oakindo, who commanded it, informed me, that its destruction was effected with much difficulty. . . . The town has since been partly rebuilt, but it has not much trade, as it has not been commonly resorted to by Europeans.'
49 Dalzel, *The History of Dahomey*, pp. 182–7.

50 ibid., p. 196.
51 'Adahoonzou' as Dalzel calls him, is the Kpengla of Dahomey traditions. He reigned from 17 May 1774 until 17 April 1789 (cf. E. Dunglas, 'Contribution à l'histoire du Moyen-Dahomey, Royaumes d'Abomey, de Ketou et de Ouidah', *Etudes Dahomeennes*, vol. 1. (Porto Novo 1957).
52 Dalzel, *The History of Dahomey*, p. 207.
53 ibid., pp. 206-7.
54 Dalzel, in ibid., p. 201, reports it as a Dahomey victory with 2000 Ketu prisoners brought to Abomey. Dunglas ('Contributions à l'histoire du Moyen-Dahomey', pp. 68-9) and Parrinder (*The Story of Ketu*, p. 431) give the very different Ketu version, in which the Dahomeans are said to have sacked a Ketu village, but not to have engaged the Ketu army (cf. also Le Hérissé, *L'ancien royaume du Dahomey*, pp. 307-8) Note: Dunglas's ms., though not published until 1957, was completed by 1951, the date of his death. Parrinder's account is largely a translation of his colleague Dunglas.
55 Dalzel, *The History of Dahomey*, p. 229.
56 Parrinder, *The Story of Ketu*, Dunglas, 'Contributions à l'histoire du Moyen-Dahomey' and P. Allison, 'The last days of Old Oyo', *Odu, a Journal of Yoruba and Related Studies*, vol. 4, p. 26.
57 Dunglas, 'Contributions à l'histoire du Moyen-Dahomey', vol. 2, p. 32.
58 Le Hérissé, *L'ancien royaume du Dahomey*, pp. 319-20; Dunglas, op. cit., vol. 2, pp. 56-7.
59 Dunglas, op. cit., vol. 2, pp. 56-7; since Robertson (*Notes on Africa*, p. 283) says there was not much trade in Badagri, a decline in the amount of trade there may have led to da Souza's move; by the early 1820s its fortunes had evidently improved once again.
60 R. L. Lander, *Records of Captain Clapperton's Last Expedition to Africa*. introduction.
61 Allison, 'The last days of Old Oyo', p. 16.
62 Clapperton, *Journal of a Second Expedition into the Interior of Africa*.
63 Lander, *Records of Captain Clapperton's last expedition to Africa*.
64 R. L. and J. Lander, *Journal of an Expedition to Determine the Course and Termination of the Niger* (3 vols., London 1832).
65 ibid., vol. 1, p. 68.
66 cf. Johnson, *A History of the Yorubas*, p. 226.
67 J. H. Blair, Intelligence report on the Iboro Administrative Area (Unpublished typescript 1938); I have confirmed only the Iboro foundation legend.
68 T. J. Adewale, 'The Ijanna episode in Yoruba history', *Proceedings of the Third International West African Conference* (Ibadan 1949), p. 251. This document, *History of Ijanna*, had disappeared by 1950 and had perhaps been destroyed in 1949, when the then District Officer, Ilaro, short of office space, burnt most of the old files and records in the Ilaro District Office.

Salu's 'history' differs from the version I heard in Ijanna in 1950, when he had been dead for some time and the right to tell the history belonged to the head of a different lineage, one Odu, Apena and Bale of Ijanna. (Not that

Salu necessarily had had the right to tell it at any time – he seems to have had a most forceful character and to have had little respect for conventions when they were inconvenient.) The legend I was given said that the people of Ijanna came from Owo, a now vanished town in Southern Oyo, led by Ejegun, a hunter, who found a suitable place to settle in the Egbado forest. This tradition matches closely a version given to Hatch in 1935-6. W. R. Hatch, Intelligence report upon the Ilaro Group of the Egbado people in the Ilaro Division of the Abeokuta Province (Unpublished typescript, 1936), Appendix IV. No mention was made to me of earlier inhabitants of the region.

69 S. O. Biobaku, 'An historical sketch of the Egba traditional authorities', pp. 35–7; Johnson, *A History of the Yorubas*, p. 17.

70 Maps in the following books are useful here: Dapper, *Umstandliche und eigentliche Beschreibung von Africa*; J. Ogilby, *Africa: Being an accurate Description of the Regions of Aegypt, Barbary, Lybia, and Billedulgerid* (London 1670); Bosman, *A New and Accurate Description of the Coast of Guinea* – the map in the English edition 'by H. Moll, Geographer'; Labat, *Voyage du Chevalier Des Marchais*; and Barbot, *A Description of the Coasts* – map to book iv.

Snelgrave (in C. A. Walckenaer, 'Collection des relations de voyages par mer et par terre, en différentes parties de l'Afrique, depuis 1400 jusqu'a nos jours', in *Voyages en Guinée*, Paris 1842, vol. viii, p. 452) reports war between Ijebu and Dahomey in 1730.

71 A. Churchill and J. Churchill, *A Collection of Voyages and Travels, some now first printed from original manuscripts others now first published in English* (6 vols., London 1732), vol. 6, p. 22.

72 Johnson, *A History of the Yorubas*, p. 188.

73 cf. Adewale, 'The Ijanna episode', passim. We find the same pattern in 1825: Clapperton, *Journal of a Second Expedition*, 'Puka (Ipokia) has once been a large town, surrounded by a wall and a ditch; the wall is now down and all the house in ruins. . . .' (p. 5). 'Owing to a Brazilian brig having arrived at Badagri for slaves, the people (of Ijanna) have been preparing themselves for two days to go on a slaving expedition to a place called Tabbo (Ijebu?), lying to the eastward' (p. 13). 'All the towns from Janna to Ekaw are situated in the bosom of an inaccessible road; the approach is through an avenue defended by stockades with narrow wicket gate and only one entrance; but Liabo only had a mud wall and ditch in addition to the stockades.' (p. 18) '. . .leaving Choco . . . a war is now carrying on only a few hours ride from us: not a national but a slaving war.' (p. 20) Crowther noted in a letter reproduced in T. J. Hutchinson (1858, p. 276): 'It was the king's prerogative in old time to make war, and that every third year; and a certain proportion of the slaves and spoils taken in such wars were due to him.'

74 S. O. Biobaku (*The Egba and their neighbours*, Chapter 1), considers that the Alafin placed his agent; (the *ajele*, chosen also from among the *ilari*), in the Egba towns at the same time, but he puts the date, without recording his reasons, some years earlier).

75 cf. W. R. Hatch, Intelligence report upon the Ilaro Group of the Egbado people in Ilaro Division of the Abeokuta Province.
76 The Olu of Ilaro in 1830 evidently still experienced the presence of the Onisare as something of an affront to his dignity. John Lander recorded: 'The chief (of Ilaro) wished to impress strongly on our minds his own dignity and power, he said he was greater than the Governor of Janna, inasmuch as the latter was a slave to the king of Katunga, but himself was a free man.' R. L. and J. Lander, *Journal of an Expedition to Determine the Course and Termination of the Niger*, p. 76.
77 Nevertheless we cannot equate the period of rule of the first Onisare (c. 1820–30) with that of any one Alafin, because 'No one was allowed to die at the death of the last king, as he did not die a natural death; having been slain by one of his sons: not the present king.' Clapperton, *Journal of a Second Expedition*, p. 49.
78 Clapperton's party was met at Ipokia by a party of armed men led by three horsemen, sent to escort them to Ijanna. The party was led by 'an Eyeo war chief. . . . The two men who appeared next in authority to himself were stout good-looking men, natives of Bornou; they were dressed in the fashion of that country, with blue velvet caps on their heads. Being Mohamedans, they could not be prevailed upon to drink spirits, but the captain and his men drank each two drams,' in ibid.
79 'I cannot omit bearing testimony to the singular and perhaps unprecedented fact, that we have already travelled sixty miles in eight days with a numerous and heavy baggage, and about ten different relays of carriers, without losing so much the value of a shilling public or private; a circumstance evincing not only somewhat more than common honesty in the inhabitants, but a degree of subordination and regular government which could not have been supposed to exist among a people hitherto considered barbarians', ibid., p. 13.

The Landers were held up for a week in Badagry at the start of their journey, on the 'report that the old King of Jenna, who it will be recollected, behaved so very kindly to Captain Clapperton's last mission, is dead; and although a successor has been appointed to fill his place, he is not yet arrived from Katunga.' R. L. and J. Lander, *Journal of an Expedition to Determine the Course and Termination of the Niger*, p. 24.

7 Effects of the Atlantic slave trade on some West African societies

1 P. D. Curtin, *The Atlantic Slave Trade, A Census* (Madison: 1969).
2 Johannes Postma, 'The Dutch Participation in the African Slave Trade; Slaving on the Guinea Coast, 1675–1795' (Unpublished Ph. D. thesis, Michigan State University 1970). A. van Dantzig, *Het Nederlands Aandeel in de Slavenhandel* (Bussum: 1968).
3 Even for these two groups, when the available evidence is analysed with the application of the concept of opportunity cost, these apparent short-term gains become long-term losses. Applying macro-economic analysis, it is

easy to show that the kind of relationship which the export slave trade encouraged between the much greater group of raided societies and the much smaller group of slave-raiding and slave-selling societies was not, in the long run, conducive to sustained economic development in both groups of societies. The long-term cost is the greater still when it is considered that evidence abounds to show that in the absence of the export slave trade normal commodity trade would have developed, during the period, between Europe and Africa. This would have encouraged between the two groups of societies a relationship that was conducive to sustained economic development in both societies. *Ed.*

4 Algemeen Rijksarchief, The Hague, Nieuwe West Indische Compagnie (WIC), 101, Engelgraaff Robberts to Assembly of Ten, Elmina, 15 August 1712 (translated in *Dutch Documents Relating to the Gold Coast and Slave Coast, 1680–1740*, p. 111), reporting on the tense political situation in 1712: '...if the Akimse get into trouble', he noted, 'the principal gold mine will come to a standstill, and the Aquamboese will lose the little respect they still have for that state, and compel the entire Lower Coast, in particular Accra, to trade with cowries in stead of with gold, keeping the gold in their country....'

5 Pacheco Pereira, in R. Mauny (ed.), *Esmeraldo de Situ Orbis*, 1956, p. 134.

6 K. A. Ratelband (ed.), *Vijf Dagregisters van het Kasteel São Jorge da Mina* (The Hague: 1953), entry for 11th December 1646.

7 A. G. Hopkins, *An Economic History of West Africa* (London: 1973), p. 104. Hopkins quotes W. Rodney's article on 'Slavery and other forms of social oppression on the Upper Guinea Coast in the context of the Atlantic Slave Trade', included in this book.

8 W. Bosman, *Naauwkeurige Beschryving van de Guinese Gout- Tand- en Slave Cust*, 3rd ed. (Amsterdam: 1709), vol. II, p. 115.

9 I. Wilks, 'Akwamu, 1650–1750', (Unpublished MA thesis, Cardiff 1958). In my opinion Wilks somewhat exaggerated the influence of Akwamu on Whydah by suggesting that the Akwamu empire 'included' Whydah, basing this idea on a passage on a canoe the king of Whydah asked the king of Akwamu to send to him to be filled with presents (see *Dutch Documents 1680–1740*, p. 98; P. Nuyts to Ass. of Ten, 25 May 1707). The kings of Whydah liked to show off with their riches, and I see this passage rather as a sign that the king of Whydah wanted to assure himself of the continuing mercenary services of Akwamu. Normally a tributary does not 'beg' to be allowed to pay his tribute!

10 Bosman, *Naauwkeurige*, vol. II, p. 186; in the English ed. of 1712 (p. 396–7) the phrase about the 'Tyrannical rule of Ardra' is not translated; the 'Ardrasian Negroes' are merely reported to have 'made complaints'.

11 I. A. Akinjogbin, in *Dahomey and its Neighbours, 1708–18*, suggests the existence of the Yoruba '*ebi* social theory' a hierarchy of a kind of father-son' relationships between chiefs, which would have governed political relations on the slave coast and in its hinterland.

12 Rawlinson Collection, 745–7, Bodleian Library, Oxford; 'Correspondence

from the outforts to Cape Coast Castle, 1681-99', letter no. 1274, Andrew Crosbie, Guidah 1 September 1682. (Listed in D. P. Henige, *A Guide to Rawlinson c. 745-7*, (Madison: 1972), p. 20).
13 ibid., id., letter 1319, 'Ardra Paquett', Arthur Windover, Appa, 17 July 1682. (Henige, *A Guide to Rawlinson*, p. 20.)
14 See WIC 180, 'Letters & Papers from Ardra', correspondence Van Hoolwerff and V. Gros, in *Dutch Documents 1680-1740*, p. 14–22.
15 Bosman, *Naauwkeurige*, vol. II, p. 183, 185.
16 WIC 98, W. de La Palma to Assembly of Ten, 5 September 1705, encl. no. 3: 'Copy of an Agreement made with His Majesty the King of Fida, 25 April 1703', *Dutch Documents 1680-1749*, p. 74–5.
17 C. Agbo, *Histoire de Ouidah, du XVIe au XXe Siècle*, Avignon, 1959.
18 Wilks, 'Akwamu, 1650-1750'.
19 WIC 104, Mins. of Council Meeting, Elmina, 17 February 1718; 'Oral report by Bookkeeper-General Ph. Eytzen on his return over land from Fida', in *Dutch Documents 1680-1740*, p. 134.
20 This explanation of the motive of Dahomey in conquering the coastal states may be compared with that put forward by Robin Law. According to Law, Dahomey invaded and conquered the coastal states because they were trying to establish an effective monopoly of the direct trade with the European slave traders, which adversely affected the trade of hinterland slave suppliers, such as Dahomey. See Law, *The Oyo Empire*, p. 220. Ed.
21 A. Le Hérissé, *L'ancien royaume du Dahomey; moeurs, religion et histoire*, (Paris: 1911). p. 295 ff.
22 Reproduced in W. Smith, *A New Voyage to Guinea*, London, 1744.
23 WIC 138, Correspondence H. Hertogh, 1730-38, in *Dutch Documents 1680-1740*, p. 163-9, 193-7, 205-6, etc.
24 K. Polanyi, *Dahomey and the Slave Trade. An Analysis of an Archaic Economy*, Seattle (London: 1966); R. S. Smith, *Kingdoms of the Yoruba* (London: 1969), *passim*.
25 Smith, *Kingdoms of the Yoruba*, p. 125.
26 ibid., p. 124.
27 R. A. Kea, 'Firearms and warfare on the Gold and slave coasts from the 16th to the 19th century,' *Journal of African History*, vol. XII (1971), p. 2.
28 P. E. Isert, *Voyages en Guinée* (Paris: 1793), p. 119.
29 WIC 111, Des Bordes and Council to Assembly of Ten, Elmina, 14 April 1738; encl.: 'Declaration of Soldier J. J. Steirmark dd. 4 December 1737', *Dutch Documents 1680-1740*, p. 222 ff.
30 D. Westermann, *Die Glidji Ewe in Togo* (Berlin: 1935), p. 127.
31 E. Donnan, *Documents Illustrative of the History of the Slave Trade to America*, (Washington: 1931), vol. II, p. 14, quoting Barbot (supplement) in Churchill's *Voyages*, vol. V.
32 Hopkins, *An Economic History of West Africa*, p. 109.
33 Isert, *Voyages en Guinée*, p. 120.
34 P. Roussier, *L'Établissement d'Issiny, 1687-1702* (Paris: 1935), p. 67. A

recent contribution by J.-C. Nardin and H. Spirik to the VIIIth Congress of Anthropological and Ethnological Sciences (Tokyo and Kyoto 1968) published by the Science Council of Japan, 1970, vol. III, p. 78-87, entitled 'Un Nouveau document pour l'étude des populations lagunaires de la Côte d'Ivoire au début du XVIIIe siècle: le Voyage de Jean Godot à Assinie (1701)' throws some interesting new light on the career of Aniaba or Hannibal.

35 Cf. note 18.
36 WIC 54, Assembly of Ten to De La Palma, Amsterdam, 19 March 1704; the Directors reported that after having received information from his predecessors that the Coast of Guinea was very appropriate for the cultivation of cotton, they had written to the Director on the Island of Curaçao, 'who consequently has sent thither the required instruments for the purification of cotton, as well as a Negro called Swarte Pieter (Black Peter)....' who had experience in this field.

8 The trade of Loango in the seventeenth and eighteenth centuries

1 P. Broecke, *Reisen naar West Afrika (1605-14)*, (ed.) K. Ratelband, (The Hague 1950), pp. 66 n. 2, 71.
2 Broecke, ibid., p. 72; A. Battell, *The Strange Adventures of Andrew Battell in Angola and the Adjoining Regions*, (ed.) E. Ravenstein (London 1901), p. 9; F. Pigafetta and D. Lopez, *Description du Royaume de Congo et des Contrées Environnantes (1591)*, (ed.) W. Bal (Louvain 1963), p. 32.
3 The significance and size of this local trade is made clear by Dutch reports when they occupied Luanda, 1641-8. They quickly discovered the complexities of the trade network which they had inherited from the Portuguese. An early report said that without supplies of palm-cloth and *nzimbu* shells, the slave trade 2-300 miles in the interior could not go on. Oude (old) West Indische Compagnie (The Hague), no. 57, Loango to Brazil (26 February 1642), no. 56, Luanda to Brazil (September 1642), Zegers to Governors of the First (Oude) Dutch West India Company (1643).
4 Broecke, *Reisen naar West Afrika*, p. 45.
5 D. Birmingham, *Trade and Conflict in Angola* (Oxford 1966), p. 79, cites the report of Pedro Sardinha on the palm-cloth trade in 1611.
6 Broecke, *Reisen naar West Afrika*, p. 72; Governors of the First (Oude) Dutch West India Company to Luanda (6 October 1645).
7 Broecke's journal records the development of these Dutch trading interests.
8 Broecke, *Reisen naar West Afrika*, pp. 64, 70.
9 P. Heyn, *De West Afrikaanse Reis van Piet Heyn, 1624-5*, (ed.) K. Ratelband (The Hague 1959), p. xcii n.2.
10 Battell, *The Strange Adventures*, pp. 43-4.
11 Broecke, *Reisen naar West Afrika*, p. 67; O. Dapper, *Naukeurige*

Beschrijvinge der Afrikaensche Gewesten (Amsterdam 1676), 2nd edition, p. 149.
12 Broecke, *Reisen naar West Afrika*, pp. 67, 70; S. Brun, *Samuel Brun's Schiffarten, 1642* (ed.) Naber (The Hague 1913), pp. 12–13.
13 Battell, *The Strange Adventures*, pp. 47, 51; Brun, *Samuel Brun's Schiffarten*, p. 12; Dapper, *Naukeurige Beschrijvinge*, pp. 151.
14 Brun, *Samuel Brun's Schiffarten*, p. 22; Dapper, *Naukeurige Beschrijvinge*, pp. 155, 200.
15 Some of the traditions concerning the origins of the Vili of Loango have been published by the following: R. Lethur, *Étude sur le Royaume de Loango et le Peuple Vili* (Pointe-Noire 1952), also published as *Les Cahiers Ngonge*, vol. II (Lovanium 1960), pp. 21–2; K. Laman, *The Kongo* (Stockholm 1953), vol. I p. 17; vol. II p. 137; J. Cuvelier, 'Traditions Congolaises', *Congo*, vol. II (Brussels 1930), pp. 470–72; A. Doutreloux, *L'Ombre des Fétiches: Société et Culture Yombe* (Louvain 1967), pp. 34–7.
16 Accounts of Loango provinces are given by Battell, *The Strange Adventures*, pp. 52–9, and Dapper, *Naukeurige Beschrijvinge*, pp. 143–7, 159.
17 Brun, *Samuel Brun's Schiffarten*, p. 13.
18 P. Bohannan, *Africa and Africans* (New York 1964), p. 218.
19 Broecke, *Reisen naar West Afrika*, p. 64.
20 See pp. 203, above.
21 Brun, *Samuel Brun's Schiffarten*, p. 22; Broecke, *Reisen naar West Afrika*, p. 45; Dapper, *Naukeurige Beschrijvinge*, pp. 157–8, 194, 233.
22 Paludanus, *Beschrijvinge van de Gantsche Cust van Guinea, Manicongo, etc.*, (ed.), C. P. Burger and F. Hunger (The Hague 1934), p. 7.
23 Broecke tells of Loango copper coming from the *Insiques* (the Teke kingdom elsewhere referred to as *Ansiko*), Dapper refers to the copper mines of *Sondy*: see Broecke, *Reisen naar West Afrika*, p. 70; Dapper, *Naukeurige Beschrijvinge*, p. 158.
24 Dapper, *Naukeurige Beschrijvinge*, p. 158.
25 *Oude West Indische Compagnie*, no. 46, Cappelle to Governors of the First Dutch West India Company (March 1642). Part of this document has been published by L. Jadin, 'Rivalités luso-néerlandaises au Sohio, Congo, 1600–75', *Bulletin de l'Institut Historique Belge de Rome*, vol. XXXVII (Brussels 1966), pp. 85–101.
26 Battell, *The Strange Adventures*, pp. 52, 58–9.
27 Oude West Indische Compagnie, no. 46, Cappelle to Governors, (March 1642).
28 Dapper, *Naukeurige Beschrijvinge*, pp. 158, 216, 219; J.-B. Labat, *Relation Historique de l'Ethiopie Occidentale*, vol. 3 (Paris 1732), p. 415.
29 Dapper, *Naukeurige Beschrijvinge*, pp. 159–60; L. B. Proyart, *Histoire de Loango, Kakongo et autres Royaumes d'Afrique* (Paris 1776), pp. 126–7.
30 Dapper, *Naukeurige Beschrijvinge*, p. 146.
31 Battell, *The Strange Adventures*, p. 44; Broecke, *Reisen naar West Afrika*, p. 64.

32 This question is further discussed on p. 218 of this book.
33 Broecke, *Reisen naar West Afrika*, pp. 29-30, 44.
34 ibid., pp. 28-9.
35 Heyn, *De West Afrikaanse Reis van Piet Heyn*, pp. lxxxii, xcii.
36 Oude West Indische Compagnie, no. 23, Minutes of the Zeeland Chamber (5 January 1637).
37 F. Mauro, *Le Portugal et l'Atlantique au XVII_e siècle, 1570-1670* (Paris 1960), p. 161.
38 Oude West Indische Compagnie, no. 8, Governors of the First Dutch West India Company to Elmina (28 November 1639).
39 References to Dutch trade with Loango can be found in the 'Journal of Louis Dammaert, under-factor on the Guinea Coast, 1652-6', in *Algemeen Rijksarchief*, vol. XXII, (The Hague 1898); also Oude West Indische Compagnie, nos. 8, 10, 55, 56.
40 G. Sautter, *De l'Atlantique au Fleuve Congo, une Géographie du Sous-Peuplement*, vol. II (Paris 1966), pp. 620-1; Sautter discusses the question of pre-Kongo inhabitants of the Niari valley in the light of oral traditions collected in the area. For the arrival of the Kongo in the area, see also M. Soret, *Les Kongo Nord-Occidentaux* (Paris 1959), p. 21, and J. Cuvelier, *Documents sur une Mission Française au Kakongo (1766-76)*, (Brussels 1953), p. 8.
41 Labat, *Relations Historique de l'Ethiopie Occidentale*, vol. 3, pp. 421-5.
42 *Gemeente Archief*, no. 802, Report on the trade of the West India Company, (Rotterdam).
43 Dapper, *Naukeurige Beschrijvinge*, p. 158.
44 J. Cuvelier, 'Contribution à l'histoire du Bas-Congo', *Bulletin de l'Institut Royal Colonial Belge*, vol. XIX (Brussels 1948), pp. 895-921; Cuvelier quotes Father Antonio de Monteprandone, who in 1651 wrote of 'the pagans from Loango many of whom come every year to San Salvador to trade and very often I preach to them at that capital'.
45 Report on the trade of the West India Company.
46 In discussing the slave trade period at Loango, it is useful to consider it within the wider context of the slave trade on the coast north of the Congo river and south of Mayumba. The term Loango Coast can be conveniently used in this wider sense, meaning the coasts of the three kingdoms of Loango, Kakongo, and Ngoyo, with their three ports of Loango Bay, Malemba, and Cabinda.
47 Treasury Records, T70/78, fo. 113, 114, Public Records Office (London).
48 Bibliothèque Nationale, PIII, Div.2, 12/1 (Paris). The figures are given on a manuscript map by de Monségnor.
49 'Journal of the *Flore*', *Archives du Ministre de la Marine*, 4JJ, 71/35 (Paris).
50 Middelburgsche Commercie Compagnie, no. 459, letter from Malemba, 12 February 1749 (Middelburg).
51 The figure is based on the journals, letters, and account books of the ships of the Middelburgsche Commercie Compagnie, which visited the Loango Coast in these years.

52 Archives Coloniales, C6/24 (Paris).
53 L. Degranpré, *Voyage à la Côte Occidentale d'Afrique fait dans les années 1786 et 1787*, vol. I (Paris 1801), p. xvii.
54 Birmingham, *Trade and Conflict in Angola*, p. 157.
55 E. Donnan, *Documents Illustrative of the Slave-Trade*, vol. II (Washington 1931), pp. 597-8.
56 Degranpré, *Voyage à la Côte Occidentale d'Afrique*, vol. II, pp. 12-13, 25, 37.
57 ibid., vol. I, p. xxvi.
58 ibid., vol. II, p. 14.
59 E. Froment, 'Trois Affluents Français du Congo: Rivières Alima, Likouala et Sanga', and 'Un Voyage dans l'Oubangui', *Bulletin de la Société de Géographie de Lille*, vol. VII (Lille 1887), pp. 458-74, and vol. XI (1889), pp. 180-216; C. de Chavannes, *Un Collaborateur de Brazza: Albert Dolisie. Sa Correspondence avec l'Auteur* (Paris 1932), p. 102. Chavannes quotes a letter from Dolisie dated 19.5.1885; C. de Chavannes, 'Exposé Sommaire d'un Voyage dans l'Ouest Africain', *Bulletin de la Société de Géographie*, vol. VI, (Lyons 1886), pp. 65-96.
60 E. Pechuel-Loesche, *Volkskunde von Loango* (Stuttgart 1907), p. 4.
61 M. Plancquaert, *Les Jaga et les Bayaka du Kwango* (Brussels 1932), pp. 72-4.
62 P. S. de Brazza, 'Voyage dans l'Ouest Africain, 1875-1887', *Le Tour du Monde,* vol. LIV (July-December 1887), (Paris), p. 289, and vol. LVI (July-December 1888), pp. 1-64; Sautter, *De l'Atlantique au Fleuve Congo*, vol. II, p. 622.
63 Degranpré, *Voyage à la Côte Occidentale d'Afrique*, vol. II, p. 5.
64 ibid., vol. I, p. xxiv.
65 An English fort built in 1722 was destroyed by the Portuguese in 1723; a Portuguese fort built in 1783 was destroyed by the French in 1784.
66 Degranpré, *Voyage à la Côte Occidentale d'Afrique*, vol. I, p. 166.
67 Birmingham, *Trade and Conflict in Angola*, pp. 131-2. The traders from the Loango Coast were often referred to as *Mubires*. See L. Jadin, 'Aperçu de la situation du Congo ... d'après le Père Cherubino de Savona', *Bulletin de l'Institut Historique Belge de Rome*, vol. XXXV (Brussels 1963), p. 408; the word is probably derived from *Muvili*, meaning 'a Vili', since a 'b' and an 'r' and an 'l' are frequently interchangeable in Bantu language.
68 Birmingham, *Trade and Conflict in Angola*, pp. 133-4, 137.
69 The figures are based on the account-books of sixteen ships of the Middelburgsche Commercie Compagnie, Middelburg which traded on the Loango Coast between 1757 and 1795.
70 Pechuel-Loesche, *Volkskunde von Loango*, p. 219.
71 ibid., p. 221.
72 Degranpré, *Voyage à la Côte Occidentale d'Afrique*, vol. II, pp. 48-9.
73 Pechuel-Loesche, *Volkskunde von Loango*, p. 222.
74 ibid., pp. 221-2.
75 ibid., p. 222.

76 This account is based on the journals of the ships of the Middelburgsche Commercie Compagnie.
77 Proyart, *A History of Loango*, p. 150.
78 The office of Mambouk was traditionally in the hands of the man second in line in the succession to the throne; see Battell, *The Strange Adventures*, p. 50, and Dapper, *Naukeurige Beschrijvinge*, p. 161. At Cabinda, the Mambouk seems to have retained important functions. He was the royal official in charge of negotiations with the Portuguese in 1783.
79 Archives du Ministre de la Marine, B4/267, Journal of the Usbele, 23 July–23 August 1783 (Paris).
80 Archives Coloniales, C6/24, Report of S. Marois, 1784 (Paris).
81 Archives du Ministre de la Marine, B4/267, Journal of M. Marigny, 1784.
82 Pigafetta and Lopez, *Description du Royaume de Congo et des Contrées Environnantes*, p. 31; Battell, *The Strange Adventures*, p. 42; Dapper, *Naukeurige Beschrijvinge*, p. 159.
83 Degranpré, *Voyage à la Côte Occidentale d'Afrique*, vol. I, pp. xxvi–vii, 166.
84 ibid., vol. I, p. 166.
85 See p. 213 in this book.
86 J. Pouabou, 'Le Peuple Vili ou Loango', *Liaison*, vol. LIX (Brazzaville 1957), pp. 57–9.
87 Degranpré, *Voyage à la Côte Occidentale d'Afrique*, vol. I, p. 109; Proyart, *A History of Loango*, p. 128.
88 Dapper, *Naukeurige Beschrijvinge*, p. 159.
89 ibid., p. 167.
90 See p. 208 in this book.
91 Broecke, *Reisen naar West Afrika*, p. 66; Brun, *Samuel Brun's Schiffarten*, pp. 13–14; Dapper, *Naukeurige Beschrijvinge*, pp. 149, 169.
92 Dapper, *Naukeurige Beschrijvinge*, p. 169.
93 The account books of the Middelburgsche Commercie Compagnie give the names of brokers who supplied slaves. These include the names of members of the royal council, princes, and common people.
94 Degranpré, *Voyage à la Côte Occidentale d'Afrique*, vol. I, pp. 105–7.
95 Dapper, *Naukeurige Beschrijvinge*, pp. 159–60.
96 Proyart, *A History of Loango*, p. 126.
97 ibid., p. 126–7.
98 ibid., p. 126.
99 This is clear from ships' journals. Visits to the Maloango and the Manikakongo are mentioned in Middelburgsche Commercie Compagnie, pp. 215, 487, 800, 803, 825, 989; and in Archives du Ministre de la Marine, 4JJ, 73/66.
100 Account books of Middelburgsche Commercie Compagnie ships, for example, 456, 795, 803, 809, 825.
101 Battell, *The Strange Adventures*, p. 50.
102 Dapper, *Naukeurige Beschrijvinge*, p. 161.
103 Proyart, *A History of Loango*, pp. 128–31.

104 ibid., p. 173.
105 Degranpré, *Voyage à la Côte Occidentale d'Afrique*, vol. I, p. 173.
106 J. Vansina, *Kingdoms of the Savanna* (Madison 1966), p. 194.
107 Archives du Ministre de la Marine, BB4/252, Report of Linois (20 May 1806). Linois found that French trade at Loango had virtually stopped. See also J. K. Tuckey, *Narration of an Expedition to Explore the River Zaire* (New York 1818), p. 126. Tuckey, who visited Malemba in 1818, was told that only one ship had visited that port in the previous five years. Only at Cabinda did the slave trade thrive under Portuguese influence.
108 E. Bouet-Willaumez, *Commerce et Traite des Noirs aux Côtes Occidentales d'Afrique* (Paris 1848), pp. 191, 197.
109 W. F. W. Owen, *Narrative of Voyages to Explore the Shores of Africa, Arabia and Madagascar* (New York 1833), vol. II, pp. 165, 171, 175. Owen refers to meetings with *Mafulas* in the Congo river, at Cabinda, and at Loango Bay. A *Mafula* he defines as 'a title bestowed on the governor of a district, or town, appointed by the king'. It seems probable that this is the same word as Mafouk, also sometimes referred to as Mafouka.

9 The Portuguese slave trade from Angola in the eighteenth century

1 Curtin has estimated Portuguese slave exports from the West African coast at 611,000 between 1701 and 1800. Portuguese exports from Angola during this same period, were over double that, or 1,414,500, thus representing 70 per cent of the total slaves shipped. As for Angola's relationship to the total volume of the slave trade, its 1.4 million represented 26 per cent of total African exports of all nations in the eighteenth century. These estimates are taken from Philip D. Curtin, *The Atlantic Slave Trade, A Census* (Madison: University of Wisconsin Press 1969), p. 211, table 63.
2 While the port of Luanda was not colonized by the Portuguese until 1575, slave trading in the region was already a fully developed system in the first half of the century. With effective occupation, and the keeping of more exact records, as well as formal contracts, it would appear that exports for the next century may have gone from 5000 to 10,000 per annum, though the reliability of these estimates is questionable. Edmundo Correia Lopes, *A Escravatura (subsidios para a sua historia)* (Lisbon: agência geral das colónias 1944), pp. 85-7.
3 While port registers for either city are unavailable for either Benguela or Luanda in any number in the 1790s (see Appendix tables I and II) a rough idea of exports can be obtained from Rio de Janeiro port registers. Since Rio de Janeiro accounted for over half of the exports in this period, its figures can be considered a reasonable reflection of trade conditions. Thus in the period 1795 to 1800, Benguela exports to Rio de Janeiro accounted for 38,990 slaves out of a total of 90,329 shipped from Angola to that port, which represented 43 per cent of the total exports. See Herbert S. Klein, 'The trade in African slaves to Rio de Janeiro, 1795-1811; estimates of mortality and patterns of voyages,' *Journal of African History*, vol. X, no. 4

(1969), p. 545. It would seem that by the first decade of the nineteenth century, Benguela probably came close to supplying half the total exports from the region, since its total share of the imports into Rio de Janeiro from 1795 to 1811 was 50 per cent; ibid., p. 541.

4 The Portuguese tried to settle Cabinda permanently several times, and even succeeded in establishing a fort there in 1783, but this was destroyed by the French a year later. For the details of the Portuguese expedition of the 1780s, see the initial exploration report of Antonio Maximo de Souza Marques in *Arquivo Histórico Ultramarino* [Hereafter cited as AHU], Angola, caixa 37, report dated 16 March 1780. On the setting up of the fort, see the letters of the Governor at Luanda to the Crown in 1783 in AHU, Angola, cx. 38, letters dated 10 and 11 August 1783. This apparently was not the first such settlement attempt by the Portuguese, according to Degranpré, and the French when they destroyed the fort built in 1783 did not replace it with one of their own. L. Degranpré, *Voyage à la Côte Occidentale d'Afrique fait dans les années 1786 et 1787* (2 vols.; Paris: Dentu 1801), vol. I, pp. 31–32. By the second decade of the nineteenth century, however, the Portuguese must have more firmly established themselves at Cabinda, for in both 1814–15, and 1817–18 the port registers of Luanda list a sizeable number of vessels which temporarily stopped at Luanda on their way from Brazil to Cabinda. The figure was nine ships in 1814, three in 1815, four in 1817 and eleven in 1818. AHU, Angola, cx. 62, 31 January 1815; and cx. 64, 31 January 1816; cx. 65, 14 January 1818; cx. 66, n.d. for 1818 report.

5 Klein, 'The trade in African slaves', p. 540. This was the average for the 162,498 slaves shipped from both Benguela and Luanda in the 1795–1811 period.

6 One of the few systematic recordings of length of voyages was given by the British consuls in Rio de Janeiro. They reported on the voyage time of all slavers that arrived in the port of Rio de Janeiro from 2 January to 23 December 1821. This showed that the twenty-two ships that arrived from Luanda averaged 36.3 days in the crossing. The five ships that sailed from Benguela averaged 36.0 days, and finally the 7 ships that came from Cabinda averaged 35.8 days. Great Britain, *Parliamentary Papers* (1845), vol. XLIX, 'Slave trade-slave vessels' report printed 25 February 1845, pp. 9–10. The major importing months at the end of the century for Rio de Janeiro were the southern equatorial seasons of spring and summer. Klein, 'The trade in African slaves', p. 539.

7 In the total slave exports for the eight years of 1812, 1815, 1817, 1822–26, for which surviving records provide ports of destination, Pernambuco, Maranhão, and Pará increased their share to 37 per cent of exports. Rio de Janeiro continued to dominate with 54 per cent of the total trade, with Bahia suffering a decline to only 6 per cent. The rest was taken by southern Brazilian ports. These figures are taken from AHU, Angola, maço 16 and from Manuel Dos Anjos da Silva Rebelo, *Relações entre Angola e Brasil, 1808–1830* (Lisbon: Agência-Geral do Ultramar 1970), quadro no. 2, after p. 81. The Silva Rebelo table has several errors in it, including arithmetic

ones, which I have corrected by referring to the originals of several years in the AHU. For 1822 he has the Ceará total incorrectly listed; it should be 465. In 1826 the original report lists no shipments to Maranhão and a year-end total of only 11,658. This makes the final total for his table 102,441, instead of 104,630, with two slaves shipped to Cabinda in 1822 and therefore not listed.

8   For the very special trade that developed between Bahia and the Gold and slave coasts, see the major study by Pierre Verger, *Flux et reflux de la traite des nègres entre le golfe de Bénin et Bahia de todos os santos, du dix-septième au dix-neuvième siècle* (Paris: Mouton 1968), especially chapters vi and following. In the nineteenth century, twice as many ships went to the Guinean coast from Bahia as went to the Angolan area, ibid., pp. 655–7. On the Dutch response to this special trade see Johannes Postma, 'The Dutch Participation in the African Slave Trade: Slaving on the Guinea Coast, 1675–1795' (Unpublished Ph.D. dissertation, Department of History, Michigan State University 1970), pp. 90–92, 108, 124–6.

9   Between 1795 and 1811, 96 per cent of the slaves exported from Africa to Rio de Janeiro came from the ports of Angola, Klein, 'The trade', p. 540.

10 ibid., p. 543.

11 Average cargo capacity for the 166 sailings of the *Curveta* was 351 adults per vessel; for the *Galera*, with 137 sailings, the average was 457 adults. The *Navio* (translated in the eighteenth century as ship) was third in importance with 75 sailings or an average of 427 adults per vessel. The *Bergantim* (or brig), however, only accounted for 17 sailings, or 3 per cent of the total, and carried a low average of 288 adults per sailing.

12 According to the 1684 decree, which was printed and is to be found in several collections of documents in the AHU, the rule was that (according to chapter vi) 'If it is a decked ship in which there are portholes through which the Negroes can easily receive the necessary fresh air, then capacity below decks should be 7 adults (cabeças) for every two tons; not having said portholes, the capacity should be only 5 slaves per two tons below decks.' It also allowed that for either type of ship, they could carry another 5 slaves per ton above deck. The law also provided detailed listings of the type and quantity of food and water to be carried by the slaver in order to provide three meals per day per slave. Provisions for housing sick slaves apart from the rest and detailed registration by port officials for all of these provisions were also required. See Lei 3, 18 March 1684, in AHU, Angola, cx. 10. This ship's capacity law remained in effect throughout the eighteenth century, and was only changed by the decree (*alvará*) of November 24, 1813, which changed the tonnage to a uniform listing of 5 slaves per two tons. See the typical post-1813 slave ship's registration papers in AHU, Angola, maço 14 'Passaportes.'

13 It has been estimated that the average tonnage of all English shipping engaged in the Atlantic trade from Europe to North America in the mid eighteenth century was less than 150 tons per vessel. Douglass C. North, 'Sources of productivity change in ocean shipping, 1600–1850,' *The Journal*

of Political Economy, vol. LXXVI, no. 5 (September to October 1968), p. 958.

14 AHU, Angola, cx. 17, letter of Provedor de Fazenda Real [Superintendent of the Royal Treasury] of Luanda to the crown dated 19 February 1728.

15 In some 56 expeditions financed by the Dutch West India Company between 1681 and 1751, the percentage of children under fifteen years of age was only 8 per cent. Postma, 'The Dutch slave trade,' pp. 177–8. Postma noted that West India Company officers advised slave captains to buy children only at the last minute before sailing and only if space was left. Postma, ibid., p. 179.

16 The records of the Companhia Geral de Pernambuco e Paraiba show that of the 49,344 slaves shipped by the Company from Africa between 1761 and 1786, only 508 were listed as children, or only 1 per cent. These figures probably do not include infants at the breast (*crias de peito*), which would probably have accounted for another 250 or so children. Even so, this would only bring the total up to 2 per cent. António Carreira, *As companhias pombalinas de navegacão, comercio e tráfico de escravos entre a costa africana e o nordeste brasileiro* (Porto: N.P. 1969), p. 261.

17 These figures are calculated from previously unanalysed data in the Arquivo Nacional, Rio de Janeiro, Policia, Codice 242.

18 These accounts are found in Biblioteca Nacional de Lisboa [Hereafter cited as BNL], Colecção Pombalina, Codice 617.

19 AHU, Bahia, cx. 37, document dated 18 December 1727.

20 BNL, Colecção Pombalina, Codice 617, folio 222.

21 To give some idea of other costs to Captain Proença e Sylva, his records note that in October of 1759 he was charged for export taxes, maintenance, passage, branding and registration fees for shipping one slave to Recife the sum of 16$480, with 8$000 of that figure due to transportation charges (ibid., folio 174). This must have been a fairly standard set of charges, for another male adult slave he sent in February of that year to Recife, also cost him 16$480 to ship to his factor in that city. In addition, the slave apparently sickened on his arrival and medical costs added another 2$690 in expenses before he could be sold. The final sale price was 70$000, leaving a gross profit of 50$830 (ibid., folio 114). Also in 1759 he shipped to Pernambuco another 5 slaves. Of these, one died at sea and another two were shipped as his personal property to a relative in Lisbon. This left two young female slaves whom he sold for 120$000. His total costs for shipping the five slaves and maintaining them until their sale or shipment to Portugal was 78$955, which still left him with a gross profit of 41$045. The charge for maintaining a slave in Recife while waiting for shipment to Portugal was 60 reis per diem. (ibid., folio 116v). In 1761 and 1762 he shipped nine slaves to Rio de Janeiro, of which lot about five died. The rest sold at a total profit of 254$898 (ibid., folio 193). In this same account with his factor in Rio de Janeiro, it is noted that he has bought and sold letters of credit to Brazil over the past several years.

22 In one report to the Crown, (AHU, Angola, cx. 21, n.d.), Angolan officials noted that the total cost of nine varieties of woollens and textiles, which

Notes and references to page 234   325

would go to make up the cost of one slave, were priced in Lisbon at 26$400. These same types and quantities of goods in Luanda cost 48$300. Their cost at delivery point in the interior was 80$000. What is not clear from the table is whether this is the price they valued the goods at for the African purchaser, or whether this 80$000 represented the base cost at Luanda plus shipping costs to the interior. My own impression is that the former is more probable. If this is so, then taking 48$300 as the cost to the Luanda merchant of European goods used to purchase slaves, and another 16$480 at his costs for shipping him to Recife (see note 21), then the total costs would be 64$780, bringing his net profit on the sale of the slave in Recife to 5$220. This would give him a profit of only 8 per cent on his investment for this slave. This would seem too small a return, especially given the fact that he would have to expect in normal operations the total loss of investment on several slaves. Also, using this same purchase price of 48$300 per slave for the seven slaves shipped by him to Rio de Janeiro in 1762 (Table 20), and assuming the three young children were adults and also sold at 90$000 (total gross income being 360$000), thus equalizing their sale prices with the assumed adult purchase price of 48$300 for each one, the net loss on this voyage was 109$111. On the basis of this very limited evidence, I assume that the report exaggerated the costs of the textiles in order to obtain benefits in reduced prices from the crown.

23 In 1795, for example, of the 337 Portuguese vessels which left the harbour of Lisbon (out of a total of 958 ships), only fourteen went to Africa, as opposed to fifty-one that sailed for Brazil. At the same time, of the 348 Portuguese vessels that entered port in that year (out of a total of 1,036 ships), only two were listed as coming from Africa, and these two were from the Cape Verde Islands. At the same time, 98 were listed as arriving from Brazil. Arquivo Geral da Marinha (Lisbon), caixa 'Entradas e saidas de Navios, Registro do Porto de Lisboa, 1741–1800', in undated mappa. In the same collection of port registers, there is a listing of sailing times for all ships from port of departure. These show that the average length of voyage from Brazil was quite long. In the registers for 1797, for example, of four ships which came from Bahia in April to June of that year, the average sailing time was eighty-one days; the two ships coming from Recife, Pernambuco averaged 73 days; and the two ships coming from Rio de Janeiro to Lisbon averaged 109 days.

24 Luanda in 1773 had a population of 612 troops and 1519 civilians. Of the troops, 140 were Mulattoes and seventy-two were Negroes, while the civilian town population consisted of the following breakdowns:

	Free population of Luanda		Total slave population by owner (Male and Female)
	Men	Women	
Whites	214	37	787
Free Mulattoes	106	32	187
Free Negroes	143	4	9
Total	463	73	983

These population statistics are found in AHU, Angola, cx. 36 documents numbered 19 and 25 and both dated 27 March 1773.

25 In the wheat flour sold in Luanda in 1800 and 1801, for example, Brazilian imported sacks accounted for 22 per cent and 19 per cent respectively of all wheat flour sold, the rest being locally produced. AHU, Angola cx. 51, 1 April 1801 and cx. 53, 16 June 1802.

26 In the mid 1780s, for example, the Angolans were importing 1340 barrels of Gerebita per annum, with the bulk of this production (or 76 per cent) coming from Rio de Janeiro. For three-year importation figures (1782-1784) see AHU, Angola, maço 13, 5 January 1785.

27 Birmingham, *Trade and Conflict*, p. 138.

28 Though evidence on this from Luanda is not presently available, data from Benguela would seem to support this assertion. Thus when the *Curveta* 'Nossa Senhora de Agua de Lupe, e Bom JESUS dos Navigantes' sailed for Rio de Janeiro on 22 January 1763 it carried slaves which had been purchased on its account as far back as the preceding October, with the bulk being purchased in December. AHU, Angola, cx. 30, document no. 8.

29 Birmingham, *Trade and Conflict*, pp. 138-9.

30 For a typical example of such a tax contract, see the printed contract given to Jacinto Dias Braga for the collection of the *novo imposto* (a tax of 1$200 per slave exported) in all the ports of Angola for a six-year period (the typical term of all tax contracts) to begin on 5 January 1742. AHU, Angola cx. 23, dated 7 September 1740.

31 These taxes were the *direito real, direito novo, novo imposto* and the *preferencia*.

32 For these decrees see Arquivo Nacional, Torre de Tombo, Manuscritos Miscellaneos, no. 926, folio 252.

33 See, for example, the contract given to Domingos Dias de Silva and his associates for the collection of the new unified head tax which was granted for a six-year term beginning on 5 January 1766. The cost to the tax farmer and his associates was the annual payment to the crown of the sum of 88:300$000. Given the estimated 12,000 slaves shipped per annum in the 1760s, this would give the tax farmer a gross income of 104:400$000, for a net profit of 16:100$000. A copy of the contract is in AHU, Angola, cx. 30, dated 6 September 1765. For an explanation of Portuguese currency in the eighteenth century, see the Note to Table 20.

34 The founding charters of the two companies will be found in Carreira, *As companhias pombalinas*, appendix, documents 'E' (pp. 313-36) and 'H' (pp. 347-72). A contemporary copy of the original charter for the Maranhão Company can be found in Arquivo Geral da Alfandega de Lisboa, Codice 51, libro 1, folios 8-21v. A detailed study of all aspects of the Maranhão company, in which the slave trade assumed only a minor role, is found in Manuel Nunez Dias, 'Fomento ultramarino e mercantilismo: a Companhia Geral do Grão-Pará e Maranhão (1775-88),' *Revista de Historia* (São Paulo) vol. XXXII no. 66 (Abril-Junho, 1966), pp. 359-428; this is Part I of a study which extends over ten parts in as many issues.

35 Carreira, *As companhias pombalinas*, p. 261.
36 ibid., p. 91.
37 The lower averages are possibly due to the shortness of the periods being considered, and also to the poor quality of recording. Too many ships had identical names, identical ship type identifications, and therefore were impossible to follow accurately in the subsequent listings. Since captains usually sailed for only one trip, it was impossible to distinguish several ships. An example of this was the listing under Corvetes with the name of 'Nossa Senhora da Conceipcão, Santo Antonio e Almas.' Between 1762 and 1767 there were three different ships with that name and vessel type designation, all of which operated in Luanda. In other cases, when names were the same and ships' types were different, thus facilitating identification, later listings often changed the ship's designation, especially from the generic *navio* to a more precise term.
38 Klein, 'The trade', p. 544 and Verger, *Flux et reflux*, p. 658.
39 Carreira, *As companhias pombalinas*, pp. 254, 261.
40 ibid., p. 52-3.
41 In data reconstructed from the Maranhão Company records, Carreira has been able to determine the sex of some 20,141 slaves who were carried by Company vessels between 1756 and 1788, with the resulting breakdown being 7572 females and 12,569 males, which means a 38 per cent contingent of females. ibid. pp. 94-5. Postma, in calculations made for fifty-six West India Company vessels that carried slaves from Africa in 1681 to 1751, found 8629 females (or 29 per cent) out of a total of 29,532 slaves who were transported. Postma, 'The Dutch . . . slave trade,' pp. 177-8. He also notes that 'as a rule, WIC [West India Company] captains had instructions to purchase a slave cargo consisting of two-thirds men and one-third women slaves.' ibid. p. 179. Unger in his study of a Dutch free trading company found a rather high ratio of 41 per cent (or 10,249) women, out of the total of 25,051 slaves shipped by the company vessels. Unger, 'Bijdragen tot de geschiedenis. . . ,' Finally, one of the few breakdowns by sex available in New World importation records can be found in Havana port registers. Here between 1790 and 1794, 25,959 slaves were imported, of which 25 per cent (or 6535) were women. Herbert S. Klein, 'North American Competition and the Characteristics of the African Slave Trade to Cuba, 1790 to 1794,' *William & Mary Quarterly*, 3rd series, vol. XXVIII no. 1 (January 1971), p. 98, Table VI. In the period from August 1815 to September 1818, (with the exception of a missing register for April 1817), some 61,851 slaves were introduced into the port of Havana. Of this number, only 19,988 (or 32 per cent) were women. These registers are to be found in the Archivo General de Indias (Seville), Audiencia de Santo Domingo, legajo 2207.
42 Postma notes that the Dutch slave trade was virtually wiped out by the fourth Anglo-Dutch war of 1780 to 1784 (Postma, 'The Dutch . . . slave trade,' pp. 160ff). Also, the French slave trade equally suffered a disastrous decline as a result of international conflicts. The trade was temporarily halted as a result of the Seven Years War, and then was totally suppressed as

a result of the wars of the French Revolution which stopped French slavers from operating after 1792. For the impact of the Seven Years War see Gaston-Martin, *Nantes au xviiie siècle: L'ère des negriers (1714 to 1774)* (Paris: Félix Alcan 1931), ch. vi; and for the developments in the 1790s see J. Meyer, 'Le commerce negrier nantais (1774 to 1792),' *Annales: économies, sociétés, civilisations*, vol. XV (1960), pp. 120-9.

43 A brief glimpse of Bahian investors in slave ships is given in the studies of Marieta Alves, 'O comércio marítimo e alguns armadores do século xviii na Bahia,' Revista de História (São Paulo), vol. XXXIV, no. 69 (1967), pp. 91-8.

44 By the early nineteenth century, average cargo size was rapidly going up in the exports from Angolan ports. Thus in the five-year period from 1812, 1814 to 1817, average cargo size was 464 slaves per ship. Silva Rebelo, *Angola e Brasil*, quadro no. 1, after p. 81. As for total volume, this rose to an annual of 14,038 in the 13 years from 1812, 1814 to 1820 and 1822 to 1826. ibid.

45 Nevertheless, some nineteenth-century data give the impression of a rather thriving merchant community in the early years of the century. Thus the Luandan merchant Francisco Luís Vieira (who was also a colonel in the local militia) claimed in official documents before the crown that he had exported 11,074 adult slaves and thirteen children to Brazil in the period 1822 to 1825. Another militia officer and local merchant, José Severino de Sousa, officially swore to the crown that he had shipped 20,018 adult slaves to Brazil between 1811 and 1816; and a third sought admission to the Order of Christ on the basis of having exported 4825 slaves to Brazil between 31 October and 31 January 1805. ibid., p. 94.

46 In 1815, for example, Luanda imported 996.9 million reis worth of goods from Brazil and Portugal (the latter accounting for only 11 million of the total), and exported only 937.5 million reis to Brazil in slaves, wax and ivory. Of the Brazilian imports, 765.9 million reis were accounted for by Rio de Janeiro, 202.7 million by Pernambuco and 17.1 million by Bahia. Of the exports, 884.8 million reis (or 94 per cent) was accounted for by slave exports, with wax being second at 45.5 million and ivory taking just 7.1 million reis, AHU, Angola, cx. 63, report dated 31 January 1816. By value, the most important products imported were textiles, followed by Gerebita, foodstuffs and tobacco, and gunpowder (which since 1808 was manufactured in the new Royal Powder Factory in Rio de Janeiro). For a detailed evaluation of goods, see Silva Rebelo, *Angola e Brasil*, quadro 3 following p. 179. On the Rio de Janeiro gunpowder factory and its exports to Angola see ibid. pp. 155ff.

10 The impact of the slave trade on East Central Africa in the nineteenth century

1 For a full treatment of the British anti-slave campaign in the Western Indian Ocean, see G. S. Graham, *Great Britain in the Indian Ocean, 1810-50* (Oxford 1967), especially chapters 2, 3, and 5.

2   Arquivo Histórico Ultramarino, Lisbon, Moc., Cx. 62, Silva Guedes, 'Relação do Marfim e mais generos q̃ se despacharão nesta Alf.ᵃp.r Sahida p.ᵃ os Portos da Azia no mes de Agosto de prezente ano de 1817'. The exact figure is 3959 *arrobas* and 10¾ *arráteis*. Of this, 70.4 per cent went to Daman, 17.3 per cent to Diu, and 12.3 per cent to Bengal.
3   ACL., Azul Ms. 648, no. 17. It is worth noting, too, that the duty paid on ivory in 1818 was now raised to 6 per cent *ad valorem*.
4   AHU., Cod. 1394, fo. 15-17, Brito Sanches to Conde dos Arcos, Moç., 10 October 1819.
5   Owen, *Narrative of Voyages to Explore the Shores of Africa, Arabia and Madagascar; performed in HM ships* Leven *and* Barracouta (2 vols., London 1792), vol. I, p. 191.
6   S. X. Botelho, *Memoria Estatistica sobre os Dominios Portuguezes na Africa Oriental* (Lisbon 1835), pp. 371-3.
7   Santana, *Documentação Arulsa Moçambique de Arquivo Histórico Ultramarino* (2 vols., Lisbon 1964-7), vol. II, p. 835. Moreover, the price of Mozambique ivory remained well above that paid at Zanzibar during these years. In 1832 it was 28 to 33 dollars per *arroba* of large ivory, equivalent to 30.6 to 36.1 dollars per *frasila (faraçola)* of the same, which was higher even than the price current at Bombay. See A. C. P. Gamitto (trans.) I. Cunnison, *King Kazembe and the Marave Cheva, Bisa, Bemba, Lunda, and other peoples of Southern Africa being the Diary of the Portuguese Expedition to that Potentate in the years 1831 and 1832*, (2 vols., Lisbon 1960), vol. II, p. 84; A. M. H. Sheriff, 'The rise of a commercial empire: An aspect of the economic history of Zanzibar, 1770-1873' (Unpublished Ph.D thesis, SOAS, University of London 1971), p. 469, graph II.
8   Bordalo, Francisco Maria and Lopes de Lima, José Joaquim. *Ensaios sobre a Estatistica das Possessões Portuguezas no Ultramar*. II Serie, Livro IV, 'Ensaio sobre a Estatistica de Moçambique' (Lisbon 1859), p. 167.
9   For a detailed description of British attempts to restrict the Brazilian and Portuguese slave trade at this time, see Leslie Bethell, *The Abolition of the Brazilian Slave Trade: Britain, Brazil, and the Slave Trade Question, 1807-69* (Cambridge 1970), chapters 1-2.
10 See Caledon to Vansittart, Cape of Good Hope, 27 June 1810, in George McCall Theal (ed.), *Records of South-East Africa* (9 vols. London 1898-1903), vol. IX, p. 12; PRO., FO. 84/122, Robert Hesketh to Lord Palmerston, London, 3 August 1831, enclosure no. 2, 'State of the slave trade on the northern coast of Brazil'.
11 William Milburn, *Oriental Commerce* (2 vols., London 1813), vol. I, p. 59.
12 ACL., Azul Ms. 648, no. 17. See also AHU., Moç., Cx. 61 and Cx. 62, Silva Guedes, *despachos* issued for twelve Brazilian merchant vessels, Moç., 9 February 1817 to 26 March 1818.
13 Arquivo de Casa de Cadaval, Cod. 826 (M VI 32), D. Fr. Bartolomeu dos Mártires, 'Memoria Chorographica da Provincia e a Capitania de Moçambique na Costa d'Africa Oriental Conforme o estado em que se

achava no anno de 1822', fos. 29–30. I am most grateful to the Marquésa de Cadava for allowing me to see this important manuscript and to Fr. Francisco Leite de Faria, Keeper of the Arquivo, who enabled me to use it in Lisbon. Lengthy extracts have been published with an introduction by Virgínia Rau, 'Aspectos étnico-culturais da ilha de Moçambique em 1822', *Studia*, vol. 11 (1963), pp. 123–62, especially 148–51. Cf. AHU., Moç., Cx. 64, Pedro Simião, 'Mappa das Embarcaçoens, que entrarão e Sahiráo do Porto de Mossambique no ano de 1819', Moç., 31 December 1819.

14   PRO., FO. 84/17, Henry Hayne to Marquis of Londonderry, Rio de Janeiro, 16 January 1822, enclosing, 'Slaves imported at Rio de Janeiro during the year 1821'; Mártires, 'Memoria', fo. 35.

15   PRO., CO.415/7, A. No. 172, pp. 12–13, Captain Acland's Journal no. 2, Moç., 9 October 1826; see also ibid., p. 34, Captain Polkinhome's Journal, post-12 December 1826.

16   AHU., Cod. 1425, fo. 3–5, Paulo José Miguel de Brito to Sheikh of Quitangonha, Moç., 9 and 17 March 1830.

17   Mártires's 1819 figures yield a higher mortality rate (27.7 per cent) than the 23.3 per cent which Herbert Klein has obtained from Brazilian notarial records for all slaves shipped (4665) and imported (3577) from Portuguese East Africa during the transitional period of 1795–1811, but the British consular figures for Mozambique and Quelimane importations in the 1820s (which together totalled 74,173 embarked and 64,688 landed, with 9485 deaths at sea), yield a much lower mortality rate of 12.8 per cent. If these figures are at all reliable, they suggest that from about 1820 the Atlantic slave trade from East Africa became a much less hazardous business than in previous years. See Klein, 'The trade in African slaves to Rio de Janeiro, 1795–1811: Estimates of Mortality and Patterns of Voyages', *Journal of African History*, vol. X no. 4 (1968), p. 540; Table 5 and sources.

18   Leslie Bethell, *The Abolition of the Brazilian Slave Trade: Britain, Brazil, and the Slave Trade Question, 1807–1869* (Cambridge 1970), Appendix.

19   I have calculated the percentage of slaves imported from Portuguese East Africa during 1828–30 by dividing the total figures supplied by Bethell by the Foreign Office statistics cited in Table 5 for those years for both Mozambique and Quelimane. See ibid., p. 71. For references to the slave trade from Mozambique to Brazil in the 1830s, see ibid., pp. 79, 85, 127, 150, 168.

20   H. Lynne to Stopford, HM Sloop *Eclipse*, 21 May 1812, and C. R. Moorsom to Christian, HMS. *Andromache*, Simon's Bay, 24 May 1825, both in Theal, *Records*, vol. IX, pp. 16, 51; AHU., Moç., Cx. 57, *autos da visita* issued to eleven vessels with British passports, from Mauritius and the Seychelles; AHU., Cod. 1386, no. 1167, António de Araujo de Azevedo to Marco Caetano de Abreu e Meneses, Rio de Janeiro, 18 June 1814; ibid., no. 1213, Marquês de Aguiar to same, Rio de Janeiro, 31 July 1815; AHU., Cod. 1380, fo. 240–3, Brito Sanches to Conde dos Arcos, Moç., 27 September 1819; AHU., Cod. 1391, no. 1414, Arcos to Brito Sanches, Rio

de Janeiro, 11 February 1820; AHU., Cod. 1394, fo. 69, Brito Sanches to Arcos, Moç., 15 July 1820.
21 PRO., CO. 415/7, A. no. 172, pp. 14–15.
22 ACL., Azul Ms 847, 'Estado das Relações Commerciaes da Capitania de Mossambique ate o dia 21 de Agosto de 1829 dado pelo Juiz de Fora de Mossambique Dionisio Ignacio de Lemos Pinto em sua informação de 2 de Novembro de 1829 dirigido ao Gov.or e Cap.am General da d.a Capitania Paulo José Miguel de Brito', fo. 13.
23 AHU., Moç., Cx. 64, Simião, 'Mappa', Moç., 31 December 1819.
24 See AHU., Cod. 1379, fos. 43, 46, 50, 90–1, being licences granted to eight Swahili and Arab traders to embark slaves at Mozambique, the average request being for fifty slaves, 14 March–12 April 1810, 1 February and 16 March 1812; ibid., fo. 66, licence granted for buying forty slaves to 'Massane Bunu Portador da Rainha Vaine de Bom-Bottoque', 8 January 1811; AHU., Moç., Cx. 60, *requerimento*. Said bin Saif, from Zanzibar, to go to Madagascar, granted, Moç., 2 April 1817; ibid., *Requerimento*, Sidi Hasan, returning from Madagascar, to go to Zanzibar, granted, Moç., 25 September 1817; PRO., Admiralty 1/69, no. 63, Joseph Nourse to John Wilson Croker, HMS. *Andromache*, at Sea, in the Mozambique Channel, 15 December 1823; Mártires, 'Memoria', fos. 31–2, also in Rau, 'Aspectos', pp. 152–3; PRO., CO.415/4, no. 61, 'Interrogatories addressed to Mr Copall and Mr Coppall's Answers relative to the State of Madagascar', nos. 200 and 202, Port Louis, 8 October 1827.
25 Owen to Croker, HMS. *Leven*, Mozambique, 9 October 1823, in Theal, *Records*, vol. IX, pp. 32–3; cf. ibid., pp. 18, 50; F. T. Texugo, *A Letter on the Slave Trade still carried on along the Eastern Coast of Africa . . .* (London 1839), p. 34; Eduardo Correia Lopes, *A escravatura (subsidios para a sua história)* (Lisbon 1944), p. 169. In assessing Texugo's evidence it is worth knowing that he was a political exile from Portugal: see AHU., Cod. 1444, no. 198, [Crown to Governor of Mozambique], 27 June 1839.
26 See Mabel V. Jackson, *European Powers and South-East Africa: A Study of International Relations on the South-East Coast of Africa, 1796–1856* (London 1942), pp. 195–6, 198–201, 222; Marquês da Bemposta Subserra, *et al*, Untitled memorandum on Portuguese East Africa directed to the Crown, Lisboa, 28 April 1856, pp. 19–20; Lyons McLeod, *Travels in Eastern Africa; with the Narrative of a Residence in Mozambique* (London 1860), vol. I, pp. 304–11, 313, 316–21, 325; James Duffy, *A Question of Slavery* (Oxford 1967), p. 41.
27 AHU., Moç., Cx. 49, petition of Joaquim da Rosário Monteiro, granted, [Moç.], 28 April 1807; AHU., Moç., Cx. 50, Prov. Govt. to Crown, Moç., 22 October 1807.
28 ACL., Azul Ms. 847, fos. 11, 16; AHU., Moç., Cx. 59 and Cod. 1380, fos. 152–3, Abreu e Meneses to Azevedo, Moç., 1 October 1815; ibid., fo. 189, José Francisco de Paula Cavalcanti de Albuquerque to Conde da Barca, Moç., 23 September 1817.
29 Jackson, *European Powers*, p. 189.

30 Owen to Croker, HMS *Leven*, Mozambique, 9 October 1823, in Theal, *Records*, vol. IX, p. 33; Thomas Boteler, *Narrative of a Voyage of Discovery to Africa and Arabia, performed in His Majesty's Ships Leven and Barracouta, from 1821 to 1826* (London 1835), vol. I, pp. 248–9; Owen, *Narrative*, vol. I, pp. 292–3; PRO. CO. 415/7, A. no. 172, pp. 34–5, Polkinhome's Journal.

31 PRO., CO. 415/9, A. no. 238, 'Correspondence and Documents furnished to Captains *Polkinhome* and Acland ... 29 September 1827 relative to the Slave Trade on the Coast of Africa', Document no. 1, article no. 4; see also AHU., Cod. 1414, no. 1837, José António de Oliveira Leite de Barros to Botelho, Ajuda, 19 April 1828.

32 See sources for Table 22; for the annual figures, see Allen F. Isaacman, *Mozambique – The Africanization of a European Institution: The Zambezi Prazos, 1750–1902* (Madison 1972), p. 92, Table 8.

33 ibid., pp. 88, Table 6, p. 93.

34 Texugo, *Letter*, p. 34; for references from the 1840s, see Coupland, *East Africa and Its Invaders*, pp. 496–8.

35 For the Makua conflicts, see AHU., Cod. 1478, fo. 233, Caetano José Resende to Mendonça, Ibo, 1 September 1811; AHU., Moç., Cx. 55, Mendonça to Resende, Moç., 1 October 1811; AHU., Cod. 1380, fo. 79, same to Galveâs, Moç., 11 December 1811; AHU., Cod. 1385, no. 1116, Aguiar to Mendonça, Rio de Janeiro, 20 May 1812; AHU., Moç., Cx. 57, Manuel Onofre Pantoja to Abreu e Meneses, Ibo, 23 February 1813; ibid., Costa Portugal to same, Ibo, 23 February 1813; AHU., Cod. 1377, fo. 154, Abreu e Meneses to Pantoja, Moç., 12 August 1814. There is a rich body of documentation on the Sakalava raids against the coast of East Central Africa during this decade: see AHU., Moç., Cx. 54, 55, 56, 58, 59, 60, 64, 66, and Cod. 1380, 1394, 1479; BNL., FG., Cod. 8470; Mártires, 'Memoria', fos. 39–42.

36 PRO., CO. 415/9, A. no. 238, Document no. 1, article no. 6; AHU., Cod. 1402, fo. 105, Prov. Govt. to Caldas, Moç., 14 February 1824; Boteler, *Narrative*, vol. II. pp. 55, 64; Owen, *Narrative*, vol. II, pp. 9–10, 14; PRO., CO. 415/7, A. no. 172, pp. 3–4, Acland's Journal no. I, Ibo, 24 June 1826; Sanatana, *Documentaçao*, vol. I, pp. 119, 457.

37 AHU., Cod. 1413, fo. 110, Botelho to José Amanti da Lima, Moç., 2 June 1829; AHU., Cod. 1427, fo. 8, Brito to Bernardes, Moç., 5 October 1830; AHU., Cod. 1207, fo. 91–2, *portaria*, Joaquim Pereira, Moç., 29 August 1840; PRO., FO. 84/1050, FO to McLeod – Slave Trade Draft no. 2, 5 January 1858.

38 PRO., FO. 63/836, McLeod to Malmesbury, Hyde Park, 30 November 1858.

39 Owen, *Narrative*, vol. I, p. 199.

40 Texugo, *Letter*, p. 34.

41 Teixeira Botelho, História, vol. II, pp. 164–5; C. G. L. Sullivan, *Dhow Chasing in Zanzibar Waters and On the Eastern Coast of Africa. Narrative of Five Years' Experience in the Suppression of the Slave Trade* (London

Notes and references to pages 252-5   333

1873), pp. 21-4; PRO., Admiralty 1/5596, T. V. Anson to B. Reynolds, HMS. *Eurydice*, Simon's Bay, 3 March 1849.

42 Jackson, *European Powers*, p. 222; Lyons McLeod, *Travels in Eastern Africa: with the Narrative of a Residence in Mozambique* (2 vols., London 1860), vol. I, pp. 247-9; see also, Bordalo, *Ensaio*, p. 49.

43 PRO., FO. 63/836, McLeod to Sir J. Grey, Mozambique, 2 March 1858; *ACU.*, p.n.o., vol. III (1862), p. 95. See Newitt, 'Angoche, the slave trade and the Portuguese, c. 1844-1910', *Journal of African History*, vol. XIII, no. 4 (1972), pp. 659-72.

44 AHU., Cod. 1385, no. 1074, Galveâs to Mendonça, Rio de Janeiro, 4 June 1811; AHU., Moç., Cx. 55, same to same, Rio de Janeiro, 5 June 1811; AHU., Moç., Cx. 54, Mendonça to Galveâs, Moç., 31 October 1811; AHU., Cod., 1380, fo. 110, Abreu e Meneses to same, Moç., 5 February 1813.

45 AHU., Cod. 1394, fos. 31-2, Brito Sanches to Arcos, Moç., 11 November 1819.

46 Mártires, 'Memoria', fos. 17-18.

47 ibid.

48 AHU., Cod. 1391, no. 1437, and Moç., Cx. 67, Arcos to Brito Sanches, Rio de Janeiro, 2 August 1820; ibid., Brito Sanches to Arcos, Moc., 10 November 1820; AHU., Cod. 1394, fo. 78 and Moç., Cx.67, same to same, Moç., 7 December 1820; ibid., same to same, Moç., 8 and 9 December 1820; Mártires, 'Memoria', fo. 27, also in Rau, 'Aspectos', pp. 142-3. In January 1823, a British naval officer reported that 'The Merchants who had recently gone into the interior to purchase slaves, I was informed, had been murdered, and their goods seized'. Joseph Nourse to Croker, HMS. *Andromache*, At Sea, 5 January 1823, in Theal, *Records*, vol. IX, p. 18.

49 See Santana, *Documentação*, vol. I, p. 169; AHU., Moç., maço 11, Brito to Conde de Basto, Moç., 8 August 1830; AHU., Cod. 1432, fos. 19-20, same to same (?), Moç., 27 October 1830.

50 Santana, *Documentação*, vol. II, p. 381.

51 ibid., vol. II, pp. 625, 756.

52 ibid., vol. II, p. 381.

53 There is a mass of documentation on this subject, much of it presented, in detail in ibid., vol. II; for specific references, see Santana's index.

54 AHU., Cod. 1425, fo. 11, Brito to the Mauruça, Moç., 30 October 1830.

55 AHU., Moç., maço 11, Sousa Ferreira to Brito, Mossuril, 22 and 24 November 1830.

56 ibid., same to same, Mossuril, 25 November 1830.

57 AHU., Cod. 1425, fo. 12, Brito to the Mauruça, Moç., 14 December 1830.

58 AHU., Cod. 1432, fos. 23-4, Brito to Manuel da Silva Gonçalves, Moç., 8 January 1831. The chief of Simuco, or Samuco, was called Nampustamuno, a Makua name, but correspondence to him was translated into Swahili. AHU., Cod. 1425, fos. 26-7, Brito to Chief of Samuco, Moç., 10 August 1831, and fo. 41, Prov. Govt. to same, Moç., 21 August 1832.

59 AHU., Cod. 1440, and unfoliated, Silva Gonçalves to José António Pereira, Moç., 13 and 19 March 1833; ibid., *portaria*, Prov. Govt., Moç., 23 April 1833; ibid., Prov. Govt. to Dez. or Ouv. or Geral, Moç., 23 April 1833; ibid., Silva Gonçalves to Interim Commander of the Mainland, Moç., 3 May 1833.
60 BNL., Cod. 8470, fo. 61, Selimane bin Agy to Prov. Govt., Quitangonha, 1 December 1833; AHU., Cod. 1440, Silva Gonçalves to António de Vasconcelos e Carvalho, Moç., 3 December 1833.
61 ibid., Silva Gonçalves to Pereira, Moç., 25 January 1834.
62 Bordalo, *Ensaio*, p. 37.
63 Owen, *Narrative*, vol. I, p. 192.
64 Bordalo, *Ensaio*, p. 50.
65 Maria José Galvão Mousinho de Albuquerque, *Moçambique, 1896-8* (Lisbon 1934; 1st ed., 1899), p. 61, no. 1, where he gives the date of the Matibane campaign as 1857; cf. Ministério dos Negocios da Marinha e Ultramar, *A Campanha contra os Namarraes. Relatorios enviados ao Ministerio e Secretario d'Estado dos Negocios da Marinha e Ultramar pelo Commissario Regio da Provincia de Moçambique* (Lisbon 1897), p. 5, where Mousinho dates it to 1854, while noting that 'there are no written documents to this point'; *ACU.*, p.n.o., vol. VII (1866), pp. 28-9.
66 Jeronymo Romero, *Supplemento á Memoria Descriptiva e Estatistica do Districto de Cabo Delgado com uma Noticia Ácerca do Estabelecimento da Colonia de Pemba* (Lisbon 1860), pp. 117-19.
67 For a capsule account of McLeod's activities at Mozambique, see Duffy, *A Question of Slavery*, pp. 51-3.
68 McLeod, *Travels in Eastern Africa*, pp. 316-17.
69 Bordalo, *Ensaio*, p. 133.
70 McLeod, *Travels*, I. pp. 317-21; see Duffy, *A Question of Slavery*, pp. 53-4.
71 Frederic J. Elton, *Travels and Researches among the Lakes and Mountains of Eastern & Central Africa*, (ed.) H. B. Cotterill (London 1879), p. 195.
72 ibid., pp. 199-200.
73 ibid., p. 195. Very little is known about the slave trade to Madagascar at this time. The Anglo-Malagasy Treaty|of 1817 specifically prohibited it, but the Malagasy took this to mean only the export of slaves from the island. Treaties aside, in the 1860s perhaps 3000 to 4000 slaves were exported annually to Mauritius, the United States of America, and the West Indies. There was a flourishing system of slavery in Madagascar, the economy of which Mutibwa has described as 'dependent largely on the use of slave labour'. Thus there was a vigorous slave trade until the final imposition of French colonial rule over Madagascar at the end of the nineteenth century. It is important to note, however, that slave labour on Madagascar did not serve only the domestic economy of the island. The Hova hierarchy was deeply involved in commercial agriculture for export, especially in the rice trade to Mauritius, and the entire economy was oriented outward after the early 1860s. Like the slave trade to Zanzibar,

then, that to Madagascar cannot be dismissed simply as the product of an anomalous Arab or Malagasy slave economy, but must also be seen in the context of Madagascar's becoming an economic satellite of the West. See Phares M. Mutibwa, 'Patterns of Trade and Economic Development in Nineteenth Century Madagascar', *Transafrican Journal of History*, vol. II, no. 1 (1972), pp. 37–40, 51, 59, n. 12. For another source on the volume of this slave trade, see Captain Colomb, *Slave-Catching in the Indian Ocean. A Record of Naval Experiences* (London 1873). According to Colomb, the general term for African slaves at Madagascar was 'Mozambiques'. ibid., p. 309. More specifically, Elton writes:

> That there are thousands of Makua slaves on the west coast of Madagascar, and that they are sold and bartered to the Hovas for service is a matter of notoriety to everybody who knows Mozambique and anything about the Sakalava, whose principal trade consists in the purchasing of the slaves from the dhows and re-selling them to their neighbours.

Elton, *Travels*, p. 162; see also, Hubert Descamps, *Histoire de Madagascar*, 2nd ed. (Paris 1961), pp. 87, 295, map 12.

74 Elton, *Travels*, pp. 145, 196–9, also 215; cf. Daniel J. Rankin, *Arab Tales translated from the Swahili language into the Túgulu Dialect of the Mákua Language, as spoken in the Immediate Vicinity of Mozambique. Together with comparative vocabularies of five dialects of the Makua language* (London, n.d.), p. xii; O'Neill, 'Journey from Mozambique to Lakes Shirwa and Amaramba', *Proceedings of the Royal Geographical Society*, vol. VI (1884), pp. 643, 735.

75 The name *namarral* (pl. *namarrais*), the etymology of which I have been unable to ascertain, was given to the Makua confederacy headed by chief Mucutomuno, whose aggressive behaviour first made an impression at Mozambique in about 1875 or 1876. Mello Machado identifies the *namarrais* as Central Makua and gives their localities as Monapo, Quixaxe, and Mossuril. During the later eighteenth century, the stronghold of Mucutomuno was Cambira, in the same general country to the west of Mossuril and northwest of Mutomunho as Monapo. So although all sources agree that they were recent arrivals in the immediate coastal strip opposite Mozambique Island, they may only have shifted their centre of activities coastward in the last quarter of the nineteenth century, rather than having come from the far interior. See O'Neill, 'Journey from Mozambique', pp. 632–3; A. J. de Mello Machado, *Entre os Macuas de Angoche – Historiando Moçambique* (Lisbon 1970), p. 111, maps facing pp. 16 and 61, and Table 1, facing p. 112; see E. Alpers, *Ivory and Slaves in East Central Africa* (London 1975), Chapter 5, p. 153; António Camizão, *Indicações Geraes sobre a Capitania-Mór de Mossuril – Governo de Moçambique: Appendice ao Relatorio de 1 de Janeiro de 1901*. (Mozambique 1901), p. 16; cf. Nancy Jane Hafkin, 'Trade, Society, and Politics in Northern Mozambique, *c.* 1753–1913' (Unpublished Ph.D. thesis, Boston University 1973), pp. 365–9. For a full account of local resistance to the

imposition of Portuguese colonial rule, see ibid., Chapter 11.
76 ACL., Azul Ms. 847, fo. 10.
77 AHU., Cod. 1394, fo. 16, Brito Sanches to Arcos, Moç., 10 October 1819; for passing references to the Yao, see AHU., Moç., Cx. 59, *requerimento*, Muhamad Hasan, n.d., with enclosure, Moç., 12 August 1815; AHU., Cod. 1380, fos. 235-6, Prov. Govt. to Arcos, Moç., 19 February 1819.
78 Mártires, 'Memoria', fos. 27, 63, also in Virgínia Rau, 'Aspectos étnico-culturais da ilha de Moçambique em 1822', *Studia*, vol. II (1963), pp. 143-4, 158-9.
79 Eugène de Froberville, 'Notes sur les moeurs, coutumes et traditions des amakoua, sur le commerce et la traite des esclaves dans l'Afrique Orientale', *Bulletin de la Société de Géographie*, 3ᵉ Série, vol. VIII (1847), pp. 323-4, and n. 1. For kidnapping and caravan protection, see J. Lewis Krapf, *Travels, Researches, and Missionary Labours, during an Eighteen Years' Residence in Eastern Africa* (London 1860), pp. 423-5.
80 See Santana, *Documentação*, vol. I, pp. 163, 300-1.
81 Manuel Joaquim Mendes de Vasconcelos e Cirne, *Memoria sobre a Provincia de Moçambique*, Ministério dos Negócios da Marinha e Ultramar, Documentos para a História das Colónais Portuguezes (Lisbon 1890), p. 6.
82 Botelho, *Memoria*, p. 311, but see also p. 389; cf. anonymous article, 'Botelho *on the Portuguese Colonies*', *The Edinburgh Review, or Critical Journal*, vol. LXIV (1837), p. 421. For Botelho's retort, see his *Segunda Parte da Memoria Estatistica sobre os Dominios Portuguezes na África Oriental* (Lisbon 1837), p. 59. See also, Texugo, *Letter*, pp. 34-5.
83 Bemposta Subserra, 'Resumo sôbre a Província de Moçambique', *Boletim da Sociedade de Geografia de Lisboa*, vol. LV, pp. 7-8 (1937), p. 303.
84 Manuel Joaquim Mendes de Vasconcelos e Cirne, *Memoria sobre a Província de Mocambique*, Ministério dos Negócios da Marinha e Ultramar, Documentos para a História das Colónias Portuguezes (Lisbon 1890), p. 41; John Rebman, *Dictionary of the Kiniassa Language* (ed.) L. Krapf (St Chrischona 1877), pp. iv-v; for the Wapogera, see Cullen T. Young, *Notes on the History of the Tumbuka-Kamanga Peoples of the Northern Province of Nyasaland* (London 1932), pp. 25-6.
85 Livingstone, *Narrative*, pp. 125-6, 363, 496-7; Peirone, *O Tribo Ajaua*, p. 25; *ACU.*, p.n.o., vol. III (1862), p. 87.
86 PRO., FO. 63/836, McLeod to Malmesbury, Hyde Park, 30 November 1858.
87 Gastão de Sousa Dias, (ed.), *Silva Porto e a Travessia do Continente Africano* (Lisbon 1938), pp. 148-66 and map at end.
88 In the early 1860s the ivory exported through the customs-house at Mozambique rose dramatically from less than half that handled at Zanzibar in 1859 to almost three times that total (see p. 265 in this book). This rise seems to have been stimulated as part of a concerted official effort to replace the slave trade with 'legitimate' commerce, and was marked by gradually rising prices that were at this time below those obtaining at

Zanzibar. These favourable prices may have attracted Indian and European ivory merchants back to Mozambique. From the available statistics, however, it is quite clear that most of this ivory was coming from Quelimane, Inhambane, and Lourenço Marques. In particular, the enormous rise in exports in 1863 was attributed to the opening up of 'the vast hinterland between Inhambane and Lourenço Marques'. Only at Quelimane was there a direct impact on the trade of East Central Africa, and by 1890 the Yao were major traders there. For the 1861-3 ivory figures and prices, see *ACU.*, p.n.o., vol. III (1862), pp. 85-8; ibid., vol. VII (1866), p. 57. For prices at Zanzibar, again see Sheriff, 'Rise of a Commercial Empire', p. 469, Graph II.

89   ANTT., Junta do Comércio, maço 62, n.º d'ordem 122, report on the trade of Mozambique by António José Baptista de Sala, Lisboa, 24 May 1824.
90   Gamitto, *King Kazembe*, vol. II, p. 197.
91   David Livingstone, *Missionary Travels and Researches in South Africa* (New York 1858), p. 680.
92   *ACU.*, p.n.o., vol. V (1864), p. 14.
93   See, for example, AHU., Moç., Cx. 60, Aguiar to Conde de Sarzedas, Rio de Janeiro, 25 January 1816; AHU., Moç., Cx. 66, *requerimento* of twelve Banyan traders, [Moç.], n.d., but *c.* 1817; AHU., Moç., Cx. 63, Arcos to Cavalcanti de Albuquerque, Rio de Janeiro, 4 July 1818; AHU., Moç., Cx. 64, Cardenas to Governor, Moç., 27 September 1819; A.H.U., Cod. 1402, fo. 41, Prov. Govt. to Simião and António José Segundo, Moç., 6 November 1821; AHU., Cod. 1413, fo. 8, João Faustino da Costa to José António Marcelino Pereira, Moç., 26 July 1827; ibid., fo. 105. Botelho to Silva, Moç., 6 May 1829; AHU., Moç., maço 11, petition of Lauchande Cancadas, granted, Moç., 18 October 1830; AHU., Cod. 1445, no. 2117 (or 2108), António Abrucísio Jarvis de Atongonia to Governor of Mozambique, Paço do Ramalhão, 12 September 1835; Botelho, Sebastião Xavier. *Memoria Estatistica sobre os Dominios Portuguezes na Africa Oriental* (Lisbon 1835), p. 376 and *Resumo para servir de introducção a Memoria Estatistica sobre os dominios portuguezes na Africa Oriental* (Lisbon 1834), pp. 11-14; Texugo, *Letter*, pp. 38-9, 41; Santana, *Documentação*, vol. II, p. 482.
94   See O'Neill, 'On the Coast Lands', p. 602, for reference to the growth of coastal trade in oilseeds, rubber, ivory, copra, and wax 'in the hands of these subjects of British and Portuguese India, and the complete web which has been woven upon it by them'.
95   J. M. Gray, *History of Zanzibar from the Middle Ages to 1856* (London 1962), pp. 194-6; Sheriff, 'Rise of a commercial empire', especially chapter 4; Nicholls, C. S. *The Swahili Coast - Politics, Diplomacy and Trade on the East African Littoral, 1798-1856*, St Antony's Publications no. 2 (London 1971), chapter 12; Alpers, *Ivory and Slaves in East Central Africa*, chapter 3, p. 87.
96   ANF., Affaires Étrangères BIII 438, Ladislas Cochet, 'Importations et exportations de principales merchandises en 1856', Zanzibar, 2 January

1857; cf. Nicholls, *Swahili Coast*, p. 371. See also, Norman R. Bennett and George E. Brooks, Jr. (eds.), *New England Merchants in Africa, A History through Documents, 1802 to 1865* (Boston 1965), pp. 246, n. 83, 385.

97 Nicholls, *Swahili Coast*, pp. 370–71. The most authoritative analysis of the ivory trade at Zanzibar is Sheriff, 'Rise of a Commercial Empire'.
98 Richard Francis Burton, *Zanzibar; City, Island and Coast*, 2nd vol. London 1872), pp. 510–11.
99 James Prior, *Voyage along the Eastern Coast of Africa, to Mosambique, Johanna, and Quiloa; . . . in the Nisus Frigate* (London 1819), pp. 80, 64; cf. W. H. Smyth, *The Life and Service of Captain Philip Beaver, late of Her Majesty's Ship Nisus* (London 1829), p. 279.
100 See AHU., Cod. 1374, fos. 96–7, Caldas to Abreu e Meneses, Ibo, 3 December 1816; AHU., Cod. 1377, fo. 210, Cavalcanti de Albuquerque to Sultan of Kilwa, Moç., 29 March 1817; AHU., Moç., Cx. 60, Sultan of Tungio to Caldas, Tungui, 24 May 1817; ibid., Caldas to Cavalcanti de Albuquerque, Ibo, 13 November 1817; BNL., FG., Cod. 8470, fo. 71. Salimo Bono Sahi Bono Saude Usaiude Seleman to Governor of Mozambique, Zanzibar (?), n.d., but c. 1817–18; Freeman-Grenville, *The East African Coast – Select Documents from the First to the Earlier Nineteenth Century* (Oxford 1962), pp. 224, 198–9; TNA., Mafia District Book; Fortuné Albrand, 'Extrait d'un Mémoire sur Zanzibar et sur Quiloa', *Bulletin de la Société de Géographie*, 2ᵉ Serie, vol. X (1838), p. 82; Nicholls, *Swahili Coast*, pp. 130–1; Kent, *Early Kingdoms in Madagascar*, 1500–1700 (New York 1970), p. 297.
101 Albrand, 'Extrait', pp. 81, 75; also Nicholls, *Swahili Coast*, p. 213.
102 See BM., Add. Ms. 41, 265, vol. V, fos. 3–6, R. T. Farquhar to Imam of Muscat (*sic*), Port Louis, 10 May 1821; ibid., fos. 7–8, same to Marquis of Hastings, Port Louis, 11 May 1821; ibid., fos. 67–70, 'Memorandum connected with the final Suppression of the Slave Trade on the *East* Coast of Africa', c. December 1821; PRO., CO. 415/7, A. no. 171, pp. 1–5, 16–19, 'Observations by Captain Owen on the Slave Trade in August 1824 . . . with Dorval's remarks thereon, 30 May 1827', articles 1–6; ibid., A. no. 172, pp. 5–8, 17–20, 25–9.
103 Santana, *Documentação*, vol. II, p. 784.
104 G. S. P. Freeman-Grenville, *Select Documents* pp. 224–5; Boteler, *Narrative*, vol. II, p. 47.
105 Nicholls, *Swahili Coast*, p. 86.
106 Freeman-Grenville, 'The Coast', p. 131.
107 See chapter 5, p. 164 in this book.
108 Hamerton's letter is quoted in Gray, 'A History of Kilwa: Part II', p. 35.
109 See Nicholls, *Swahili Coast*, p. 215; Sheriff, 'Rise of a Commercial Empire', p. 171.
110 Krapf, *Travels*, p. 423.
111 Burton, *The Lake Regions of Central Africa* (New York 1861), vol. II, p. 377.
112 Norman R. Bennett, and George E. Brooks, Jr. (eds.), *New England Merchants in Africa, A History through Documents, 1802 to 1865* (Boston

1965), p. 479.
113 Krapf, *Travels*, p. 424.
114 See, for example, Santana, *Documentação*, vol. II, pp. 835, 881.
115 Bennett and Brooks, *New England Merchants*, p. 502.
116 Burton, *Zanzibar*, vol. II, p. 347.
117 Elton, *Travels*, chapter 2. For still another major work on the suppression of the East African slave trade from this time, see François Renault, *Lavigerie, l'Esclavage africain et l'Europe, 1868-1892* (Paris 1971).
118 C. E. B. Russell (ed.), *General Rigby, Zanzibar and the Slave Trade* (London 1935), pp. 333, 352.
119 Quoted in Coupland, *The Exploitation of East Africa, 1856*-1890 (London 1939), p. 140, from the Report of the Select Committee of 1871.
120 Carl Claus von der Decken, *Reisen in Ost-Afrika in der Jahren 1859 bis 1865*, (ed.) O. Kersten (Leipzig and Heidelberg 1869), vol. I, book 2; David Livingstone, *Last Journals* (ed.) Horace Waller (2 vols., London 1874), vol. 1, pp. 70, 79.
121 Richard Francis Burton, *The Lands of Cazembe: Lacerda's Journey to Cazembe in 1798* (London 1873) pp. 37, 39, footnotes only.
122 Burton, *Lake Regions*, vol. II, p. 376, and *Zanzibar*, vol. II, pp. 346-7.
123 Carl Claus von der Decken, *Reisen in Ost-Afrika in der Jahren 1859 bis 1861* (ed.) Otto Kersten (4 vols. Leipzig and Heidelberg 1869), vol. 1.
124 Petro Kilekwa, *Slave Boy to Priest: The Autobiography of Padre Petro Kilekwa*, trans. from Cinyanja by K. H. Nixon Smith (London 1937), p. 9; A. C. Madan, *Kiungani* (Zanzibar 1886), pp. 14-23, 33-4; Rashid bin Hassani, 'The Story of Rashid bin Hassani of the Bisa Tribe, Northern Rhodesia', recorded by W. F. Baldock, in Margery Perham (ed.), *Ten Africans*, (London 1936), pp. 92-5.
125 Colomb, *Slave-Catching*, pp. 28-30; John Hanning Speke, *Journal of Discovery of the Source of the Nile* (London 1863), p. 7.
126 James Mbotela, *Uhuru wa Watumwa* (Nairobi 1967; 1st ed., London 1934), p. 10. There is an English translation available as *The Freeing of the Slaves in East Africa*, but I was unable to obtain it when writing this section. Madan, *Kiungani*, p. 46.
127 Colomb, *Slave-Catching*, p. 29; Madan, *Kiungani*, pp. 30, 51, 56; African Studies Association Oral Data Archives, Archive of Traditional Music, Indiana University, Bloomington: Allen F. Isaacman Collection, interviews with Capachika Chúau, 10 October 1968 (Translated Tape no. 14, side no. 2; Edited Tape no. 11, side no. 1) and Chiponda Cavumbula, 16 October 1968 (TT. no. 15 [2]; ET. no. 11 [2]), both conducted in the region of Makanga.
128 Isaacman Collection, joint interview with Chetambara Chenungo and Wilson John, 15 October 1968 (TT. no. 15 [2]; ET. no. 11 [2]), and interview with Chiponda Cavumbula: Madan, *Kiungani*, p. 39.
129 Colomb, *Slave-Catching*, p. 28.
130 Yohannah B. Abdallah, *The Yaos*, Arranged, edited, and translated by M. Sanderson (Zomba 1919) p. 31.
131 Isaacman Collection, interviews with Simon Biwi, 10 October 1968, region

of Makanga (TT. no. 14 [2]; ET. no. 11 [1]), Capachika Chúau, and Chiponda Cavumbula; joint interviews with Calavina Couche and Zabuca Ngombe, 14 October 1968, region of Makanga (TT. no. 15 [1]; ET. no. 11 [2]), and Chetambara Chinungo and Wilson John; Rashid bin Hassani, 'The Story of Rashid bin Hassani of the Bisa Tribe, Northern Rhodesia', p. 91; Abdallah, *The Yaos*, p. 32.

132   Madan, Kiungani, pp. 24, 34, 36; Kilekwa, *Slave Boy*, p. 13; Rashid bin Hassani, 'Story', p. 98.

133   For slave prices, see, for example, Steere, *The Universities' Mission to Central Africa. A Speech delivered at Oxford* (London 1875), pp. 8–9; and cf. Colomb, *Slave-Catching*, pp. 55–9. For prices at the coast, see Nicholls, *Swahili Coast*, pp. 201–2, 209–11, 216–17. For an example of an Arab who was trading for slaves on credit, and the way in which this affected a young Makua when agents of the money-lender came to collect on the Arab's debt, see Madan, *Kiungani*, p. 40.

134   Isaacman Collection, interviews with Capachika Chúau and Chiponda Cavumbula. It is not at all clear what is meant by a *peça* here. According to Burton, *Zanzibar*, vol. II, p. 419, 'The Takah or piece varies greatly. That of "Merikani", American domestics, is generally of 30 yards.' He also notes that the *taka* ranges down to twenty yards of cloth. This would indicate an unusually high price for slaves among the Chewa of Makanga. If, however, a *peça* is taken to indicate a *doti* of either two yards of wide cloth or four yards of narrow, then the price of a slave in Makanga, while still high, is within the range of prices cited by Abdallah and others.

135   Abdallah, *The Yaos*, pp. 31–2; Kilekwa, *Slave Boy*, p. 10; Madan, *Kiungani*, p. 46.

136   ibid., p. 34.

137   See Alpers, *Ivory and Slaves in East Central Africa*, chapter 1, pp. 5–6;

138   Froberville, 'Notes sur les Va-Ngindo', *Bulletin de la Société de Géographie*, 4e Série, vol. III (1852), pp. 426–7.

139   See TNA., Masasi District Book, 'The Ekoni Clan (Makua Tribe) of Masasi-District', trans. of an article in Swahili by Marko Gwaja in *Mambo Leo* (June 1936); TNA., Secretariat 42186, 'Preliminary Report', p. 9.

140   See also Isaacman, *Mozambique*, pp. 89–90.

Select bibliography

Afigbo, A. E., 'Trade and trade routes in nineteenth-century Nsukka', *Journal of the Historical Society of Nigeria*, vol. VII, no. 1 (December 1973).
Ajayi, J. F. Ade and Smith, Robert, *Yoruba Warfare in the Nineteenth Century*, 2nd ed., Ibadan 1971.
Akinjogbin, I. A., *Dahomey and its Neighbours, 1708-1818* Cambridge 1967.
Amin, Samir, 'Underdevelopment and dependence in Black Africa - their historical origins and contemporary forms', *Social and Economic Studies*, vol. XXII, no. 1 (1973).
Anstey, Roger, *The Atlantic Slave Trade and British Abolition, 1760-1810* London 1975.
Arhin, Kwame, 'The structure of Greater Ashanti, 1700-1824', *Journal of African History*, vol. VIII (1967).
Austen, Ralph A., 'The trans-Saharan slave trade: a tentative census', in Henry A. Gemery and Jan S. Hogendorn (eds.), *The Uncommon Market: Essays in the Economic History of the Atlantic Slave Trade*, New York 1979, pp. 23-76.

Beachy, R. W., *The Slave Trade of Eastern Africa*, London 1976.
Birmingham, David, *Trade and Conflict in Angola: The Mbundu and Their Neighbours under the Influence of the Portuguese, 1483-1790*, Oxford 1966.
Boahen, A. Adu, 'The coming of the Europeans (c. 1440-1700)', in A. Adu Boahen, *et al*, (eds.), *The Horizon History of Africa*, New York 1971, pp. 305-27.
Boserup, Ester, *The Conditions of Agricultural Growth: The Economics of Agrarian Change Under Population Pressure*, London 1965.

Curtin, P. D., *Economic Change in Precolonial Africa: Senegambia in the era of the Slave Trade*, Madison 1975.

Daaku, K. Y., 'The Slave Trade and African Society,' in T. O. Ranger, (ed.), *Emerging Themes of African History*, London 1968.
Daget, Serge, 'British repression of the illegal French slave trade: some considerations', in Gemery and Hogendorn (eds.), *The Uncommon Market*, pp. 419-42.
Davidson, Basil, *Black Mother: Africa, The Years of Trial*, London 1961.

Dike, K. O., *Trade and politics in the Niger Delta 1830-5: An Introduction to the Economic and Political History of Nigeria*, Oxford 1956.

Eltis, David, 'The Export of Slaves from Africa, 1821-43', *Journal of Economic History*, vol. XXXVII, no. 2 (1977).

Fage, J. D., *A History of Africa*, London 1978.

Fisher, Allan G. B., and Fisher, Humphrey J., *Slavery and Muslim Society in Africa: The Institution in Sudanic Africa and the Trans-Saharan Trade*, London 1970.

Fynn, J. K., *Asante and its neighbours 1700-1807*, London 1971.

Gemery, Henry A. and Hogendorn, Jan S., 'The economic costs of West African participation in the Atlantic slave trade: a preliminary sampling for the eighteenth century', in Gemery and Hogendorn (eds.), *The Uncommon Market*, New York 1979, pp. 143-61.

Graham, J. D., 'The slave trade, depopulation and human sacrifice in Benin history', *Cahiers d'Etudes Africaines*, vol. V (1965).

Henige, David and Johnson, Marion, 'Agaja and the slave trade: another look at the evidence', *History in Africa*, vol. III (1976).

Hopkins, A. G., 'Economic imperialism in West Africa: Lagos, 1880-92', *Economic History Review*, vol. XXI (1968).

Hunwick, J. O., 'Black Africans in the Islamic world: an under-studied dimension of the black diaspora', *Tarikh*, vol. V, no. 4 (1978).

Igbafe, Philip A., 'Slavery and emancipation in Benin, 1897-1945', *Journal of African History*, vol. XVI, no. 3 (1975).

Inikori, J. E., 'Slave Trade: A Retardative Factor in West African Economic Development, 1451-1870', in Mahdi Adamu (ed.), *Economic History of the Central Savanna of West Africa*, Zaria, forthcoming.

Inikori, J. E., 'The Origin of the Diaspora: The Slave Trade from Africa', *Tarikh*, vol. V, no. 4 (1978).

Klein, Martin, 'Social and economic factors in the Muslim revolution in Senegambia', *Journal of African History*, vol. XIII, no. 3 (1972).

Klein, Martin, and Lovejoy, Paul E., 'Slavery in West Africa', in Gemery and Hogendorn (eds.), *The Uncommon Market*, pp. 181-212.

Latham, A. J. H., *Old Calabar 1600-1891: The Impact of the International Economy upon a traditional Society*, Oxford 1973.

Law, R. C. C., *The Oyo Empire c. 1600-c. 1836: A West African Imperialism in the Era of the Atlantic Slave Trade*, Oxford 1977.

Law, R. C. C., 'Royal Monopoly and Private Enterprise in the Atlantic Trade: The Case of Dahomey,' *Journal of African History*, vol. XVIII, no. 4 (1977).

LeVeen, Phillip E., 'The African slave supply response', *African Studies Review*, vol. XVIII, no. 1 (1975).
Lovejoy, Paul E., and Hogendorn, Jan S., 'Slave Marketing in West Africa', in Gemery and Hogendorn (eds.), *The Uncommon Market*, pp. 213-35.

Martin, Phyllis M., *The External Trade of the Loango Coast 1576-1870*, Oxford 1972.

Richards, W. A., 'The Import of Firearms into West Africa in the eighteenth century', *Journal of African History*, vol. XXI, no. 1 (1980).
Rodney, Walter, *A History of the Upper Guinea Coast, 1545-1800*, Oxford 1970.
Rodney, Walter, *How Europe Underdeveloped Africa*, Dar es Salaam 1972.
Ryder, A. F. C., *Benin and the Europeans, 1485-1897*, London 1969.

Wallerstein, Immanuel, 'The three stages of African involvement in the world-economy', in Peter C. W. Gutkind and Immanuel Wallerstein (eds.), *The Political Economy of Contemporary Africa*, Beverly Hills 1976, pp. 30-57.
Wilks, Ivor, 'The Mossi and Akan states to 1800', in J. F. Ade Ajayi and Michael Crowder (eds.), *History of West Africa*, 2nd ed., vol. I, London, 1976.
Wilks, Ivor, *Asante in the Nineteenth Century: The Structure and Evolution of a Political Order*, Cambridge 1975.
Wrigley, C. C., 'Historicism in Africa: slavery and state formation', *African Affairs*, vol. 70 (1971).

Index

abolition of slavery, 243-51, 257-8
Adewale, T. S., 181, 311-12
age of slaves, 22, 24, 59, 225, 229-32, 237-40, 324
agriculture, commercialized, 17-18, 31, 44, 205; *see also* commodity trade; economic development
Akinjogbin, I. A., 162, 284, 307, 314, 341
Al-Bakri, 76-7, 81, 289
Allison, P., 177, 311
Al-Omari, 77, 289, 291
Alpers, E., 26, 242, 275, 279
analysis of slavery, 155-6
Angola, 22-3, 73, 221-41; firearms to, 152-3
Anstey, R., 20, 341
Arab trade, 156, 298-9; *see also* Muslim
Arhin, K., 46, 283, 341
aristocratic slavery, 74-90
Ashanti wars, 46
Atlantic slave trade: and East Africa, 242-73; effect on West African societies, 187-201; and Oyo Yoruba, 167-86; and Upper Guinea Coast, 61-73
Austen, R., 20-22, 278, 341

Baol, 92, 107-25
barbarism hypothesis, 45-7
Barbot, J., 169, 173, 306-10
Barry, B., 106, 108
Battell, A., 204, 316
Bazin, J., 86, 293
Beachy, R. W., 27, 279, 341

Becker, C., 100, 284
Benin, 22-3, 75, 158, 162, 167-9, 172-3, 306; commodity trade, 40; firearms to, 138, 142-3, 145; wars in, 288
Bethell, L., 247, 330
Biobaku, S. O., 50, 182, 312
Bocarro, G., 273
Bohannan, P., 206, 317
Bonnafe, P., 97-8, 296
Bonny, 22-3; firearms to, 138-9, 142-7, 151
Bordalo, F. M., 244, 256, 334
Boserup, E., 17, 275, 341
Bosman, W., 191-2, 196, 308-9, 314-15
Boutiller, J. L., 94, 294
Bowen, T. J., 71, 308
Bradbury, R. E., 173
Brazil, slave export to, 21, 26, 223, 226-38, 242-52, 277, 321-2, 328
British: abolitionists, 243-51, 257-8; firearms from, 126-53; slave trade, 114, 117, 191-3, 202, 211-14, 277-8
Burton, R., 268, 278, 338-9

Calabar, 22-3; firearms to, 138, 140, 142-3, 145, 151-2
Caldwell, J. C., 29-33, 173, 177-81, 280-1
Cameroon, firearms to, 138, 140, 142-3, 145, 152
Canot, Captain, 67, 69-70, 287-8
capacity of ships, 225-30, 236, 239-40, 323, 328
Capiteyn, J. E., 198

346 *Index*

Carreira, A., 235–6, 327
children *see* age of slaves
Clapperton, H., 169, 308, 311–13
climatic change, 17, 30
clothes for slaves, 233
colonial period: in Sahelo-Sudanic Africa, 91–4; trade, reorganization of, 125; *see also* British; Danish; Dutch; French; Portuguese; Spanish commodity trade, 36, 39–41, 53–8, 314, 328, 336; in Angola, 234; in East Africa, 242–4, 250, 263–6; in Guinea, 40–1, 64; lack of, 94–9; in Loango 202–10; Sahelo-Sudanic 80, 83–5, 93, 96–7; in Senegal, 124; in West Africa, 40, 189–90, 198; *see also* firearms
Congo, firearms to, 138, 140, 142–3, 145, 152–3
currency, 205–6
Curtin, J. C., 19–21, 29, 47, 50, 160–61, 187, 222–4, 276, 281, 284, 306, 313, 321, 341

Dahomey, 94, 96, 165, 171–7, 194–5; human sacrifice in, 48–9, 284
Dalzel, A., 176, 306–7, 310–11
Damel, 101–25
Danish slave trade, 134, 140, 145
Dapper, O., 169, 308, 317, 320
Davenport, W., 138–9, 150–3
De Almada, A., 64–5, 287–9
death *see* mortality
de Mondevit, S., 273
Degranpré, L., 211–13, 319–20
Delafoss, M., 84
demographic impact of slave trade, 16–38; in Angola, 221–2; in Senegal, 119; in West Africa, 155, 160–3, 199–200, 291, 295; *see also* numbers of slaves
Dike, K. O., 13, 40, 275, 282, 342
disease, 17, 30, 257
domestic slavery, 61–73
Dorval, C., 249–50

Dutch slave trade, 134, 171, 192–3, 202–4, 208–14, 232

East Africa, 242–73; commodity trade in, 242–4, 250, 263–6
economic development and slave trade, 14–16, 34–6, 51–60; in Loango, 202–20; in Sahelo-Sudanic area 74–99; in Senegal, 119–20; in West Africa, 154, 159, 162–3
Eltis, D., 21, 342
Elton, F., 259, 334–5, 339
empires, Sahelo-Sudanic, 76–83
endemic nature of slavery, 154–66; *see also* internal slavery
English *see* British

Fage, J. D., 25–9, 39, 41, 47–8, 55, 57, 62, 70, 154, 175, 279–85, 289, 310, 342
Falconbridge, A., 135, 303
female slaves *see* sex of slaves
Fernandes, V., 63–4, 287–8
firearms trade, 51, 113, 116, 126–53, 195–6, 214–15, 301–6
Fisher, A. G., and H. J., 41, 282, 294, 342
Flint, J. E., 163, 307
focus and analytical framework of discussion, 14–19
food for slaves, 93
Freeman-Grenville, G. S. P., 267, 338
French slave trade: and colonialism, 91; in East Africa, 147, 250–1, 254; and firearms, 134; in Loango, 202, 211–16; in Senegal, 107, 112–18; in West Africa, 191, 193

Gabon, 22–3
Gambia, 22–3, 150
Gamitto, A. C. P., 264, 337
Ghana, 34–5, 76, 84–5
gifts, 123
Gold Coast, 22–3, 72, 157–8, 163,

188–201; firearms to, 138, 140, 142–3, 150
Guinea coast, 37–41, 61–73, 94, 157–9, 164; commodity trade on, 40–1, 64
guns *see* firearms

Hatch, W. R., 173, 310
history *see* slave trade
Hopkins, A. G., 50, 53, 190, 283–5, 314–15

Ibn Batuta, 81, 291
Igbafe, P. A., 45, 283, 342
Indians of Mozambique, 264–5
indigenous slavery *see* internal slavery
industrial development, lack of, 14–16, 56
Inikori, J. E., 21, 126, 276, 281, 285, 342
internal consequences of slave trade *see* economic development; social structure
internal slavery, 38–45, 61–73; *see also* endemic nature of slavery
Irving, W., 131
Isert, P. E., 196, 315
Islam *see* Muslims
Ivory Coast, 94

Jobson, R., 72, 289
Johnson, S., 168, 183, 308, 310, 312

Kayor, 91, 100–25
Kilwa, 265–9
kingdoms *see* empires
Kjekshus, H., 46, 283
Klein, H., 220
Klein, M., 42–4, 50, 52, 91, 93, 282–3, 285, 291, 294, 322, 342
Krapf, J. L., 268

Lander, R., and J., 168, 177–81, 186, 307, 311–13

land-scarce societies, 17–18
land-surplus societies, 17–18, 31, 39, 56, 99
Latham, A. J., 45, 275, 283, 285, 342
Law, R. C., 306–9
LeVeen, P. E., 50, 284, 343
Levine, D., 18, 276
Loango Coast: commodity trade, 202–10; firearms trade, 135, 138–40, 142–3, 145; slavery in, 202–20
loans, 112
Lovejoy, P., 42–3, 283, 342–3
Lugard, F. D., 38, 282

McLeod, L., 251–2, 257–8, 334
Macuana, 252–60
Madagascar, 259, 334–5
Makua of Macuana, 252–60
male slaves *see* sex of slaves
Mali, 77, 80–81, 85
Mannix, P., 62, 71
Martin, P. M., 139, 202, 275, 303, 343
Martin, V., 100, 284
Masina, 87–9
Mauny, R., 20–1, 156, 161, 278, 289, 306
medicine, 33
Meillassoux, C., 39, 41–2, 50, 74, 289–90, 292, 294–5
merchant cities, 83–91
Milburn, W., 245, 329
military states, 41–51, 74–99; *see also* war
Monteil, C., 85, 162, 292–3, 306
Moors *see* Arabs; Muslims
Moroccan invation, 78–9, 85
mortality of slaves, 26–7, 32–3, 232, 280, 330
Morton-Williams, P., 167
Mossi, 79–81
Mossuril, Yao trade to, 260–4
Mosto, C., 96
Mozambique, 26–7, 243–65

348 Index

Muslim slave trade, 20–5, 59, 106–7, 122–3; *see also* Arabs

neighbouring communities, relations with, 122–5
Nigeria, 31, 35, 40, 44–5, 73, 167–87, 285
Norris, R., 155, 306, 310
North Africa, 78–9, 84–5
numbers of slaves exported, 19–38; from East Africa, 245–50, 261, 266–9; from Sahelo-Sudanic area, 94–5; from Senegal, 107–12; from West Africa, 321–2; *see also* demographic impact
Nyasa, 40–1, 269–73

Ormond, J., 69
Oyo Yoruba, 41, 167–86

Pachecho Pareira, D., 158, 306, 311
Park, M., 64, 71–2, 78, 287–8
Parrinder, E. G., 171, 308–9, 311
plague, 17, 30
political consequences of slave trade, 45–51, 59; *see also* social structure
population *see* demographic change; numbers of slaves
Protuguese slave trade: in Angola, 221–41; in East Africa, 243–74; and firearms, 134; in Guinea, 64, 68, 71–3; in Loango, 202–3, 208–16; in West Africa, 157–8, 189
Postma, J., 188, 278–9, 313, 327
price *see* value
proletarianization, 18
punishment of slaves, 71, 98, 164

Rattray, R. S., 62, 70, 155, 306
Rebman, J., 263
Richards, W. A., 126, 343
rights of slaves, 62, 155–6
Rinchon, P. D., 61, 70
Roberts, J., 137
Robertson, G. A., 168, 307, 310

Rodney, W., 38–9, 41–2, 61, 157, 275, 282, 306
Romero, J., 256, 334
Ronen, D., 48–9, 284
Rouch, J., 77, 289–90
Rout Jr, C. B., 19–21, 276
Ryder, A. F., 158, 306, 343

sacrifice, human, 48–9, 284
Sahelo-Sudanic Africa, 39, 74–99
savagery hypothesis, 45–7
Say's Law, 53, 285
Segu, 86–7, 89
Senegal, 31, 51, 92, 94, 100–125
Senegambia, 64, 72, 75, 91; firearms to, 138–40, 142–3, 145, 150
sex of slaves, 22–5, 31, 59, 148–50, 238, 272, 327; in Sahelo-Sudanic area, 82, 89–90; in West Africa, 161
share-cropping, 44
Shaw, T., 29–30, 280
Shelburne, Lord, 130, 134, 141
Sierra Leone, 40, 62, 91; firearms to, 138–40, 142–3, 145, 150
'slave coast', 188–201 *passim*
'slave towns', 66–7
slave trade: from Angola, 221–41; from East Central Africa, 242–73; introduction to, 13–60; from Loango, 202–20; and Oyo Yoruba, 167–86; in Sahelo-Sudanic Africa, 74–99; from Senegal, 100–125; from Upper Guinea, 61–73; from West Africa, 154–66, 187–201
Snelgrave, W., 172–4, 309–10, 312
social oppression, 61–73
social structure and slave trade, 100–2, 120–2, 187–202, 210–20; *see also* political consequences
Senegal, 100–25
Spanish slave trade, 20–25, 59, 64, 277
state slavery, 74–99 *passim*
Stein, R., 21
Sudan, 39, 41, 62, 74–99, 156, 159

taxes, 113-14, 120, 180, 214, 234-5, 263
Tegn, 101-25
Terray, E., 97, 295-6
time of sea journey, 322
trade *see* Atlantic trade; commodity trade; slave trade
transport, 15, 34-6

United States, slave export to, 32-3, 90, 155, 160, 166
Upper Guinea *see* Guinea

value of slaves, 93, 197-8, 231-3, 244, 272, 294, 324-5, 340
van Dantzig, A., 187, 284
van der Broecke, P., 203, 316-18
Vansina, J., 220, 292, 321
Vaz, F., 69
von der Decken, C. C., 270, 339

Wadstrom, C. B., 65, 69, 287-8
wars, 17, 25-9, 46-51, 288; East African, 262, 270-1; in Guinea, 66; Oyo Yoruba, 169-77, 184-6; Senegalese, 100-25; *see also* military states
West Africa, 28-30, 36; commodity trade, 40, 189-90, 198; firearms trade, 126-53, 195-6; map of, 204; slave trade in, 52, 154-201, 280, 291, 293
West Indies, 24, 227, 248, 277
Westermann, D., 196, 315
Whydah, 22-3, 314
Wilks, I., 34, 314-15, 343
Windward Coast, 22-3; firearms to, 138-40, 142-3, 145, 150
Wolof states, 100-125 *passim*

Yao trade, 40-41, 260-4
Yoruba wars, 27-8, 51, 91

Zanzibar, 265-9

For Product Safety Concerns and Information please contact our EU
representative GPSR@taylorandfrancis.com
Taylor & Francis Verlag GmbH, Kaufingerstraße 24, 80331 München, Germany

www.ingramcontent.com/pod-product-compliance
Lightning Source LLC
Chambersburg PA
CBHW071152300426
44113CB00009B/1176